THE CLAY SANSKRIT LIBRARY
FOUNDED BY JOHN & JENNIFER CLAY

EDITED BY

RICHARD GOMBRICH

WWW.CLAYSANSKRITLIBRARY.ORG
WWW.NYUPRESS.ORG

Artwork by Robert Beer.
Typeset in Adobe Garamond Pro at 10.25 : 12.3.+pt.
Printed and Bound in Great Britain by
TJ International, Cornwall on acid free paper

THE EPITOME OF QUEEN LĪLĀVATĪ

VOLUME TWO

BY JINARATNA

EDITED AND TRANSLATED BY

R.C.C. FYNES

NEW YORK UNIVERSITY PRESS
JJC FOUNDATION
2006

First Edition 2006

The Clay Sanskrit Library is co-published by
New York University Press
and the JJC Foundation.

Further information about this volume
and the rest of the Clay Sanskrit Library
is available at the end of this book
and on the following websites:
www.claysanskritlibrary.org
www.nyupress.org

Volume 1: ISBN 978-0-8147-2741-6
Volume 2: ISBN 978-0-8147-2742-3

Library of Congress Cataloging-in-Publication Data
Jinaratnaśrī, 13th cent.
[Līlāvatīsāra. English & Sanskrit]
The epitome of Queen Lilavati / by Jinaratna ;
edited and translated by R.C.C.Fynes.
p. cm. – (The Clay Sanskrit library)
Poem.
In English and Sanskrit; includes translation from Sanskrit.
Includes bibliographical references and index.
Volume 1: ISBN 978-0-8147-2741-6
Volume 2: ISBN 978-0-8147-2742-3
I. Fynes, R.C.C. II. Title III. Title: Series.
PK3794.J45L5513 2005
891'.21–dc22 2004029511

CONTENTS

SANSKRIT ALPHABETICAL ORDER

Vowels:	*a ā i ī u ū ṛ ṝ ḷ ḹ e ai o au ṃ ḥ*
Gutturals:	*k kh g gh ṅ*
Palatals:	*c ch j jh ñ*
Retroflex:	*ṭ ṭh ḍ ḍh ṇ*
Dentals:	*t th d dh n*
Labials:	*p ph b bh m*
Semivowels:	*y r l v*
Spirants:	*ś ṣ s h*

GUIDE TO SANSKRIT PRONUNCIATION

a	b*u*t
ā, â	f*a*ther
i	s*i*t
ī, î	f*ee*
u	p*u*t
ū, û	b*oo*
ṛ	vocalic *r*, American p*ur*dy or English p*re*tty
ṝ	lengthened *ṛ*
ḷ	vocalic *l*, ab*le*
e, ê, ē	m*a*de, esp. in Welsh pronunciation
ai	b*i*te
o, ô, ō	r*o*pe, esp. Welsh pronunciation; Italian s*o*lo
au	s*ou*nd
ṃ	*anusvāra* nasalizes the preceding vowel
ḥ	*visarga*, a voiceless aspiration (resembling English *h*), or like Scottish lo*ch*, or an aspiration with a faint echoing of the preceding vowel so that *taiḥ* is pronounced *taih^i*
k	lu*ck*
kh	blo*ckh*ead
g	*g*o
gh	bi*gh*ead
ṅ	a*n*ger
c	*ch*ill
ch	mat*chh*ead
j	*j*og
jh	aspirated *j*, he*dgeh*og
ñ	ca*ny*on
ṭ	retroflex *t*, *t*ry (with the tip of tongue turned up to touch the hard palate)
ṭh	same as the preceding but aspirated
ḍ	retroflex *d* (with the tip of tongue turned up to touch the hard palate)
ḍh	same as the preceding but aspirated
ṇ	retroflex *n* (with the tip

	of tongue turned up to touch the hard palate)
t	French *t*out
th	ten*t h*ook
d	*d*inner
dh	guil*dh*all
n	*n*ow
p	*p*ill
ph	u*ph*eaval
b	*b*efore
bh	a*bh*orrent
m	*m*ind
y	*y*es
r	trilled, resembling the Italian pronunciation of *r*
l	*l*inger
v	*w*ord
ś	*sh*ore
ṣ	retroflex *sh* (with the tip of the tongue turned up to touch the hard palate)
s	hi*ss*
h	*h*ood

CSL PUNCTUATION OF ENGLISH

The acute accent on Sanskrit words when they occur outside of the Sanskrit text itself, marks stress, e.g. Ramáyana. It is not part of traditional Sanskrit orthography, transliteration or transcription, but we supply it here to guide readers in the pronunciation of these unfamiliar words. Since no Sanskrit word is accented on the last syllable it is not necessary to accent disyllables, e.g. Rama.

The second CSL innovation designed to assist the reader in the pronunciation of lengthy unfamiliar words is to insert an unobtrusive middle dot between semantic word breaks in compound names (provided the word break does not fall on a vowel resulting from the fusion of two vowels), e.g. Maha·bhárata, but Ramáyana (not Rama·áyana). Our dot echoes the punctuating middle dot (·) found in the oldest surviving forms of written Indic, the Ashokan inscriptions of the third century BCE.

The deep layering of Sanskrit narrative has also dictated that we use quotation marks only to announce the beginning and end of every direct speech, and not at the beginning of every paragraph.

An asterisk (*) in the body of the text marks the word or passage being annotated.

CSL PUNCTUATION OF SANSKRIT

The Sanskrit text is also punctuated, in accordance with the punctuation of the English translation. In mid-verse, the punctuation will not alter the *sandhi* or the scansion. Proper names are capitalized. Most Sanskrit metres have four "feet" *(pāda):* where possible we print the common *śloka* metre on two lines. In the Sanskrit text, we use French *Guillemets* (e.g. *«kva saṃcicīrṣuḥ?»*) instead of English quotation marks (e.g. "Where are you off to?") to avoid confusion with the apostrophes used for vowel elision in *sandhi*.

Sanskrit presents the learner with a challenge: *sandhi* ("euphonic combination"). *Sandhi* means that when two words are joined in connected speech or writing (which in Sanskrit reflects speech), the last letter (or even letters) of the first word often changes; compare the way we pronounce "the" in "the beginning" and "the end."

In Sanskrit the first letter of the second word may also change; and if both the last letter of the first word and the first letter of the second are vowels, they may fuse. This has a parallel in English: a nasal consonant is inserted between two vowels that would otherwise coalesce: "a pear" and "an apple." Sanskrit vowel fusion may produce ambiguity. The chart at the back of each book gives the full *sandhi* system.

Fortunately it is not necessary to know these changes in order to start reading Sanskrit. For that, what is important is to know the form of the second word without *sandhi* (pre-*sandhi*), so that it can be recognized or looked up in a dictionary. Therefore we are printing Sanskrit with a system of punctuation that will indicate, unambiguously, the original form of the second word, i.e., the form without *sandhi*. Such *sandhi* mostly concerns the fusion of two vowels.

In Sanskrit, vowels may be short or long and are written differently accordingly. We follow the general convention that a vowel with no mark above it is short. Other books mark a long vowel either with a bar called a macron (*ā*) or with a circumflex (*â*). Our system uses the macron, except that for initial vowels in *sandhi* we use a circumflex to indicate that originally the vowel was short, or the shorter of two possibilities (*e* rather than *ai*, *o* rather than *au*).

When we print initial *â*, before *sandhi* that vowel was	*a*
î or *ê*,	*i*
û or *ô*,	*u*
âi,	*e*
âu,	*o*
ā,	*ā* (i.e., the same)
ī,	*ī* (i.e., the same)
ū,	*ū* (i.e., the same)
ē,	*ī*
ō,	*ū*
āi,	*ai*
āu,	*au*
', before *sandhi* there was a vowel *a*	

FURTHER HELP WITH VOWEL SANDHI

When a final short vowel (*a*, *i* or *u*) has merged into a following vowel, we print ' at the end of the word, and when a final long vowel (*ā*, *ī* or *ū*) has merged into a following vowel we print " at the end of the word. The vast majority of these cases will concern a final *a* or *ā*.

Examples:

What before *sandhi* was *atra asti* is represented as	*atr' âsti*
atra āste	*atr' āste*
kanyā asti	*kany" âsti*
kanyā āste	*kany" āste*
atra iti	*atr' êti*
kanyā iti	*kany" êti*
kanyā īpsitā	*kany" ēpsitā*

Finally, three other points concerning the initial letter of the second word:

(1) A word that before *sandhi* begins with *ṛ* (vowel), after *sandhi* begins with *r* followed by a consonant: *yatha" rtu* represents pre-*sandhi* *yathā ṛtu; atra' rṣiḥ* represents pre-*sandhi atra ṛṣiḥ.*

(2) When before *sandhi* the previous word ends in *t* and the following word begins with *ś*, after *sandhi* the last letter of the previous word is *c*

and the following word begins with *ch*: *syāc chāstravit* represents pre-*sandhi syāt śāstravit*.

(3) Where a word begins with *h* and the previous word ends with a double consonant, this is our simplified spelling to show the pre-*sandhi* form: *tad hasati* is commonly written as *tad dhasati*, but we write *tadd hasati* so that the original initial letter is obvious.

COMPOUNDS

We also punctuate the division of compounds (*samāsa*), simply by inserting a thin vertical line between words. There are words where the decision whether to regard them as compounds is arbitrary. Our principle has been to try to guide readers to the correct dictionary entries.

WORDPLAY

Classical Sanskrit literature can abound in puns *(śleṣa)*. Such paronomasia, or wordplay, is raised to a high art; rarely is it a *cliché*. Multiple meanings merge *(śliṣyanti)* into a single word or phrase. Most common are pairs of meanings, but as many as ten separate meanings are attested. To mark the parallel senses in the English, as well as the punning original in the Sanskrit, we use a *slanted* font (different from *italic*) and a triple colon *(⁝)* to separate the alternatives. E.g.

Yuktaṃ Kādambarīṃ śrutvā kavayo maunam āśritāḥ
Bāṇa|dhvanāv an|adhyāyo bhavat' îti smṛtir yataḥ.

"It is right that poets should fall silent upon hearing the Kádambari, for the sacred law rules that recitation must be suspended when *the sound of an arrow ⁝ the poetry of Bana* is heard."

Soméshvara·deva's "Moonlight of Glory" I.15

EXAMPLE

Where the Deva·nágari script reads:

कुम्भस्थली रक्षतु वो विकीर्णसिन्दूररेणुर्द्विरदाननस्य ।
प्रशान्तये विघ्नतमश्छटानां निष्ठ्यूतबालातपपल्लवेव ॥

Others would print:

kumbhasthalī rakṣatu vo vikīrṇasindūrareṇur dviradānanasya /
praśāntaye vighnatamaśchaṭānāṃ niṣṭhyūtabālātapapallaveva //

We print:

Kumbha|sthalī rakṣatu vo vikīrṇa|sindūra|reṇur dvirad'|ānanasya
praśāntaye vighna|tamaś|chaṭānāṃ niṣṭhyūta|bāl'|ātapa|pallav" êva.

And in English:

"May Ganésha's domed forehead protect you! Streaked with vermilion dust, it seems to be emitting the spreading rays of the rising sun to pacify the teeming darkness of obstructions."

"Nava·sáhasanka and the Serpent Princess" I.3 by Padma·gupta

INTRODUCTION

The Epitome of Queen Lilávati *(Līlāvatī/sāra)* is an epic poem composed by Jina·ratna, a Jain scholar-monk. Jina·ratna completed his poem in the year 1285CE in western India, in Jábali·putra, modern Jhalor in the state of Rajasthan. As its title suggests, "The Epitome of Queen Lilávati" is an epitome of a much larger work, "The Story of the Final Emancipation of Lilávati" *(Nivvāṇa/līlāvaī/kahā)*, composed in Prakrit in 1036 by Jinéshvara, also a Jain monk.

In this second and concluding volume of Jina·ratna's "The Epitome of Queen Lilávati" the Jain monk Sámara·sena continues the narration to King Simha and Queen Lilávati which he began at the end of the first canto. After relating the consequences of addiction to the pleasures of taste, smell, sight, and hearing, he describes King Víjaya·sena and his four friends' taking of initiation as Jain monks and their subsequent rebirths. Among the many memorable characters encountered in the course of Sámara·sena's narration are Prince Jitári, who became addicted to hunting, Mádana·manjúsha and Mádana·shaláka, the two master-of-magic princesses, and Sudárshana, the wonderful talking parrot. At the conclusion of Sámara·sena's narrative in canto seventeen, King Simha and Queen Lilávati themselves take initiation. The concluding cantos of Jina·ratna's epic describe how Sámara·sena, Simha, Lilávati and the other leading characters gain omniscience and final liberation.

Jainism and the Jain universe

Jainism already had a history of some 1,600 years when Jina·ratna wrote "The Epitome of Queen Lilávati." It is far from being a monolithic religion; it has continued to develop, and within it there are several sects or traditions that share the central beliefs of Jainism but have differing views about religious practice. The main division is between the White Clad *(Śvet'|âmbara),* whose ascetics wear white robes, and the Sky Clad *(Dig|ambara)*, whose fully initiated monks go naked. The White Clad tradition is itself divided into a number of groups or sects *(gaccha)*. Jina·ratna belonged to a sect of the White Clad tradition known as the Very Acute Ones *(Kharatara gaccha)*, probably because of their skill in debate.

Although abounding in memorable characters and lively incidents, "The Epitome of Queen Lilávati" has a serious goal: nothing less than to provide embodied beings with the enlightenment that will liberate them from the everlasting cycle of continued death and rebirth. An understanding of the Jain beliefs concerning embodiment and the means to liberation from it is essential for a full understanding of the text. There are four possible classes of embodiment for a being: as a god, a human, a hell being, or as an animal or plant. The nature of a being's embodiment is determined by its actions in its previous embodiments. This is the theory of karma; karma means action.

Jainism shares with other heterodox Indian religions the belief that the ethical content of one's actions predetermines the status of one's future embodiments. However, Jains developed the belief, unique to them, that karma is a fine material substance that somehow 'flows in' and clings to the soul of the embodied being, obscuring the soul's natural qualities of bliss and omniscience and causing and determining the nature of its embodiment. To gain final liberation from the cycle of death and rebirth it is necessary to prevent the influx of new karma and to expunge the existent karma from one's soul. The only way to do this is by the following the path of self-denial and asceticism taught and exemplified by the Fordmakers, so called because their teaching provides a ford which enables embodied beings to cross the ocean of existence.

Traditional Jain belief holds that the omniscient Fordmakers periodically reactivate the truths of the Jain religion. The Fordmakers are also known as Jinas, meaning Conquerers, because their omniscience has been gained as a result of their conquest of their desires and passions by means of a life of harsh asceticism; hence a Jain is one who follows the religion of the Conquerers. Although they have superhuman characteristics as a result of their superior spiritual status, the Fordmakers are human, born of human parents. By their preaching the Fordmakers create the fourfold congregation, made up of Jain monks, nuns, laymen, and laywomen.

Despite the traditional Jain belief in the uncreated and eternal verities of the religion, it is clear that the historical origins of Jainism began with the most recent Fordmaker, Maha·vira, who lived and preached in the areas bordering the lower Ganges valley in the fifth century BCE, and that the other Fordmakers, with the possible exception of the one immediately preceding Maha·vira, are components of a complex mythology which was not fully elaborated until many years after Maha·vira's death.

The drama of the soul's embodiment is played out in a universe the Jains described as follows: uncreated and eternal, it is envisaged as a vast three-dimensional structure in the shape of a gigantic man standing with his arms akimbo. At the level of its chest and neck is the upper world, where the heavens are situated, the homes of the gods; at the level of its waist is the middle world, a flat disc on which are innumerable concentric rings of land separated from each other by oceans, the inner land-masses being the home of human beings and animals and plants; below its waist are the hell grounds, the homes of the hell beings. The central island of the middle world is "Rose-apple Tree Island," in which the continent of Bhárata is situated; Bhárata, the Indian subcontinent, is where most the action of "The Epitome of Queen Lilávati" is set. Over the upper world is an upturned canopy above which the liberated souls remain forever, in a state of permanent bliss and omniscience, never to be reborn.

The rules of rebirth are fairly simple: a human being can be reborn as another human being, or animal or plant in the middle world, as a god, or as a hell-being. Life as a god or as a hell-being is not permanent. Since the Jain universe is uncreated and self-existent there are no permanent creator gods. A god may enjoy countless blissful years in heaven, but the time it spends there is determined by its karma; once the fruit of its karma has been used up, it falls from heaven to be reborn in the middle world. Likewise with hell beings; they may spend countless years in a hell, but once their time there is over, they too are reborn in the middle world. Even though life as a god is pleasant, it is not permanent and it is not conducive to liberation. Only human beings can gain liberation, and the way for them to gain it is to lead the life of an ascetic a Jain monk or nun.

JINA·RATNA AND JINÉSHVARA

What little is known about Jina·ratna he states himself in the colophon he placed at the end of his poem, in which he gives the lineage of the succession of monastic teachers and pupils from Vardhámana, the teacher of the Jinéshvara who was the author of "The Story of the Final Liberation of Lilávati," to another Jinéshvara who was Jina·ratna's own teacher.

Jina·ratna studied literature, logic, and the canonical texts of the White-clad Jains with Jinéshvara and other monks. In the colophon he acknowledges the help he received from others in the preparation and correction of the text of "The Epitome of Queen Lilávati." Jina·ratna states that he assisted a poet named Lakshmi·tílaka in his composition of the poem "The Deeds of the Self-enlightened Ones" *(Pratyeka/buddha/carita),* completed in 1255.

More is known about Jinéshvara, the author of "The Story of the Final Emancipation of Lilávati." His poem was written not in Sanskrit, but in a Prakrit, a literary Middle Indo-aryan language known as Jain Maha·rashtri; it was over three times the length of Jina·ratna's epitome. No manuscript of "The Story of the Final Emancipation of Lilávati" is known to have survived; it was perhaps rendered otiose by Jina·ratna's composition of "The Epitome of Queen Lilávati." Jinéshvara was a pupil of Vardhamána, the founder of the sect of the Very Acute Ones.

Vardhamána and Jinéshvara were leaders of a reform movement in Jainism; they argued that a Jain monk should imitate the practice of early Jainism by continually wandering and only stopping in temporary lodging houses, except in the rainy season when extended travel was impossible. Their opponents were Jain monks who did not travel, but instead remained in temples or monasteries. Vardhamána and Jinéshvara criticised what they saw as the laxity of the temple-dwelling monks. In 1024 Jinéshvara was victorious in a debate with temple-dwelling monks held under royal auspices at Patan in Gujarat. Those who followed the practice recommended by Vardhamána and Jinéshvara became known as the dwellers in lodging houses.

"The Story of the Final Emancipation of Lilávati" was highly regarded by the successors of Jinéshvara as being conducive to final liberation, and Jina·ratna in his introductory verses to "The Epitome of Queen Lilávati" describes how his interest in Jinéshvara's poem was stimulated by his own teacher. Jina·ratna states that he began to write his epitome at the request of those who wished to concentrate on its narrative alone.

Genre and sources

When Jain ascetics preached to lay people they used popular stories to illustrate the truths of the Jain religion. In many cases the stories were well-known folk tales to which a Jain moral was added. Eventually the stories were gathered into the written collections to which western scholars have given the generic name: Jain narrative *(kathā)* literature. The primary purpose of Jain narrative literature was to edify through amusement; consequently the stories are racy, and in some cases the moralising element is rather tenuous. These stories were gathered into independent anthologies or 'treasuries' *(koṣa)* and also used in composing biographies of important figures in Jainism: Fordmakers, kings, and exemplary ascetics and lay people.

The main feature of Jain narrative literature is its concern with past and future lives. The fate of the embodied soul is of fundamental importance for Jainism, and there developed a genre of soul biography, in which the adventures of a soul are related through the course of several of its embodiments. The soul biographies usually relate the stories of a pair of souls, which are reunited and interact with each other over a series of parallel lifetimes.

Jinéshvara's "The Story of the Final Emancipation of Lilávati"—the immediate source of "The Epitome of Queen Lilávati"—was in turn influenced in its form and in some of its material by an earlier work, Uddyótana's "Garland of Kuválaya" *(Kuvalayamālā),* a Prakrit poem composed in 779, which related the soul biographies of a group of characters who exemplified the vices of anger, pride, deceit, greed and delusion.

Language

By writing in Sanskrit, the pan-Indian language of learned discourse, Jina·ratna gave The "The Epitome of Queen Liĺávati" a far wider readership than was possible for The Story of the Final Emancipation of Liĺávati, written in Jain Maha·rashtri, a language with a more restricted currency.

Prakrit, meaning 'artless' or 'unrefined', is the generic name given to the various dialects of Middle Indo-aryan. In contrast, Sanskrit means 'refined' or 'elaborated'.

Even though it epitomizes a larger work, Jina·ratna's poem is epic in its length as well as its theme. It consists of some 5340 verses, most of them couplets of thirty-two syllables, known as *śloka*s; this is the metre par excellence of Sanskrit epic.

Sanskrit metres were quantitative, like the metres of Classical Greek and Latin poetry; their rhythms were based on the order of long and short syllables and not on stress, as in most modern English verse. Like other composers of Jain narrative verse, Jina·ratna is innovative in his use of this metre in that he sometimes omits the caesura or pause after the first and third feet and sometimes uses unusual patterns of short and long syllables.

Moreover, Jina·ratna displays his mastery of Sanskrit poetics by interspersing more complex lyric metres throughout his poem; for example, Canto Seventeen is entirely written in the lyric 'earth' *(pṛthvī)* metre.

Not only does Jina·ratna employ rare words and unusual grammatical forms drawn from Sanskrit lexicons and grammars, but he also incorporates into his poem words taken from contemporary spoken vernaculars. Jina·ratna's language in the narrative portions of the poem is fast moving and direct, but it is far more ornate in his descriptions of cities, mountains, desert wildernesses, battles, festivals, and other topics with which a Sanskrit epic should be embellished. Some attempt has been made to convey these different registers of language in this prose translation, but the full range of Jina·ratna's poetic resource can only be enjoyed in the original Sanskrit.

Some passages are not in Sanskrit but in literary Prakrits; a notable example is the conversation of the demons in Canto Four, written in *Paiśācī*, "Demon Language".

Lilávati was the beautiful wife of King Simha of Raja·griha. Simha sponsored a debate by the advocates of various religions and a Jain named Jina·datta was victorious. Later, the Jain monk Sámara·sena visited the city, and King Simha went to hear him preach. On the king's asking him why he had renounced the world, Sámara·sena began to relate the story of king Vijáya·sena, and his four friends Jaya·shásana, Shura, Puran·dhara, and Dhana. One day the Jain teacher Súdharman held a preaching assembly which Vijá-ya·sena and his four friends attended. Sudharman began to preach about the bad consequences of anger and violence, pride and false speech, theft and deceit, sexual immorality and delusion, greed and possessiveness, and, in turn, the consequences of addiction to the pleasures of each of the five senses, touch, smell, taste, sight, and hearing, in each case pointing to a member of the assembly as an example and describing his past lives. Sámara·sena then related how king Vijáya·sena, his four friends, and the people in the assembly described by Súdharman took initiation as Jain monks. King Simha and Queen Lilávati themselves then took initiation as Jain ascetics. The final cantos of the poem describe how they and the other leading characters achieved the state of omniscience which is a precursor of final liberation from death and rebirth.

Acknowledgements

I wish to record my gratitude to Muni Jambuvijaya and Paul Dundas. This second volume of "The Epitome of Queen Lilávaviti" is dedicated, as was the first, to my wife Michelle in acknowledgement of her help and support.

Manuscripts and editions

"The Epitome of Queen Lilávati" is known from a single manuscript preserved in the *Kharatara Gaccha Bhandar* (the Library of the Very Acute Ones) at Jaisalmer, Rajasthan. There is some damage to its first and last leaves and occasional lacunæ within the main body of the text, but it is otherwise in good condition. In 1983 H. C. Bhayani published an excellent printed edition of the manuscript with a glossary of rare and unusual words found in the text, together with an English précis of the narrative prepared by N. M. Kansara. Bhayani's edition was based on a photocopy of the manuscript held by the Rajasthan Oriental Institute in Jodhpur. That photocopy has apparently since disintegrated, so I am particularly grateful to Muni Jambuvijaya for providing me with a further photocopy of the manuscript.

Bibliography

The best one-volume introduction to Jainism is Dundas, P. *The Jains*, 2nd. ed, London, 2002: Routledge.

For a beautifully illustrated description of the full complexities of the Jain universe, see: Caillat, C. and Kumar, R. *The Jain Cosmology*, Basle, 1981: Ravi Kumar.

Manuscripts of this poem are held in the *Kharatara Gaccha Bhandar* (the Library of the Very Acute Ones) at Jaisalmer in Rajasthan. See page

151 of the library catalogue: PUNYAVIJAYAJI, MUNI SHRI *Jesalmer Collection: New Catalogue of Sanskrit and Prakit Manuscripts,* Ahmedabad, 1972: L.D. Institute of Indology, 36.

Jina·ratna (BHAYANI, H. C. ed.) *Līlāvatī-Sāra: A Sanskrit Abridgement of Jineśvara Sūri's Prakrit Līlāvaī-Kahā,* Ahmedabad, 1983: L.D. Institute of Indology 96.

CANTO 8
THE CONSEQUENCES OF THE SENSE OF TASTE

8.1 Ath' âpare 'hni Vijayasen'|ādinām̩ sabhā|sadām
Sudharma|svāmy upādikṣat sudhā|dhārā|kirā girā:

«sparśanasya sva|rūp'|ādi, rājan, nyakṣeṇa kīrtitam.
adhunā rasanasy' âitad vistareṇa prakīryate.
jātu kasy' âpi viṣaya|sat|tvaram̩ karaṇ'|ântaram.
rasanam̩ tu sad" âpy evam̩—tat teṣv etat su|dur|jayam.

yad uktam:

rasan" âkṣeṣu, yogeṣu mano, mohaś ca karmasu,
vrateṣu brahma; catvāri jīyante kṛcchrataḥ khalu.

8.5 rasanā|svairiṇī c' êyam̩ rasān viṭa|naṭān iva
yath"|êṣṭam upabhuñjānā na tṛṣyati, su|dṛpyati.

rasāḥ punar a|viruddha|viruddh'|ātmatayā dvidhā.
tatr' â|viruddhā ghṛt'|ādyā, viruddhā madir'|ādayaḥ.
tatr' ādyeṣv api lāmpaṭyam anarthāya prajāyate.
sudhā|laulyāc chira|cchedam̩ Rāhor āhuḥ purā|vidaḥ.
viruddheṣu tu vāñch" âpi duṣṭā, laulye tu kā kathā?
n' êṣṭo janaṅgamaḥ sparṣṭum apy, āśleṣṭum̩ kim ucyatām?
rasanā|rasa|lāmpaṭya|paṭy|āvṛta|mat'|īkṣaṇāḥ
a|pey'|â|bhakṣya|rasikāḥ patanti narak'|âvaṭe.

ON THE NEXT DAY reverend Sudhárman instructedVí- 8.1
jaya·sena and the others seated in the assembly with a voice pouring forth a stream of nectar:

"Your Majesty, the nature and so forth of touch have been described in their entirety. Now those of the organ of taste will be described in detail. For everyone, the speed of the duration of a sense object is different from the organ of sense. But taste is always like this—among them it is very difficult to subdue.

Since it is said:

Taste among the senses, mind among the activities, delusion among the karmas, chastity among the vows; these four
are subdued only with great difficulty indeed. This sense of 8.5
taste, a woman traveling where she wills, enjoying at pleasure objects of taste, like actors taking the role of gourmet companion, is never sated but exults in her delight.

Objects of taste are divided into two kinds: adverse and non-adverse. Of these, the non-adverse are clarified butter and suchlike, and the adverse are liquor and suchlike. Lust for even the former produces undesirable consequences. Those who know the events of yore say that Rahu's head was cut off because of his lust for nectar. Even the wish for the adverse is certainly culpable, but what can one say of the ardent passion for them? An untouchable is not desired to be touched; why speak about embracing? Their mind's eye covered by the blindfold of their craving for objects of taste, delighting in the taste of what is forbidden to be drunk and eaten, they fall into the cavern of hell.

tathā hi:

8.10 aihik'|āmuṣmik'|âpāya|kāriṇīm api vāruṇīm
rasa|jñā vivaś'|ātmānaḥ pibanti ca vamanti ca.
madirā|mada|rākṣasyā grasta|caitanya|vaibhavāḥ
patanti dāsa|pādeṣu nindanti ca gurum api.
vādit'|ānana|vāditrā nṛtyanti ca niraṅkuśāḥ.
rathyāsu suptā vadane lihyante śunakair api.
kādambarī|pibāḥ pāpā māṃsa|peśy|upadaṃśinaḥ
kroḍa|saṭṭā|lāvakīyaṃ rasaṃ ca bruvate sudhāṃ.

kravy'|âdinaḥ kravya|kṛte go|riṅgāyanti, vāgurāṃ
lānti, dru|mūlaṃ śrayante, rakṣanty ambu mṛg'|āptaye.
8.15 gala|jāl'|ādibhir ghnanti nirghṛṇā matsa|kacchapān,
vītaṃsa|pañjar'|ādyaiś ca pāpā hiṃsanti pakṣiṇaḥ.
caṇak'|ādīn viprakīrya vaśīkṛti|kaṇān iva,
viśvāsya krūrāḥ kroḍ'|ādīn kṣiṇvate kṣaṇa|tṛptaye.
bhindanti madhu|jālāni, saraghā ghātayanti ca.
phalaṃ ca pañc'|ôdumbaryā sandhānāni ca bhuñjate.
ananta|kāyikān, rātri|bhojanaṃ, navanītakam,
kukkuṭy|aṇḍaka|rasaṃ ca rasayanti ras'|ôttṛpaḥ.
pāpīyāṃsaḥ ke 'py a|bhakṣyaṃ bhakṣayanti ca kevalam,
yāge chāg'|ādi|kadanaṃ vadanti ca sura|śriye.
8.20 ‹na māṃsa|madyayor doṣo, na rājñāṃ mṛgay"|ādiṣu,
pravṛttir eṣā bhūtānāṃ vāyos tiryag|gatir yathā.
kiñ ca jīvo n' âsti. tad|a|bhavāt kasya śubh'|â|śubhe?
tataś c' âśnīta māṃs'|ādi svairam› ity ūcire pare.

Like so:

Gourmets, deprived of self-control, drink and vomit wine, although the cause of misfortune in this world and the next. Their power of thought seized by the demoness of intoxication by liquor, they fall at the feet of their servants and even abuse the respectable. And whistling tunes, they dance wantonly. Having fallen asleep in the streets, they are even licked in the face by dogs. Drinking wine and relishing gobbets of flesh, the wretches declare that the flavor gathered from hogs and crows is nectar. 8.10

Eaters of flesh, to obtain flesh, make cattle creep. They prepare traps, fix roots of trees and conceal water to get
deer. With rods, nets and so on, they cruelly kill fish and 8.15
turtles, and with cages, coops and so on, the wretches harm birds. By scattered chickpeas, et cetera, like seed for the enchantment to one's will, they gain the confidence of hogs and such and slaughter them for a moment's pleasure. They shatter honeycombs and destroy the bees. They eat the fruit of the five kinds of fig tree and eggplants. And delighting in savors, they savor root vegetables containing numerous lives, midnight feasts, clarified butter and the yolk of hens' eggs. And some very wicked people not only eat what is forbidden to be eaten but even say that the slaughter of goats and suchlike at religious ceremonies is for the fortune of the gods.

'There is no fault in eating meat or drinking wine, nor 8.20
in the hunting of kings and such, since this behavior is the animal condition of the appetite of beings. And moreover, the soul doesn't exist. Since it doesn't exist, to what pertains

ity|ādi|vākyaiḥ pravartya hims"|ādau ghasmarān narān
svayaṃ puraḥsarībhūya nayante narake sukhāt.
tatr' âti|duḥ|sahaṃ duḥkhaṃ ciraṃ soḍhvā kathañ cana
tata utpadya siṃh'|ādau palal'|āsvāda|lampaṭe
duṣ|karma|bhāritā yānti narake bhairave punaḥ.
rasanā|rākṣasī|vaśyā kaṃ na kleśaṃ karoty aho!»

8.25 rasan"|êndriya|lāmpaṭye dṛṣṭ'|ântaḥ spaṣṭam ucyate:
«rājan śrī|Vijayasena, mantry asau Jayaśāsanaḥ.»

tato gurūn namaskṛtya mantrī vyajñāpayat: «prabho,
kiṃ kathaṃ prāṅ mayā cakre? śrāvaya śravaṇau mama.»

tato jñāna|ratna|dīpa|prakāśa|bhuvan'|ôdaraḥ
śrī|Sudharmā|gaṇa|dharas tam ūce vāgmināṃ varaḥ:

«asti śrī|Dhātakī|khaṇḍe pratīcya|Meru|Bhārate
maṇḍalaṃ Kośalā nāma kil' â|khaṇḍala|maṇḍalam.
ata ev' Ârhatāṃ kalpa|kalyāṇaka|mahā|diṣu
milaty akhilam apy atra kil' â|khaṇḍala|maṇḍalaṃ.

8.30 śrī|Sukāñcī|purī tatra su|kāñc" îva bhuvo babhau,
jajñe yasyā jhaṇat|kārair vācālaṃ harid|ambaram.

good and bad? So eat meat and such at your pleasure.' Thus say others.

With these and other assertions, they impel greedy men to acts of violence, et cetera, and, themselves forming the vanguard, lead them willingly to hell. Having there for a long time endured suffering extremely difficult to endure, they somehow ascend from there, and as a lion or such addicted to the taste of flesh, burdened with bad karma, they enter a fearful hell once more. What affliction will subjection to the demoness of taste not create!"

Asked by His Majesty Víjaya·sena for an actual instance 8.25
of lust for the sense of taste, he said, "Your Majesty, that minister Jaya·shásana."

Thereupon the minister bowed to the teacher and said, "Lord, cause my ears to hear what I did in my former lives."

Then, the vault of the world illuminated by the light of the jewel of his knowledge, reverend Sudhárman, the leader of the flock, eminent among the eloquent, said to him:

"In the lovely Grislea-Tormentosa-Tree Island, in the Bhárata continent at the western Mount Meru, there is a country named Kóshala, truly an unbroken circle. For the very reason that it joins without a gap the four quarters of the blessed precepts of the reverend Jinas, in this it is truly
an unbroken circle. In it is a city, lovely Sukánchi (Lovely 8.30
Girdle), like a lovely girdle for the world, whose tinkling seems to fill the circumference of the quarters of the sky.

Arhad|dharm'|âvacūlo 'tra Ratnacūlo 'śubhan nṛpaḥ;
yat|samyaktv'|âcalasy' âgre svaḥ|śailo 'pi cal'|âcalaḥ.
bāhyaṃ dṛṣṭv" êv' âri|cakraṃ vinamad dharma|vaibhavāt,
tasy' ântar|aṅgam api tat svayaṃ neme bhay'|āturam.
tasya prema|guṇa|ratn'|āvalī Ratnāvalī priyā,
yat|samyaktva|jhalat|kāro dinaṃ praty adhik'|âdhikaḥ.
tasyā rūpaṃ vapur|bhūṣā, śīlaṃ tasy' âpi bhūṣaṇam,
tasy' âpi bhūṣā samyaktvaṃ, saṃvego 'sy' âpi bhūṣaṇam.

8.35 adya śvo vā parivrajyāṃ rājyaṃ hitvā jighṛkṣatoḥ,
rājyaṃ ca bhuñjator bhāga|phala|karm'|ôdayāt param,
mitho 'viyukta|manasor yathā yugala|dharmiṇoḥ,
yayuḥ sahasrā ghasrāṇāṃ tayor ek'|âha|helayā.
anyadā suṣuve devī kumāraṃ sphāra|kāntikam,
Jitārir iti nām' âsya suṣuve ca mahī|patiḥ.
samaye ca kal"|ācāry'|âbhyāśe 'bhyāsyat kalāḥ kalāḥ,
viśeṣāc ca dhanur|vedam a|nirvedaṃ sa rāja|sūḥ.
kal"|âkūpāra|pārīṇaṃ yauvana|śrī|taraṅgitam
taṃ bhūpo bhūpa|kanyābhiḥ pramodād udavāhayat.

8.40 kul'|âdhvan" ânāgatā y" âdhyāpak'|âdhyāpitā na yā,
māṃs'|āśitāṃ kalām enāṃ pāṭhito 'sau rasa|jñayā.

There, a pendent crest for the Jain religion, King Ratna·chula was resplendent; even the mountain of heaven moved before the mountain of his righteousness. Having just beheld him, the discus of his foreign enemy bowed down through the power of his religion, and his internal enemy submitted of his own free will, sick with fear. His wife, whose necklace of jewels consisted of the excellencies of her affection, was Ratnávali (Necklace of Jewels), the rays of the brilliance of whose righteousness grew ever brighter by each day. Her beauty was her body, and its ornament was her morality. Its ornament was her righteousness, and its ornament was her desire of final emancipation.

Wishing to abandon the kingdom and lead the life of 8.35
religious mendicants that day or the next, nevertheless enjoying the kingdom through the acceptance of the karma that was the fruit of their fortune, their minds mutually undivided as of a virtuous couple, their thousands of days passed as lightly as a single day.

One day, the Queen brought forth a prince of abundant beauty, and the King brought forth his name, Jitári. And at the appropriate time the King's son, in the presence of a master of arts, studied the various arts, and especially the art of archery, with unflagging zeal. When he had crossed to the far shore of the ocean of the arts and was billowing with the loveliness of youth, the King married him with great joy to the daughters of kings.

Although it did not arrive by the path of his family and 8.40
was not taught by his teacher, he was taught by his tongue that art that was fed by flesh.

tataś ca:

dur|dānta|rasan"|âśven' âpahṛto '|patha|gāmukaḥ
ku|mitrair mṛgay"|âṭavyāṃ so 'vasthānam akāryata.

tathā hi:

‹cala|vedhya|vyadh'|âbhyāsas
teṣāṃ bhī|krodha|bodhanam,
vapur|dārḍhyaṃ, śrama|jayaś
c' êty ādyā mṛgayā|guṇāḥ.

kiñ ca:

n' âsty ātmā, tad|a|bhāvāc ca na karma na paraṃ januḥ.
tad, deva, mānyatāṃ sv'|êcchā; kṛty'|â|kṛtya|kathā vṛthā›

pāpa'|rddhi|vyasanī so 'tha dav'|âgnir iva saṃharan
a|saṅkhyān prāṇinaḥ saṅkhy"|âtītāṃ pāpa'|rddhim ārjayat.

8.45 rasanā|rasa|nāṭyena
naṭito 'sau tataḥ piban
madhūni bahudhā, kṣaudraṃ
bhakṣayan sarva|bhakṣy abhūt.

pāpo mitraiḥ sa|pīty" âsau tato dhāvati, gāyati,
dig|ambaro nṛtyati ca, tad|akīrtis tath" âiva ca.

tato nir|aṅkuśa|lasad|rasanā|laulya|sāgaram
taṃ kumāraṃ tathā vīkṣya pitarau tematus tamām.
sva|putr'|ân|ārya|kāry'|âugh'|āsañjit'|â|śubha| saṃhati|
sambhāvit'|ôgra|naraka|pāta|sambhūta|manyunā
ajasra|sravad|uṣṇ'|ôṣṇa|bāṣpa|dūn'|āsya|paṅkajā chinna devī
bhūpam ath' ôpetya sa|gadgadam ado 'vadat:

And so:

Carried away by the badly tamed horse of taste, he traveled the wrong way and was led by bad friends to take residence in a hunting-forest.

Like this:

'Practicing hitting living targets, arousing their fear and anger, the toughening of the body and the overcoming of fatigue are the principal elements of hunting.

Moreover:

The soul does not exist and because of its nonexistence there is no karma or future birth. So, Your Highness, one should respect one's own desire.'

Then, addicted to hunting, destroying, like a forest fire, countless animals, he acquired an accumulation of sin beyond counting. Then, deluded by the acting of the senti- 8.45
ment of taste, repeatedly drinking spirits and eating honey, he became omnivorous. Then, while drinking with his friends, the wretch ran, sang and danced naked, and in this way gained a bad reputation for it.

Thereupon, having seen the Prince thus an ocean of addiction to the sense of taste, which was sporting free from control, his parents became extremely distressed. Then, entirely overcome by the flood of her son's ignoble objects, with distress arisen from his falling into a fearful hell because of his close connection with inauspicious deeds, the lotus of her face withered by the constant stream of her very hot tears, the Queen approached the King and, between her sobs, said this:

8.50 ‹mahā|pāp'|ād ato ghorān naraka|dvārato drutam
vāryatāṃ vāryatāṃ vatso. m" âiva, svāminn, upekṣyatām.›
rāj" ākhyad, ‹devi, su|janair bahuśo 'py eṣa vāritaḥ,
n' âsmān nivartate pāpād, upadeśyas tad eṣa na.›
devy ūce, ‹cintyatāṃ ko 'py upāyas tatra punaḥ, prabho.
ratn'|ākarasya ratnāni dhīmato dhīr navā navā.
s'|ôpakrame karmaṇi c' ôpāyo 'pi syāt phale|grahiḥ.
putro 'sti deva|pādānāṃ kumāro, vāryatāṃ tataḥ.›
sa|khedaṃ punar ūce rāṭ, ‹ka upāyo 'tra sāmpratam?›
mantrī Vimalamaty|ākhyo 'tr'|ântare bhūpam abravīt:
8.55 ‹ekad" āhūyatāṃ, deva, kumāro 'tra sva|sannidhau.
deva|rājñyos tad" ālāpe vakṣye 'ham api kiñ cana.›
rājñā sadyaḥ samāhūtaḥ kumāro nṛpam ānamat
siṃh'|āsane 'tha sv'|āsanne tena premṇā nyaveśitaḥ.
‹kaccit, kumāra, kuśalaṃ sarv'|âṅgaṃ tava samprati?›
iti pṛṣṭo mudā pitrā putro 'vādīt kṛt'|âñjaliḥ:
‹yasya prasādāt kuśalaṃ jṛmbhate jagatī|tale,
tasya su|svāminaḥ putre kuśalaṃ mayi niścalam.
tāta|pādair adhunā tu hūto yen' âsmi hetunā,
tan|nivedana|prasādaṃ labdhuṃ lubdhe śrutī mama.›

'Let our child be kept back, kept back without delay from the terrible gates of hell, a great misfortune. Don't let him be neglected like this, husband.' 8.50

The King said, 'My Queen, good people have repeatedly tried to prevent him, but he does not abstain from this wickedness, consequently he cannot be instructed.'

The Queen said, 'Then let some other plan of dealing with him be thought up, Your Majesty. A jewel mine produces ever new jewels and a wise man ever new wisdom. And since the action is linked with expediency, a plan would be successful. He is Your Majesty's son, so let him be prevented.'

The King replied dejectedly, 'What plan can be successful in this matter?' At that moment a minister named Vímala·mati said to the King:

'Let the Prince be summoned one day, Your Majesty. 8.55
Then, in his presence, during Your Majesty's and the Queen's conversation, I shall say something.'

The King immediately summoned the Prince. He bowed to the King, who affectionately seated him next to himself on a lion-throne.

Asked with pleasure by his father, 'I hope you are completely healthy right now, Prince?,' the son replied, his hands folded in respectful salutation:

'Good health is firmly fixed in me, the son of that good king, by whose grace good health spreads over the surface of the earth. But for what reason have I been summoned to my respected father? My ears are eager to obtain the grace of his communication.'

8.60 vyājahār' âtha pṛthv"|īśaḥ, ‹śṛṇu, vatsa, vivakṣitam.
an|arvak|pāra|saṃsāra|pārāvāra|bhay'|ākarāt,
pradīpta|bhavan'|ākārād adya śvo vā vinaśvarāt
gṛha|vāsān moha|pāśān nirviṇṇaṃ mama mānasam.
nṛ|janma|kalpa|vṛkṣasya mahā|vrata|mah"|âṅkuṭaiḥ
mah"|ānanda|phalaṃ, vats', āditsate mānasaṃ mama.
tat, kumāra, mahī|bhāraṃ dur|dharaṃ dhara samprati!
Śeṣa|rāja iv' êdānīṃ viśrāmyāmy asmy a|viśramam.›

iti śrutvā muhuḥ smitvā kumāro nṛpam abhyadhāt:
‹tāta, prastūyate vaktuṃ kiñ cit prastuta|vartmani,
8.65 yadi prasāda|vimukhās tāta|pādā bhavanti na.›
‹vatso yath"|êṣṭam ācaṣṭām,› ity ācaṣṭa sphuṭaṃ pitā.

tataḥ kumāro Jitāriḥ pāp'|ôpādhyāya|pāṭhitām
caṇḍāṃ tāṇḍavayāmāsa vitaṇḍāṃ sva|pituḥ puraḥ.

‹janm'|ântar'|ârjita|phala|bhokt" ātmā ced bhavet, pitaḥ,
tad yujyate sarvam idaṃ, tad|a|bhāve tu niṣphalam.
yad v" âstv ātmā bahu|vādi|prayukta|hetu|jālataḥ,
tath" âpi kartā n' âiv' âsau, bhuṅkte 'sau prāk|kṛtaṃ yataḥ.
kṛta|nāś'|ākṛt'|āpatti|doṣād ātmā karotu vā.
kin tu na jñāyate kṛtyaṃ śubh'|â|śubha|nibandhanam.

Then the King declared, 'Listen, my son, to my stated 8.60
intention. My mind has grown disgusted with the life of a householder, the cause of fear to the boat that plies from here to the far shore of the ocean of existence, the cause of the kindling of the abode today or its perishing tomorrow, the snare of delusion. My son, my mind desires to obtain the extremely blessed fruit of the wishing-tree that is human birth by means of the long hooked pole of the great vows of asceticism. So, Prince, take up the burden, difficult to bear, of governing the world, forthwith. I shall now cease from labor without ceasing, like Vishnu, the lord of the serpent.'

As soon as he heard this the Prince smiled and said to the King, 'Father, I would like to say something about the
path that has been undertaken, if my respected father is 8.65
not averse to the granting of the favor.' His father stated distinctly, 'My son may state what he wishes.'

Then Prince Jitári, in his father's presence, began to beat out the cruel and fallacious argument that he had learned from the preceptors of evil.

'If the Self enjoys the fruit obtained during life, father, then all this would be fitting, but, given the nonexistence of the Self, it is fruitless. But suppose the Self exists according to the deceptive argument employed by a big-talker, nevertheless it is not the actual creator, since it enjoys what was made previously. Or let the Self act as a consequence of the condition formed at death. It still isn't known if what it is to do is connected with good or evil.

8.70 arth'|āpatty" âtha budhyeta śubh'|â|śubha|karī kriyā,
dṛśyante tārak'|ādīnāṃ yad vimānā nabhas|tale.

śubha|kriyā|phalam idaṃ yad eṣ' ûtpattir aṅginām.
tāta, tāny apy a|saṅkhyāni, devā apy eṣv a|saṅkhyakāḥ.

prati|kṣaṇam a|saṅkhyātāś cyavante ca bhavanti ca.
tad etad ghaṭate tarhi ced yāyus tatra pāpinaḥ.
yato '|saṅkhyās ta ev' êha, hiṃsā tat svar|nibandhanam.
balād āpatitaṃ, tāta, hiṃsr'|ādyais taj jitaṃ jitam.
kiñ c' â|hiṃsrā yatayo 'tra te mitā eva yad bhuvi,
tatas te syuḥ kuṣṭhi|paṅgu|bhikṣākās te mitā eva.

8.75 tathā hetv|anurūpaṃ syāt kāryam etat su|viśrutam,
kāya|kleśāt tatas, tāta, syāt sukha|prabhavaḥ katham?
tat sarva|śāstra|tattva|jña|maulinā svāminā vṛthā
«dīkṣiṣye samprat' îty» uktaṃ. tad ā|candraṃ mahīṃ pṛṇu!›

‹sarvath" ân|upadeśyo 'yam› iti bhū|bhṛti maunini,
sa|khedaṃ s'|âsram ūce 'tha devī Ratnāvalī sutam:

‹hā hā putra! kim aparaṃ vairāgyasya vratasya ca,
tvat|pituḥ kāraṇaṃ hanta tava duś|ceṣṭitaṃ vinā!

Now, whether an action is the cause of good or evil may 8.70
be understood by inference from circumstances, since the mansions of the stars and suchlike can be observed in the firmament of the sky.

This is the fruit of auspicious actions, that beings take their birth in them. And, father, they are countless and the gods in them are countless, too.

At every moment, they fall away and come into existence in countless number. Since this thing takes place, then those fraught with sin go there. Since they are indeed countless, then violence here is the connection to heaven. Happening through necessity, father, it is ever gained by the violent and suchlike. Besides, since nonviolent ascetics are few indeed in this world, consequently they become leprous and crippled beggars. They are few indeed.

And since this is very well known, that the effect is con- 8.75
formable by the cause, how, father, could the source of comfort come from the affliction of the body? Therefore, Your Majesty, the crest-jewel of those who know the principles of all the textbooks, spoke foolishly when you said you would take initiation forthwith. So continue to protect the earth as far as the moon.'

Then, as the King thought in silence, 'He is absolutely unteachable,' Queen Ratnávali, weeping and full of care, addressed her son:

'Oh, oh, my son! What is superior to the vow of asceticism, and this would be your father's endeavor, except for your bad conduct, alas!

api ca:

tri|loka|khyāta|yaśaso devasy' âitasya nandanaḥ,
dhig! daivena kṛtaḥ kiṃ tvaṃ yady a|bhavyo 'si, putraka?
8.80 bhaviṣyasi kathaṃ, vatsa, bhav'|âbdhau kṣipta enasā?
yat praty|akṣaṃ bhavasy evaṃ. hā hatā sā janany api!
kalaṅkito 'dya bhavatā pitṛ|vaṃśo 'ti|nirmalaḥ.
hā putra, bhagnikā mātā tvayy a|bhavye karotu kim?
vatsa, yady api bhavyo 'si tath" âpi bhava|bhājanam.
katham āsanna|bhavyasya syur ullāpā amū|dṛśāḥ?
tat prasādaṃ kuru, vatsa, mā mudhā bhūḥ sva|vairikaḥ!
pāpād amuṣmād virama! ramasva Jina|vartmani!›

kumāro 'th' āha sa|krodhaṃ, ‹mātas, tvaṃ yadi dhārmikī,
tad a|priyaṃ karkaśaṃ ca kim evaṃ mayi bhāṣase?
8.85 dur|bhāṣiṇī tu nirbhāgya|manyā dhany" âsi na kvacit.
sarvath" ôpekṣaṇīyā tat tvam evaṃ bhāṣase mudhā.

kiṃ c' âsmy an|ucit'|ācāra|phalam āpsyāmi? kiṃ tava?
ya āskhalati tasy' âiva bhajyate danta|mālikā.›

mantrī Vimalamaty|ākhyo 'th' ācakhyau taṃ, ‹sva|mātari,
kumāra, mā kupo, 'patya|sneha ity aparādhyati.
mṛgī|gav'|âsvā|śakuni|kalaviṅka|dvik'|ādayaḥ
apatya|sneha|naṭitāḥ, paśya, kiṃ na hi kurvate!›

And besides:

What if you, the son of this king whose glory is celebrated by the triple universe, are destined by fate, alas, to be in-
capable of final emancipation, my dear son? How will you 8.80
exist, my child, sunk by sin in the ocean of existence, since you are evidently so! Alas, your mother is destroyed, too! Now you have disgraced your immaculate paternal lineage. Alas, my son, what will your sister, mother, do, if you are not capable of final emancipation? My child, even if you are capable of final emancipation, there's still the participating in existence. Would coaxing like this be necessary for one whose emancipation was close at hand? So be good-natured, my son. Don't make the mistake of being your own enemy. Desist from this bad conduct! Delight in the way of the Jina!'

Then the Prince said angrily, 'Mother, if you are so righteous, why are you saying these harsh and unpleasant things
about me? But, uttering abuse, you are to be regarded as in- 8.85
auspicious. You are completely lacking in good fortune. So, in speaking vainly in this manner, you are to be entirely disregarded.

And besides, am I the one who'll obtain the fruit of improper conduct? What about yours? The one who stumbles forward is the one who receives a garland of the teeth.'

Thereupon the minister named Vímala·mati said, 'Don't be angry with your mother, Prince, because her affection for her offspring has missed its mark. See, what won't does, cows, mares, kites, cuckoos, crows, et cetera, perform through affection for their offspring!'

kumāra|nirapekṣ'|ôkti|bāṇa|vṛndair arun|tudaiḥ
śrī|Ratnacūlo rāṇ mauna|vrata|bhaṅgam akāryata.

8.90 tato 'vadan nṛpas, ‹tvadvad
yady upekṣ" âsti nas tvayi,
rājyaṃ dadmaḥ kathaṃ? tasmāt
tat kuryā yena naḥ sukham.›

ath' âbhāṇi kumāreṇa, ‹deva|pādā diśantu me
yat kiñ can' âpy an|ucitam ācarāmy avakīrṇivat.›

rājñ" ōce, «putra, ye ghasrā Jina|dharm'|âvakeśinaḥ,
te garīyo|duḥkha|lakṣ'|âmbho|dhi|bhrama|nibandhanam.
prāpte nṛtve sarva|dharma|karma|nirmāṇa|karmaṭhe
na hi nirmantu|jantūnāṃ yukti|yuktaṃ pramāpaṇam.
naktaṃ|dinaṃ śabaravad aṭavyāṃ vasatas tava,
rājya|śriyā guṇaḥ ko nu cintā|maṇi|vayasyayā?
8.95 nānā|vidhāni peyāni khādyāny api ca santi te.
mal'|âvilair ninditaiś ca madya|māṃsair alaṃ tataḥ!

jīva|ghāte 'n|ārya|kārye yan|nimittaṃ tav' ôdyamaḥ,
tal labhyate dhanen' âpi, svayaṃ hiṃsā tato vṛthā.
ahar|niśam idaṃ, vatsa, yad ākheṭaka|kheṭanam,
tac ca prācīna|puruṣa|merāṃ lumpati mūlataḥ.
kula|merām atiyatāṃ kathaṃ śāstiṃ vidhāsyasi,
svayaṃ bhindan sva|maryādāṃ yādovaj jaḍa|saṅgataḥ?

The pain of the fleet of arrows that was the statement about disregard made by the Prince caused His Majesty King Ratna·chula to break his vow of silence.

Thereupon the King said, 'How can I have disregard for 8.90
you, as you say? I am bestowing the government of the kingdom on you. Therefore, undertake it in order to please me.'

Then the Prince said, 'Let my respected father show me in what respect my conduct has been at all improper, like one violating a vow of chastity.'

The King said, 'My son, those cruel beings who are barren of the Jain religion are bound to wander in the ocean of a hundred thousand extremely heavy sorrows. Once one has gained human birth, which provides the capability of performing every religious action, the slaughter of innocent beings is not at all fitting. Abiding day and night in a wilderness, like a savage, what quality do you now share with the rank of king, which has the power of a wishing-jewel?
And your drink and even your food is of various prohib- 8.95
ited kinds. So, have done with alcohol and meat, impure, polluted and forbidden!

And the aim of your effort, at the ignoble action of the slaughter of a being, can be gained by money alone, so violence is needless. And since, my son, this devotion to hunting continues day and night, it will completely obliterate the goal of previous human birth. How will you ordain chastisement on those who transgress the bounds of their family morality, since you yourself break your own bank, like a river, through association with the waters of stupidity?

tad an|uttāna|cittena praśastena divā|niśam,
deśa|kośa|catur|aṅga|camū|cintā viracyatām.

8.100 kiñ c' â|hiṃsreṇa dharma|jña|
miśreṇa bhavat", ânagha,
ā|candr'|ârkam idaṃ rājyaṃ
prājyaṃ nyāyyaṃ prabhujyatām!›

smitvā Jitāriṇ" âbhāṇi, ‹s'|â|śaṅkaḥ praharen na yaḥ,
tasya vāṇijakasy' êva na hi rājati rājatā.›

ath' ākhyad Vimalamatir mati|vaibhava|gīḥ|patiḥ:
‹dev'|āmātyaiḥ sva|pratibhā|pratibhātam udīryate.
śrūyate svāmibhiḥ samyak, sampradhārya vidhīyate.
na punas teṣu vijñaptyā prasādaḥ pratihanyate.
tad abrūve 'smi kumārāya sāraṃ sv'|ânubhav'|āspadam.
yadi samyak śrī|kumāro 'vadhatte, su|prasadya me.›

8.105 kumāro 'py abhyadhād, ‹dhīman,
sva|medh'|ôdbuddham ucyatām.
rājñāṃ dhiyaḥ saciva|dhīḥ
sa|dhrīcī hi divā|niśaṃ.›

mantry ūce, «nandan'|ôdyāne, deva, sva|pura|maṇḍane,
muni|vṛndārakair nityaṃ sevyo vṛndārakair api
saṃsār'|âmbudhi|tāraṇ'|âika|taraṇiḥ,
prodyan|manaḥ pary|av'|â-
vadhy|udvīkṣita|viśva|viśva|saraṇiḥ,
siddhānta|cintā|maṇiḥ,
nānā|labdhi|mahā|nidhir nara|sura|
śreṇī|vasat|saṃnidhiḥ,
kalye 'bhyait kila jaṅgamaḥ sura|taruḥ,
śrī|Suvrataḥ sad|guruḥ.

So, with an unsupine and happy mind, day and night let your care be disposed on the country, the treasury and
the army of four divisions. And besides, stainless one, let 8.100
this kingdom, the subjects and justice be protected by you, respected as one who knows the right, by means of nonviolence, for as long as the moon and sun exist.'

Jitári smiled and said, 'He who does not attack fearlessly is, like a merchant, in no degree resplendent with the rank of kingship.'

Then Vímala·mati, a master of eloquence through the power of his intelligence, said, 'The manifestation of their intelligence is uttered by a king's ministers. Kings hear what is right, deliberate, and make the decision. But their generosity is not impeded by a request. So I myself will tell the Prince the main point, which has the authority of his own experience. If His Highness the Prince comes to the right conclusion, reward me generously.'

The Prince said, 'Wise man, let what has arisen from 8.105
the power of your intelligence be spoken. The thoughts of kings and the thoughts of ministers certainly face the same direction, day and night.'

The minister said, 'Your Highness, in the garden of delight, the ornament of your city, ever attended by his eminent monks and also by the gods, a unique helper for the crossing of the ocean of existence, a path for the entire universe beheld with upraised perception as far as the limit of the senses, a wishing-jewel of true doctrine, a huge treasury of manifold profit, his vicinity beset with throngs of men and gods, at daybreak, came the true teacher reverend Súvrata, truly a walking tree of the gods.

taṃ c' ānantum ahaṃ tad" âiva gatavān.
romāñcitas tri|prada-
kṣiṇyā cāru|mahī|rajas|tilaka|vi-
bhrājiṣṇu|pañc'|âṅgakaḥ,
bhaktyā vanditavān su|sādhu|pariṣad|
vibhrājitaṃ śrī|guruṃ,
marty'|â|martya|sabh"|ântare samucita|
sthāne tatas tasthivān.

tataś ca mandara|kṣubdha|dugdh'|âmbhodhi|gabhīra|dhīḥ
śrī|Suvrata|guruś cakre deśanāṃ kleśa|nāśinīm.
8.110 atr'|ântare galat|kuṣṭha|galit'|âṅguli|nāśikaḥ,
sphuṭit'|âṅga|sravat|pūti|dhārā|saṃsikta|bhūtalaḥ,
madhu|jālakavad viṣvaṅ|makṣikā|kambal'|āvṛtaḥ,
caṇḍālavat śiṣṭa|lokaiḥ sampark'|ālāpa|varjitaḥ,
cal'|âcala|kṛmi|kul'|ākulit'|âkhila|vigrahaḥ,
a|jñāni|janat"|ākrośyas tāsv a|sabhy'|ôkti|bhīṣaṇaḥ,
duṣ|karm'|ôdaya|dṛṣṭ'|ânto, vidvan|nirveda|mandiram,
Vasumitro nāma pumān āyayau tatra parṣadi.
śrī|Suvrataṃ sūri|rājaṃ namaskṛtya kṛt'|âñjaliḥ,
sa ca vijñāpayāmās' âuṣṭha|sphor'|ônmitayā girā:
8.115 «yathā duḥkhy asmi, bhagavaṃs,
tath" ânyo 'py asti kaś cana?»
bhagavān āha, «he bhadra,
s'|âvadhāno niśāmaya.

At that very moment I came to bow before him. Respectfully walking around him three times, my body desiring to shine with the ornamental marks made by the dust of his approval, I was brought by you to pay my respects to the venerable teacher, resplendent among his assembly of true ascetics, and then stood in an appropriate place among the assembly of men and gods.

And then, his understanding as deep as the ocean of milk that was churned by the sacred mountain, reverend Súvrata began to expound the teaching that destroys distress.
At that moment, his nose, finger and toes crumbled away 8.110
by leprosy, sprinkling the ground with stinking pus oozing from the cracks in his body, covered with a cloak of bees facing all directions, his touch and conversation shunned by the other people, as if he were an untouchable, his body filled with a mass of worms continually writhing, an object of abuse for ignorant people, a cry of horror for the impolite among them, an example of bad karma becoming manifest, for the wise an abode of indifference to the world, a man named Vasu·mitra arrived at that assembly.

And, having bowed with his hands folded in salutation to reverend Súvrata, the best of learned doctors, he spoke in a voice meted out through trembling lips:

"Is any other possessed of as much distress as I am, rev- 8.115
erend sir?" The reverend doctor said, "Now, my good man, listen with attention.

anantara|bhave 'py āsīd yat te duḥkhaṃ kim apy aho!
tad anantatame bhāge 'py etad duḥkhaṃ na vartate.
yatas tvay" â|pratiṣṭhāne mahā|duḥkham anukṣaṇam
trayas|triṃśi|sāgarāṇi nirantaram asahyata.
tataś c' ântar|ṃuhūrt'|āyur matsī|garbhe jhaṣo 'bhavaḥ.
tato 'bhūr a|pratiṣṭhāne trayas|triṃśy|abdhi|jīvitaḥ.
ṣaṭ|ṣaṣṭiṃ sāgarāṇy evaṃ duḥkhaṃ soḍhvā nirantaram,
a|jīrṇa|duṣ|karma|śeṣāc chunī|garbham upāgamaḥ.
8.120 kālāj jātā kāla|śunī tad|bālye 'mṛta tat|prasūḥ.
dur|dānt'|ābhīra|ḍiṃbhaiḥ sā yodhyate sma śva|potakaiḥ.
tat tīkṣṇa|danta|nakhara|prahārair dārit'|âṅgikā
kṣut|tṛṣṇ'|ārtā mṛtā, jajñe Rāṣṭravardhana|pattane,
ā|janma|niḥsvātā|sadma|yoga|rāj'|ākhya|vaṇṭhataḥ
Mahilasya gṛha|dāsyāṃ cauryaga|kṛtta|naśy atha,
tvag|doṣa|dūṣit'|âṅgyāṃ ca, prājaniṣta bhavān sutaḥ.
tad|doṣāt prācya|duṣ|karma|śeṣataś c' êti kuṣṭhy abhūḥ.»

kuṣṭhy āha, «bhagavan, kena karmaṇā bhava|pañcake
duḥkh' îty abhūvaṃ? prasady' āviṣkuru, jñāna|bhāskara!»
8.125 sūrir ūce, «bhadra|mukha, tvam atr' âiva hi Bhārate
śrī|Kāñcanapura|svāmi|Nabhovāhana|bhūpateḥ
devyāḥ Kanakamañjaryāḥ putro 'bhūḥ Kanakadhvajaḥ.
mātā|pitṛbhyāṃ mene sa sva|vaṃś'|âlaṅkṛti|dhvajaḥ.

Ah! How great besides was your distress in the endless cycle of existence, for this here pain does not proceed without the inherited portion of fortune very close at hand. For, in the hell without a solid ground for thirty-three aeons you endured extreme pain increasing at every moment. Then, in the womb of a female fish, you became a fish with a life span of less than an hour. After that you lived for thirty-three aeons in the hell without a solid ground. Having endured constant pain for sixty-six aeons, because your remaining bad karma was not worn away, you entered the womb of a bitch.

In course of time, a black bitch was born. Her mother 8.120
died in her childhood. She used to fight with puppies, the offspring of untamed mongrels. Then, her body rent by sharp teeth and claws, sick with hunger and thirst, she died, and was conceived in the town of Rashtra·vardhana, in the womb of a slave girl in Máhila's house, who, through being crippled, was known as a mistress of yoga, an abode of poverty from birth, her nose cut off by a bandit, and her body defiled by skin disease. You were born her son. Because of her faults and because of the remainder of your previous bad karma, you became a leper."

The leper said, "Reverend sir, through what action in the field of battle of existence did I become so unfortunate? Graciously make it manifest, you sun of knowledge."

The reverend doctor said, "Good sir, in this very land of 8.125
Bhárata, you became the son of King Nabho·váhana, the lord of lovely Kánchana·pura, and Queen Kánaka·mánjari. Named Kánaka·dhvaja (Golden Banner) by his parents, he was a banner ornamenting his lineage.

sa ca rākṣasavan māṃsa|priyo, hiṃsā|parāyaṇaḥ,
golikā|dhanuṣā pakṣi|kulaṃ vivyādha śaiśave.
śyenaiḥ śakunta|śakuni|mukhān ākāśa|cāriṇaḥ,
jālaiḥ kacchapa|matsy'|ādīṃś c' âgrahīj jala|cāriṇaḥ.
mṛg'|ādīnāṃ ca mṛgayāṃ svayaṃ mṛgayubhis tathā
nirmimāṇaḥ sa n' âtṛpyad, bhasmaka|vyādhimān iva.

kiṃ bahunā?

8.130 na sa prakāraḥ ko 'py asti, yen' âsau māṃsa|lolupaḥ
jala|sthal'|âmbara|carān n' âvadhīd Daṇḍapāṇivat.
jugupsate dharma|gurūn, sādhūn upahasaty api.
mitr'|ādyair vārito 'vādīn, ‹n' âsty ātmā, na bhav'|ântaram.›
‹prajñāpanīyo n' âiv' âyam› iti śiṣṭair upekṣitaḥ,
apekṣitaś ca pāpiṣṭhaiḥ, so 'janiṣṭa niraṅkuśaḥ.
tataś ca tādṛg|duṣ|karm'|ârjita|duṣ|karma|bhāritaḥ
nimamajj' âpratiṣṭhāne narak'|âbdhau. sa c' âsi, bhoḥ.»

tat tādṛg|guru|māṇikya|dhāmnā dhvasta|tad|āvṛteḥ
jāti|smṛti|nidhis tasy' ôjjaghaṭe '|cintya|vīryataḥ.

8.135 sv'|āihik'|ôdanta|dṛṣṭ'|ântād guru|vāc" ânumāpitāt
jāti|smṛtyā sva|saṃvittyā niścikye prāg|bhavān asau.

And he, like a demon, was addicted to meat, violence his principal aim. In his childhood he killed flocks of birds with ball from a catapult. He caught denizens of the air, jay, finches, et cetera, by means of hawks, and denizens of water, turtles, fish, et cetera, by means of nets. And thus on his own and with huntsmen, he never had his fill of going on hunts for deer, et cetera, like one possessed of continually eating sickness.

What need of more?

There was no method with which he, ravenous for flesh, 8.130
did not kill those going by water, land or air, like Death with his stick in hand. He detested the teachers of righteousness and derided ascetics. Warned by his friends and such, he would say, 'The soul does not exist. There is no afterlife.'

Disregarded by the cultivated on the grounds that he was not fit to be associated with, but sought after by the wickedest, he became out of control. And then, weighed down by the bad karma acquired by such bad actions, he sank into the ocean of the hell without a solid ground. And you are he, good sir."

Then, his obstruction of it destroyed by the glory of that jewel of a teacher, the treasury of the memory of his former lives was opened, with its inconceivable power.

Because of this account of his doings here in this world 8.135
related by teacher, made conformable by this memory of his former lives together with his understanding, he gained firm conviction through his former existence.

so 'tha vyajñāpayat sūriṃ,
«niḥsandigdham idam, prabho.
Kanakadhvaja|nāstikya|
phalam āsvāditaṃ mayā.
tad atra, bhagavann, asmi bhava|bhramaṇa|rīṇa|dhīḥ.
sarv'|āhāra|parīhārād, yuṣmad|deva|nṛp'|āśrayāt,
prāṇa|tyāgaṃ cikīrṣāmi vuvūrṣāmi ca sad|gatim.»
gurur ākhyad, «idaṃ kartuṃ jāgarti tava yogyatā.»
tatas tasya guroḥ pārśve 'n|aśanaṃ pratipadya saḥ
gṛdhra|pṛṣṭha|vidhānen' âvatasthau sthema|parvataḥ.
8.140 tatra gṛdhra|kaṅka|kāka|vṛka|śvāna|śiv"|ādhibhiḥ
bhakṣyamāṇaḥ śubha|dhyānāt kṣīṇ'|āyuḥ kalpa ādime
vimān'|âdhipatir devo Vibhākaravibho 'bhavat,
sadya|prayukt'|âvadhiś ca tad|guroḥ pārśvam āgamat.
«sa ev' âhaṃ kuṣṭhī
sakala|janatā|dur|bhagatamaḥ,
prasādād vaḥ pūjyāḥ
sapadi divi|ṣad|bhūvam abhajam»
iti vyāhṛty' ôccaiś
caraṇa|kamalaṃ Suvrata|guror
namajjitvā nāṭyaṃ
vyaracayad agāt sv'|āspadam asau.
ity puṇy'|â|puṇya|phalaṃ may" âdy' âdhyakṣam īkṣitam.
kumāra, bahu|manyasva, manyasva pitṛ|bhāṣitam.›
vihasy' āha kumāro 'tha, ‹mantrin, kuhaka|mohitaḥ
māṃ mohayitum ārabdho, Jitārir mohyate na hi.›

Then he addressed the reverend doctor, "There is no doubt about this, my lord. I have enjoyed the fruit of Kánaka·dhvaja's atheism. This being the case, reverend sir, my mind has become detached from wandering in existence. By means of abandoning all food, with close reliance upon you and the king of the gods, I wish to abandon life and I desire to gain a good destination." The reverend teacher said, "Your ability to do this is evident."

Then, in the presence of the teacher, having undertaken the renouncement of food, he remained a motionless mountain, abandoning himself to vultures, according to precept.
There devoured by vultures, herons, crows, wolves, dogs, 8.140
jackals, et cetera, his life having ended in meditation on auspicious matters, in the first Good Works heaven, he became the god Vibhákara·vibha, the king of a celestial mansion, and, immediately employing his supernatural faculties, went to the side of that teacher.

Having loudly declared, "I am that very leper, the most unfortunate of all people. By your grace, may you be blessed!, I suddenly partook of the realm of the dwellers in heaven," he bowed to the lotus-feet of the teacher Súvrata, performed a dance and returned to his own abode.

Thus I have now made clearly evident the consequences of auspicious and inauspicious actions. Pay high regard to it, Prince, and regard what was said by your parents.'

Then the Prince laughed and said, 'Minister, deceived by trickery, you tried to deceive me, but Jitári is not deceived at all.'

8.145 kāla|daṣṭa iv' â|sādhya upadeśa|rcām asau,
iti niścitya sacivo jujuṣe joṣam añjasā.

tato rājā Ratnacūḍaś, cūḍa|ratnaṃ vivekinām,
‹śarīra|ceṣṭām ādhatsv' êty› uvāca nija|nandanam.

‹mahā|prasādo dev' êty› abhidhāy' ôtthāya rāja|sūḥ
samāsasāda sv'|āvāsaṃ jita|kāśī sva|cetasā.

atha devī sa|nirvedaṃ medin"|īśaṃ vyajijñapat:
‹dharm'|ân|abhijñas tvat|sūnuḥ kathaṃ, deva, bhaviṣyati?›

rāj" ākhyad, ‹devi, kaḥ kasya svaḥ paro v" âtha vā na kaḥ
saṃsāra|nāṭake 'muṣmin saṃdṛbdhe karma|sūtriṇā?

8.150 āntar'|âri|jito 'py eṣa Jitāriḥ kīrtito mṛṣā,
na c' āropita|tāratvaṃ śuktik'|ârdhaṃ tad|artha|kṛt.
duṣ|karma|saṃnipāty eṣa yogyo dharm'|āuṣadhasya na.
tad asya cintayā, devi, mā viṣādaṃ kṛthā vṛthā.

tad asya rājya|dānen' āihikaṃ kāryaṃ samāpyate,
pāratrikaṃ tu pravrajy"|âṅgīkārāt paripūryate.›

Yaśobhājana|mantry ūce catuṣ|karṇaṃ mahī|bhuje:
‹bhāvit'|Ârhad|vacanānām etad, dev', âti|yujyate.
svāmin, kumāraḥ kin tv eṣa rājyasy' ârho na sarvathā.
devo jānāty eva tasya rājya|kāry'|ôtsahiṣṇutām.

8.155 tataḥ sīm"|āla|bhū|pālaiḥ sambhavī deśa|viplavaḥ;
tataḥ saṅghasya caityānāṃ dharmasy' âpi ca viplavaḥ.

Having come to the conclusion that he, like one bitten 8.145
by a black snake, was incurable by the recitation of advice, the minister instantly chose silence.

Then King Ratna·chula, the crest-jewel of the prudent, told his son to go and care for his bodily needs.

Then, saying, 'You are very gracious, Your Majesty,' the Prince left and returned to his own abode, mentally raising his fists in victory.

Then the Queen said to the King despondently, 'Your son lacks knowledge of religion. What will become of him, Your Majesty?'

The King said, 'My Queen, what future wealth has a person, or rather what does he not have, in this drama of
existence, bound together by the thread of karma? And since 8.150
he is vanquished by his internal enemy, he was named in vain Jitári, he whose enemy is vanquished, and his failure to ascend the vessel of salvation has reduced his wealth to half a pound. One who is totally cast down by bad karma, he is not fit for the medicine of religion, so don't be vainly depressed by your care for him.

So, by presenting him with the kingdom, duty in this world will be completed, but the duty of the other world is fulfilled by the undertaking of renouncement.'

The minister Yasho·bhájana said to the King in private, 'This is highly conformable to the teaching of the holy Fordmakers. But this prince, Your Majesty, is by no means fit for the kingship. Your Majesty understands the strenuous
business of government. Thence would come the overthrow 8.155
of the kingdom by powerful neighboring kings; thence the overthrow of the congregation, temples and religion. Your

dev'|ādiṣṭaṃ n' ôcitaṃ, tat pālyatāṃ tāvad urvy asau,
Yaśo|rāja|kumāraḥ syād yāvad urvī|dhuran|dharaḥ›
‹Yaśobhājana, sādhv etad yaśo|bhājanam eva naḥ.›
iti pratiśrutya rājā prāgvat svaṃ rājyam anvaśāt.
so 'nyadā vyasan'|āsakto rājya|kārya|parāṅ|mukhaḥ
Jitārir aśva|thaṭṭena yayāv ākheṭakaṃ prati.
gacchatā tena dṛṣṭv" âgre mukto 'śvo jambukaṃ prati.
aparair aśva|vāraiś ca tato 'sau mṛga|dhūrtakaḥ.
8.160 ṛju|mārgeṇa dhāvitvā jhaṭity eva nivartate.
kāṭeṣu līyate, tūrṇaṃ nirgacchati ca vāmataḥ.
pravṛtya dakṣiṇen' āśu ṭato 'pi ca nirvartate.
yādṛśā te 'bhidhāvanti, valaty eṣa tatas|tataḥ.
śṛgāla|siṃhena tena nṛ|siṃhā api te kṣaṇāt
śṛgālatām anīyanta, dur|gatau yogyatām api.
taṃ hantum evam eteṣām abhyāyatāṃ parasparam,
kumār'|âśvo Jasaravi|hayen' āsphalito 'dhikam.
kumār'|âśvo 'gra|kāyena nabhasy ullalito bhṛśam,
kumāraṃ pātayāmāsa dṛṣad|dṛḍha|mahī|tale.
8.165 gāḍh'|âbhighātena tena kumāraś cūrṇit'|âṅgakaḥ,
kumbhī|pāke 'ti|sukhataḥ praveśāy' êva vedhasā,
kṣaṇād vipanno Jitārī rasa|laulya|ku|mitra|yuk,
raudra|dhyāna|hay'|ārūḍho narakaṃ prāpadād imam.

Majesty's instruction was not suitable, so continue to govern this land until Prince Yasho·bhadra becomes able to govern the land.'

'Yasho·bhájana (Distributor of Glory), this is an excellent distribution of my glory.' Having thus agreed, the King governed his kingdom as before.

One day, intent on sin, averse to the duties of government, Prince Jitári went to a hunting ground with a troop of horsemen. As he was proceeding, he saw a jackal in front and sped his horse toward it. And then that deceiver of an-
imals was chased by the other fine horses. Forced to run in 8.160
a straight path, he immediately ran away. He entered some holes, and quickly came out in the other direction. And then, moving to the right, he quickly ran away again. As they likewise chased him, he ran from here to there. And they, although lions of men, were in a moment brought by that lion of a jackal into the state of being a jackal, despite it being fit for a bad rebirth.

As they galloped together in order to kill him, the Prince's horse collided violently with the horse of Yasho·ravi. The Prince's horse reared up violently into the air with the forepart of its body, and threw the Prince onto the surface of the ground, as hard as rock.

His body pulverized by the power of the impact, as if 8.165
it were fitting him very easily into a cooking pot, Jitári died instantly from the blow, and, the association of this bad friend, addiction to taste, mounted on the horse of meditation on violence, entered that cooking-pot hell.

tatra sāgaram ekaṃ so 'nubhūy' â|śarma kevalam,
Magadheṣu śry|agādheṣu, grāme Gobbara|nāmani.
kuṭumbinaḥ Satyahareḥ Sarvadevī|priy'|ôdare
duhitṛtvena sampede Jitārir narakāt tataḥ.
sā ca Satyamatir nāmnā yauvane paryaṇīyata
Satya|nām'|âbhidhānena kuṭumbi|tanu|janmanā.
8.170 kramāt tasyāḥ suto jajñe, Nāgadev'|âbhidhaḥ sa ca.
jāto 'ṣṭa|vārṣikaḥ pitroḥ pratyāśā|valli|pādapaḥ.
anyadā tad|gṛhe kā cic cārikā samupāgatā
tāṃ lobhayāmāsa nānā|śakti|kautuka|darśanaiḥ.
‹asman|mate milasi cet tan na bhogam avidyayā.
upabhuṅkṣe sadā sarv'|êndriya|śarma yadṛcchayā.›
tayā ca prāg|bhav'|âbhyasta|rasan'|êndriya|laulyataḥ
mene tad|uktaṃ. s" âth' ākhyat, ‹siddhir jyeṣṭha|sut'|ârpaṇāt›
Satyamaty" âbhāṇi, ‹katham idaṃ, mātar, vidhīyate?
pāpo vai vetsi, vatse, na kā mātā kaś ca nandanaḥ?›
8.175 ‹yady etad ucitaṃ na syād, kathaṃ svaṃ putram ārpayam
pūjyābhyo yoginībhyaḥ? kiṃ jyeṣṭhaḥ putro na me priyaḥ?
kiñ ca gehe nivasatā, manye, syur bahavo 'ṅgajāḥ.
nanv īdṛk siddhir iti me! vacanaṃ m" ânyathā kṛthāḥ.›

Having experienced there for an aeon only unhappiness, in a village named Góbbara, in the Mágadha country with its lovely deeps, in the womb of Sarva·devi, the wife of Satya·hari, a farmer, Jitári was endowed with daughterhood after being in hell. And named Satya·mati in her youth she was married to Satya, the son of a farmer.

In due course she bore a son named Naga·deva, and he 8.170
grew to be eight years old, a tree for the creeper of his parents' hopes.

One day, a certain wandering nun came to her home and excited her greed by displaying the various wonders of her power.

'If you meet my mind, then it won't be with ignorance of pleasure. You will enjoy spontaneous happiness with all your senses.'

And she agreed to what she said because of her addiction to the sense of taste practiced in her former life, and the other said, 'The accomplishment of magic power comes through the sacrifice of an eldest son.'

Satya·mati said, 'How can this be accomplished, mother? True, he is naughty, my dear, but don't you know what mother and son are like?'

'If this were not the proper thing to do, how would I have 8.175
sacrificed my own son to the demonesses who were to be worshipped? Was not my eldest son dear to me? Besides, in the home there will be many sons, I suppose. Surely, such is my power! Don't go back on your word.'

tayā pratiśrute jyeṣṭhas tat|putro vidadhe baliḥ.
śikṣitā śākinī|mantraṃ tābhiḥ s" âbhakṣayaj janam.

anyadā jagṛhe tābhir Mahilasya kuṭumbinaḥ
priyaḥ putro Vāmadevas, ten' āhūtāś ca māntrikāḥ.

ekena māntrikeṇ' âth' ākṛṣṭā sākṣād imāḥ samāḥ,
uktāś ca, ‹mukta ev' âsmin jīvitaṃ vo, 'nyathā na hi.›

8.180 tato muktaḥ sa pāpābhir atha grāmyair janair jage.
etāḥ sākṣān|mārayas tan n' ôjjhyā grāma|hit'|âiṣibhiḥ.

‹kin tu bhiṇṭair veṣṭayitvā pradīpyantām imā samāḥ,
yen' âkhilasya grāmasya sampanīpadyate śivam.›

tataś ca tās tathā kartuṃ nīyamānā vyalokayan
śāntā māhā|satīḥ sādhvīr mūrtā iva śama|śriyaḥ.

Satyamatyā tay" âcinti, ‹dhanyā vandyā imā param,
yā īdṛk|pāpa|viratāḥ puṇyā atra paratra ca.

aham tu niṣkṛpā, pāpā, kula|dvaya|kalaṅkinī
ih' âivaṃ maraṇaṃ prāpy' āpsyāmy amutra tu dur|gatim!›

8.185 muhur|muhuś cintayantī s" âivaṃ grāmeyakaiḥ kṣaṇāt
pradīpitā Satyamatī tābhiḥ saha palālavat.

tena sādhvī|guṇa|gaṇa|grahaṇe sa|hṛdā hṛdā,
upārjya sā manuṣy'|āyur, vipadya ca samādhinā,

puryām atr' âiva Kauśāmbyāṃ Buddhisāgara|mantriṇaḥ
priya|patnyā Jayadevyāḥ kukṣau tanayatām agāt.

She agreed, and her eldest son was sacrificed as an offering. The demonesses taught her the demoness spell, and she devoured people.

One day, they captured Vama·deva, the dear son of the farmer, Máhila, and he summoned soothsayers.

One of the soothsayers made the demonesses appear before their eyes and told them, 'You will live if he's freed, otherwise you won't.'

Thereupon he was released by those wicked females and 8.180
called by the village people. Then those goddesses of pestilence made manifest were not released by those well-wishers of the village. 'Rather, let them be wrapped in hemp and set on fire together, so that happiness be firmly attained for the entire village.'

And then, as they were being led away to suffer thus, they beheld Jain nuns, free from passion, highly virtuous, like images of the glory of tranquility.

Satya·mati thought, 'Henceforth these virtuous, venerable ladies who are so devoid of sin are to be honored in this world and the next. But I, pitiless and wicked, am the disgrace of two families. Alas, alas, after thus attaining death here, I shall attain a bad destination in the other world!'

Constantly thinking thus, Satya·mati was suddenly set 8.185
alight by a villager, together with the others, like a demon made of straw. Therefore, in her comprehension, with sincere heart, of the multitude of the virtues of the nuns, she attained human life, and having died in meditation, in this very city of Kaushámbi, she attained sonhood in the womb of Jaya·devi, the dear wife of the minister Buddhi·ságara.

kramena tanayo jajñe, jajñe sapadi mantriṇā
vardhāpitena dhātreyyā mantriṇī|baddha|sakhyayā.
pāritoṣika|dānena sacivas tām avardhayat.
dadhate na ciraṃ santo hy upakār'|âdhama'|rṇatām.

8.190 mah"|ôtsavair nava|navaiḥ prīṇayitv" âkhilaṃ puram
Jayaśāsana ity asya nāma|dheyam adhāt pitā.
sa ca tvam eṣa, saciva. svayaṃ samyag vibhāvaya.»
Sudharma|svāmin" êty uktaḥ sa īh'|ādau praviṣṭavān.

kṣaṇaṃ mūrcchā|vyājān
manasi calite prāg|bhava|diśaṃ,
samāyāte jāti|
smaraṇa|sahite tatra sapadi.
tad|ākhyātaṃ buddhvā
punar api yathāvat su|caritaṃ,
prabhuṃ natvā vyajñā-
payata muditaḥ s' âiṣa sacivaḥ:

«niḥ|sandigdham idaṃ prabh'|ûktam akhilaṃ.
svāmiṃs, tad ādiśyatām
īdṛk kaśmala|karma|marma|bhiduraṃ
kiñ cid rahasyaṃ mama.
īdṛk saumya|Jin'|ēśvarasya caraṇaṃ
yogyo 'smi ced, dehi tad.»
«yogyaḥ samprati, kin tu kiñ cid aparaṃ
tāvat kṣaṇaṃ śrūyatām.»

iti śrī|nirvāṇa|Līlāvatī|mahā|kath"|êti|vṛtt'|ôddhāre Līlāvatī|sāre Jin'|âṅke rasan'|êndriya|vipāka|vyāvarṇano nāma aṣṭama utsāhaḥ

In due course, a son was born, and the minister was congratulated on being a father by the midwife, the firm friend of the minister's wife. The minister enriched her with the presentation of a gratuity. Good men certainly do not remain long in debt for a favor given them.

As the entire city was filled with ever-renewed festivities, 8.190
his father gave him the name Jaya·shásana.

And you are he, minister. Reflect on yourself rightly." Thus addressed by reverend Sudhárman, he became engaged in consideration of what was for and against.

Suddenly, in the semblance of a swoon, his mind stirred in the direction of his former existences and, having arrived there, it was instantly endowed with the memory of his former lives. And having reawakened with a conscious understanding of what he had said, and, duly, of the right way of life, that very minister bowed to the lord, and joyfully declared:

"There is absolutely no doubt about the entirety of what was said by your lordship. So, reverend doctor, let some such protection be assigned me that will destroy the vital of impure karma. If I am worthy, grant me that way of life such as of the excellent Lord Jina." "You are now worthy, but listen to the rest for a moment."

Here ends the eighth canto, entitled "The Consequences of the Sense of Taste," of the Jain epic *The Epitome of Queen Liláváti*, an abridgment of the events of *The Epic Story of the Auspicious Final Emancipation of Liláváti.*

CANTO 9
THE CONSEQUENCES OF THE SENSE OF SMELL

9.1 Ath' âpare dyavi śrīmān Sudharma|prabhur abhyadhāt
ghrāṇa|laulya|vipākaṃ. «bho niśāmaya diśāṃ, vibho.
nānā|parimal'|āsakto ghrāṇa|duṣṭa|bhujaṅgamaḥ
pratyāsanno 'n|artha|sārtha|nidānaṃ, vaśyito na cet.
mūrcchām a|tucchāṃ datte 'sau, caitanyam apahanti ca.
aśnāti prāṇa|pavanaṃ, śvabhra|pātaṃ tanoti ca.

tathā hi:

elā|lavaṅga|kakkola|tvag|jāti|phala|garbhitam
pañca|saugandhikaṃ gandha|lubdhas tāmbūlam icchati.
9.5 elā|pāṭala|karpūra|pramukhair vāsitaṃ payaḥ,
drākṣ"|ādi|pānakaṃ kāpiśāyanaṃ ca pipāsati.
su|gandhi|nāga|raṅg'|āmra|mātuliṅg'|ādi sat|phalam,
karpūra|candana|rasa|vāsi|pūgī|phal'|ādi ca,
elā|karpūra|cūrṇ'|ādi|vāsitaṃ modak'|ādi ca,
karpūra|pūritaṃ varṣ"|ôpal'|ādi ca jighatsati.

candra|candana|kastūrī|ghusṛṇ'|ādi|vilepanam,
saurabhya|lubhyad|bhramara|mālāḥ kusuma|mālikāḥ,
kṛṣṇ'|âgaru|prabhṛtibhiḥ keśa|vastr'|ādi|vāsanam,
su|gandha|lakṣa|pāk'|ādi|tail'|âbhyaṅgaṃ ca sarvataḥ,
9.10 cañcarīka iv' â|śrāntaṃ ghrāṇ'|êndriya|vaṃśavadaḥ,
prati|kṣaṇaṃ vardhamān'|â|tuccha|mūrccho 'bhilaṣyati.

THEN, ON THE following day, the reverend Lord Su- 9.1
dhárman expounded the consequences of addiction
to smell. "Pay attention, Your Majesty, good sir.

One addicted to various fragrances, a pimp corrupted by smell, is close at hand to the cause of a company of unworthy matters, if he does not gain self-control. He gives himself a major delusion and steals away his intelligence. He consumes his breath of life and prepares his descent into hell.

Like so:

Greedy for perfume, he craves five-fragranced betel leaves
filled with cardamom, clove, aromatic berries, cinnamon
and nutmeg. And he desires to drink milk scented with 9.5
heaps of cardamom, fragrant pink flowers and camphor,
and wines made from grapes, et cetera, and liquor made
from honey. He desires to consume nutmeg, oranges, man-
goes, citron fruits and suchlike, pomegranates, and areca
nuts and suchlike flavored with the essence of camphor and
sandalwood, and round sweets scented with the powder
of cardamom, camphor and suchlike, and hailstone sweets
filled with camphor.

Subjugated to his sense of smell, he craves unweariedly 9.10
like a bee unguents of camphor, sandalwood, musk, saffron,
et cetera, garlands of flower with swarms of bees desirous
of their sweet scent, the perfuming of his clothes, hair, et
cetera, with black aloes and such, and being anointed all
over with fragrant oils made from boiled citrons, et cetera,
his severe delusion increasing at every moment.

etac ca vipulāṃ lakṣmīṃ vinā sampadyate na hi.
vipulā śrīś ca na prāyo vin" ārambha|parigrahau.
tad" āsaktaś ca vikalo rāga|dveṣa|visaṃsthulaḥ,
kṛty'|â|kṛty'|ândha|badhiraḥ patati prāṇa|saṃśaye.
duṣ|karma|bandhān nibiḍān narake 'sau viḍambyate.
tataḥ kathañ cid udvṛttaḥ ku|tiryaṅ|nṛṣu jāyate.
tatr' âpi gandha|sambandha|lubdha|ghrāṇ'|âhi|saṅgataḥ
bhave bhave varāko 'sau duḥ|sahaṃ duḥkham aśnute.

9.15 rājann, atra ca dṛṣṭ'|ânta eṣa śreṣṭhī Purandaraḥ.»
sa natv" ōce, «sva|caritaṃ śuśrūṣe tvan|mukhāt, prabho.»
deva|dundubhi|nirghoṣa|sa|nābhi|dhvani|ḍambaraḥ
«ākarṇyatāṃ, naigam'|êś'» êty uvāca gaṇa|bhṛd|varaḥ.
«Jambū|dvīpo dvīpa|rājo yojana|lakṣa|nāyakaḥ.
lavaṇas tad|dvi|guṇ'|ēśaḥ samudrāṇāṃ dhuri sthitaḥ.
tato 'pi Dhātakī|khaṇḍo dvīpas tad|dvi|guṇ'|âdhi|sūḥ.
tataḥ paratra kāl'|ôdas tad|dvi|guṇa|mat'|īśvaraḥ.
tataś ca Puṣkaravara|nāmā dvīpas tṛtīyakaḥ
cakāsti yojana|laksa|ṣo|ḍaśak'|âdhi|nāyakaḥ.

And this certainly can't be achieved without extensive wealth. And generally extensive wealth is not without attachment and possessiveness.

Then, addicted and destitute, agitated by rage and hatred, blind and deaf through doing what shouldn't be done, he falls into peril of life. Because of the density of the bad karma he has attracted to himself, his is afflicted in hell. Having somehow arisen from there, he is born among low animals and men. There, too, through close association with the snake of the sense of smell, because of his craving to be in close embrace with perfume, in every existence he attains pain, difficult to endure.

And, Your Majesty, as an example of this, here is the 9.15
merchant Puran·dara." He bowed and said, "I wish to hear my story from your mouth, my lord."

His loud voice reverberating like the beating of the kettledrums of the gods, the excellent leader of the congregation said, "Listen, leading merchant."

"Rose-apple Tree Island is the head of the islands, owner of a diameter of a hundred thousand leagues. The salt ocean, possessing a diameter twice the size of that, stands at the head of the oceans. And after that is Grislea-Tormentosa-Tree Island, master of a diameter twice the size of that. In the next place after that is the black ocean, possessor of a measurement twice the size of that. And after that, the third island, named Lotus Island, shines resplendent, master of sixteen hundred thousand leagues.

9.20 na jāne, kena cit, kasmāc cid vivādāt kadā cana
mānuṣ'|ôttara|śailena sīmnā dvedhā vyabhājy asau.
pūrv'|ârdhe tatra ca prācī|pratīcyor mandara|dvayam.
sapta sapta Videh'|ādyā varṣāś ca prati|mandaram.

prāṅ|mandara|pratibaddhe kṣetre Bharata|nāmani
cakāśe madhyama|khaṇḍa|bhūṣā śrī|Vijayāpurī,
yā vapra|śṛṅga|skhalana|bhīty" ârkeṇ' âpy a|laṅghitā,
parikhā|vāri|śamita|śeṣa|bhū|vahana|klamā
yakṣa|harmya|tal'|ālīn'|ācārya|tāla|pratiṣṭhayā
ekayā yatra divi ca saṅgītakam ajāyata.

9.25 tasyāṃ śasya|krama|lakṣmīr Arisiṃho mahī|patiḥ,
yan|nāma|mantras trāsāya pratyarthi|kariṇām, aho!
preyasī tasya Padmaśrīḥ k" âpy a|bhaṅgura|saurabhā,
naktaṃ|diva|vikāśinyāṃ yasyāṃ rāj" âty|arajyata.
sa ca kṣoṇī|patir ghrāna|viṣay'|āsakta|mānasaḥ
sāraṃ saurabhyam ev' âikam indriy'|ârtheṣv amanyata.

tathā hi:

jala|ja|sthala|j'|âneka|kusum'|āmoda|ṣaṭ|padaḥ, chinna
sarva'|rtu|ramya|nān"|âṅga|rāga|vicchitti|kovidaḥ,
naika|jātīya|kusuma|druti|snān'|âti|pāvanaḥ,
gandhasāra|ghanasāra|paṭavās'|âdhivāsitaḥ,

I don't know by whom, as a result of what dispute, or when, it was parted in two by a mountain ridge marking the final boundary of human beings. And in that first half are two mountains, one in the east, one in the west. And by each of the mountains lie seven continents, Vidéha and the others. 9.20

In the continent named Bhárata, attached to the eastern mountain, the lovely city of Víjaya·puri* shines forth, the ornament of the central region, which was unsurmounted even by the sun through its fear of teetering from the pinnacles on its ramparts, and which had tired out the primeval serpent, the supporter of the world, through the labor of preparing its moat of water; in which, and also in heaven, a symphony was created at the inauguration of a temple of the demigod, through the clapping of the teachers situated on its roof.

In it was a king named Ari·simha (Lion for His Enemies), 9.25 whose sovereign power was of excellent descent, and whose name was, bravo!, a spell for protection against the elephants of his enemies. His mistress was Padma·shri. The King was passionately delighted with whatever intense perfume arose by day or night. And that King, his mind addicted to the sense of smell, actually paid regard to the essence of fragrance alone among the sphere of the objects of the senses.

Like so:

A bee for the fragrant perfume of the various flowers grown in land and water; skilled in marking the body with and applying the various unguents enjoyable in every season; being highly cleansed with baths softened with many

9.30 āma|karpūra|kastūrī|śrī|kṛṣṇ'|âguru|candanaiḥ
keśa|vastra|vapur|vāsa|veśma|vās'|âti|lālasaḥ,
samucchalat|parimala|vāsit'|â|śeṣa|diṅ|mukhaḥ chinna gan-
dha|skandhaś cariṣṇur nu vyacarat sa yad|ṛcchayā.
guṇī|kṛt'|â|śeṣa|śeṣa|hṛṣīka|viṣay'|ôtkaraḥ
sa priya|prābhṛte 'py āsīt surabhau rābhasikya|bhāk.

itaś ca Puryāṃ śrīmatyāṃ, bhīmatyāṃ na kadā cana,
rājā śrī|Vimalakīrtis, tasya Kīrttimatī priyā.
Kamalāvatī tat|putrī catuḥ|ṣaṣṭi|kalāvatī,
an|aupādhika|saubhāgya|saugandhy|āḍhya|vapur|latā.
9.35 adhītinī kāma|śāstre, rati|kelī|vicakṣaṇā,
tasmai śrī|Arisiṃhāy' âth' ôpatasthe svayaṃvarā.

sa tāṃ mahā|ḍambareṇ' ôpayeme medinī|patiḥ,
tayā punaḥ sa saṃyeme 'ṅga|saurabha|mukhair guṇaiḥ.
Lakṣmīm a|lakṣmīm, Āryāṃ c' ân|
    āryāṃ, varṇāt til'|ôttamām,
Rambhāṃ rabhā|giraṃ mene
    sa tay" ân|upama|śriyā.

tataḥ sa bhūpaḥ Padmaśrī|pramukhaṃ prema|mandiraṃ
avarodham avarodhaṃ sukha|śrīṇām amanyata.
śayane jāgare sthāne prasthāne bhavane vane
dine din'|ânte chāy" êva tasy' âbhūt s" anuyāyinī.

kinds of flowers; scented with perfumed powder of sandalwood and camphor, which was a bee for the honey of
perfume; absolutely craving for his hair, clothes, body, rai- 9.30
ment and house to be perfumed with fine camphor, musk, fragrant black aloes and sandal; his face moving in all directions to enjoy the fragrance rising upward from the grinding of aromatic substances, he passed his time at will, an actual walking mass of perfume. The mass of all the other objects of his senses made subordinate to that remaining one, the King was excessively desirous of perfume, even as an offering for his favor.

Now, in lovely Puri, in which there was never any fear, lived a king, His Majesty Vímala·kirti. Kírttimati was his wife. Kamalávati was their daughter, mistress of the sixty-four arts, the creeper of her body rich in the fragrance of her
unsurpassable beauty, a skilled student of the sport of love 9.35
as described in the manual of erotics, she made a choice of His Majesty Ari·simha at her assembly of suitors.

The King married her with high-sounding assertations, but he was under her control, because of her excellencies, chief of which was the beauty of her body. And in comparison with her beauty he considered Lakshmi to be without fortune, honorable Párvati to be dishonorable, in outward appearance the smallest particle, and Rambha to have a voice like a cow.

Thenceforth, the King considered the apartment made excellent by Padma·shri, a temple of affection, to be an obstacle to the good fortune of his pleasure. Sleeping, staying at rest, moving forth, in the palace, in the forest, at

9.40 bhoginī s" âtha Padmaśrī pradveṣa|viṣa|pūritā
tasyāś chidrāṇi mṛgyantī divā|niśam akhidyata.
tām uccāṭayituṃ, bhūpaṃ vaśīkartum ath' âiṣikā
māntrikāmṣ tāntrikān yoginy|ādikān apy upācarat.

yoga|cūrṇaṃ carikayā dade tasyāḥ pare dyavi,
ūce ca, ‹gandhe prakṣipya deyaṃ nasi yathā viśet.›

Padmaśrīs tat sughandeṣu
nyasya gandhān dadau prabhoḥ.
te gandha|lobhād āghrātā
bhū|bhujaḥ prāviśan nasi.
taiś ca cūrṇa|lavair mando grahilaḥ syāt paṭur vaśaḥ.
tadā ca sa nṛpo mandas tato 'bhūd grahilo bhṛśaṃ.

tataś ca:

9.45 hasati rodati pūt|kurute nṛpo
bhramati gāyati tāratara|svaram,
sva|mukha|vādana|tāla|puraḥ|saraṃ
nivasanena vinā parinṛtyati.
śapati nindati pūjyatamān api
praharate 'nucarāṃś ca nirāgasaḥ.
nanu mah"|āuṣadhi|mantra|gaṇā|gaṇā
viphalatām upayānti vidhiṃ vinā.

tato 'mātyaiḥ sa saṃyamya cikṣipe dāru|pañjare.
hūtā vaidyā mantra|tantra|yoga|cūrṇa|vido 'pi ca.
sva|sva|kriy"|ārambhitaiś ca na c' âbhūt praguṇo nṛpaḥ.
tatr' âtha mantriṇo 'bhūvan nirāśā vigat'|ādarāḥ.

day, at night, like his shadow, Kamalávati was his constant attendant.

But the mistress, Padma·shri, filled with the poison of hostility, hunting for her weak spots, remained depressed, day and night. And in order to ruin her and subdue him to her will she approached sorcerers, wizards and witches, et cetera. 9.40

And on the following day a nun gave her magic powder and said, 'Sprinkle it in perfume and apply it to his nose as he is sleeping.'

Padma·shri put it in perfumes, and applied the perfumes to the King. Because of his greed for perfume, those scents entered the King's nose. And by means of those particles of powder one becomes idiotic and mad with violent intent. Then, because of it, the King became idiotic and violently mad.

And then:

The King laughed, wept, blew raspberries, wandered about, sang in a very shrill tone, and danced about without any clothes, the attendant rhythm produced by sound from his own mouth. He cursed and reviled even the most respectable and struck his blameless servants. Surely, indeed, powerful drugs, spells and witches do not achieve success without a stratagem! 9.45

Thereupon the ministers restrained him and placed him in a wooden cage. And they summoned doctors skilled in spells, sorcery and magic powder. And he was not made sound by any of them, each employing his own remedy. Then the ministers had no more hope in him, their regard for him gone.

sampradhārya tataḥ samyak sarvaiḥ sāmanta|mantribhiḥ
tan|mūrty|antaravad rājye ’sthāpi putro ’rikesarī.

9.50 tato ’rikesarī rājā saṃjajñe rāja|kesarī,
krama|vikrama|śālitvād adhṛṣyo vairi|kuñjaraiḥ.
nirbhāgyā sā ca Padmaśrī naṃṣṭv” âgāt tāta|mandiram.
pati|kārmaṇa|pāpm” âsyāḥ papāt’ çtr’ âiva mūrdhani.

sa c’ Ârisiṃho grahilo, ’n|ādarān manda|rakṣitaḥ,
nirgatya bhrāmyan dikṣv āpa puraṃ Kṣitipratiṣṭhitam.
ārakṣaiḥ pratyabhijñāya, so ’risiṃho ’yam ity, asau
grahilo darśayāñcakre Vijayarāja|bhū|bhujaḥ.

ten’ ôcchalat|krodha|vahni|jvāla|pāṭala|cakṣuṣā
tad|dhūma|laharī|sadhryaṅ|bhrakuṭī|bhīṣmam aucyata:

9.55 ‹re, so ’yaṃ nitya|vairī nas tat khar’|āropaṇād ayam
pure vigopy’ âivam|evaṃ, bahir evaṃ viḍambyatām.›

tataś c’ âbhidadhe mantra|maulinā śrī|Subuddhinā:
‹dev’, âvadhāryatāṃ tāvan nīti|pūtaṃ vaco mama.
mṛtasya māraṇe, deva, su|bhaṭasya yaśo na hi.
grahilaś ca mṛta ev’ êty ādeśo ’n|ucitaḥ prabhoḥ.

api ca:

nirāyudhasya vyasanaṃ, prāptasya, gṛham eyuṣaḥ,
raṇa|kṣetre patitasya vadho ’rer api n’ ôcitaḥ.

Then, having duly deliberated, all the ministers and barons appointed to the kingship his son Ari·késarin, who was like another image of him. Then King Ari·késarin be- 9.50
came a lion of a king, having become distinguished by the heroism of his proceedings, not ventured to be attacked by the elephants of his enemies. And, lacking any portion, Padma·shri disappeared and went to her father's home. Her criminal sorcery against the King assuredly fell on her own head.

And Ari·simha, mad and negligently guarded through the lack of regard for him, escaped, and wandering in all directions came to the city of Kshiti·pratíshthita . The police, having recognized that the madman was Ari·simha, exhibited him to King Víjaya·raja.

His eyes red with the flames of the fire of his rising anger, with a fearful frown accompanied by billows of its smoke, he said:

'Hey, this is my constant enemy. So, after mounting him 9.55
on a donkey, let him be mocked in such and such a way within the city, and then let him be degraded like so outside.'

Then the chief minister, honorable Subúddhi, said, 'Your Majesty, just consider for a moment my advice, pervaded with statecraft. Your Majesty, a true soldier has no glory at all in the killing of one already dead. And because a madman is indeed dead, Your Majesty's command was unfitting.

And besides:

The slaughter of one without a weapon, who has met defeat, who has come to one's home, has fallen in the field of battle, even of an enemy, is not right, Your Majesty.

kiñ c' Ârikesarī rājā putro 'sya viditaḥ prabhoḥ,
etasy' âivaṃ kṛte 'vaśyaṃ tav' â|mitrī|bhaviṣyati.

9.60 tat|senay" âpi devasya, trāsitāyā bhuvo dhruvaṃ,
jala|sthal'|âdri|durgāṇi muktv" ânyac|ccharaṇam na hi.

«kṛta|pratikṛtaṃ kartuṃ tava sāmpratam īśmahe,
vayaṃ na tvā|dṛśāḥ, kin tu tad|asmad|deśato vraja.»
bhāṇayitv" êti datvā ca śambalaṃ preṣyate 'sakau.
evaṃ|kṛte prabhoḥ kīrtiḥ Kārttik'|êndu|vijitvarī.›

rājñā tathā kārite 'sau bhraman Kheṭapuraṃ yayau,
rājye kṛta|prasādena paryajñāyi naṭena ca.

jyot|kṛtya bhāṣitas tena, ‹svāminn, evaṃ kim aṭyase?›
sa vicetāḥ pratibrūte n' âiv', â|sambaddham eva vā.

9.65 jñātaṃ tena, dhātu|doṣ'|ādin" âsya mati|vibhramaḥ
jajñe, bambhramyate tena. sa nato 'cintayan naṭaḥ:

‹āpannānām uttamānāṃ ye 'tr' ân|upakṛtā api
upakurvanti, ta ime jagatyāṃ nara|bhāskarāḥ.

āpad|gatānāṃ dur|daivād ye t' ûpakṛta|pūrviṇām
pratyupakurvate, te tu kiñ cid ānṛṇyam īyati.

And besides, if King Ari·késarin, his son, is informed that he has been treated like this, he will certainly become your enemy. And that King's army, making the pillar of the earth 9.60
tremble, will shatter the fortified places of the water, land and mountains, and there will be no other defense at all.

"We are able to pay you due recompense for what you have done, but we will not give that order. Rather, go from this, our country"—having caused him to be addressed so and given him provender, send him on his way. Having acted thus, Your Majesty's glory will surpass the full moon of Autumn.'

The King having thus effected that, he continued wandering and came to Kheta·pura, and was recognized by an actor, owing to the royal favor shown him in his kingdom.

He greeted him and asked, 'My lord, why are you wandering about like this?' He, his wits gone, either replied nothing at all or nonsense.

The actor realized that his mind had become disturbed 9.65
by sickness of the bodily humors and suchlike and was being made to wander about by it. Depressed, the actor thought:

'Those of the excellent who perform benefits for the unfortunate, although they have not been benefited in the matter, they are the ones who are human suns for the universe. But those who perform benefits in return to those who had previously performed benefits but through adverse fate have fallen into disaster, they merely obtain requital of a debt.

ye t' ûpakārake 'py uccair dur|daśā|vivaś'|ātmani
n' ôpakāra|parās, te syur ṛṇa|dāsā bhave bhave.
tad enam upakurve 'smi. yady eṣa praguṇo bhavet,
tad|rājyaṃ me 'sya prasādād bhavit", ân|ṛṇat" âthavā.›
9.70 tato 'sau sva|gṛhe ten' ôpacere 'bhyaṅga|bhojanaiḥ,
na paṭv abhūt, tato Dhanvantari|vaidyasya darśitaḥ.
‹svāmy eṣa no. na jāne 'smi, kuto 'py evaṃ daśāṃ gataḥ.
tad, āpta, samyak kathaya yath" âiṣa syād drutaṃ paṭuḥ.›
ittham naṭa|prakaṭite tat|sva|rūpe bhiṣag|varaḥ
śāstr'|ânubhava|cakṣurbhyāṃ taṃ vīkṣāmāsa sarvataḥ.
śailūṣam avadac c' âivaṃ, ‹vāta|pitta|kaph'|ôdbhavaḥ
vikāro n' âsya, tal|liṅg'|â|bhāvād viṣa|vikāravat.
na bhūta|śākinī|doṣo 'py atra ko 'pi nirīkṣyate.
sambhāvyate tad etasya doṣaḥ kārmaṇa|sambhavaḥ.
9.75 kārmaṇaṃ c' âsya nāsāyāṃ nāsāṃ spṛśati yan muhuḥ.›
naṭen' ôce, ‹kārmaṇasya tvaṃ jānāsi pratikriyām?›
Dhanvantarir ath' ācakhyau, ‹kārmaṇānām aśeṣataḥ
vidhiṃ prati|vidhiṃ vedmi.› tato 'vādīn naṭaḥ punaḥ:
‹puṇy'|ātmann, eṣa rāj" āsīc. ced amuṃ kuruṣe paṭum,
dāridrya|mudrā dravati tadā sapta|kulāt tava.›

But those who are not intent on giving benefits to the performer of a benefit whose mind has lost its will and is in an extremely bad situation, they become debt-slaves in existence after existence. So I will benefit him. If he becomes healthy, through his favor his kingdom will be mine, or at least freedom from debt.'

Thereupon he was nursed by the actor in his own home 9.70 with massages, with ointments and with meals, but he did not become healthy. So he showed him to Dhanvan·tari, a doctor.

'This is my king. I don't know how he came to be in such a situation. So, trustworthy friend, duly tell me, how will he quickly become healthy?'

His condition thus described by the actor, the excellent doctor examined him all over with eyes experienced in the medical treatises.

He spoke thus to the actor: 'His bodily condition did not result from wind, bile and phlegm since its symptoms, unlike poisoning, are missing. There is no sign in him of any illness caused by ghosts or witches. Therefore, his illness is being produced by the application of magic. There is magic 9.75 in his nose which is constantly afflicting his nose.' The actor said, 'Do you know a remedy for the magic?'

Then Dhanvan·tari said, 'I understand the action and counteraction of all magical processes.' Thereupon the actor asked once more:

'Pure-souled one, this man was my king. If you make him sound, the stamp of poverty will flee from seven generations of your family.'

tataḥ proce 'gadaṅ|kāraḥ, ‹karomy enam an|āmayam,
tvaṃ ced akta|nihuḍuṅkī|dugdham ānayase, sakhe.
Trilāha|viṣaye sā ca, tuṅge Go|śṛṅga|parvate.
tasyā amūny abhijñānān'› îty avādīd bhiṣag|varaḥ.
9.80 naṭaḥ pratīta|puruṣāṃs tan|nimittam ath' ādiśat,
taiś ca tad auṣadhī|dugdham āninye sva|gṛhād iva.
vaidyena vidhinā tac ca prayuktaṃ tasya bhū|bhujaḥ.
praśānta|kārmaṇ'|ôdgāraḥ so '|cirāt praguṇo 'bhavat.
‹aho tava parijñānam! aho tava cikitsitam!›
iti praśaṃsan śailūṣo doṣa|jñaṃ bahv apūjayat.
‹kathaṃ|kāram ih' âsm'? îti› rājñ" ôkte bharato 'bhyadhāt
sv'|ânubhūtaṃ vyatikaram Arisiṃhāya bhū|bhuje.
tato rāj" âvadad, ‹yāmaḥ sva|puryām adhun" âiva hi.›
naṭo 'vādīd, ‹evam eva gacchatāṃ, deva, no '|śubham.
9.85 yato rājyaṃ nidhānaṃ ca para|hasta|gataṃ yadi
na labhyate labhyate vā parayā śakti|sampadā.›
tato 'risiṃho 'vādīd, ‹kiṃ prāpta|kālam ih' âdhunā?›
tau ca Dhanvantari|naṭau taṃ vyajijñapatām iti:
‹yad āvayor gṛhe lakṣmīḥ, sa prasādas tav' âiva hi,
yat sarāṃsi prapūrṇāni, tat payoda|vijṛmbhitam.
tad imāṃ sva|ramāṃ, deva, mānay' âtr' âiva tiṣṭha ca.
āvāṃ punas tatra yāvaḥ svāmi|kāryasya siddhaye.
naṭa|vṛttyā pradhānānāṃ kariṣyāmi bhidām aham,
vaidyas tu tasya bhūpasya bhaiṣajāt kīrti|śeṣatām.›

Then the doctor said, 'I will render him healthy, if you bring the juice of the oily drum plant, my friend. And it is found in the Tri·laha region, on the peak of Cow-horn Mountain. These are its signs of recognition.' Thus spoke the doctor.

The actor assigned wise men to the task, and they brought 9.80
the juice of that medicinal plant, as if from their own homes. And under the direction of the doctor it was applied to the King. He vomited forth the allayed magic, and instantaneously became sound.

'Hurrah for your knowledge! Hurrah for your skill!'—praising him thus, the actor paid high honor to the doctor.

On the King's asking, 'How did I come to be here?,' the actor explained to King Ari·simha his misfortune and its consequence.

Then the King said, 'Let's go to my city right this moment.' The actor said, 'If we go just like this, we will not be successful. Since the kingdom is the deposit of a treasure, if 9.85
it has fallen into the hands of another, it will either not be obtained, or be obtained by a subsequent successful effort.'

Then Ari·simha said, 'Hasn't the time arrived here and now?,' and those two, Dhanvan·tari and the actor, said to him:

'As the good fortune in our homes is assuredly your graciousness, so when lakes are full it is through the opening of the clouds. So, paying respect to your own good fortune, Your Majesty, stay right here. On the other hand, we two will go there to effect Your Majesty's business. By the employment of acting, I will produce discord among the nobles, and the doctor through the use of drugs will

9.90 ‹asmad|vijñapty" âiva pādo 'vadhāryas tatra.› bhū|bhujā
ity uktvā naṭa|vaidyau tau jagmatur Vijayāṃ purīm.

naṭena ghaṭitaṃ nāṭyam Arikesariṇaḥ puraḥ.
tatr' āgate rasa|bandhaṃ s'|ûktam ekaṃ naṭo 'paṭhat.
kṛtaṃ vetti, guṇān vetti, vetti vijñāpitaṃ su|dhīḥ,
sevakasya sthitiṃ vetti, svāminas tasya k" ôpamā.

prajage, nanṛte vyāpya tad ev' âsy' ânucāribhiḥ.
raṅga|prasaṅgāt punar apy apāṭhīt pāṭha|vin naṭaḥ:
‹yatra jāte pitā śete na śaṅkā|śaṅku|varjitaḥ,
tasya kāśa|sumasy' êva niṣphalaṃ janma janminaḥ.›

9.95 tad eva ca su|vistārya pragītaṃ pārśva|sāribhiḥ.
rasa|sthairyam avatāry' āpaṭhat s'|ûktaṃ punar naṭaḥ.
‹«bhikṣāṃ deh'» îti vilapan ghaṭa|karpara|pāṇikaḥ
pitā bhrāmyaty ari|gṛhe yasy' âsy' â|jananir varam.›

punaḥ prastāvam āsūtrya sūtra|dhāra|śiro|maṇiḥ,
nivāry' ôccaiḥ kalakalaṃ su|bhāṣitam abhāṣata:
‹parākrameṇa labhyante rājya|śrī|kīrti|nāyikāḥ,
pitarau na hi labhyete parākrama|śatair api.›

produce the report that that King has only a short time to live.'

The King having said, 'By our sure request, let your feet be known there,' the actor and the doctor went to Víjaya·puri. 9.90

The actor prepared a play to be performed before that King. When he arrived there, the actor recited a speech, full of eloquence. Intelligent, he learned what had been done, he learned his qualities, he learned what was ordered, he learned the situation of his followers, what was closest to that King.

Then he sang and danced, surrounded by his company. As an interlude in the performance, the actor, a knower of speeches, recited a speech once more:

'At his birth, a father rests not without the sting of fear that the birth of his son will be fruitless, like the flower of the *kasha* plant.'

And then he performed an elaborate musical number with his company by his side. Then, causing delight in his eloquence, he once more recited a speech: 9.95

'The father, a beggar crying, "Give alms!," and holding a begging bowl, comes wandering to the home of his enemy. Better that he had never been born!'

Once more, the crest-jewel of leading actors, having strung together a prologue, quelled the loud applause and proclaimed an excellent saying:

'A kingdom, wealth, fame and a mistress are obtained by a bold attack, but parents cannot be obtained at all even by a hundred bold attacks.'

kath"|ântar'|âvatāreṇa punaḥ śailūṣa|bhūṣaṇaḥ
su|bhāṣita|sudhā|sāraṃ sudh"|ākara iv' âmucat:

9.100 ‹yac|cchriyo 'nya|jano bhuṅkte, vidiśe bhikṣate pitā,
tena bhūr bhārayāñcakre mātur yauvana|hāriṇā.›

atho nivārya bharataḥ kolāhala|halāhalam,
su|bhāṣita|sudhā|vṛṣṭiṃ vitene Vainateyavat:

‹adham'|âdhamasya puṃsas tasy' āsyaṃ ko nu paśyatu,
pitā yasy' âri|bhavane bhikṣ"|ârthaṃ cāṭu bhāṣate?›

ity apar'|âparaiḥ sūktair naṭ'|ôktaiḥ tasya bhū|bhujaḥ
prabhinnaṃ na hi rom" âpi Mudga|śaila iv' âmbudaiḥ.

punaḥ prastāvam ānīya raṅgād raṅg'|âvatārakaḥ
sadasyānāṃ hṛdi nyāsyat s'|ûkti|mukt'|āvalīm iti:

9.105 ‹yasy' ôtsaṅge śiraḥ kṛtvā sarva|svaṃ vinivedya ca
śete su|nirvṛtaḥ svāmī, mantriṇas tasya k" ôpamā?›

su|prakramam upakramya krama|vedī kuśīlavaḥ
papāṭha pāṭhaka|praṣṭhaḥ sūktaṃ śreṣṭhatamaṃ punaḥ:

‹dhig, dhik tān mantriṇo, yeṣāṃ jīvatām api su|prabhuḥ
dig|ambaro varākaś ca bhikṣākaś ca bhramed bhuvi.›

Again, with the representation of another story, that ornament of actors, like a mine of nectar, let flow the essence of the nectar of an eloquent saying:

'When another person enjoys the wealth while the father 9.100
begs in a foreign country, that, stealing away the youth of the mother, creates a burden for the earth.'

Then the actor, having quelled the hubbub of applause, produced the rain of the nectar of an eloquent saying, like Vainatéya the famous poet:

'Who, now, would look on the face of that worst of the worst of men whose father speaks kind words in the abode of his enemy for the sake of alms?'

By those various speeches thus spoken by the actor, not a hair of that King was changed, like Bean Mountain by the clouds.

Again that incarnation of acting, having spoken a eulogy from the stage, deposited a necklace of an eloquent saying in the hearts of the audience.

'What comparison is there with that minister whose 9.105
King, having placed his head in his lap and presented him with all his wealth, lies quite at ease?'

The actor, who understood rhetorical disposition, produced a well-disposed speech, and then that excellent reciter recited a most excellent saying once more:

'Shame, shame on those ministers whose good King, although they are still alive, naked, wretched and a beggar, wanders over the earth.'

punaḥ kṣaṇ'|ântaraṃ kṛtvā, hṛtvā rolaṃ ca sarvataḥ,
kuśīlavo 'ti|kuśalaḥ sa idaṃ s'|ûktam uktavān:
‹dhik|kṛtā dhīr dhī|sakhānāṃ teṣāṃ, yeṣām adhīśvaraḥ
raṅkavad vairi|geheṣu bhikṣāyai parisarpati.›

9.110 prastāv'|ântaram ārabhya, racit'|âñjali bhāratiḥ
su|bhāṣitam abhāṣiṣṭa śiṣṭa|ceṣṭita|sṛṣṭi|kṛt:
‹«deva, tvam eva naḥ svām"» îty
ākhyātāṃ rājya|ge prabhau
tad|bhraṣṭe t' ûpekṣakāṇāṃ
mantriṇāṃ syād a|jīvaniḥ.›
tat tādṛk|s'|ûkta|racanā|cāturī|caturaṃ vacaḥ
niśamya mantribhir jajñe, ‹brūte sākūtam eva, bhoḥ.›
punaḥ|punar|nava|nava|pratibhā|pratibhā|svaraḥ chinna
naṭ'|ēśvaraḥ s'|ûkta|khāniṃ prakramād udajīghaṭat:
‹prāṇair apy upakurvanti svāminaṃ ye mah"|âujasaḥ,
na saṃhatā na bhinnāś ca śrī|sāmantā jayanti te.
tathā:

9.115 teṣāṃ kaḥ prekṣatām āsyaṃ sāmantānāṃ samantataḥ,
prabhu|prasādān āsvādya pāpā ye sva|prabhu|druhaḥ?
tathā:
yaḥ prāṇair api gṛhṇāti svāmine vijaya|śriyam,
śucer, dakṣ"|ânuraktasya tasya bhṛtyasya k" ôpamā?
pāpāḥ padātayo 'līk'|āḍambarāś cāṭu|kāriṇaḥ,
svāmi|prasādān ādāya druhyanti svāmine 'tra ye.›

Once more, having made a short interval and accepted applause from all directions, that very skillful actor recited this eloquent saying:

'Reproached is the wisdom of those wise ministers whose King, like a starveling, hovers around the houses of his enemies for the sake of alms.'

Having spoken another eulogy, his hands folded in respectful salutation, the actor, effecting a shower filled with learning, proclaimed an eloquent saying: 9.110

'May death come to those ministers who, while the King was in the kingdom, declared, "You are our King!," but, when he was deprived of it, disregarded him.'

Then, having heard the speeches, charming with the clever composition of such sayings, the ministers realized, 'He is assuredly speaking with an intentional meaning, sirs.'

His voice a splendor of novel images renewed again and again, that lord of actors in due course opened up a mine of eloquent sayings:

'Those barons of great might who assist their King even with their lives will conquer, unwounded and unshattered.

Thus:

Who would look upon the face of those barons who, having enjoyed together their King's favor, are the wicked enemies of their King? 9.115

Thus:

What comparison is there with that servant who, even with his life, wins for his master the glory of victory, brilliant and beloved for his ability? Wicked are those soldiers who, full of bombast and making flattering speeches, receive their King's favor but bear enmity to that same King.'

tato nṛpaṃ vinā sarvaiḥ sāmant'|ādyair abudhyata,
s'|âbhiprāyam ayaṃ nāṭya|kapaṭena naṭo 'vadat.
ath' ōce mantri|sāmantair, ‹ati|kālam ajāyata.
aye, naṭa, tato nāṭyam idaṃ saṃvṛṇu saṃvṛtam.›
9.120 te mantriṇaḥ sura|guror gṛhe gatvā mitho 'bhyadhuḥ:
‹bheda|kṛt ko 'py, asau tan na hitāya svasya, n' âpi naḥ.
nirghāṭyate bhīṣayitvā tad ayaṃ vanya|sattvavat.›
tatas tatra naṭo hūtaḥ pṛṣṭo, ‹devo 'dhunā kva, bhoḥ?›
‹ko 'yaṃ devo, 'smi pṛccheyaṃ,
mantrinn?› ity avadan naṭaḥ.
‹devo 'risiṃho, 'syāḥ puryāḥ
svām"› îty ūce 'tha mantriṇā.
sa ‹kiṃ, ken' âpy arpito me
yat pṛcchye 'smi?› naṭo 'bhyadhāt.
‹tvay" âṭatā kv' âpi devo
dṛṣṭaḥ syād› iti mantry avak.
naṭo 'brūt' âtha, ‹«devaḥ kv'? êti» vaḥ sākūtam īritam,
anyathā bhavatā «devo dṛṣṭaḥ kv' âp'? îti» yuktimat.›
9.125 mantry ūce, ‹yat|kṛte yatnas tad ev' âpahnute ku|dhīḥ,
su|dhīs tu sādhayann eva tat|kāryaṃ vakti kiñ cana.›
ākhyan naṭaḥ, ‹prekṣaṇena hṛd āvarjya bhavā|dṛśām,
kuṭumbaṃ vartaye, mantrin, kāryam ity eva me nanu.
sambhāvayāmi tat siddhiṃ. n' ânyat kāryaṃ mam' âdhunā.
a|sambaddham iv' ākhyātaṃ tad, amātya|vara, tvayā›

Then, except for the King, everyone, the barons and the rest, realized that that actor had spoken with an intentional meaning, under the pretext of acting.

Thereupon the ministers and the barons said, 'Too much time has passed. So come now, actor, put an end to this ambiguous acting.'

The ministers went to the temple of the teacher of the 9.120
gods and agreed mutually, 'If anyone creates dissension, then it won't be for the advantage of himself or for the rest of us. He must be frightened and driven away, like one whose nature is savage.' Then the actor was summoned to that place and asked, 'Where is the King now, good man?'

'Might I ask, minister, who is this King?' said the actor. Then the minister said, 'King Ari·simha, the king of this city.'

The actor said, 'Why and by whom have I been brought here to be asked that?' The minister said, 'You might have seen the King somewhere on your travels.'

Then the actor said, 'You asked "Where is the King?" on purpose, otherwise "Have you seen the King somewhere?" would have been appropriate.'

The minister said, 'That was done on purpose, because an 9.125
ill-disposed person actually conceals it, but a well-disposed person, while accomplishing his business, says something about it.'

The actor said, 'Once I have delighted with a show the minds of good people such as you, my only concern is to look after my household, that's for sure. That's what I'm about to accomplish. I have no other business right now. What you've said seems incoherent, excellent minister.'

sacivo 'brūta, ‹he dhūrta, pralapsy atra kiṃ vṛthā?
yato 'sti yat tav' ākūtaṃ, taj jñātaṃ tvat|su|bhāṣitaiḥ?
kiñ c' âsmākam ap' îṣṭaṃ śrī|svāmi|pād'|âbja|sevanam.
tad viśrabhya kiṃ na vakṣi vṛttāntaṃ svāminaḥ sphuṭam?›

9.130 viśrabhy' âtha naṭo 'vādīd, ‹devaḥ Kheṭapure 'sti, bhoḥ.
nirāmayo, rājya|lakṣmyai Cakrapāṇir iv' ôtsukaḥ.›

aho, mantri|mates taikṣṇyaṃ, draḍhīyastvaṃ ca kiñ cana.
naṭa|hṛd vajra|ghaṭitaṃ yay" âbhedyata līlayā.

tato mantry|ādibhiḥ proce, ‹tvam ito 'pasara drutam!
are naṭa, na naṣṭaś ced, vinaṣṭo 'si tato dhruvam!›

prāṇa|prahāṇa|bhīty" âtha nāṭayan bhaya|nāṭakam
kāka|nāśaṃ naṭo naṣṭo 'risiṃh'|ântikam āsadat.

dvitīye 'hany amāty'|ādyā Arikesariṇ" ôditāḥ,
‹kv' âsau naṭo Bharatavan, nāṭya|veda|vidāṃ varaḥ?›

9.135 sa tair ūce, ‹prabho, 'smākaṃ taṃ sadyo 'pi jighāṃsatām,
kin tu dev'|â|kīrti|bhītyā pracchannaṃ tac cikīrṣatām,
kathañ cit jñāta|vṛttānto naṭo naṃṣṭvā kva cid yayau,
yata ete mahā|dhūrtā ākār'|êṅgita|vedinaḥ.›

The minister said, 'Hey, you trickster, why are you prattling vainly about this, since what you intended was made known by your eloquent sayings? And besides, it is our desire to serve the lotus-feet of His Majesty. So, with confidence, why don't you tell us the news about the King openly?'

Then the actor, his confidence won over, said, 'The King 9.130
is in Kheta·pura, good sirs. He is free from illness and, like discus-bearing Vishnu, is keenly desirous of the Fortune of the kingdom.'

Bravo for the keenness of the minister's intelligence and for his perseverance to some extent! The actor's mind, although formed from adamant, was cleaved by it with ease.

Then the ministers and the others said, 'Get away from here quickly! Hey now, actor, if you don't disappear, then you're surely a dead man.'

Then, because of the fear of relinquishing his life, acting the drama of fear, the actor disappeared as if with the flight of a crow and reached the presence of Ari·simha.

On the following day, Ari·késarin asked the ministers and the others, 'Where is that actor, like Bharata, the chief of those who know the texts on acting?'

They said to him, 'Your Majesty, we were desirous of 9.135
killing him quickly, but through fear of disgrace befalling Your Majesty, we just wanted to interrogate him; somehow the actor found out what was happening and, having disappeared, went somewhere else. These eminent swindlers can read bodily gestures and facial expressions.'

‹vyāpādyate kim ity eṣa?› rājñ" ôkte mantribhir jage:
‹pāpo 'yaṃ bheda|kārī no jala|kānta iv' âmbhasām.
kiṃ na śrutaṃ svāminā yat putraṃ sāmanta|mantriṇaḥ,
pattīṃś c' āśritya ten' ôktaṃ? tato vadhyatamo 'sakau.›
rājñ" ôktaṃ, ‹bhoḥ, kva cit tātaḥ? kuśalī vartate kim u?›
tair ūce, ‹'numito 'st' îti naṭ'|ôktiḥ. s" ânyathā katham?›
9.140 tato 'rikesarī rājā sāśaṅkaṃ dadhyivān iti:
‹na jñāyate, naṭe tasminn ete kim api cakrire.›
gūḍh'|âbhisandhy ath' ācāṣṭa
gambhīraṃ dhīra|dhīr nṛpaḥ:
‹bhavadbhir na kṛtaṃ suṣṭu
yad asau me na melitaḥ.
yatas tan|mukhatas tāt'|ôdante samyag viniścite,
rājyaṃ ca prāpite tāte syān me sat|putra|dhuryatā.
śrī|tāte ca rājya|bhāji mama rājyam a|saṃśayam
tad anviṣy' ānīya tātaṃ, rājye sthāpayata drutam.›
tato 'mātyaḥ Surasūr' îty amṛśat, ‹kim u māyayā?
sad|bhāvād atha rājñ" êdaṃ ākhyātaṃ tat parīkṣyate.
yataḥ:
9.145 bhū|bhuj|aṅgasya yo mantrī viśvasya syāt pramadvaraḥ,
tasmād eva hi so 'vaśyaṃ vinaśyaty a|cirād api.›

On the King's asking, 'Why was he about to be put to death like that?,' the ministers said, 'That criminal was making splits among us, like the wind among the waters.

Didn't Your Majesty hear what he said about the son and the soldiers of the barons and the ministers? Because of that, he is absolutely deserving of capital punishment.'

The King said, 'Good sirs, where is my father? He's now healthy, isn't he?' They replied, 'The actor's statement was a guess. How could it be otherwise?'

Then Ari·késarin the King thought, 'Whatever they did 9.140
concerning that actor is not certain.'

Then the King, whose intelligence was deep, speaking with a secret purpose, said gravely, 'It was not fitly done by you that he was not brought before me. Since, news of my father having been properly obtained from his mouth, and my father having been brought back into possession of the kingdom, the office of legitimate son would have been mine. Upon His Majesty my father's partaking of the kingdom, the kingdom would be mine without any doubt. So go and find my father and cause him to put in possession the kingship forthwith.'

Then the minister named Sura·suri said, 'Why bother with illusion? Now, let what Your Majesty said be considered under the actual circumstances.

Since:

If an entrusted minister of a king's council were to become 9.145
negligent, for that very reason he would soon be ruined.'

mantry ūce, ‹n' êti rāṇ|nītir yad rājyaṃ kriyate 'nyasāt?
rājy'|ânīhas tāpasaḥ syān nyasy' ânyasmin nṛpa|śriyam.›

rāj" âcintayad, ‹asy' ôktiḥ kṛṭtim" â|kṛttim" âthavā.
tataḥ parīkṣyo 'sau samyak, svarṇavadd hṛt|kaṣ'|ôpale.

yataḥ:

ced viśrabdhaḥ pradhānānāṃ rājā vyājān vitanvatām,
mṛgayūnāṃ mṛga iva, tad" âvaśyaṃ vinaśyati.›

ath' āha nṛ|patir, ‹mantriṃs, tāte rājya|dhuran|dhare
na me 'bhūj jātv a|kalyānaṃ, tad etad ucitaṃ na hi?

9.150 kiñ ca loke sādhu|vādaḥ pitū rājya|samarpaṇāt?
tātasy' ân|antaraṃ rājyaṃ mam' âvaśyaṃ kram'|āgatam.›

sacivo 'vocata, ‹vibho, rāja|nītir iyaṃ na hi:
yadi svāmī priya|tātas tatr' âiva prātu tat|priyam?
tātasy' ân|antaraṃ rājyaṃ tav' âiv' êti na niścitam.
priya|devy|aṅgajaḥ prāyaḥ kumāro bhū|bhujāṃ priyaḥ.
tatra rājye niviṣṭe ca ced vidhāsyasi viḍvaraṃ,
tad idānīm eva, deva, rājyaṃ tyājyaṃ na sarvathā.›

nṛpo 'th' âbrūta, ‹śṛṇuta, bho bhoḥ, sāmanta|mantriṇaḥ.
mṛṭasy' âpi pituḥ piṇḍā dīyante kula|putrakaiḥ.
9.155 yasya sarva'|rddhi|pūrṇasya jīvann eva pitā punaḥ
bhikṣate para|geheṣu kulīnaḥ sa kathaṃ bhuvi?›

The minister said, 'Isn't it according to the rules of kingship that the kingship may be determined on another? If one becomes disinclined to undertake the kingship through asceticism, then the rank of king is deposited on another.'

Thereupon the King thought, 'His statement is either feigned or sincere. Therefore, he must be duly tested like a gold coin on the touchstone of his heart:

Since:

If a king trusts in his ministers while they are spreading traps, then he is destroyed, like a deer trusting in its hunters.'

Then the King said, 'Minister, nothing inauspicious befell me while my father was governing the kingdom, so isn't this fitting, then?

And besides didn't the world applaud at my father's hand- 9.150
ing over of the kingdom? The kingdom certainly came to me in due course, in direct succession from my father.'

The minister said, 'Your Majesty, isn't this the rule of kingship: if one's dear father was a king, then that rank falls to that very one? There is no doubt that the kingship came to you in direct succession from your father. Generally, the prince who is the son of a beloved queen is the beloved of kings. And even if you intend to create dissension in this settled kingdom, you should by no means abandon the kingdom at this very moment.'

Then the King said, 'Listen, barons and ministers, good sirs. When a father is deceased, funeral rites for him are
performed by sons of eminent family. But how can he, 9.155
abundant with all prosperity, whose father begs in the homes of others, be eminent in the world?'

Devarakṣita|nām" âtha mugdhaḥ sāmanta|nandanaḥ,
‹samīcīnaṃ vakti deva evam ev' âitad› ity avak.

tataḥ kṛtaka|toṣeṇ' Ârikesari|mahī|bhujā
sarvaḥ sv'|âṅga|pariṣkāro dade 'smai pāritoṣikam.

tat|pitā Devarājo 'tha dadhyau, ‹kāryaṃ vināśitam
hah"! âmunā yan nṛpo 'smad|bhāvam evaṃ parīkṣate.›

sāmantena tataḥ putro 'bhāṇy, ‹a|nyāyaṃ praśasya, re,
nṛpa|prasādaṃ gṛhṇāsi. rāja|nītiṃ na budhyase.
9.160 devas tuṣyatu vā, mā vā, nītir eva praśasyate.
nītis tv anyā|dṛśī loke, nṛpāṇāṃ punar anyathā.
mad|dṛk|pathād apasar' ādatse cet pāritoṣikam.›
bhīta|bhītena ten' âtha tan muktaṃ dandaśūkavat.

tato bhūpen' âbhidadhe, ‹bho bhoḥ, sāmanta|mantriṇaḥ,
kim eṣa pakṣo vo 'p' îṣṭo?› ‹nyāyaḥ sarv'|ēpsitaḥ, prabho.›

rājā sa|roṣam ācaṣṭa, ‹kīdṛg nyāyo 'yam ucyate?
yad v" âvāmāni yuṣmābhis tātas, tad bibhith' âmutaḥ!›

Surasūrir ath' āmātyaḥ pṛthvī|nāthaṃ vyajijñapat:
‹tiryaṅ|mātram ih' ônmiṇṭho duḥkham ālānyate karī.
9.165 nara|siṃhasya devasya sva|cchandasya kim ucyatām?
paraṃ vācyaṃ hitaṃ bhṛtyair bhāvi daiva|kṛtaṃ punaḥ.
tac ca praveditaṃ tāvat svāmino hita|cintakaiḥ.
svāmi|rucyaṃ tu dur|daiva|prelitaṃ ko niṣedhatu?
kevalaṃ tatra n' âsmākaṃ, svāminn, anumatiḥ kva cit
yac c' âvamānitas tāto 'tra pramāṇaṃ prabhuḥ punaḥ.

Then Deva·rákshita, the stupid son of a baron, said, 'What he's saying is the absolute truth, Your Majesty.'

Then King Ari·késarin, with simulated satisfaction, gave him a gratuity, adorning his entire body.

Thereupon his father, Deva·raja, thought, 'Oh, no! The business has been ruined by him, since this is the way the King is testing our disposition.'

Then the baron addressed his son, 'Hey, you've gained royal favor by commending what is not right. You don't understand royal policy. Let the King be pleased or not, it's 9.160
the policy that is to be commended. But policy in ordinary life is of one kind; that of kings is another. Disappear from my sight if you accept that gift.' Then, absolutely terrified, he dropped it like a snake.

Then the King said, 'Barons and ministers, good sirs, do you approve of this argument?' 'Justice is desired by all, Your Majesty.'

The King said angrily, 'What kind of justice is this you are talking about, otherwise you would have feared the consequences of neglecting my father!'

Then the minister Sura·suri addressed the King, 'Among the class of animals, in this case an elephant with a keeper feels distress at his restraint. What can one say about a king, 9.165
a lion of men, acting at his own free will? But the blame of others later becomes inevitable for servants. And so much was made known by those concerned for His Majesty's welfare. But who could deny that His Majesty's brilliance was dimmed by adverse fate? In that only were we not approved, Your Majesty. And if that was disregard for your father, Your Majesty is the judge once more.

tad atra kāryena vayaṃ praṣṭavyāḥ svāmin" âdhunā?
siddham ev' ôpadeṣṭavyaṃ, puṇya|sṛṣṭaṃ bhaviṣyati.›
‹kiṃ bhaviṣyati?› rājñ" ôkte ‹devo jānāti ke vayam.
kin tu kartavyam asmākaṃ, svāminā deśyam añjasā.›
9.170 ādideśa tato rājā, ‹tātam ānayata drutam.›
‹deva, ko yātu?› rāj" ōce, ‹yasy' ôtsāhaḥ, prasarpati.›
‹«kasy' ôtsāho» na dev'|ājñā devat"|ārādhane, prabho.
tad yasya yogyatā tatra svāmī tasya prasīdatu.›
rāj" ākhyat, ‹kīdṛśā yūyaṃ niṣṭhurāḥ kṛta|ghātinaḥ,
ye na smaranti tātasya prasādān praty|ahaṃ kṛtān?›
‹dev', āsatāṃ tāta|kṛtāś cira|kāla|tiro|hitāḥ.
n' âiva smariṣyanti, deva, kṛtān api hitān amī.
yato vayaṃ paṭṭa|bhaktā, bhaktā na puruṣe punaḥ,
yo yadā paṭṭam adhyāste, tasy' âiva hita|cintakāḥ.›
9.175 moda|mādyan|mano|'mbho|dhir, vikasan|netra|paṅkajaḥ,
kānti|kallolit'|āsy'|ênduḥ sa rāj'|êndus tato 'vadat:
‹aye saciva|sāmantāḥ, samantād yūyam īkṣitāḥ,
paraṃ pīyūṣavat kv' âpi na vikāro vyalokyata.
aho, vaḥ śemuṣī k" âpi gambhīrā sāgarād api.
itthaṃ nirmathane so 'pi vikṛtiṃ yāti, na tv iyam.
lok'|ôttaraṃ kim apy etad aikya|matyaṃ bhavā|dṛśām,

But why are we being questioned about this matter by Your Majesty now? When what should be ordered is actually accomplished, there will be a successful result.'

The King asked, 'What will it be?' 'Your Majesty knows who we are. But let Your Majesty order right now what we are to do.'

Then the King ordered, 'Bring my father home quickly.' 9.170
'Who should go, Your Majesty?' The King said, 'The one who is eager to go will set forth.'

'"Who is eager?" is not a royal command to propitiate the deity Your Majesty. So let Your Majesty favor the one who is fit for this matter.'

The King said, 'Are you so cruel and unmindful of past favors that you don't remember the favors that my father granted daily?'

'Your Majesty, let those favored by your father remain far removed for a long time. Nor will these here be mindful, Your Majesty, of the benefits done. Since we are devoted to the crown, but not devoted to the person, the person who assumes the crown, he's the one to whom our thoughts are devoted.'

Then, the ocean of his mind reveling with joy, the lotus 9.175
of his eyes beaming, the moon of his face billowing with brightness, that moon of a king said:

'Well done, ministers and barons, you've been inspected all over, but nowhere, as in nectar, was there seen any deviation. Bravo for your intellect, certainly deeper even than the ocean. At the churning thus, the latter underwent change, but not the former. It has been manifestly proclaimed that

sarveṣāṃ viduṣāṃ c' âikā dhīr ity ābhāṇakaḥ sphuṭaḥ.›
sarv'|âṅgīṇāṃ svāmi|bhakti|devīm arcayituṃ kila
sarv'|âṅgīṇam alaṅkāraṃ tebhyaḥ prītaḥ prabhur dadau.
9.180 jīvikāṃ dvi|guṇāṃ cakre teṣāṃ tuṣṭaḥ prajā|patiḥ,
īdṛṣāṃ su|pradhānānām a|kṣayitvam ap' îṣyate.
sa tu Dhanvantarir vaidyo naṭavad Vijayāṃ purīm
prāpa pṛthvī|patiṃ c' âitam upatasthe sva|vidyayā.
prasāda|pātra|dvārā c' āsannā sevā nṛpe 'bhavat.
rājñaś c' â|jīrṇa|doṣeṇ' âpāṭavam sasṛje 'nyadā.
sa c' â|nivṛtte 'pi doṣe rājñaḥ pathyam adāpayat,
rāja|vaidyais tan niṣiddhaṃ, tac ca vyajñāyi mantribhiḥ.
dadhye ca taiḥ, ‹parīkṣyo 'yaṃ,
kim ajño, 'th' âri|gṛhyakaḥ.›
rājā vyajñāpy ath' āmātyair,
‹vaidyo 'yaṃ no na sammataḥ.
9.185 kim eṣa tāta|gṛhyo 'th' â|vijña eva cikitsati?
parīkṣyas tad ayaṃ, deva.› so 'vak, ‹kathaṃ parīkṣyate?›
‹deva, ken' âpi viśvāsya bhāṇyate so, «nṛpaṃ yadi
viṣ'|ādinā hansi tadā tubhyaṃ svarṇam iyad dade.»
ced abhyupaiṣyati, tadā jñāsyate tāta|gṛhyakaḥ.›
rāj" ākhyal, ‹lobhato 'nyo 'pi, mantrinn, aṅgīkaroty adaḥ.›

this single-mindedness and unanimous intelligence of all your learned selves is somewhat more than worldly.'

The delighted King gave them ornaments for their entire bodies, such as to adorn to the entire body of a queen through the devotion of her king. The pleased King doubled 9.180
their salaries, wishing for the continued prosperity of such good courtiers.

Now, Dhanvan·tari the doctor, like the actor, went to Víjaya·puri and attended on that King with his medical knowledge. His close attendance on the King was a means to being an object of his favor. One day he produced an illness in the King which had the consequence of indigestion. And that illness continuing unchecked, he placed the King on a diet, which was forbidden by the royal doctors, and which was discovered by the minister.

And they thought, 'He must be tested to see if he is incompetent or if he is in the service of an enemy.' The ministers informed the King, 'We do not approve of this doctor. Is he in the service of your father or is he incompetent 9.185
as he gives his medical treatment? So he must be tested, Your Majesty.' He replied, 'How will he be tested?'

'Your Majesty, someone must gain his confidence and say to him, "If you kill the King with poison or suchlike, then so much gold will be given you."

If he agrees, then he will be known to be in the service of your father.' The King said, 'But one other than that, minister, would agree through greed.'

‹satyaṃ, deva, tath" âpy êṣa jñāsyate vacana|cchalāt.›
tataḥ purodhasā samyak śikṣitena sa bhāṇitaḥ.

Dhanvantaris tato 'vādīn, ‹mā vādīr iti me puraḥ!›
‹iyad dāsye tava svarṇaṃ, kuru, vaidya, mam' ôditam!›

9.190 na viśvasitaṃ tasy' âiṣa, ‹m" âiṣa!› vakt' îti māyayā.
tato vaidyena so 'bhāṇi, ‹kim ity evaṃ vyavasyasi?›

ūce purodhā, ‹āneṣye 'risiṃhaṃ prācya|bhū|patim.›
a|viśrabdho 'brūta vaidyo, ‹'mum ev' ôpāssva, tena kim?›

purohito 'vadad, ‹eṣa pratyanīko mam' âdhikam.
tad vairy asau mayā māryo ghātuken' âpi niścitam.›

vaidyo 'bhyadhād, ‹Arisiṃho jānāsi kv' âpi tiṣṭhati?›
dhūrto 'brūta, ‹tasya pārśve yānty, āyānti narā mama.›

ākhyad vaidyo, ‹rāḍ|viruddham
iti me n' âbhidhāḥ, sakhe?›
‹mā bhaiṣī, vaidya, yad idaṃ
bahu|sāmanta|sammatam.

9.195 ced brūṣe tāṃs tadā sarvān ānayāmi tav' ântike.›
bhiṣag jagau, ‹mam' ânena rājñā kin tu vināśitam.

upadrutā yadi yūyaṃ, tato 'haṃ kiṃ karomy adaḥ?›
ākhyad dhūrto, ‹'risiṃho rāṭ tava rājyaṃ pradāsyati.›

vaidyo 'vādīt, ‹tān manuṣyān mama tāvat pradarśaya.
tataḥ samyag vicārya âhaṃ bhaṇiṣyāmi yath"|ôcitam.›

'That's true, Your Majesty. Then he must be tested by means of duplicitous speech.' Then the doctor was addressed by a duly instructed chaplain.

Thereupon Dhanvan·tari said, 'Don't speak like that before me!' 'I will give you so much gold, Doctor. Do what I've said!'

Not trusting him, the doctor said deceptively, 'Not him!' 9.190
Then the doctor asked him, 'Why are you thus determined?'

The chaplain said, 'I want to bring back Ari·simha, the former King.' Not trusting him, the doctor asked, "It's that king you should be serving, so why?"

The chaplain said, 'This King is extremely hostile to me. So I have resolved that this enemy will be killed by some murderer.'

The doctor said, 'Do you know where Ari·simha is staying?' The liar said, 'My men come and go to and from his presence.'

The doctor said, 'Didn't you say that the King was hostile to you, my friend?' 'Don't worry, Doctor, because many barons are of the same mind. If you agree, then I'll bring 9.195
them all to your presence.' The doctor said, 'Nevertheless, I was ruined because of that King. If you are oppressed, what can I do in this matter?' The liar said, 'King Ari·simha will give you a kingdom.'

The doctor said, 'Just show me those men. Then, having duly deliberated, I will speak as is fitting.'

śikṣayitvā ke 'pi narās tatas tasya purodhasā
ānītās, taiś ca vaidyo 'sāv ukto, ‹rājā diśaty adaḥ.›
cakrena kiñ cid ādiṣṭam. so 'vak, ‹kiñ cin na vedmy aham.›
tair ūce, ‹vakṣi kiṃ mithyā, yan naṭas tvaṃ ca rāṇ|narau?›
9.200 tato vihasya ten' ōce, ‹samādiśati kiṃ prabhuḥ?›
śikṣitais tair abhāṇy, ‹evaṃ tat kāryaṃ sādhaya drutam.›
ūce vaidyaḥ, ‹kṛt'|ôpāyo varte, siddhis tu daivataḥ.›
keśa|grāhaṃ gṛhītv" âtha taiḥ so 'pātyata bhū|tale.
baddhvā nītaḥ puro rājñas, tad|uktaṃ ca nyavedi taiḥ.
rājñā sa|roṣam ūce 'sau, ‹saty'|ôktau te 'sti jīvitam!›
mṛtyu|bhītyā tena sarvam ūce. rājñā vigopya saḥ
khar'|āropa|pura|bhrānty|ādinā nirviṣayī|kṛtaḥ.
naṭavat so 'pi kṛṣṇ'|āsyo 'risiṃh'|ântikam āgamat.
mithas te vyamṛśan kāryaṃ, kāryaṃ kim adhunā nanu?
9.205 naṭo 'vag, ‹vivara|rasa|siddhyā kṛtvā mahad balam
rājyam uddālyate tasmād, yathā loptraṃ malimlucāt.›
rāj" ākhyad, ‹rasa|siddhir me siddh" âiv' âsti.› tataś ca te
bhūri svarṇaṃ samutpādya catur|aṅgāṃ camūṃ vyadhuḥ.

Some previously instructed men were brought by the chaplain, and they said to the doctor, 'The King commands this.'

Something was ordered by the troop. He said, 'I don't know anything.' They said to him, 'Why are you falsely denying that you and the actor are servants of the King?'

Thereupon he smiled and said, 'What does His Majesty 9.200
command?' They, as instructed, said to him, 'Accomplish this task quickly.'

The doctor said, 'I'll act as the means for the task, but success will come through fate.' They grabbed him by the hair and pulled him to the ground.

They bound him and took him before the King, and informed him of what he had said. The King said angrily, 'Your life depends on your true statement!'

Extremely frightened, he told all. Sentenced by the King to be publicly humiliated, he was mounted on a donkey, paraded around the city, et cetera, and then banished.

Like the actor, he, his face black, returned to the presence of Ari·simha. They took mutual counsel about what was to be done next.

The actor said, 'Having prepared a great army by means 9.205
of the skill of alchemical transformation, the kingdom will be snatched from him like booty from a thief.'

The King said, 'Skill in alchemy is actually my skill.' Then, having produced gold from the ground, they prepared an army of four divisions.

kṛtvā kośaṃ mahā|camvā sva|rājya|graha|hetave
Arisiṃhaḥ siṃha iva pratasthe svāṃ purīṃ prati.
tam āgacchantam ākarṇya kesar" îv' Ârikesarī
sadyaḥ sarv'|âbhisāreṇa pratipede 'bhaymitratām.
saṃlagne pradhane dvayor api tayor
nirdainyayoḥ sainyayoḥ,
datv" ādāya ca na prahāram abhito
'tṛpyan bhaṭāḥ kāmivat,
hastibhyām abhiyujya saṃyati catur|
dante samāsūtrite,
śastrā|śastri|kathāṃ, hahā, pitṛ|sutāv
etau ciraṃ cakratuḥ!
9.210 krodhen' ândha|tamo 'rikesari|nṛpo
hast'|îndra|sat|koṣṭhakāt
kunt'|âgreṇa Kṛt'|ânta|danta|tativat
tīkṣṇena bhīṣmena ca
aty|uccaiḥ samudakṣipat sva|pitaraṃ.
kin tv eṣa raudr'|āśayāt
kaṣṭaṃ kaṣṭatame jagāma narake
pātāla|kūpe kila.
naśyamānaṃ tac ca pitṛ|śibiraṃ bhaya|kātaram,
dhīrayitv" ādade rāṭ sa pitṛ|śrīḥ putram eti yat.
sa c' Ârisiṃho nṛ|patir atr' âiva ghrāṇa|laulyataḥ
rājya|bhraṃś'|ādi samprāpa, paratra narakaṃ punaḥ.
narake prathame tatra sāgaraṃ duḥkha|sāgaram
vigāhy' âjani kṛṣṇ'|âhir bhīṣaṇo Malay'|âcale.

Having created a treasury, Ari·simha, like a lion, with a great army set out for his city in order to take his kingdom.

Having heard him approaching, Ari·késarin, like a lion, immediately advanced with all his companion forces to attack the enemy.

The battle of the two armies commenced, both free from apprehension. Neither giving nor receiving any blow, everywhere the warriors enjoyed themselves like lovers. Having attacked with their two elephants, their four tusks locked together in combat, for how long did those two, father and son, alas!, fight together, sword to sword!

Dark with the blindness of anger, King Ari·késarin, from 9.210
the safe stronghold of his king of an elephant, with the tip of his spear, sharp like the baring of the teeth of Death, and fearful, stabbed his father very deeply. But Ari·simha, because his mind was set on savagery, underwent torment in a tormenting hell, the one in the pit under the world, to wit.

And since his father's camp was disappearing, disheartened by fear, the King renewed its confidence and preserved it, since the rank of the father had come to the son.

And King Ari·simha here in this world, because of his addiction to smell, met with the loss of his kingdom, et cetera, and afterward in the next world, hell. Having plunged into an ocean of pain for an aeon in that first hell, he was reborn a terrifying black snake in the Málaya mountain.

yasmiṃś candana|bhū|ruhāṃ param, aho,
ek'|ātapa|traṃ padaṃ,
yasmin kinnara|gītayaḥ śruti|sudhāḥ
stabhnanti khe khe|carān,
yat|saurabhya|ramāṃ pragṛhya maruto
vismāpayante diśaḥ,
śliṣyante, bata, yatra candana|latā
naikair bhujaṅgaiḥ samam.

9.215 tatra nāraka|jīvo 'hiḥ prāgvad gandh'|âti|lolupaḥ
candana|druṣu sa bhrāntv" âdhik'|âdhika|su|gandhiṣu,
udyat|parimal'|ôllola|plāvit'|âśeṣa|dik|taṭe
ek'|âṅge, sarale, tuṅge 'sajad gośīrṣa|pādape.

sa c' ânyadā kāṣṭha|taḍbhiś chettum ārambhi pādapaḥ.
tad|utsaṅgam avarudhya stithaḥ so 'hir na muñcati.
yadā te chettum āyānti, tadā dhāvati tān prati.
tato dūra|sthitair eva taiḥ so 'vidhyata patriṇā.
vedan"|ārto 'patat pṛthvyāṃ. tair bāṇe dayay" ôddhṛte
tān eva pratyadhāvat sa, bhay'|ārtās te palāyitāḥ.

9.220 sa ca prahāra|niḥspando dadṛse caraṇa'|ṛṣiṇā
dadau cārāṇya|kāruṇyāt sa tasy' Ârhan|namas|kṛtim

ten' âpi śraddadhe samyak|saṃjñinā dharaṇ'|êndravat.
parāpt'|â|vyakta|samyaktvo namas|kṛti|paro 'mṛtaḥ.

In which the rank of sovereignty supreme, yes!, belongs to the sandalwood trees; in which the singing of the celestial musicians, nectar for the ears, arrests the gods as they travel in the sky; having carried away the wife that is the scent of which, the winds astonish the four quarters; in which, gosh!, the tendrils of the sandalwood trees are mutually embraced by multitudes of snakes.

There, the snake whose soul had been the hell-being, as 9.215
before, extremely fond of perfume, after wandering among the sandalwood trees, which became ever more fragrant, would cling to a straight and tall sandalwood tree, its sandal perfume causing as far as the horizon to be filled with waves of rising fragrance.

One day lumberjacks began to cut down that tree. The snake blockaded the part where its branches met, reared up, and did not retreat. And when they approached to cut down that tree, it darted toward them. Whereupon they, standing at distance, obviously, pierced it with an arrow. Pained by the piercing, it fell to the ground, and they compassionately drew out the arrow. It darted toward them again, and they, stricken with fear, ran away.

A wandering ascetic saw it lying motionless because of 9.220
the blow, and through his ascetic compassion taught it the prayer in praise of the Worthies.

And he was given faith by that possessor of right knowledge, like a king. And having attained a state of unripened righteousness, he died intent on the prayer in praise of the Worthies.

tato 'tra Bharate, puryāṃ śrī|Kauśāmbyām ih' âiva hi,
Bhogāvaty|Amarāvatyor madhya|bhū|bhaginī|śriyi,
Purandarayaśaḥ|śreṣṭhi|priyāyāḥ kukṣi|paṅkaje
sa Purandaradattāyā āyayau rāja|haṃsavat.
kāla|kramāt suto jajñe. jajñe vardhāpanaṃ mahat.
Purandara iti tasya nāma|dheyaṃ vyadhīyata.
9.225 sa ca tvam ev'. âdhun" âpi gandha|gṛdhnuḥ ṣaḍ|aṃhrivat,
rājñaḥ puryāś c' âti|mānyo dhatse śreṣṭhi|padaṃ mahat.
tataś c' êh' âpohaṃ
sapadi kalayan śreṣṭhi|tilakaḥ
kṣaṇaṃ mohāj jāti|
smaraṇam alabhat prātibham iva.
svayaṃ sākṣāt ten' âdhy-
avasita|nija|prāg|bhava|vidhir,
vahad|bāṣpaḥ sūri|
krama|kamalam ānamya sa jagau:
prasādād vaḥ, svāmin,
sapadi samabhūvaṃ samucitaḥ
su|mārge prasthātuṃ
kim api Jina|candra|prakaṭite.
prabho, n' âtaḥ sthātuṃ
kṣaṇam api sahe, tat kuru kṛpāṃ!
prapāṃ prāptas tṛṣṇaś
cirayati payaḥ pātum iha kim?›»

iti śrī|nirvāṇa|Līlāvatī|mahā|kath"|êti|vṛtt'|ôddhāre Līlāvatī|sāre Jin'|âṅke ghrāṇ'|êndriya|vipāka|vyāvarṇano nāma navama utsāhaḥ.

Then, in this continent of Bhárata, here in this very city of lovely Kaushámbi, the lovely middle-earth sister of the city of the snake demons and the city of the gods, he approached like a royal swan the lotus of the womb of Puran·dara·datta, the wife of the merchant Puran·dara·yashas, and, in due course of time, was born a son. A great celebration was held, and the name Puran·dara was bestowed upon him.

And you are indeed he. Even now, greedy for perfume 9.225
like a bee, highly esteemed by the King and by the city, you hold the high rank of merchant-banker.

And then straightaway he became engaged in proper consideration of what was for and against, and, after swooning for a moment, that ornament of merchants obtained memory of his existences as if by intuition. The conduct of his former lives was clearly ascertained by him. Streaming with tears, he bowed to the lotus-feet of the reverend teacher, and said:

'Through your grace, reverend sir, I have suddenly become to a great extent fit to set forth on the right path illuminated by the moon of the Jina. Lord, I am not able to wait one moment longer, so have compassion. Would a thirsty man having come to a well wait here to drink water?'"

Here ends the ninth canto, entitled "The Consequences of the Sense of Smell," of the Jain epic *The Epitome of Queen Liláavati*, an abridgment of the events of *The Epic Story of the Auspicious Final Emancipation of Liláavati.*

CANTO 10
THE CONSEQUENCES OF
THE SENSE OF SIGHT

10.1 Śrī|Sudharmā muni|rājo vyājahāra Purandaram:
«pravrājayiṣyase, saumya. kṣaṇaṃ cakṣur|gatiṃ śṛṇu.

ayam ātmā viparīta|śikṣeṇ' ēkṣaṇa|vājinā
ādau sva|dāra|sarv'|âṅg'|ôpāṅga|mārga|sthiti|spṛṣā,
paścāt paṇy'|âṅganā|gātra|vilās'|â|patha|yāyinā,
tataḥ parakalatr'|ādik'|â|patha|prasthiti|śritā,
atha kutsita|naṭy|ādi|līlā|vipatha|gāminā,
parastān mantri|sāmanta|rāṭ|priyā|prāntara|vrajā,
10.5 tato 'pi sv'|êccha|pān'|ādi|kāntā|kāntāra|dhāriṇā,
adhik'|âdhika|vegena pātyate narak'|âvaṭe.

kiñ ca:

svarṇa|rūpya|citra|lepya|dārv'|âśm'|ādi|mayīṣv api,
strīṣv akṣṇā bhramito mūḍho mudhā pāpena lipyate.

āstāṃ strī|rūpam anyac ca ramaṇīyaṃ gṛh'|ādikam,
cakṣuṣā darśitaṃ dṛṣṭv" âpy ayam ātm" âti muhyati.

api ca:

gandh'|ādayo hi viṣayāḥ saṃvedyante kadā cana,
kadā cana tato 'vaśyaṃ vikārāy' êndriy'|ântaram.

unmīlitaṃ tu cakṣuś cet, paśyaty eva śubh'|â|śubhaṃ
rāga|dveṣau tatas, tasmāc cakṣur|a|kṣīṇa|śaktikam.

REVEREND Sudhárman, the leader of the monks, said 10.1
to Puran·dara, "You will be given initiation as a Jain
monk, good sir. Listen for a moment to the course of ad-
diction to sight.

That soul, by the badly trained horse of sight, firstly, by
its touching the limbs of the entire body of his own wife,
afterward, by its going along the path of lust for the bodies
of prostitutes, thereafter by its resorting to the wrong path
of adultery and suchlike, then, by its proceeding along the
wrong path of sporting with vile dancing girls and suchlike,
later on, by its traveling along the long desolate road of
the wives of ministers, barons and kings, and then by its 10.5
holding at its own will to the wilderness of the mistress of
an innkeeper and suchlike, going ever and ever faster, is
made to fall into the wilderness of hell.

And besides:

Confounded by looking at gold, silver, paintings, unguents, wood, precious stones, and mares, and women, vainly led astray, it is defiled by wickedness.

Let there be present a wife, silver, any other lovely thing, a house, et cetera, that soul, having seen what is shown by the eye, goes far astray.

What's more:

Whenever objects of the senses, smell and the others, those, are experienced, whenever, then the power of the sense organ changes for the worse.

But if an eye is open, it certainly sees good or bad, beloved or enemy, so because of that its power is undiminished.

kiṃ bahunā?

10.10 na tathā sv'|ântaraṃ vaśy'|â|vaśyaṃ syād guṇa|doṣa|kṛt,
yathā cakṣus tatas teṣu pradhānam idam eva hi.
tad avaśye 'sminn avaśyaṃ dur|gatir dehināṃ bhavet,
yath" âsya Dhanadevasya Subhadrā|kukṣi|janmanaḥ.»

Dhanadevas tato 'vādīc, «caksuḥ|pratyayataḥ katham
bhave 'bhrāmyam ahaṃ, svāmin, prasadya pratipādaya.»

tataḥ Sudharmā Saudharm'|âdhipa|saṃsevya|saṃnidhiḥ
saṃnidhir jñāna|ratnānāṃ jagāda, «śṛṇu samprati.

śrī|Puṣkaravara|dvīpe pratyak svarṇ'|âdri|saṃyuji,
Bharate madhyame khaṇḍe 'bhūt Kāñcanapuraṃ puram,
10.15 prākāraḥ kāñcano yatra saṃkrāntaḥ parikh"|âmbhasi,
bibhṛte kāñcan'|âmbhoja|śriyaṃ kāñcana|śāśvatīṃ.

âiśvarya|tarjita|Ghanavāhano Ghanavāhanaḥ
tatra rājyaṃ praśaśāsa sphurad|dambholi|pāṇikaḥ.
Rambhā|garbha|sa|garbh'|ôru Rambhādevy asya vallabhā,
vallabhā sarvato yasyā lajjā śīla|śriyāḥ sakhī.

sa ca rājā sva|bhāvena cakṣuś|cara|niveditāḥ
prati|pratīkaṃ lāvaṇya|puṇy'|âṅgīḥ paśyati striyaḥ.
vicitra|nāyikā|citra|śālikāś citra|śālikāḥ,
prati|stambhaṃ danta|dāru|putrikā apy akārayat.
10.20 pṛṣṭhataḥ pārśvato 'gre ca sarvato 'py aṅganā|sakhaḥ

What need of more?

The powers of the other senses, whether controlled or out of control, do not produce excellencies or faults to the same extent as sight, since that is the one that is principal among them. Then, that being necessary, a bad rebirth becomes necessary for embodied beings, just as for Dhana·deva here, born from the womb of Subhádra." 10.10

Then Dhana·deva said, "Kindly explain, reverend sir, how, as a result of my sense of sight, I myself wandered in existence."

Then Sudhárman, his presence fit to be worshipped by the god of the Good Works heaven, a treasure of the jewels of knowledge, said, "Listen now.

In lovely Royal Lotus island, facing the adjoining Golden Mountain, in Bhárata, in the middle region, was a city, Kánchana·pura, in which the golden rampart reflected in the water of the moat bore the radiance of a golden water lotus and the golden earth. 10.15

Ghana·váhana (Rider of the Clouds), threatened of the sovereignty of Shiva, the rider of the clouds, governed the kingdom there, the thunderbolt of Indra flashing in his hand. His beloved wife was Rambha·devi, her midriff as narrow as the midriff of Rambha. Extremely beloved to her was modesty, the companion of the splendor of morality.

And that King, according to his natural disposition, used to look at every part of the bodies of women whose bodies were pleasant in their charms, whom he experienced by the motion of his eyes. And he had prepared painted chambers with murals of mistresses of love and painted chambers with models of women made of ivory and wood attached to the sa nārī|kuñjara iva vireje rāja|kuñjaraḥ.

anyedyur dyu|sadāṃ prabhor iva naṭās
tatr' āgatā udbhaṭās,
taiḥ śrīmān Ghanavāhano nara|patiḥ
prekṣā|kṣaṇaṃ yācitaḥ.
ten' âpy adbhuta|nāṭya|kauśala|kalā|
lāmpaṭya|paṭv|ātmanā
sāmantaiḥ sacivaiḥ purī|vara|naraiḥ
sārdhaṃ mud" âdīyata.

nādayanto 'tha brahm'|âṇḍaṃ tauryikāḥ sama|hastakaiḥ
tūryāṇy avādayan. nṛttā nartakyaḥ pakṣa|sārikāḥ.

mūla|pātraṃ Kāmadattā tato raṅgam avātarat,
sabhā|sadāṃ hṛdi punas tad|didṛkṣā|mano|rathaḥ.
vighnaṃ yuva|cakorāṇāṃ ca jyotsnāṃ pralilikṣatām
svam uttarīyaṃ muktv" âsau lāsyaṃ prākramata svayam.

10.25 yatr' Ôm" âpy anumā, yatra nāṭya|vedaś ca tuccha|vāk,
yat stambhanaṃ viśva|dṛśāṃ, jaitraṃ tantraṃ smarasya yat,
tad|aṅgahāra|karaṇa|cārī|caraṇa|cañcuram
udyat|kaṭ'|âkṣa|puṣp" âsau tatra nṛttam avartayat.

tasyā rūpa|kalā|vāgbhir a|nimeṣa|nirīkṣaṇaḥ
śata|koṭi|datām icchuḥ satyo 'bhūd Ghanavāhanaḥ.

na kevalaṃ vapur|vācos tad|vidyābhiḥ, sabhā|sadām
manaḥ|kaper api ciraṃ stambha|mudrā vyajṛmbhata.

pillars. And everywhere attended by women, behind, at his sides and in front, that bull-elephant of a king looked like a bull-elephant among his females. 10.20

One day, excellent actors, as if of the king of the gods, arrived there and asked His Majesty King Ghana·váhana to grant a moment for their show. He, himself having a keen desire to experience the art of wonderful dramatic performance, granted it with joy, together with the barons, ministers and leading citizens.

The musicians made the globe of the world resound as they played their trumpets with the accompaniment of guitars. Dancing girls performed a dance with lutenists at their side.

Then Kama·datta played the principal role on the stage, but in the minds of the audience was the desire of seeing her. She removed her blouse, an obstacle to the young *chakóra* birds desirous of licking her splendor, and herself began to perform a dance of love.

Flowering with the rising up of side glances, there she performed a dance, which even Uma was unable to equal, compared to which the treatises on dancing were idle talk, which was the conquering spell of Love, paralysis for all spectators. 10.25

His gaze rendered unblinking by her figure, art and voice, Ghana·váhana genuinely wanted to give her a billion.

Not only by the spells of her body and voice—the gesture for stilling the monkey of the minds of the audience was exhibited for a long time.

tato rājā dade tasyā adhikaṃ pāritoṣikam,
sāmant'|āmātya|paurā apy ucit'|âbhyadhikaṃ daduḥ.

10.30 tataḥ pūrv'|âhṇe, 'par'|âhṇe, pradoṣe 'tha mahā|niśi
rājā muhur navam iv' âgāpayat tām, anartayat.
divyaṃ bhojy'|âṅga|rāg'|ādi, divyaṃ bhūṣ"|âṃśuk'|ādi ca
svato 'dhikaṃ prati|dinaṃ tasyai prādān nar'|ēśvaraḥ.
tasyā dadānaḥ svarṇ'|ādi manīṣitam anekaśaḥ
na paścān n' âgrataḥ paśyaty akṣi|rāg'|ândhavan nṛpaḥ.

tata ūce mitho 'mātyai, ‹rājyam etad vinaṅkṣyati,
yataḥ kośa|kṣaye rājño bhāvī tantra|kṣayo dhruvam.
tat|kṣaye 'ri|parābhūtis, tato janapada|kṣayaḥ.
tataḥ sāmanta|muktasya bhāvinī vana|vāsitā.
10.35 asyāṃ padyām iva nadyāṃ rāṇ nīlī|rāgatāṃ gataḥ,
na nivartayituṃ śakyaḥ kiṃ kāryaṃ sāmprataṃ tataḥ?

yataḥ:

gaṇayanti n' âpa|śabdaṃ,
na vṛtta|bhaṅgaṃ, kṣayaṃ na c' ârthasya
rasikatven' ākulitā
veśyā|patayaś ca kavayaś ca.›

ākhyad Yaśaskar'|āmātyaḥ, ‹sarv'|ân|artha|khanir naṭī.
etāṃ viṣ'|ādinā hiṃst' ân|artho na syād yataḥ kva cit.›

Then the King gave her an extravagant gratuity, and the barons, ministers and townsmen gave to her more generously than was fitting.

And from then on, in the morning, in the afternoon, in 10.30
the evening, at midnight, at every moment, the King would have her sing and dance, as if it were a new thing. Every day, the King gave to her divine food and unguents and such, and divine ornaments and clothes and such, finer than his own. And as the King continued to give her manifold objects of desire, gold and such, he did not see behind or in front, as if blinded by his heart's desire.

Thereupon the ministers spoke together, 'This kingdom will be utterly ruined, since on the destruction of the treasury there will be certain destruction of the King's army. On the destruction of that, there will be defeat by the enemy and the destruction of the country. Then the consequence of it being abandoned on all sides will be dwelling in the
forest. The King has fallen deeply in love with her, as with 10.35
an advancing river, and is not able to be brought back. What is the proper thing to do about it?

Since:

Those rendered unrespectable by infatuation, the husbands of prostitutes or poets, think nothing of harsh speech, the violation of good conduct or the destruction of wealth.'

The minister Yashas·kara said, 'The dancing girl is a mine of all badness. By exhausting her the badness will be destroyed, and there will be nowhere from where it might come.'

Subuddhir abhyadhatt' âtha, ‹jñāsyat' îdaṃ nṛpo yadi,
tadā na naḥ prāṇa|rakṣā, yad eṣa viṣamo 'dhikam.›
tato Vimalamatin" âbhidadhe, ‹bhaiṣṭa mā mudhā
svayaṃ vijñapyate svāmī, cet tām tyakṣyati tac chubham.
10.40 na cet, tad" âsau caturth'|ôpāya|sādhyo bhaviṣyati.
sarve viraktāḥ sāmantā atr' êty etan na duṣ|karaṃ.›
ity aika|matyān niścitya mitho granthi|grahaḥ kṛtaḥ,
prāptāś ca te bhū|pa|pārśve. 'vag mantrī Matiśekharaḥ:
‹ekam ākhyānakaṃ, deva, prabhor vijñapyam asti naḥ.
niśāmayatu tat svāmī vidhāy' âvahitaṃ manaḥ.›
Ghanavāhana|bhūm'|īśa ākhyād, ‹ākhyāhi, dhī|nidhe.›
tato bhaṇitum ārebhe mantrī śrī|Matiśekharaḥ:
‹śrī|Vasantapure jajñe Jitaśatrur mahī|patiḥ
Sudarśan" âsya devy ādyā, dvitīyā Priyadarśanā.
10.45 Jayasiṃhaḥ suto 'gryāyā, anyasyā Jayamaṅgalaḥ.
tau ca jātau kal"|âmbho|dhī rājy'|ôcita|vapur|latau.
ubhābhyām api devībhyāṃ svasya svasy' âṅga|janmanaḥ
rājā rājy'|âbhiṣekāya vyajñapyata tato 'nyadā.
pṛthvī|patir ath' âbhāṇīd, «yuvāṃ dve api me priye,
tadvat priyau sutāv etau kalā|kūpāra|pāragau.
tayoḥ śreyastaro yas tu, sthāpayiṣyāmi taṃ pade.
yuṣmat|samakṣaṃ parīkṣāṃ kurve sarv'|ēpsitaṃ hy adaḥ.»

Then Subúddhi declared, 'If the King finds out about it, then there will be no protection for our lives, since he will be extremely cross.'

Then Vímala·mati said, 'Don't argue to no purpose. The
King himself will be informed that if he gives her up, that
will be well and good. But, if not, then he will be over- 10.40
come by the fourth stratagem of assault. All the barons are
disaffected about this. Thus informed, it won't be difficult.'

Having thus come to a unanimous conclusion, they made a mutual bond and arrived at the presence of the King. The minister Mati·shékhara said:

'Sire, we have a little story to tell Your Majesty, so let Your Majesty listen, having composed your mind attentively.'

King Ghana·váhana said, 'Tell it, you treasure of intelligence.' Then the minister honorable Mati·shékhara began to speak:

'In lovely Vasánta·pura lived King Jita·shatru, His first
Queen was Sudarshaná, his second Priya·dárshana. Jaya·si- 10.45
mha was the son of the first, Jaya·mángala of the other. And
the two had become oceans of the arts, the tendrils of their
bodies suitable for the kingship.

Then one day each of the Queens asked the King to consecrate her own son to be heir apparent to the kingship.

The King said, "You two are both dear to me, just as dear as these two sons, both having reached the far shore of the ocean of the arts. But I will appoint to the position the one of the two who is more excellent. In your presence I will enquire to what each of them is actually devoted."

āhūto Jayasiṃho 'tha, sa c' āyātas tad" âiva hi.
rājñ" ôktaś ca, «vinodena kena, putr', âdhunā sthitaḥ?»
10.50 so 'vak, «prekṣā|vinodena.»
«sāraṃ kiṃ, putra, janmanaḥ?»
ten' ōce, «deva, rāja|śrīs.»
«tasyāḥ sāraṃ ca, putra, kim?»
«pañca|prakāra|viṣaya|sevanaṃ, tāta, n' âparam.»
ūce rājā, «rājya|lakṣmyāḥ sādhanaṃ, vatsa, kiṃ nanu?»
putro 'vak, «prākṛtam karm'» ê-
ti kṛtvā saṃkathāṃ kṣaṇam
viśṛṣṭo Jayasiṃho, 'th' ā-
kārito Jayamaṅgalaḥ.

samāgataḥ sa sahasā rājñā dāpitam āsanam.
tātaṃ natv" āsanaṃ spṛṣṭvā pāṇin" âsiṣṭa bhuvy asau.
sa|harṣam atha rājñ" ōce, «vats', āsanam alaṅkuru.»
so 'vocad, «deva|pādānāṃ purato bhūr mam' āsanam.»
10.55 rājñ" ôktaś ca, «vinodena kena, vats', âdhunā sthitaḥ?»
so 'vak, «tāta, rāja|nīti|rahasya|pariśīlanaiḥ.»
rāj" âvocata, «putra, tvaṃ somālo na śram'|ôcitaḥ.»
smitv" āha putraḥ, «kiṃ tarhi nītim adhy'|āpitaḥ, pitaḥ?»
nṛpo 'vak, «kiṃ phalaṃ nīte?» «rājya|śrī|pālanaṃ, pitaḥ.»
«rājyasya kiṃ phalaṃ, putra?» « tāta, dharmasya sādhanam.»

Then Jaya·simha was summoned, and he came immediately, and the King asked him, "With what pastime are you engaged now, my son?"

He said, "With the pastime of shows." "What is the best part of life?" "The fortune of a king, Your Majesty." "And what is the best part of that, my son?" 10.50

"Resorting to the five kinds of sense object, father, nothing else." The King said, "What, then, my son, is the furtherance of the fortune of the kingdom?"

The son said, "The usual business." After a moment of conversation, Jaya·simha was dismissed and Jaya·mángala summoned.

When he arrived, he was instantly offered a chair by the King. He bowed to his father, touched the chair with his hand and sat on the ground.

Then the King joyfully asked him, "My son, ornament the seat!" He said, "The ground before Your Majesty's feet is my seat."

The King asked, "With what pastime are you engaged now, my son?" He said, "Father, with the subtleties of statecraft." 10.55

The King said, "My son, you are tender. You are not suitable for hard work." The son smiled and said, "But why then are you engaged in instructing the statecraft, father?"

The King asked, "What is the profit in statecraft?" "The maintenance of the fortune of the kingdom, father." "What is the profit of the kingdom, my son?" "The furtherance of religious duty, father."

«dharmasya sādhanaṃ, vatsa, dev'|ârcā|vrata|dhāraṇe?»
«tāta, rāja|rakṣitāḥ syur vrati|deva|tad|arcakāḥ.»

rāj" ākhyat, «putra, rājyasya phalaṃ viṣaya|sevanam?»
«rājño viṣayiṇas, tāta, rājya|śrīḥ katham edhate?»
10.60 «vatsa, puṇyena rājya|śrīr naśyed viṣayinaḥ katham?»
«deva, pauruṣa|hīnasy' â|sambhavī puṇya|sambhavaḥ.»

«nītiḥ kā, putra?» «rājya|śrī|pālikā, tāta, kathyate.
sāmantānām a|viśvāso, viṣay'|āsakti|varjanam,
niṣphala|tyāga|tyāgaś ca, mantri|mantr'|ôpajīvanam,
nity'|ôdyogo, rath'|âśv'|êbha|patti|nitya|nirīkṣaṇam,
prātiveśika|rājebhyaḥ prītiḥ parataraiḥ saha,
nityaṃ ca cara|cakṣurbhiḥ prativeśy|upalambhanam,
sad|bhāv'|ôktir mantriṇāṃ, na sāmant'|ôtkarṣa|varjanam,
paura|mānaḥ krodha|māna|māyā|lobha|vinigrahaḥ,
10.65 dyūta|bhūta|parīhāro, nidr"|ân|aṅga|dviṣaj|jayaḥ;
iti nītis, tāta, rājy'|ôdyāna|pīyūṣa|sāraṇiḥ.»

tad amī mantriṇaḥ sarve vivadante 'tra bhūriśaḥ.
tad devo vaktu, ko nāma kumāro rājya|bhājanam.›

"Is the furtherance of religious duty, my son, in the maintenance of vows and the worship of the gods?" "Father, ascetics and gods, and acts of worship to them, are protectors of the kingdom."

The King said, "My son, is resorting to the object of the senses the fruit of the kingship?" "Father, how could the fortune of the kingdom prosper whose king is a sensualist?"

"My son, how can the the fortune of the kingdom be 10.60
destroyed if the king, though a sensualist, has merits?" "Your Majesty, an inferior person cannot have merits."

"What is statecraft, son?" "It is said to be the protective guardian of the fortune of sovereignty, father. Not trusting in the barons; avoiding attachment to sensual objects; the abandonment of unprofitable liberality; dependence on the advice of ministers; constant effort; constant inspection of the chariots, horses, elephants and foot; amity with the more distant neighboring kings; constant intelligence of the neighbor by means of the surveillance of spies; the statement of the true situation is of the ministers; not shunning the vaunting of the barons; the opinion of the people being repressed because of its anger, pride, delusion and greed;
shunning the demon of gambling; overcoming the bodiless 10.65
enemy, sleep; that is statecraft, father, a river of nectar for the garden of the kingdom."

Then those ministers all began to dispute variously about the matter. So let Your Majesty declare which is the prince who should partake of the sovereignty.'

Ghanavāhana|bhūpo 'vag, ‹vivādaḥ kuta eṣa vaḥ?›
ūce 'mātyaiḥ, ‹parīhāsāt.› tato 'brūta nar'|ēśvaraḥ:
‹kaḥ kasya pakṣo vo madhye?› ta ūcuḥ, ‹pauruṣaṃ matam
Subuddhy|āder, deva, deva|gurv|ādeh puṇyam eva hi.›
tataś ca cintayāñcakre Ghanavāhana|bhū|bhujā:
‹evam any'|âpadeśena mām apy ete 'nuśāsati.
10.70 aye 'mī sundarā n' âiv' āyātāḥ; ken' âpi hetunā?
huṃ, naṭī|kāraṇād ete ghaṭitāḥ kūṭa|cetasaḥ!
ghaṭantāṃ sarva ev' âite, mantrayantāṃ ca kiñ cana,
naṭīṃ dṛṣṭi|sudhā|vṛṣṭiṃ tyakṣyāmy etad|bhayān na hi!
ke 'mī varākāḥ sacivāḥ, kaś c' âhaṃ Ghanavāhanaḥ?
tad amī pheravaḥ satyaṃ bheṣayanti mṛg'|âdhipam!›
itthaṃ vimṛśya dhātr"|īśas tān ūce, ‹n' âvadhāritam
mayā bhavat|pralapitaṃ. niścinudhvaṃ tataḥ svayam.›
dadhye tataś ca sacivair, ‹aye, jñāt'|âsmad|āśayaḥ!
kruddho drogdhu|manāś c' âiṣa, pratīkāryo drutaṃ tataḥ.›
10.75 vimṛśy' êti, tat|prasattyai vidhāya ca kath"|ântaram,
sva|sthānaṃ sacivā īyuś cikīrṣita|kṛta|tvarāḥ.
‹naṭī|vinaṭito rājā hitaṃ na hi śṛṇoty api,
rājy'|âriś c', êti nigrāhyaḥ› sāmantān iti te 'bhyadhuḥ.

King Ghana·váhana said, 'What's the reason for this dispute of yours?' The ministers said, 'For amusement.' Then the King said:

'Among you, whose side is taken?' They said, 'The manly opinion of Subúddhi and the others is certainly meritorious for kings, teachers and such.'

Thereupon King Ghana·váhana thought, 'By the example of another, they are actually scolding me. Now, then, 10.70
they didn't come just to be agreeable; what's the reason? Ah, it's because of the dancing girl that they are scolding, deceitfully-minded! Well, let them all scold and advise whatever, I will certainly not give up the dancing girl, a shower of nectar for the eyes, through fear of them! Who, on the one hand, are these wretched ministers and who, on the other, am I, King Ghana·váhana, since jackals always fear the king of the animals!'

Having thus deliberated, the King said, 'I don't understand what you're talking about, so come to your own decision.'

Thereupon the ministers thought, 'Ah, our intention has been discovered! Angry and malevolent, he must be quickly counteracted.'

Having thus deliberated and having made further con- 10.75
versation for the sake of his favor, the ministers returned to their own abodes, hastening the accomplishment of their design.

They said to the barons, 'Led a dance by the dancing girl, the King won't even listen to what is fitting, and because he has become an enemy to the kingdom, he must be suppressed.'

ta ūcur, ‹vayam etena dhūler api laghū|kṛtāḥ.
yuṣmad|bhiy" âkārṣma n' êdaṃ, yuṣmad|ukta|kṛtaḥ param.›

kṛt'|âika|matyaiḥ sāmant'|āmātyair bhūp'|âṅga|jo 'pi ca
param'|ârthaṃ nivedy' āśu vidadhe sva|vaśaṃ|vadaḥ.

tato madhyaṃ|dine 'nye|dyur ekākī Ghanavāhanaḥ
babandhe 'mātya|sāmantaiś, cikṣipe dāru|dhāmni ca.

10.80 śrī|Tribhuvanamallo 'tha dāna|śauṇḍo 'bhyudain nṛpaḥ,
hasti|malla|prati|mallaḥ pratāpen' ârka|sodaraḥ.
tataḥ saciva|sāmanta|kḷpta|nīti|parākramaiḥ
śrī|Tribhuvanamallo 'bhūd eka|mallo jagaty api.

Ghanavāhana|bhūpen' ânyadā tādṛg|daśā|spṛśā
bhāṇitā mantriṇo, ‹gatvā tīrthe svaṃ sādhayāmy aham.›

taiś ca tad|bhū|bhujaḥ proce. ten' ōce, ‹kim ih' ôcitam?›
‹dev', atr' âiva hi yat kṛtyaṃ kuryāt, tīrtha|gamo vṛthā.›

rājñ" ôktaṃ, ‹hetunā kena?› ‹deva, klībo 'yam, akṣamaḥ,
tīrthe martuṃ vadhyamāno 'nyathā 'dhāt kiṃ na pauruṣaṃ?

kiñ ca:

10.85 kariṣyati mṛto 'sau kiṃ? tiṣṭhatv atr' âiva dharma|kṛt.
api ca dviḍ|gṛhe bhikṣuḥ śrī|devaṃ laghayiṣyati.

They said, 'We have been treated as lightly as dust by him. We didn't do it through fear of you, but we will do it now you've said it.'

The barons and ministers having become of one mind, they revealed the whole business to the King's son, and he immediately became obedient to their will.

Then at noon the next day, when Ghana·váhana was alone, he was bound by the ministers and barons and cast into a wooden prison.

Then His Majesty Tri·bhúvana·malla, intoxicated with 10.80
generosity, arose as king, a protagonist against the elephant of Indra, twin to the sun in the rays of his majesty. Thenceforth, through the powers of the policy effected by the ministers and barons, His Majesty Tri·bhúvana·malla became the sole protagonist even for the universe.

One day, King Ghana·váhana, touched by the experience of such a condition, asked the ministers, 'I wish to go to a holy place and complete my life.'

And they informed their King. He asked, 'What is fitting in this case?' 'Since he may do what needs to be done right here, going to a holy place is needless.'

The King asked, 'For what reason?' 'Your Majesty, he is a sissy and too weak to die at a holy place through self-annihilation, otherwise why didn't he show manliness?

What's more:

What will he do once he's dead? Let him stay right here 10.85
performing acts of religion. And besides, a beggar in the house of your enemy, he will cause Your Majesty to be slighted.

anyac ca, vairi|milito mā dhāt kim api viḍvaram.›
rājñ" ôktaṃ, ‹ko mayā sārdhaṃ kartum īśo 'sti viḍvaram?›

kiñ ca:

pṛcchat' âitaṃ ‹kuto hetor, deva, tīrthe mumūrṣasi?›
pṛṣṭaś ca taiḥ sa|dambhen' âbhidadhe ‹dharma|hetave.›

mantriṇo 'bhyadhur, ‹atr' âiva
dharmaṃ dān'|ādikaṃ kuru.›
so 'brūta, ‹re dur|ācārā,
dharmaṃ tīrthaṃ vinā kutaḥ?›

tad|uktaṃ tai rājña ūce, rāj" âpi vyājahāra tān:
‹muñcat' âinaṃ, svairam etu sva|śaktiṃ c' âiṣa paśyatu.›
10.90 tato 'mātyair jarato 'śvān śambalaṃ ca pradāya saḥ
mukto jagāma Samarasenasya sva|ripor gṛhe.
dvāre sthitvā bhāṇitaṃ ca yathā, ‹tvāṃ Ghanavāhanaḥ
didṛkṣate› tato 'sau tac chrutvā kruddho 'bravīn nijān:

‹āsannasya ripor mūlāny an|ucchidya śayīta yaḥ,
asau prāpt'|ôdayāt tasmād dhruvam eva vinaśyati.
kiṃ vismṛtaṃ vaḥ pāpen' âmunā vayam upadrutāḥ?
kṛta|pratikṛtaṃ śīghraṃ kurut' âsya dur|ātmanaḥ.›

vyajñapy amātyaiḥ, ‹sva|gṛham āgatasya dviṣo 'pi na
kulīnaḥ prahared, deva, tad a|dṛṣṭaḥ prayātv asau.›
10.95 rājñā pratiśrute tatra tair datv" ôcita|śambalam
viśṛṣṭo 'sau. tad|upari ruṣṭo Jayapuraṃ gataḥ.

And besides, don't let him, having met with your enemy, instigate a rebellion.' The King said, 'Who is capable of making a rebellion against me?'

What's more:

Ask him, 'For what reason do you wish to die at a holy place, Your Majesty?' They asked him, and he said deceitfully, 'For the sake of religion.'

The ministers said, 'Practice religion right here, with acts of charity, et cetera.' He said, 'Hey, your conduct is bad! How can there be religion without a holy place!'

They informed the King of what he had said, and he told them, 'Release him and let him go at will, and let him see his own strength.'

Then the ministers, having given him some old horses 10.90
and provisions, let him go, and he went to the home of Sámara·sena, his enemy. He stood at the door and sent the announcement, 'Ghana·váhana wishes to see you.' Angry on hearing this, he said to his men:

'He who is lulled to sleep without cutting the roots of his enemy nearby is certainly destroyed as a consequence of his arrival. Have you forgotten that this criminal attacked us? Take speedy revenge for that on this evil-natured man.'

The ministers replied to him, 'A man of good breeding does not attack even an enemy who has come to his home, Your Majesty, so let him continue on his way without having been seen.'

The King agreed to this, so, given suitable provisions by 10.95
them, he was dismissed. Angry because of this, he went to Jaya·pura.

rājño Vijayasenasya jñāpitaṃ, Ghanavāhanaḥ
tvāṃ didṛkṣus. tatas tena pradhānānām it' īritam.
‹niṣkāśito 'tr' āgato 'yam. etad|dvār" âsya nandanam
nigṛhṇīmo.› 'bhāṇy amātyaiḥ, ‹supto 'hir bodhyate na hi.
deva, cet tad|grah'|êcchā vas, tad etena vin" âpi hi
taṃ gṛhāṇa. kim ūnaṃ te?› nṛpo 'vag, ‹nītir īkṣyatām.
upakāra|gṛhītena śatruṇā śatrum uddharet,
pāda|lagnaṃ kara|sthena kaṇṭaken' êva kaṇṭakam.›
10.100 tataḥ pradhānair mānite prāveśi Ghanavāhanaḥ,
sammāny' âbhidadhe, ‹kiṃ te samāgamana|kāraṇam?›
Ghanavāhana ācakhyāv, ‹ekānte kīrtayiṣyate.›
tato rājñā vāsa|gṛhaṃ vyayasvaṃ c' âsya dāpitam.
rājñ" ādiṣṭā rahaḥ śrotuṃ mantriṇo 'gus tad|antike.
tato raha upaviśya vyājahre Ghanavāhanaḥ:
‹sarve 'pi kariṇaḥ, śulka|sthānāni, bahudhā karāḥ
rājño Vijayasenasy', âhaṃ tv etasya padātikaḥ.
prasadya dāpayetv ekaṃ mama rājyaṃ yathā tathā.›
tac ca pradhānair āgatya sarvaṃ rājṇe nyavedyata.
10.105 rāj" ākhyat, ‹kiṃ mataṃ vo 'tra?›
Dhavalo mantry ath' âvadat:
‹devas tad|rājyam ādātuṃ
samarthaḥ svayam eva hi.
saṃgṛhyate tad|virakti|viśrambh'|ârtham asau param.›

Ghana·váhana caused King Víjaya·sena to be informed that he was desirous of seeing him, and Víjaya·sena said to his nobles:

'He has come here after being expelled. By means of him, we can overpower his son.' The ministers said, 'A sleeping snake should never be awakened. Your Majesty, if you want to overpower the son, then overpower him without this man. What is lacking in you?' The King said, 'Let regard be given to policy. One should remove an enemy by an enemy laid hold of by kindness, like a thorn sticking in the foot by a thorn held in the hand.'

Respect having been paid by the nobles, Ghana·váhana 10.100
was ushered in, and, having been given high honor, was asked, 'What is the reason for your arrival?'

Ghana·váhana said, 'It will be communicated in private.' Then the King caused him to be given an inner apartment and a disbursement. Ministers appointed by the King to listen in private went to Ghana·váhana's presence, then he entered the private place and said:

'All the elephants, the custom houses, the manifold revenues are King Víjaya·sena's and I am his foot soldier. By his grace, let him cause my kingdom alone to be given me in according manner.' And the leading men went and related all to the King.

The King asked, 'What's your opinion on this matter?' 10.105
Then the minister Dhávala said, 'Your Majesty is capable of taking his kingdom by yourself alone. But he should be welcomed for the sake of confirming his change of disposition.' The King said, 'Excellent, this is excellently said. There is no doubt in it, since whoever is afflicted by his

rājñ" ōce, ‹sādhu, sādh' ûktam evam etan, na saṃśayaḥ.
yato yo yo 'sya putreṇa dūnaḥ so 'sya miliṣyati.
vaśyito 'nena tad|deśo bhaviṣyati sukhāt svasāt.›

tan nyāyyam asya sāhāyyam ity ukte bhū|bhujā, daduḥ
amātyās tasya saṃvāhaṃ dur|vigāhaṃ surair api.
tad|balāt sa|balaṃ|manyaḥ sadyo 'tha Ghanavāhanaḥ
gatv" âdhākṣīt putra|deśam abhāṃkṣīc ca van'|êbhavat.
10.110 ye Tribhuvanamallen' âvajñātāḥ ke 'pi ṭhakkurāḥ,
militais tair jita|kāśiṃ manyo 'bhūd Ghanavāhanaḥ.

teṣāṃ grāma|pur|ādyāś ca lañcā bhṛśam amamaṃsta saḥ.
sarva|sven' âpi tasy' êṣṭaṃ tair aniryātanaṃ yataḥ.

śrī|Tribhuvanamallo 'tha vyajñapyata Subuddhinā:
‹tadā, deva, pitṛ|tyāgād ity a|prekṣā|taroḥ phalam.
tad upekaṣva n' êdānīṃ medinīṃ jananīm iva.
parākrama|kramo rāja|siṃhānāṃ hi phale|grahiḥ.›

tataḥ sarv'|âbhisāreṇa śrī|Tribhuvanamalla|rāṭ
nisvāna|vācālitā|śastaṃ sadyo 'py abhyaṣeṇayat.
10.115 sīmni sthitvā Vatsarājaṃ daṇḍa|rājaṃ pratāpavat
sapadi preṣayāmāsa taṃ prati prati|panthinam.

son will come to terms with him. The son's kingdom that is desired by this man will easily become subject to him.'

The King having declared that it was fitting to give assistance to him, the ministers gave him a fort, difficult to be penetrated even by the gods. Formidable in his forces through the strength of that, then Ghana·váhana suddenly went and destroyed his son's country, and ravaged it, like a forest elephant.

Ghana·váhana became esteemed by those of the landown- 10.110
ers who had been slighted by Tri·bhúvana·malla, who thronged to him with fists raised in victory.

Their villages and citadels and such were a gift. He valued it very highly, since they desired to make him a gift of all their wealth.

Then His Majesty Tri·bhúvana·malla was informed by Subúddhi, 'Your Majesty, this is the fruit of the tree of lack of foresight, which results from the release of your father. So neglect not now the earth as if it were your daughter. Proceeding with valor is certainly the cause of success for lions of kings.'

Then, with his whole force, His Majesty King Tri·bhúvana·malla suddenly advanced with his army, his going rendered auspicious by the sound of instruments and voices.
Having halted at the frontier, glowing with majesty, he sud- 10.115
denly sent Vatsa·raja, the general of his forces, against Ghana·váhana as he was advancing forward.

viśvasy' âpi bhayaṅ|kare raṇa|bhare
lagne tayoḥ sainyayoḥ,
sva|sva|svāmi|kṛte jaya|śriya|maho
prāṇair api krīṇatoḥ,
śrī|daṇḍ'|âdhipatiḥ prayudhya sa ciraṃ
viśvam|bharāṃ devatāṃ
paryārcīd Ghanavāhanasya śirasā
pātho|ruha|śrī|spṛśā.

tato jaya|jay'|ārāvo nisvāna|svāna|meduraḥ
Tribhuvanamalla|sainye jajñe viśv'|ôdaram|bhariḥ.

n' âika|pañc'|êndriy'|āghāta|pātaken' âti|kaśmalaḥ
prathame narake kumbhī|pāke 'gād Ghanavāhanaḥ.
tatr' âikaṃ sāgaraṃ pakvaḥ sa śuddhiṃ kiñ cid āptavān.
tataḥ kathañ cid āyuṣka|kṣayeṇa nirakāśyata.
10.120 tatr' âiva Bhārate varṣe śrī|Kāñcanapure 'tha saḥ
Dhanāvaha|sārthavāha|Dhanadevyoḥ suto 'jani.
sa kramād Dhandev'|ākhyaḥ kul'|ôcita|kal"|âñcitaḥ
Dhanaśriyā|śreṣṭhi|putryā pitṛbhyām udavāhyata.

pūrva|janma|bhav'|âbhyāsād Dhanadevaḥ sa puṅ|gavaḥ
dṛg|naśyayā samākṛṣṭo bhrāmyan prekṣaṇak'|ādiṣu
ati|śādvala|rūpāsu nava|tāruṇya|bhūmiṣu,
taruṇīṣu viśaśrāma kāmaṃ kāma|vaśaṃ|vadaḥ.
maṭhe, deva|kule, rāja|kule, śrī|rāja|vartmani
ramaṇī|rūpa|cakito n' âjñāsīt kṛtyam ātmanaḥ.

The contest of the battle of the two armies commenced, the cause of fear even to the universe, each, even with their lives, trying to make a festival for the goddess of the victory made by their respective leaders. The chief judge of the goddess of victory fought for a long while, then worshipped the goddess of the earth with the auspicious touch of the lotus that was the head of Ghana·váhana.

Then a cry of 'Victory, victory!,' dense with the sound of voices, arose in Tri·bhúvana·malla's army, filling the vault of the universe.

Ghana·váhana, extremely defiled by manifold destructive sins of the five senses, went to the cooking pot hell in the first hell-ground. Roasted there for an aeon, he somehow achieved purification. Then, by wearing away his life-determining karma, he somehow issued out of there. Then, 10.120
in this very continent of Bhárata, in lovely Kánchana·pura, he was born the son of Dhana·devi and Dhanávaha, a merchant. In due course, he, named Dhana·deva, distinguished in the arts of his family, was married by his parents to Dhana·shri, the daughter of a merchant.

Dhana·deva, because of the practice of the experience of his former lives, was a bull of a man dragged by the nose ring of the sense of sight. Driven about, subject to his passion, he reposed his passion in shows and suchlike, very verdant colors, objects of early youth, and young women. In college, in the temple, in the royal court, in the residence of His Majesty the King, trembling at the bodies of lovely women, he did not understand what he had to do.

10.125 anyadā tena dadṛśe nava|yauvana|śālinī
su|rūpā ratn'|ābharaṇ'|âlaṅkṛtā laṅkha|putrikā.
tasyām adhyupapanno 'sau, cūta|lumbyāṃ yathā śukaḥ,
tāṃ bhūri|bhūriṇ" âyācann āpat tat|tolitām api.
‹tvam asmābhir milasi cet, tat tav' âiṣā bhavet param,›
tat pratiśrutya so 'tyākṣīt sarvaṃ pitṛ|kul'|ādikam.
gīta|nṛty'|ādi tat|parśve 'bhyasya jāto mahā|naṭaḥ.
tāṃ gaurīṃ prāptavāṃś cakre dhana|da|prītim anvaham.
anyadā Vijayapuryāṃ Sudharma|kṣmā|pateḥ priyām
nirīkṣya Kamalādevīṃ naṭīṃ so 'maṃsta markaṭīm.
10.130 gṛhītvā svaṃ, viyujy' âibhyaḥ puryāṃ tatra sthito 'mṛśat:
‹melakaḥ Kamalādevyā devy" êva mama dur|labhaḥ.
duḥ|sādham abhyupāyena, su|sādhaṃ vā vipaścitām.
ākṛṣyante hy upāyena divo 'pi hi div|aukasaḥ?›
niścity' êti nṛp'|āvās'|āsanna|saurabhik'|āpaṇe
gṛhītv" âṭṭaṃ Dhanadevo 'paṇāyat kuṅkum'|ādikam.
tathā hi:
kuṅkum'|âguru|karpūra|kastūrī|candana|druti|
paṭa|vās'|âmbu|vās'|ādi vyavahārṣīt tad eva saḥ.
yasya śrī|Malaya|girer iva saurabhavī|cayaḥ
parito vāsayāñcakruḥ sarvān saurabhik'|āpaṇān.

One day, he saw the daughter of an acrobat, abounding 10.125
in early youth, her body very lovely, adorned with jewels and ornaments. He fell deeply in love with her like a parrot with a grove of mango trees, and he offered her weight in gold for her.

'But if you join us, then she will be yours.' Having agreed to that, he abandoned all, his parents and family, et cetera.

Having practiced singing and dancing at her side, he became a leading dancer. He gained that beautiful girl and day and night enjoyed the affection of the gift of love.

One day, in Víjaya·puri, having beheld Kámala·devi, the wife of King Sudhárman, he considered the dancing girl an
ape. Taking his wealth, he parted from them and remained 10.130
in that city. He deliberated, 'Conjunction with Kámala·devi, as with a goddess, will be difficult for me to attain. For the wise, what is difficult of accomplishment, by means of a stratagem, certainly becomes easy of accomplishment. Are not the dwellers in heaven actually attracted from heaven by means of a stratagem?'

Having thus determined, he took a shop in the perfume market near the King's residence and began to sell saffron, et cetera.

Like so:

There he dealt in saffron, aloes, camphor, musk, sandal, resin, perfumed powder, perfumed water and such. His billows of perfume, as if of the lovely Málaya mountain, perfumed the perfume markets all over.

kiñ ca:

10.135 tad eva surabhi|dravyaṃ vikrīṇīte sma sa pradhīḥ.
śuddh'|ânta|dāsyo bhramaryas tatr' āgur yasya saurabhaiḥ.

mah"|ârgham apy alpa|mūlyāt dadāne 'tr' âbruvann imāḥ:
‹suvarṇaṃ surabh'› îty. eṣa, ‹satyam ābhāṇakaṃ› vyadhāt.

krameṇa Kamalādevyā dāsyo 'py āgus tad|āpaṇe,
sa ca tā niścitya samyak su|vastubhir upācarat.

tasya saubhāgya|bhaṇiti|nānā|rakti|kath"|ādibhiḥ
tās tathā vāsitās tābhir, yathā devy apy avāsyata.

tataś ca tasya sarv'|âṅga|saurabh'|āditsay" ôtsukā
sv'|âbhisandhi|nidhiṃ tasmai devy alekhīt su|patrakam.

yathā:

10.140 ‹iyaj jānāti yo dhūrtaḥ, sa saṅgama|ghaṭā|paṭuḥ
sv'|êṣṭaṃ ghaṭayate. kiṃ sa kiṃ mudhā paritapyate?›

likhitvā patrakam puṭyāṃ svayaṃ kṣiptvā, niyamya ca
tai (- -) ś ca *bandhurā* ity ākhyāḥ *kūṭasya tasya* ho!
ity ādiśya praiṣi devyā dāsī, sā ca tathā vyadhāt.
Dhanadevaḥ su|dhīr dadhyāv, ‹aye 'tr' âsti raho dhruvam!›

‹kṣaṇ'|ântare samāgaccher› iti dāsīṃ visṛjya saḥ
puṭīm ucchoṭya rahasi tat patrakam avācayat.

And besides:

That man of preeminent intelligence used to sell per- 10.135
fumed substances, and to there, bees attracted by his fragrances, the maidservants of the royal women's quarters came.

Upon his giving great value for a small amount of money, they said, 'Perfume is gold.' He replied, 'The saying is true.'

Eventually Kámala·devi's maidservants too came to his shop, and he, having rightly recognized them, served them with fine substances. And just as they were perfumed by the conversation and suchlike about the various delights of his perfumes, so, too, was the Queen perfumed.

And then, anxious with the desire to have his perfume over her entire body, the Queen sent him a kind letter, a receptacle of her intention.

Like so:

'The deceiver who knows so much, keen on effecting a 10.140
union, effects his desire. Why, why does he suffer needlessly?'

Having written her letter, she placed it in a packet and sealed it, telling her maidservant, 'You should say, "Look, *here is a diadem for your forehead! : here is a harlot for your deceit!*" ' Having thus ordered her, the Queen sent her maidservant, and she said what she had been told. Clever Dhana·deva thought, 'Ah, there is certainly something secret in it!'

Telling her to come back in a moment, he dismissed the maidservant, untied the packet and read the letter in private.

tataḥ sa|harṣa|romāñcaḥ, saṃsiddh'|âbhīṣṭa|māny atha
sa tasyai jāti|kastūryā lilekha prati|patrakam.

yathā :

10.145 ‹kelī|gṛhe 'tr' âsmi pūrvam āyāsyāmi, priye, dhruvam.
tvam apy udyānikā|vyājād eyāḥ sāyaṃ, ghana|stani.›

tac ca nyastaṃ tena puṭyāṃ sā ca tasyāḥ kṣaṇ'|ântare
sameyuṣyā dade dāsyās, tayā devyāḥ samarpitā.
devy ek'|ânte ca paśyantī tad vyalokata patrakam
muhur|muhur vācayantī yāvat tiṣṭhati harṣulā.

atr'ântare kañcukinā devī vijñāpitā yathā:
‹devi, devaḥ samait' îti mā bhūd aty|ākulā tataḥ.›

abhyāyāntyās tato devyā bhraṣṭaṃ tat patrakaṃ bhuvi,
rājñā c' āgacchat" ādāya vācitaṃ hi vidher vidhiḥ.
10.150 papracche Kamalā rājñā, ‹kim etad?› iti. s" ākulā,
‹jāne n' âsmi'› îty abhyadhatta, kiṃ v" ânyad vaktu sā tadā.

pṛṣṭā dāsyaḥ, ‹kasya haṭṭād gandhān ānayat' âdhunā?›
ūcus tā, ‹Dhanadevasya.› tato rājā krudh" âbhyadhāt.

‹are re, taṃ dur|ācāraṃ kṛtta|nāśā|kara|śrutim
kharam āropy' êti|doṣa|ghoṣaṇena pur'|ântare
bhramayitv" ôcca|śūlāyām āropayata tat|kṣaṇāt!›
tato 'sau vyaṅgit'|âṅgas tais tath" âbhrami pure 'bhitaḥ.

Then, thrilled with joy, thinking that his desire was accomplished, he wrote her a letter of reply with fine musk.

Like so:

'I will go first to the play house. It's certain, my dear. In the evening, you come, too, under the pretext of going for a walk in the garden, firm-breasted lady.' 10.145

And he placed it in a packet and gave it to the maidservant, who had returned after a moment, and she presented it to the Queen. And the Queen looked at and read the letter, continually reading it out, as she stood delighted.

At that moment the chamberlain addressed the Queen, 'The King has come, Your Highness, so don't be over-agitated.'

Then, as the Queen went to meet him, the letter fell to the ground, and the King came and took it. He actually read it, for precept belongs to expedience.

The King asked Kamalávati, 'What is this?' She replied in confusion, 'I don't know,' then tried to talk about something else. 10.150

He asked the maidservants, 'From whose shop did you bring the perfume just now?' They said, 'From Dhana·deva's.' Then the King became angry and said:

'Hey, now, cut off that criminal's nose, hands and ears, mount him on a donkey and parade him around the city to the proclamation of his crime, and immediately after that impale him on the sharp point of a stake.' Then, with his limbs mutilated, he was paraded around the city.

krameṇa prāpto 'sau sādhu|pratiśraya|gṛh'|âgrataḥ.
dadarśa tatra ca munīn dāntān śāntān mah"|ātmanaḥ.
10.155 atr'|ântare sva|yogen' âguṇyata kena sādhunā.
tasya tādṛk|pāpa|bhāvi|dur|gaty|uddhāra|bandhunā.

‹Arahaṃta|namukkāro jīvaṃ moei bhava|sahassāo,
bhāveṇa kīramāṇo hoi puṇo bohi|lābhāya.›

udgṛhītaṃ ca ten' êdaṃ vaṇijā tattva|tṛṣṇajā.
guṇayann eva tad asau śūlāyāṃ h" âdhiropitaḥ.
tato 'cintya|dhāmnā tasya bhavyatva|paripākataḥ,
kaṣāy'|âlpatay", ātmīya|tādṛk|pāp'|âti|nindayā,
ā yauvanād dṛṣṭi|rāga|daurātmya|parigarhayā,
tiryaṅ|naraka|gaty|ākhya|dur|gati|dvāra|vāraṇāt,
10.160 madhyama|guṇa|sampattyā tattva|sādh'|ûpabṛṃhaṇāt,
tat|pāṭhasya parāvṛttyā sa nar'|āyur upārjayat.

kṣaṇād vipadya Kauśāmbyāṃ mahā|puryām ih' âiva hi,
Dhanasya sārthavāhasya dhana|dasya śriyām bharaiḥ
śīla|lakṣmī|su|bhadrāyāḥ Subhadrāyāś ca yoṣitaḥ
sa jīvo Dhanadevasya nandanaḥ samajāyata.
Dhanadeva iti nāma pitṛbhyāṃ tasya nirmame,
prācīna|bhava|tan|nāmnaḥ kathañ cic chravaṇād iva.
sa ca tvam eva, su|mate. sva|maty" êdaṃ vibhāvaya,
yena sv'|anubhavāt te 'pi draḍhīyān pratyayo bhavet.»

Eventually he was brought before a house where Jain monks were lodging, and there he saw the monks, self-restrained, tranquil and magnanimous. At that moment, a 10.155
certain Jain monk was reciting the prayer in praise of the Worthies, with praise of its action beneficial for the removal of the impending bad rebirth due to a sin such as Dhana·deva's.

'Praise of the Worthies releases the soul from a thousand existences, but recited with concentration it leads to the attainment of enlightenment.'

And it was taken up by that merchant, thirsty for the truth, and then he actually recited it as he was, alas!, impaled on the stake. Then, through its inconceivable power; as a result of his potential for final liberation; through the diminution of his impurity; through his extreme censure of sin such as his own; through his blame of his depravity in the sense of sight from the time of his youth; through the blocking of the door of the bad rebirths called hell-rebirth and
animal rebirth; through his attainment of middling virtue; 10.160
through the support of the truth of that monk; through the averting power of his recitation, he attained human rebirth.

After a moment he died, and in Kaushámbi, here in this very great city, the soul of Dhana·deva was reborn as the son of the merchant Dhana, generous in the bestowals of fortune, and his wife Subhádra, very glorious in the good fortune of her morality. And his parents gave him the name Dhana·deva, as if they had somehow heard the name of his former life. And you are he, certainly. You are intelligent, consider it with your intelligence, so, that by means of your own ascertainment your belief may become firmly fixed."

10.165 īh"|âpoh'|ādi kurvann
atha khalu Dhanadevaḥ sa sārth'|ādi|netā,
jāti|smṛtyā parīto
nija|janana|catuṣkaṃ yathāvad dadarśa.
śrī|sūr'|êndoḥ pad'|âbje
nyapatad atha tataḥ saṃyama'|rddhiṃ kil' āptuṃ,
vijño vyajñāpayac ca,
«vrati|tilaka, bhav'|âbdher itas tārayer mām!»
su|gurur abhayadevo,
«bhaktir acchā Jin'|ôkte,
'varatir akhila|pāpāc
c', êti kaivalya|hetuḥ
vilasati, bata, sampraty
adbhutā yogyatā, bhoḥ,
param avahiti|hṛdyaṃ
śrūyatām śrotra|vṛttam.»

iti śrī|nirvāṇa|Līlāvatī|mahā|kath"|êti|vṛtt'|ôddhāre Līlāvatī|sāre Jin'|âṅke cakṣur|indriya|vipāka|vyāvarṇano nāma daśama utsāhaḥ.

Then indeed, making proper consideration of what was for and against, et cetera, Dhana·deva, the foremost leader of merchants, filled with the memory of his former lives, saw the courtyard of his former lives as it actually was. And then, having fallen before the lotus-feet of the moon of learned doctors, he, wise to obtain the wealth of ascetic restraint, requested that ornament of monks, "Enable me to cross from here the ocean of existence." 10.165

Then the true teacher said, "Because your devotion to the word of the Jina is clear and because your abstention from all sin for the sake of emancipation is evident, oh, wonderful is your suitability to undertake this now. But listen with attentive mind to what happens with the sense of hearing."

Here ends the tenth canto, entitled "The Consequences of the Sense of Sight," of the Jain epic *The Epitome of Queen Lilávati*, an abridgment of the events of *The Epic Story of the Auspicious Final Emancipation of Lilávati.*

CANTO 11
THE CONSEQUENCES OF THE SENSE OF HEARING

II.1 Atha śrīmān Sudharm'|ēśaḥ Su|dharm'|ēśa|stuta|kramaḥ śrī|Vijayasena|rāja|mukhebhyaḥ punar ādiśat.

«śrotraṃ vaḥ prīṇyate śrotra|sva|rūp'|ôtkīrtan'|â|patham.
ko na hi prīyate 'sau sva|rūpasy' ôtkīrtanād iha?
asau śravaṇa|hariṇo gītim ākarṇya hāriṇīm
yāna|pān'|âśana|tyāgāt prāṇān na gaṇayaty api.

a|kharva|gāndharva|rāgāt śrotra|matta|mataṅgajaḥ
nibiḍaṃ bandham ātmānaṃ nayate na yataḥ sukham.
II.5 ādau śṛṇoti gīt'|ādi yuvā kautuka|mātrataḥ.
sat|kal" âiṣ" êti muditas tato 'bhyasyati, gāyati.
krama|kramāt tataś c' âiṣa tiras|kṛtya kriy"|ântaram
manute gīta|vātulo gītam ekaṃ jane phalam.
cāraṇair gāyakair bhaṭṭair aty|uccaiḥ kṛtya|varṇitaḥ
an|īdṛśo 'pi ced dṛkṣaṃ|manyas teṣu dyu|vṛkṣati.
veṇu|vīṇā|mṛdaṅg'|ādi|dhvani|ḍambara|garbhitām chinna
gīti|hālāṃ piban mūḍho, hā, dharm'|ârthau prahāpayet.

vīṇā|trisarikā|sāraṅgikā|rāvaṇa|hastakān
paṇy'|âṅganā|gāna|garbhān sudhā|pāyaṃ pibaty asau.
II.10 pāna|gāna|ras'|āveśāt prasaṅgād agrato 'grataḥ
cokṣ'|â|cokṣa|vyavahāraṃ, hā!, hārayati pātakī.

THEN THE REVEREND Lord Sudhárman, his proceeding II.1
praised by the lords of the Good Works Heaven, once more instructed them, His Majesty King Víjaya·sena at their head.

"The sense of hearing delights you as it goes along the wrong path of the praise of its own nature of hearing. Who here indeed does not delight in the praise of his own nature? The deer of hearing, having heard the doe of captivating music, through its abandonment of the way, drink and food, does not pay heed even to life.

Because of its great passion for music, the wild rutting elephant of hearing leads the self into close bondage, and
is not easily restrained. At first, a young man listens to II.5
songs and suchlike through mere curiosity. Thinking that it is a fine art, he is delighted. Then he begins to practice music. And in course of time he passes by other activity, and, devoted to music, considers music the only fruit in a person. His deeds very highly lauded by traveling minstrels, singers and bards, even if he is not like that he considers himself to be like that, and is a wishing-tree among them. Drinking the liquor of music, which is filled with the sound of the reverberation of flutes, lutes, drums, et cetera, he becomes deluded, and also destroys, alas, his morality and his wealth.

He drinks the liquor of the nectar of lutes, banjos, guitars and mandolins, accompanied by the singing of prostitutes.
Devoting himself to the flavor of liquor and music, contin- II.10
ually putting his addiction first, full of sin, alas!, he loses the distinction between pure and impure.

atha paṇy'|âṅganā|gīta|kaṭākṣa|smara|sāyakaiḥ
prabhinna|cetā grahilo, hā!, mahelāḥ karoti tāḥ.
gīt'|ādi|vyasanāt tāsāṃ sarva|svasy' âpi dāyakaḥ,
mugdho na gaṇayet kośa|kṣayaṃ rājya|kṣayaṃ na ca.

tataḥ kliśnāti koś'|ârthaṃ prajāḥ, sāmanta|mantriṇaḥ,
a|līka|kṣūṇakair vṛttiṃ padātīnāṃ bhanakti ca.
daṇḍa|hīnaḥ, kośa|hīno, muktaḥ sāmanta|mantribhiḥ
tato rājyāya dāyādaiḥ pradhānair vā sa rudhyate.

11.15 raṇāy' ôttiṣṭhamāno 'sau raudra|dhyānī, balaṃ vinā
vināśyate tair, narakaṃ yāti, gīti|taroḥ phalam.
tataḥ ku|nara|tiryakṣu gīta|vyasanato bhraman
su|mānuṣatvaṃ labhate kathañ cin madhyamair guṇaiḥ.

dṛṣṭ'|āntaḥ punar atr' âyaṃ, rājan, Sūraḥ purohitaḥ.»
purohitas tataḥ Sūraḥ sūrim evaṃ vyajijñapat:

«kathaṅ|kāraṃ mayā, svāmin,
śrotr'|êndriya|nibandhanaḥ
duḥkh'|âmbhodhir avagāḍho?
jñān'|âbdhe, pratipādaya.»

tataḥ, Siṃha|mahā|rāja, Sūreṇ' êti nivedite
su|ghoṣā|ghoṣa|nirghoṣaḥ Sudharma|svāmy ath' âbhyadhāt:

Then, his mind pierced by the arrows of Love that were the side glances of the music of prostitutes, possessed by a demon, shame!, he uses those women. Giving them even all his wealth through his addiction to their music and suchlike, gone astray, he does not reckon the decay of his treasury or the decay of his kingdom.

Then, for the sake of wealth, he harasses the subjects, barons and ministers, and with contrived delays makes breaks in the maintenance of the foot soldiers. Deprived of the means of punishment, deprived of his treasury, abandoned by the barons and ministers, he is deposed from the sovereignty by his kinsmen or the nobles. Rousing himself 11.15
to battle, meditating on dreadful matters, lacking a force he is destroyed by them. He goes to hell, the fruit of the tree of music. Then, devoted to music, wandering in bad human and animal rebirths, by means of his middling virtues he somehow obtains a good human birth.

Now, as an example of this, Your Majesty, here is the chaplain Sura." Thereupon the chaplain Sura addressed the reverend doctor thus:

"Reverend doctor, explain how I plunged into an ocean of sorrow, the bondage of the sense of hearing, you ocean of knowledge."

Then, Your Majesty Great King Simha, at Sura's requesting thus, reverend Sudhárman, his voice sounding like a trumpet, began to relate:

11.20 «Jambū|dvīpe 'tr' âiva varṣe Bhārate bhāte rājataḥ
Bharat'|ântas|tiro|māna|daṇḍo Vaitāḍhya|parvataḥ.
tatr' ôbhe bāhuvat śreṇyau nānā|pū|ratna|bhūṣaṇe.
tatr' âbhūd uttara|śreṇyāṃ Nabha|ābharaṇaṃ puram.
yat śrī|vidyā|dharair vidyā|dharībhiś ca vibhāsvaram
devair dev'|âṅganābhiś ca deva|loka iv' âśubhat.

śrīmān Kamalaveg'|ākhyas tatra vidyā|dhar'|ēśvaraḥ
sur'|ēśvara iv' ābhāsīt śata|koṭi|da|pāṇikaḥ.
sāhasaṃ yasya pādātaṃ; sad|bodho mantri|maṇḍalam;
vivekaḥ sāmanta|jātam; āstikyaṃ bāndhana|vrajaḥ;
11.25 sarv'|âdhikārī saṃvego; nirvedas tu niyoginaḥ;
Dayā|Tattva|Ruci|Kṣānti|mukham antaḥ|puraṃ tathā;
śrī|prajñapti|mahā|vidyā dṛḍha|praṇidhi|saṃhatiḥ;
nṛpati|prakriyā|mātraṃ pādāt'|ādy|aparaṃ punaḥ.

tathā:

Arhad|ājñ" âiva koṭīraṃ; syād|vādo maṇi|kuṇḍale;
puṇya|śrī|ratna|tilakas; tāmbūlaṃ sū|nṛtaṃ vacaḥ;
jaya|śrīr maṇi|keyūraṃ; dānam ratn'|âṅgulīyakam;
hāraḥ pañca|namas|kāro; līlā|vrajy" âṃhri|bhūṣaṇam;
yaśaḥ|kīrtī ca saṃvyān'|ôpasaṃvyāne samantataḥ;
tasya rājñaḥ pariṣkāra|bhāro bhāro 'paraḥ param.

"In Rose-apple Tree Island, here in this continent of Bhárata, the silver Vaitádhya mountain lies resplendent, a rod for the punishment of pride lying transversely within Bhárata. Both sides of its mighty ranges are ornamented with the jewels of various cities. On its northern range was situated the city of Nabha·ábharana, which shines with the splendor of the masters and mistresses of magic like heaven with the gods and goddesses. 11.20

There a king of the masters of magic called His Majesty Kámala·vega, his entrepôts producing a hundred billion, was as resplendent as the king of the gods. His boldness was his infantry; his true understanding, his council of ministers; his discrimination, his numerous barons; his piety, his host of kinsmen; his prime minister, desire of emancipation and 11.25 indifference to the world, his officials; likewise with place of honor in his royal women's quarters, Charity, Truth, Faith and Patience; his splendid magic power of discernment* was his endowment with the observation of what is rightly established; the measure of his rank of king, his devotion to wandering ascetics and such.

Like so:

His diadem was the teaching of the Worthies; his adherence to the doctrine of possibility and non-possibility, his two jeweled earings; his forehead ornament, the auspicious jewel of virtue; his betel, his pleasant and true speech; his fortune of victory, his jeweled arm bracelet; his charity, his jeweled finger ring; his string of pearls; his prayer of homage to the five supreme beings; his wandering in disguise, his foot ornament; and the fame of his glory, his enveloping upper garment and lower garment; but the amount of the

11.30 tri|loka|sārad|alika|ghaṭit" êva gat'|ôpamā;
sudhā|sāra|saṃbhṛt" êv' â|tulya|saubhāgya|bhājanam;
śīla|śālīnya|kaulīnya|samyaktv'|ārjava|śeva|dhi ḥ
devī Madanarekh" âbhūt tasya khecara|bhū|bhujaḥ.

tayoḥ śrī|Kamalavega|śrīman|Madanarekhayoḥ
bhuñjatoḥ puṇya|kalpa|dru|phalaṃ vaiṣayikaṃ sukham.
upary|aneka|putrāṇāṃ upayācita|tuṣṭayā
kula|devyā dve pradatte udīyāte sute kramāt.

tayor janm'|ôtsavaś cakre pitrā putr'|ôtsav'|âdhikaḥ,
Madana|pūrvā Mañjūṣā Śalāk" êty abhidh" âpi ca.

11.35 dhātrībhir lālyamāne te, khelyamāne nṛpair api,
jyotsnā|jyotsn"|ēśa|maṇḍalyāv iva vṛddhim upeyatuḥ.
adhītinyau te ca sarva|kalāsu nija|nāmavat.
yauvanaṃ Kāma|rājasya mitraṃ citram acitrayat:
rūpa|śriyā Rati|jitau, śaraj|jyotsnā|jitau tviṣā,
matyā c' âti|Sarasvatyau, Pārvatyā ati|saubhage,
kṣobhayantyau ca vidyā|bhṛt|sur'|âsura|mano|'mbudhīn
krama|krameṇa jajñāte te Smar'|âvatar'|ôcite.

jewels of the self-discipline of this king was an amount second to none.

Her equal having vanished as if formed at the destruc- 11.30
tion of the universe—as if formed from the essence of nectar; a vessel of unequaled loveliness; a treasury of morality, modesty, good breeding, righteousness and rectitude—the queen of that king of the travelers in the sky was Mádana·rekha.

They, His Majesty Kámala·vega and Her Highness Mádana·rekha, enjoyed sensual pleasure, the fruit of the wishing-tree of their merit. In due course, granted by their family goddess, pleased with their prayers concerning many sons, two daughters were born to them.

Their father celebrated a birth festival for them, surpassing the birth festival for a son, and named them Manjúsha and Shaláka, with Mádana as their forename.

Cherished by nurses, encouraged to play even by kings, 11.35
like two orbs of the moon in their splendor, the two began to grow. And they learned all the arts as if they were their own names. Youth, the friend of the King of Love, painted a picture: In the loveliness of their bodies, surpassing Passion; in their complexions surpassing the light of the autumn moon, in intelligence surpassing Sarásvati, the goddess of learning; in beauty surpassing Párvati; and in their churning the oceans that were the minds of the gods, the demigods and the masters of magic, in due course the two became suitable for the descent of Love.

sūry'|ôdaya|kṣaṇe 'nye|dyus te sva|saudhasya mūrdhani
sah' ārūḍhe vayasyābhiḥ khelituṃ naika|khelanaiḥ.
II.40 yāvat saudh'|ôpari parikrīḍante tāḥ su|nirbharam,
tāvaj jagāda Madanaśalākā vismay'|ônmukhī:
‹halā halā, vyomni dūre 'ty|a|vyakto '|śruta|pūrvakaḥ
kolāhala|dhvaniḥ ko 'pi karṇ'|âtithir abhūn mama.›
jagau Madanamañjūṣā, ‹śrutī te, bhagni, vādite.
aparā k" âpi kim api na śṛṇoty anyathā katham?›
atha kṣaṇ'|ântare 'ny" âny" âpy ūce, ‹kiñ cin niśamyate.›
atha sarvā avadadhuḥ śuśruvuś c' āsphuṭaṃ dhvanim.
sambhāvanā|bala|jñāta|tat|tad|vyatikar" âparā
tat|pura|vāsi|Kuraṅgavega|bhūr Matisundarī
II.45 vyājahāra, ‹halā, jñātaṃ leś'|ôddeśād idaṃ mayā.
kolāhalasy' âsya mūlaṃ, bhagni, kiṃ śrūyatāṃ halāḥ?
asty asminn eva Vaiṭāḍhya|bhūmī|bhṛty utttam'|âṅgavat
Siddhaṃ kūṭaṃ tatra caityaṃ prasiddhaṃ vaḥ kirīṭavat.
tatra yātr"|ârtham āyātāṃ yātām vidyā|bhṛtāṃ kila
davīyastvād a|dṛśyānām ayaṃ kalakala|dhvaniḥ.›
kṣaṇe 'tr' Âbhayasundary" ôdairye, ‹tat, sakhi, n' ân|ṛtam.
kiṃ tv ati|prājya|lok'|ôttho dhvanir eṣa vijṛmbhate.
tādṛg|janaś ca yātrāyāṃ, sā ca caitre, 'dya phālgunaḥ.
tad anyat kāraṇaṃ kiñ cid vidyā|bhṛn|melake vada!›

One day, at the setting of the sun, they ascended the terrace roof of the palace with their companions to play
various games. As they were playing about very intently 11.40
on the roof of the palace, Mádana·shaláka looked up in astonishment and said: 'My friends, my friends, far away in the sky, very indistinct, some previously unheard sound of a hubbub came a guest to my ears!'

Mádana·manjúsha said, 'It sounded in your ears, sister. Otherwise why didn't anyone else hear anything?'

The next moment, one and then another said that she had heard something. Then they all concentrated and heard the sound clearly.

Another of them, joined with the facts that she had learned through the strength of her mental powers, Mati·súndari, the daughter of Kuranga·vega, a citizen of that
town, said, 'My friends, after brief cogitation, I've found out 11.45
the cause of this hubbub. Why listen to arguments, sister?

There is on this very Vaitádhya mountain, the supporter of the world, a peak named Siddha, like its head, on which there is a famous temple, like your crest. There, for the sake of pilgrimage, the masters of magic, yes, are coming and going. This sound of murmuring comes from them, who, because of the far distance, cannot be seen.'

Straightaway Ábhaya·súndari declared, 'That is not untrue, my friend. But this sound is coming from an extremely large number of people. And the pilgrimage with so many people takes place in spring, but now it is winter, so tell us, what other reason is there for this congregation of the masters of magic?'

11.50 Matisundary avag, ‹bhūyo yātr" âiv', âtra nibandhanam:
yato 'tīta|pradoṣe me tasthuṣyāḥ saudha|mūrdhani,
a|kasmād eva me tāto 'vatīrṇo vyoma|maṇḍalāt.
mayā c' āsana|dān'|ādi tad|vel"|ôcitam ādadhe.
pitrā gṛhīt" âsmy utsaṅge, tato 'pracchi may" âsakau,
«tadā, tāta, prasthitasy' êyatī|velā kva te 'tyagāt?»
pit" ākhyat, «putri, jānāsi Siddh'|āyatanam asti yat?»
«tāta, jāne.» «tarhi, vatse, tatr' âdya prāptavān aham.»
«tāt', ânyad" âpi tatr' âiṣi, velā na tv ityatī laget,
yat prage 'dya prasthito 'si, vikāle ca samāgamaḥ.
11.55 tad adya Siddh'|āyatane vilambo 'bhūt kutaḥ, pitaḥ?»
vyājahāra pitā, «putri, s'|âvadhānaṃ niśāmaya.
asti svasti|śriyāṃ dhāma puraṃ Gaganavallabham,
yad vīkṣya svaḥ|pater, manye, tri|divaṃ svaṃ na vallabham.
prajñapty|ādi|mahā|vidyā|prabhīṣṭ'|âtula|śāsanaḥ
param'|Ārhata|rājo 'tra rājā Pavanavega|rāṭ.
sarva|vidyā|bhṛtāṃ cakrī, śreṇi|dvitaya|nāyakaḥ,
divaṃ bhuvaṃ c' ântarā yo nityam antara|rājati.
tasy' ôpayācita|śataiḥ kula|devy" âti|tuṣṭayā
devī Ratnavatī putra|ratnāt saty'|âbhidhā kṛtā.

Mati·súndari said, 'This numerous pilgrimage is taking place for this very reason: now, at the very close of evening, as I was standing on the roof of the mansion, without a why or a wherefore, father descended from the sphere of the sky. I presented him with a chair, et cetera, and said what was fitting for the occasion. Father held me in an embrace, then I asked him, "After setting out, Father, where did you spend so much time?" 11.50

Father said, "My daughter, you know that there is a temple on Siddha?" "I know, Father." "Then, my child, that's where I went today."

"Father, when you go there at other times it doesn't take so long, yet today you set off early in the morning and returned late in the evening. So what was the cause of your delay 11.55
today in the Siddha temple, Father?" Father said, "Listen attentively, my daughter.

There is a city, an abode of prosperity, Gágana·vállabha, which the king of heaven having seen, I suppose, his own heaven was no longer dear to him. His dominion equal to the range of his mighty magic power of discernment, King Pávana·vega ruled there as a supreme Jain king, emperor of all the masters of magic, a second lord of the hosts, who ruled among heaven, earth and the space between. His Queen was Ratnávati (Abounding in Jewels), her name made true by the birth of a jewel of a son, granted by the family goddess, who was supremely pleased by their hundreds of prayers of entreaty.

11.60 tasya janmani Vaiṭāḍhya|sarva|caityeṣu cakriṇā
akāle yātrā|karaṇe 'dy' ādiṣṭāḥ khe|carāḥ same.
tato 'mutr' āsanna|Siddh'|āyatane maha|nirmitau
Kamalaveg'|ādi|vidyā|bhṛtām ājñām adāt prabhuḥ.
tataḥ, putri, tatra vidyā|dharāṇāṃ melake sati
Kamalavega|khe|caro mah"|ôtsavam acīkarat.

tatra tīrthe snāna|gān'|ârcana|nartana|vandanaiḥ
punānasya janur, vatse, kāla|kṣepo 'dya me 'bhavat.
anyac ca, śvaḥ sametavyam ih' êty aṅgīkṛtaṃ samaiḥ.
avaśyaṃ tatra gantavyaṃ tat kalye 'muny anantaram.»
11.65 tato may" âbhāṇi, «tāta, śrāntā viśrāmyat' âdhunā.»
tatas tāto 'smi ca sve sve talpe 'svāpi ca līlayā.
prātas tato 'ham utthāya yuṣmat|pārśve samāgamam,
tato 'kāle caitya|yātrā|kāraṇaṃ niścitaṃ mayā.›

tato jagāda Madanaśalākā, ‹he vayasyikāḥ,
vayam api tādṛg|tīrtha|natyā syāma niraṃhasaḥ.›
‹bhagnye, tat sādhu, sādh' ûktam!›
ity upabṛṃhya tāḥ samāḥ
sva|sva|veśmasu gatvā sa,
snātvā, bhuktvā, vilipya ca,
nivasya deva|dūṣyāṇi jagmuḥ saṅketit'|āspadam.
smṛtvā vidyāṃ samutpetuḥ, Siddha|caityaṃ yayuś ca tāḥ.

For his birth, all the sky-travelers have been ordered by the emperor to perform an out-of-season pilgrimage among all the temples on Mount Vaitádhya. Then, straight after that, in the Siddha temple, the emperor ordered the masters of magic, Kámala·vega and the others, to prepare a festival. So then, daughter, the masters of magic having congregated there, Kámala·vega the sky-traveler had them prepare a great festival. 11.60

Today, in that holy place, my time was spent, my child, in celebrating the birth with bathing, singing, praising, dancing and worship. And everyone agreed to assemble there again tomorrow. So I must certainly go there immediately after dawn."

Then I said, "Father, you are tired. Please rest now." Then Father and I went to our respective beds and slept soundly. Then in the morning I arose and came to meet you, since I have found out the reason for this untimely pilgrimage to the temple.' 11.65

Thereupon Mádana·shaláka said, 'Hey, my friends, let us, too, become free from sin by means of reverence at such a holy place.'

Together they urged powerful agreement, saying, 'That is excellent, excellent, sister!,' and having gone to their respective homes, bathed, and anointed themselves, and having donned divine garments, they met at their appointed place. Remembering their magic power, they flew up and arrived at the Siddha temple.

11.70 tatra c' ân|ādi|nidhanaṃ sarva|śreyo|nibandhanam
Jin'|êndra|bimbaṃ vidhinā namasyāmāsur āśu tāḥ.
tato vidyādharī|devī|kinnarīṇāṃ vimadhyataḥ
tā namaskṛtya Madanamañjūṣ"|ādyāḥ samāsata.

Mahāśanijavaḥ pūrvaṃ prāpto vidyā|dhar'|ēśvaraḥ
tatr' âpaśyat tāṃ Madanamañjūṣāṃ smara|śevadhim.
jighṛkṣur iva tāṃ jñātvā Madanena ruṣā śaraiḥ
viddho Mahāśanijavaḥ sadyaś cint"|āturo 'jani.

tathā hi:

«kasy' âiṣ" âbhinavasya paṅkaja|bhuvo
lokottarā nirmitiḥ
kiñ c' ôccair vimalaṃ kulaṃ tilakayaty
eṣ" âdbhut'|âlaṅkṛtiḥ;
asy' âiṣā puruṣ'|ôttamasya hṛdaye
saṃdhāsyate śrī|śriyaṃ.
kiṃ v" ânyair? mama netra|patra|puṭayor
eṣā sudhāṃ varṣati.

11.75 strī|ratnaṃ tad iyaṃ yasya gṛhe, khe|cara|cakry asau.
yathā|tath" êyaṃ tad|grāhyā pratimallo 'tra ko mama?

yadvā me 'kṣṇā cañculena mano mugdhaṃ vimohitam
tad ime bodhayitv" āśu su|pathe sthāpayāmy aham.
he manaś|cakṣuṣī, tīrthe yuvāṃ yātr"|ârtham āgate,
tan niṣiddhiṃ kim ārabdhaṃ? dhig, dhig vām iti cāpalam.›

ity anuśiṣyamāṇe te balāt tām eva jagmuṣī
manaḥ|spṛśā dṛśā tasyāḥ parirabdhe mudā ciram.

And there, according to precept, they worshipped the image of the Lord Jina, a treasure without beginning or end, the foundation of every excellence. Then, having worshipped, they, Mádana·manjúsha and the others, took their places among the mistresses of magic, the goddesses and the centaur-ladies. 11.70

Maha·shani·java, a king of the masters of magic, had arrived previously, and there he saw Mádana·manjúsha, a treasury of love. Pierced by Love's arrows as if in anger because Love had realized that he wished to seize her, Maha·shani·java's mind became sick with desire:

Like so:

'The creation of her form more out-of-this-world than the springing up of a very young lotus, the one whose family, although absolutely stainless, this wonderful ornament adorns besides—in the heart of that excellent man she will deposit the fortune of prosperity. But, rather, what need of more? She showers nectar in the leaf-baskets of my eyes.
Even if this jewel of a women is in the house of him who 11.75
is the emperor of the sky-travelers, nevertheless she will be taken from him. Who can oppose me in this matter?

Or, rather: my foolish mind has been beguiled by my inconstant eye. I will enlighten them both and place them on the right path. Hey, mind and sight, you have come to this holy place for the sake of pilgrimage. Shame, shame on you, that the restraint you have undertaken is inconstant.'

Thus instructed, the two actually forcibly approached her and with the touch of mind and with sight embraced her with great delight for a long time.

tayos tādṛg|dṛg|vilāsaṃ mantrī Varamatir vidan
papraccha kañ cana, ‹sakhe, k"êyaṃ kamala|locanā?›
11.80 so 'vak ‹Kamalavegasya vidyā|dhara|pater iyam.
śrī|kanyā su|bhagaṃ|manyā, su|mukhī, vi|mukhī narāt.›
dadhyau sa mantrī, ‹mat|svāmī yath" âsyāṃ lola|locanaḥ,
mat|svāmini tath" âiṣā 'pi. tato 'bhūt priya|melakaḥ.›
atha śrī|Siddh'|āyatane yātrām āsūtrya khe|carāḥ
sarve svāṃ svāṃ purīṃ jagmuḥ Śiva|puryāṃ tu yogyatām.
Mahāśanijavaḥ s' âiṣa manda|manda|gatir yayau
sva|puraṃ Sundarānandaṃ, tan|manas tu tayā saha.
tat|saṅgam'|ôtsav'|ôpāya|śata|cintā|vrajaṃ sṛjan
śrīmān Mahāśanijavas tena vyajñapi mantriṇā.
11.85 ‹devasya hṛd|garbha|gṛhe yā viveśa balād api
sā śrī|Kamalavegasya kanyā vidyā|dhar'|ēśituḥ.
mahā|kulaṃ kal"|āsthānaṃ yuvānam api khe|caram
manyate sva|guṇ'|âhaṃyuś cañcā|sadhryañcam eva sā.
prabhuṃ tu sā tadā tādṛg|dṛg|vilāsa|saro|ruhaiḥ
vapuṣmantaṃ Smaram iva pūjayāmāsa sa|tvaram.
tato 'bhirucitas tasyāḥ svāmy avaśyaṃ na saṃśayaḥ.
tādṛśām īdṛśā bhāvā mano|bhāvaṃ vinā na hi.›

The minister Vara·mati, realizing that the glances of the two were amorous, asked someone, 'My friend, who is this lady with the lotus-eyes?'

He replied, 'She is the lovely daughter of Kámala·vega, king of the masters of magic. Proud of her good fortune, lovely-faced, she is averse to a husband.' 11.80

The minister thought, 'Just as my master's eye is desirous of her, so is hers for him. Thus there has been a meeting of lovers.'

Then, having completed their pilgrimage at the holy Siddha temple, all the sky-travelers returned to their respective cities, each comparable to the city of Shiva.

Maha·shani·java himself with a very slow gait returned to his own city, Sundaránanda, but his mind remained with her. As His Majesty Maha·shani·java was forming a way from a hundred thoughts about the means for the festival for his union with her, he was addressed by that minister:

'She who has forcibly entered the sanctuary of Your Majesty's heart is the daughter of Majesty Kámala·vega, a king of the masters of magic. And being proud of her own excellencies, she considers the young sky-travelers, although of noble family and endowed with the arts, to be like straw dolls. But then she swiftly worshipped Your Majesty, your body handsome like Love, with the lotuses of such amorous glances. And then Your Majesty was absolutely delighted with her, there's no doubt. Such sentiment of such people is certainly not without love.' 11.85

su|dhīḥ Sudarśanaḥ s' âiṣa tat tasyā varako 'dhunā
śrī|Kamalavega|pārśve preṣyate sā yad īṣyate.
11.90 pitṛ|pārśve paraṃ tasyāṃ sameyuṣyāṃ śubha|kṣaṇe
udīryaṃ sarvathā kāryam, ity ādeśyaḥ Sudarśanaḥ.
Mahāśanijaven' âtha śikṣāṃ dattvā Sudarśanaḥ
prahitas tatra tat|kārya|sādhane prahitaḥ sa hi.
tatra prāptena Madanamañjūṣ"|âdhyakṣam īritam
‹śrī|Kamalavega|rājan, Mahāśanijavo nṛpaḥ
imāṃ Madanamañjūṣāṃ mañjūṣāṃ guṇa|sampadām
bhavantaṃ yācate. tāvad devo jānāty ataḥ param.›
tato nirūpitaṃ rājñā mukhaṃ tasyās tanū|bhuvaḥ,
‹Mahāśanijavaḥ ko 'yaṃ?› tay" âpracchi śanaiḥ sakhī.
11.95 sakhyā proce, ‹priya|sakhi, yo 'sau tatra tadā tvayā
ciraṃ kaṭ'|âkṣa|mālābhiḥ sarvato 'rcita, eṣa saḥ.›
tato Madanamañjūṣā joṣam ājuṣya tasthuṣī.
tātena jagade, ‹vatse, prāpta|kālam ih' âstu kim?›
harṣ'|âśru|plāvita|dṛśā romāñc"|âñcita|gātrayā
ūce, ‹putryā pitṛ|adhīnāḥ, putryo na sva|vaśāḥ pitaḥ?›
tato jñāta|tad|ākūtas taṃ dūtaṃ proktavān nṛpaḥ:
‹javād gatv" 'śanijavaṃ vad', «ôdvaha javād imām!» ›

Sudárshana was intelligent, so he was the negotiant for her, sent to her father to ask for her hand.

Now Sudárshana was commanded to state the matter 11.90
in its entirety, in the presence of her father, at the right moment, when she had joined them. Then, after being instructed by Maha·shani·java, he was sent there, having been surely commissioned to accomplish his business. When he arrived there, he said, in the presence of Mádana·manjúsha, 'Your Majesty King Kámala·vega, King Maha·shani·java entreats you for Mádana·manjúsha here, a treasure of the riches of excellence. But just let Your Majesty come to a decision about this.'

Then, as the King observed his daughter's face, she softly asked her companion, 'Who is this Maha·shani·java?'

Her friend replied, 'My dear companion, he's the very 11.95
one whom, in that place, you adorned all over with the garlands of your lingering side glances.'

Mádana·manjúsha resorted to silence and remained like that. Her father said, 'My child, hasn't the time come for this?'

Her eyes flooded with tears of joy, her body bristling with her thrilling hair, his daughter said, 'Dependent on their father, are not daughters subject to their father's will?'

Then, having discovered her intention, the King commanded that messenger, 'Go quickly and tell Maha·shani·java to marry her quickly!'

dūtaḥ Sudarśano gatvā kārya|siddhiṃ prabhor jagau.
maha"|rddhyā sa ca Madanamañjūṣāṃ tām upāyata.

II.100 tatas tāṃ sundar'|ānandāṃ Sundarānanda|pattane
ninâya medur'|āmodo Mahāśanijavo javāt.

an|icchantī sphurad|varya|saundaryam api khe|caram
kaumāram eva Madanaśalākā vahate param.

sa śrī|Mahāśanijavas tayā vallabhayā saha
ramamāṇo rati|sukhaṃ nava|smara|kalām adhāt.

tataś ca:

nān"|ôdyāna|saro|vāpī|sarid|giri|van'|ādiṣu
tatr' Ârhat|samavasṛti|srī|Siddh'|āyatan'|ādiṣu
yātrābhiḥ su|pavitrābhiḥ puṇya|puṇya|vyay'|ârjane
vitanvantau dampatī tau dinaṃ|dinam atīyatuḥ.

II.105 *san|mārga|sthitim ātanoti nitarāṃ*
yo nimnagānāṃ kṣaṇād,
yo bhintte *ghana|bandhanāni* ca diśāṃ
samyag daśānām api,
yaś c' ôccaiḥ kamal'|ākarān vitaritum
prodghāṭayaty añjasā,
so 'nyedyuḥ prasasāra ko 'pi hi śarat|
kālaḥ kṣamā|pālavat.

tataḥ sarv'|âvarodhena nirvirodhena bhūṣitaḥ
sa reme nandan'|ôdyāne khe|car'|ēśaḥ sur'|ēśavat.

Sudárshana the messenger went and told the King that his business was accomplished. And he married Mádana·manjúsha with great abundance. Then, full of delight, Ma- 11.100
ha·shani·java quickly took that joy of beauty to his capital, Sundaránanda.

But Mádana·shaláka did not want to marry a sky-traveler, even though he was young and radiant with eminent beauty.

His Majesty Maha·shani·java, enjoying the pleasure of sexual passion with his beloved, practiced the art of renewed love.

And then:

Those two, husband and wife, passed their days, intent on the acquisition of merit through the expenditure of good works by means of holy pilgrimages among various gardens, lakes, ponds, rivers, mountains, forests, et cetera, among the holy sanctuary of Siddha and other places, there where the Worthies had held their preaching assemblies.

One day, one who in an instant provides *a firm footing* 11.105
on the right path for those who are sinking down : the right courses for the rivers to return to after the monsoon flood; who breaks up *the clouds of attachment : knots of clouds* even in the ten directions; who in a trice begins to produce lakes of dense lotuses, came forth, surely like a kind of autumn season, like a protector of the world.

Now, that king of the sky-travelers, adorned by all the ladies of his women's quarters—who were not averse!—was enjoying himself in the garden of delight.

itaś ca:

Ratna|pura|śiro|ratna|śrī|Bhānu|pṛthivī|bhujaḥ chinna tanayaḥ kāñcana|cchāyaḥ Suvratā|śukti|mauktikam,
ā janm' âpi catuḥ|ṣaṣṭyā sur'|êndraiḥ sevita|kramaḥ,
pañca|catvāriṃśa|dhanus tanur dambholi|lāñchanaḥ,
bhukt'|âpojjhita|sāmrājyaḥ saṃyama|śrī|pariṣkṛtaḥ,
a|mlāna|kevala|jñān'|ādarśa|saṃkrānta|viṣṭapaḥ,
II.110 ākāśa|gena chatreṇa puṇyen' êva virājitaḥ,
cāmarābhyāṃ yaśaḥ|kīrtibhyāṃ tv īdṛgbhyāṃ pravījitaḥ;

deva|dundubhin" ākāśe śabd'|â|dvaitaṃ pradarśayan
s'|âṃhri|pīṭhen' āsanena ratnen' âujaḥ|śriy" āśritaḥ,
dharma|cakreṇ' ântar'|âri|ghāta|cakra|ruc" âgrataḥ,
Ārhatya|saudha|dhvajen' êndra|dhvajena ca śobhitaḥ,
kevala|śrī|darpaṇena divya|bhā|maṇḍalena ca
nidhiṣv iva nava|svarṇa|kamaleṣu padau dadhat;

naikabhir deva|koṭībhiḥ samyaktvair iva dehibhiḥ
mūrtimadbhir nu cāritraiḥ saṃyutaḥ saṃyut'|âyutaiḥ,
II.115 namadbhir abhito vṛkṣaiḥ kṛta|puṇya|pravarṣaṇaḥ,
kīrty|a|māna|yaśo|rāśiś caturdh"|âmara|cāraṇaiḥ,
puṇya|skandha iv' âdhyakṣas tīrtham kila car'|â|caram
Tīrth'|ēśvaraḥ pañca|daśaḥ śrī|Dharmas tri|jagat|prabhuḥ
yug'|ādi|dev'|ādi|Jina|catuṣk'|ôtpatti|pāvane
śrī|Ayodhyā|pure puṣpa|karaṇḍe samavāsarat.

And then:

The son of King Bhanu, the crest-jewel of Ratna·pura, casting a golden shadow, was the pearl of the womb of Súvrata; even from birth his steps attended by sixty-four kings of the gods; his body forty-five yards high and marked with the sign of Indra's thunderbolt; with complete dominion over the abandonment of food; adorned by the radiance of self-restraint; the world reflected in the mirror of his unclouded omniscience; illustrious with the aerial parasol as if 11.110
with his excellence; fanned with the two fly whisks of such fame and glory;

causing a unique sound to be heard in the sky by means of the kettledrum of the gods; resorted to by the brilliant luster of a jewel of a foot-stool at his feet; adorned in front by the discus of right, splendid through the destruction of the army of internal enemies, and by the royal banner, the banner on the palace that was his state of being a Worthy; and placing his feet on fresh golden lotuses like oceans bearing an orb of divine light that was the reflection of his omniscience;

thronged by several billion gods, their bodies like perfections, actual moving images, assembled in their myriads; a 11.115
rain cloud of fulfilled meritorious action with trees bowing all around; with a hymn in praise of his immeasurable glory performed by four troops of heavenly musicians; an aggregate of excellence made manifest, an actual moving permanent ford, the fifteenth Lord of the Ford, His Majesty Dharma, the lord of the triple universe, in lovely Ayódhya, purified by the birth of Ríshabha, the first lord of the present time cycle, and by the birth of four subsequent Jinas of four, in the flower-basket garden, began his preaching assembly.

tataś ca samavasṛte dhātrīṃ yojana|mātrikīm
marud|bahu|karair vāyu|kumārāḥ kṣaṇato 'mṛjan.
siṣicur vasudhāṃ gandh'|âmbubhir bhakti|bharair iva,
rajaḥ|śāntyai śaran|meghā iva megha|kumārakāḥ.

II.120 kṣmāṃ babandhuḥ svarṇa|maṇi|
ratn'|âśmabhir udaṃśubhiḥ,
vyantarās tatra cakr'|ēśa|
saudhe vardhaki|ratnavat.

jānu|daghnīḥ su|manaso 'dho|vṛntāḥ pañca|varṇikāḥ
mumucus te divya|vṛṣṭyā. sadyaḥ sampuṣpit" êva bhūḥ.

ratna|svarṇa|mayān uccais toraṇāṃs te catur|diśi
śāla|bhañjī|dhvaja|cchatra|makara|pravarān vyadhuḥ.
tad|antare ca parito rūpya|prākāra ādadhe
bhavan'|ēśair, valayita|Prāley'|âdri|bhrama|pradaḥ.
tad|ūrdhvaṃ kapi|śīrṣāṇi kānakāni cakāśire
cāmīkar'|âravindāni Svaḥ|sravantī|pravāhavat.
II.125 sa|kūṭa|Himavac|chīla|līlo jyautiṣikaiḥ kṛtaḥ,
suvarṇa|varaṇo ratna|kapi|śīrṣas tad|antare.
vaimānikair maṇi|kapi|śīrṣaś cakre tad|antarā,
ratna|vapro ratna|girer iva sāra|samuccayaḥ.

tat|sarva|madhye 'śok'|ākhyaś caitya|pādapa unnataḥ
jambū|vṛkṣ'|ânu|janm" êva vicakre vānamantaraiḥ.
tan|mūle mahad|uccaiś ca ratna|pīṭhaṃ vyadhāyi taiḥ,
tasy' âlavāla|līlāṃ yad dadhre kānti|taraṅgitam.
tasy' ôpari vicakre taiḥ deva|cchandaś catur|mukhaḥ,
an|eka|bhaṅgi|su|bhago, vaimānika|vimānavat.

And then, in an instant, the princes of the winds purified with sweeping blasts a ground for the preaching assembly, a league in diameter. To settle the dust, the princes of the clouds, like autumn rain clouds, sprinkled the earth with perfumed waters, as if with masses of devotion. The inter- 11.120
stitial gods bound the earth in the residence for the king of the earth with mosaics of gold, rubies, jewels and precious stones, as if it were variegated with jewels.

In a divine shower they released flowers to the height of the knee with their stalks facing downward. It was as if the earth had suddenly flowered.

At the four quarters they built lofty gateways made of silver and gold, beautified with statues of *shala* wood, banners, parasols and figures of sea monsters. And all around that the mansion-dwelling gods built a silver rampart, its circumference encircling that of the Himálaya mountain. On top of it golden pinnacles shone, like golden lotuses in the stream of the heavenly Ganges. Around that the stellar 11.125
gods built a rampart of gold with pinnacles of rubies, its summit looking like the Himálaya mountain. Around that the gods of the celestial vehicles made a rampart of jewels with pinnacles of rubies, an accumulation of the riches of the mountain of jewels.

In the center of them all the interstitial gods produced a holy tree called an *ashóka*, free from sorrow, lofty, like the younger brother of the rose-apple tree at the center of Rose-apple Tree Island. At its foot they placed a very high platform of manifold jewels, which produced a billowing splendor that gave the appearance of its surrounding water channel. On top of that they built a four-faced divine

II.130 tad|utsaṅgeṣu caturo ratna|siṃh'|āsanān vyadhuḥ,
s'|âṃhri|pīṭhān Meru|śaila|śilā|siṃh'|āsana|śriyaḥ.
tat|puraś cāmara|dharau yakṣau babhatur ujjvalau,
vahan|Mandākinī|sroto Him'|âdri|śikhar'|ôpamau.
deva|cchand'|ôpari sita|cchatra|trayam arājata
milit'|Āśvina|Rādh"|Ōrja|rāk"|êndu|tritay'|ôpamam.

deva|cchandaka aiśānyāṃ ratna|raiva|pramadhyataḥ
gṛhe 'pavaraka iva viśrāmāya kṛto 'rhataḥ.
prati|vapraṃ ca catvāri catur|aśra|vimānavat
dvārāṇi rejire tatra dharmasy' êva catur|bhidaḥ.
II.135 kalpa|dru|pallavais tatra cakrur vandanda|mālikāḥ
dig|vadhūnāṃ catasṛṇām iva śoṇ'|âśma|kambikāḥ.

prati|dvāram arājanta sa|dhvajā ratna|toraṇāḥ,
sa|kīrtayo bhagavataḥ pratāpā iva sarvataḥ.
toraṇāny ubhayataś ca svarṇa|ratna|ghaṭā babhuḥ,
bhavyebhyaḥ sajjitā dharma|nidhāna|kalaśā iva.
kānakyo dhūpa|ghaṭikā ghana|dhūma|latā|mucaḥ
dvāreṣ' ûbhayato rejur yava|vāraka|vibhramāḥ.
vāpyaḥ svaccha|payaḥ|pūrṇās tatr' âbhur vikac'|âmbujāḥ,
svar|vāpya iva Tīrth'|ēśaṃ draṣṭum eyuḥ suraiḥ saha.

dais, ornamented with many figures, like a mansion of the mansion-dwelling gods.

On its level surfaces they made four jeweled lion-thrones, 11.130
each with footstools, with the splendor of the stone lion-throne of Mount Meru. At their sides a pair of demigods bearing fly whisks appeared, resplendent like peaks of the Himálaya mountain bearing the current of the heavenly Ganges. Above the divine dais three white parasols shone forth, like the three full moons of spring, autumn and winter assembled together.

To the northeast, within the rampart of jewels, they made a small divine dais, like a room within a house, for the Worthy to rest in. And at each rampart four doorways were resplendent, like quadrangular heavenly vehicles, like four en-
trances for religion in them. On them they placed festoons 11.135
of blossoms from wishing-trees, like necklaces of rubies for the four maidens of the quarters of the sky.

By each gateway, archways of jewels were resplendent with banners, like holy ones with their reputations, glowing everywhere. At each side of the archways, water pots of gold and silver were prepared for the beings, like water pots of the treasure of religion. At each side of the doorways, golden braziers of incense shone, emitting creepers of dense smoke with the appearance of blades of barley. There were ponds of very clear water with budding lotuses, as if his own pond had come to see the Lord of the Ford together with the gods.

11.140 ity|ādi vyantarāś cakruḥ sarvebhyo dhanya|māninaḥ.
su|svāmi|bahu|kāry'|āptau bahu hṛṣyanti sevakāḥ.

paurastya|deśanā|deśāt tath"|âiva|sthaṃ suraiḥ kṣaṇāt
āhṛty' êv' êti samavasaraṇaṃ tatra nirmame.
tataś ca deva|koṭībhiḥ paritaḥ parivāritaḥ
sarvath" â|dṛṣṭa|caravad dṛśyamānaḥ punaḥ punaḥ,
‹prabho, ciraṃ jaya, svāmin, nanda jīva cirād!› iti
āśāsyamānaḥ purato muhur nirjara|cāraṇaiḥ,
paribaṃbhramyamāṇeṣu bhaktito nu pradakṣiṇam
navasu svarṇa|padmeṣu nyasyann aṃhri|saro|ruham,
11.145 pūrva|dvāreṇa samavasaraṇaṃ prāviśat prabhuḥ
śrī|Dharma|nātha|Tīrth'|ēśaḥ, sākṣād iva mah"|ôdayaḥ.

niruñchayantaṃ nu calaiḥ kosumbhair iva pallavaiḥ
pradakṣiṇī|kṛtya caitya|pādapaṃ, pādap'|ôttamam
tīrthaṃ namas|kṛtya kṛtyam iva m"|āvaśyakaṃ kila
pūrva|siṃh'|āsane pūrv'|âbhimukho nyaṣadat prabhuḥ.

tri|diśi prati|rūpāṇi racayāñcakrire suraiḥ,
prabhoḥ sadṛṃśi, prabhuvad vaktṛṇi prabhu|vaibhavāt.

tato gaṇ'|êndra|pramukha|sādhavaḥ svaḥ|puran|dhrayaḥ,
sādhvyaś ca pūrva|dvār" âitya pradadus triḥ pradakṣiṇām.
11.150 tīrthaṃ ca Tīrtha|nāthaṃ ca natvā sa|pulak'|ôtkaram
diśi dakṣiṇa|pūrvasyām āsāmāsur maha"|rṣayaḥ.
tat|pṛṣṭhato 'sthuḥ svar|devya ūrdhvās tad|anusaṃyatāḥ,
prabhu|pūj'|ârtha|kamala|mukulāyita|pāṇayaḥ.

Thus and more besides the interstitial gods prepared, 11.140
their minds bestowing opulence on all. Servants are highly
delighted at the accomplishment of many tasks for a good
master.

Suddenly, as if as soon as they had been summoned, the
gods from their kingdom in the east formed an assembly
there according to rank. And then, thronged all around by
billions of gods, gazed at again and again like a previously
unseen planet, being beseeched, 'Be long victorious, Lord,
be propitious, Lord, live long!,' preceded at every step by
immortal dancers, depositing the lotuses of his feet in fresh
golden lotuses that were turning from left to right through
certain devotion, the Lord of the Ford, holy Lord Dharma, 11.145
entered the assembly by the eastern entrance, like preeminent prosperity made manifest.

As it was being lustrated by the winds like blossoms of saffron, the lord circumambulated the holy tree, and having bowed to the holy place that was the excellent tree—certainly the performance of a non-obligatory action—the lord sat facing the east in the eastern lion-throne.

In the three other directions the gods made images with the shared likeness of the lord, speaking like the lord, by means of the power of the lord.

Then the monks, preceded by the chief of the troop,
their munificence heavenly, and the nuns entered by the
eastern doorway and performed a threefold circumambu-
lation. And having bowed to the holy place and the Lord 11.150
of the Ford with a multitude of joy, the great sages sat toward the southeast. At their side the goddesses of heaven stood erect, self-controlled in regard to them, their hands

pūrvavad bhavana|pati|jyotiṣka|vyantara|striyaḥ
apāg|dvār" āgatya tadvat nairṛte 'stu yathā|kramam.
pratyag|dvāreṇa bhavan'|ēśa|jyotir|vyantar" âmarāḥ
prāgvat praviśya nyaṣadann apar'|ôdag|dig|antare.
Indr'|ādi|devā, rāj'|ādi|narā, nārya udag|diśā
pradakṣiṇayy' ēśaṃ prāgvan natv" āiśānyām upāviśat.

11.155 tisras|tisro diśi diśi babhūvur iti parṣadaḥ,
tābhiś ca śākhābhir iva babhau kalpa|drumaḥ prabhuḥ.
sarva|bhāṣ"|ânukāriṇyā, vistāriṇyā ca yojanam,
sudhā|visrāviṇy" âtha vāṇyā śrī|Dharmo dharmam ādiśat.

‹bho bhoḥ, saṃsāra|sindhau
vidhura|niravadhau majjan'|ônmajjanāni
vyātanvadbhir bhavadbhiḥ
katham api nṛ|januḥ prāpi cintā|maṇ'|îva.
samyaṅ|nītyā tad ārā-
dhayata, yad amutaḥ śuddha|samyaktva|ratn'|ādy|
āsādy' āsādayadhvaṃ
tad api śiva|padaṃ, yatra niḥsīma|śarma.›

itaś ca so 'śanijavo lalanābhiḥ samaṃ lalan
udīcyā gacchanto 'pācyāṃ vimānān vyomny udaikṣata.
‹kim etad?› iti saṃbhrānto yāvad eṣa vyacintayat
tāvat prajñapty" âsya karṇe vyajñapyata rahasyavat:

blossoming with lotuses for the purpose of worshipping the lord.

Like the former, the ladies of the mansion-dwelling, stellar and interstitial gods entered by the western doorway in order to sit according to rank in the southwest. The mansion-dwelling, stellar and interstitial gods entered by the western doorway, and, as the former, sat in the northwestern direction. The gods, Indra and the others, men, kings and others, and women entered by the northern direction, and, as the former, sat in the northeast.

Thus there were three companies in each direction, and II.155
the lord appeared like a wishing-tree with them as his branches.

Then holy Dharma began to expound religion in a voice conforming to every language, extending over a league and emitting nectar:

'Good people, by producing the means of emerging for those sunk in the ocean of existence whose sorrows are infinite, you have managed to obtain human rebirth, which is like a wishing-jewel. So strive with right conduct, and, as a result of that, having attained the jewel of right-belief, purity, et cetera, you will reach the auspicious place in which blessings are unbounded.'

And then Maha·shani·java, while sporting with his wives looked up into the western sky and saw celestial vehicles traveling to the north. As he, perplexed, wondered, 'What's this?,' his supernatural perception whispered in his ear as if it were a secret:

II.160 ‹dev', Âyodhyā|pure deva|devaṃ śrī|Dharma|Tīrtha|pam
abhyāyātaṃ mudā nantuṃ yānti khe khe|carā amī.›
ath' Âśanijavo 'vādīd
āsannān khecarān prati:
‹prabhuṃ nantuṃ gamyate, bhoḥ!›
‹satvaraṃ, deva, gamyate.›
tato vimānaṃ vikṛtya kṛtya|vit sa|paricchadaḥ
tad āruhya drutaṃ prāpa śrī|Dharma|svāmino 'ntike.
vidhinā sa prabhuṃ natvā s'|ântaḥ|pura|paricchadaḥ
upa|Śakraṃ niṣasāda Śakra|līlāṃ viḍambayan.
tatr' ântare bhagavato deśanā|ratna|rohaṇāt
ke cit samyaktva|māṇikyaṃ, deśa|vrata|maṇiṃ pare,
II.165 ke cic ca cāritra|cintā|maṇim apy upalebhire.
paryupāstir bhagavatāṃ na kasy' âpy avakeśinī.
deśan"|ôparame svāmī deva|cchandam aśiśriyat,
sarvā api pariṣadaḥ prāyaḥ sv'|āspadam aiyaruḥ.
asmin kṣaṇe samāgatya deven' âikena sādaram
ūce Madanamañjūṣā, ‹vande tvāṃ, śrāvik"|ôttame.›
tay" âpy utthāya cakre 'syā gauravāt prativandanam.
sad|ācāra|vidhau santaḥ pramādyanti kva cin na hi.

'Your Majesty, the god of gods, holy Dharma, the Lord of the Ford, has arrived at the city of Ayódhya. Those are sky-travelers, traveling through the sky to pay their joyful respects to the lord.' 11.160

Then Maha·shani·java said to his attendant sky-travelers, 'Good sirs, we must go pay our respects to the lord.' 'We'll go immediately, Your Majesty.'

Thereupon, knowing what was to be done, he prepared by magic a vehicle, and, having mounted it together with his entourage, he soon arrived in the presence of the holy Lord Dharma. Having paid his respects to the lord according to precept, attended by the ladies of his royal women's quarters, taking on the appearance of Shakra, the king of the gods, he sat alongside Shakra.

At that moment, through the germination of the teaching of the holy one, some attained the ruby of right-belief, others
the jewel of the partial vows of a layperson, and some even 11.165
the wishing-jewel of the ascetic life. Attendance upon the holy ones is unfruitful to no one at all.

On finishing preaching, the lord resorted to the small divine dais, and all the companies began to return in bodies to their respective homes.

At that moment, a god approached and respectfully addressed Mádana·manjúsha, 'I salute you, most excellent laywoman.'

And she stood and made a respectful salutation in return. Virtuous women neglect the injunctions of proper conduct on no point at all.

tad" Âśanijavasy' āsīd gṛhāy' ôtkaḥ paricchadaḥ,
tataḥ sa devo 'vag, ‹vidyā|bhṛt|pate, kṣaṇam āsyatām.›
II.170 pratiśrutaṃ khe|careṇa sureṇ' ārambhi bhāṣitum:
‹saumye Madanamañjūṣe, sāvadhānaṃ niśamyatām.
bhaginī te 'sti yā laghvī, puruṣa|dveṣiṇī kila.
sā prācya|janma|patinā vivāhy" Âmaraketunā.›
s" ākhyat, ‹kv' âsau, kathaṃ v" âsyā
janm'|ântara|patiḥ sa ca,
kim arthaṃ ca tvaṃ bravīṣi?›
devo 'vag, ‹śrūyatāṃ, śubhe.
asy' âiva Jambū|dvīpasy' Āi-
rāvate parididyute
saty'|âbhidhaṃ Candrapuraṃ
puraṃ candra|mukhī|mukhaiḥ.
tatr' āsīt Somadatt'|ākhyo dvijaḥ ṣaṭ|karma|karmaṭhaḥ,
catur|daśānāṃ vidyānāṃ tattva|vit tat|praṇetṛvat.
II.175 tasya priyā Somabhadrā, Somādityas tayoḥ sutaḥ.
sarva|vidyaḥ kṛtaḥ pitrā, sa ca sarva|jña|māny abhūt.
dīkṣita|Brahmadevasya nandanā hṛdya|darśanā
Sudarśanā tena mudā pitṛbhyām udavāhyata.
itaś ca:
samyag|jñāna|latā|vitāna|mudiraḥ,
samyaktva|ratn'|ākaraḥ,
pravrajyā|pramadā|vasanta|samayaḥ,
śaśvat|tapaḥ|śrī|priyaḥ,
nānā|labdhi|nadī|nadī|parivṛḍhaḥ,
puṇya|sva|kośo, dṛḍhas,
tatr' āgād Dṛḍhadharma|sūri|tilakaḥ,
ṣaṇḍe sahasr'|āmrake.

Then Maha·shani·java's entourage became eager for home, whereupon the god said, 'Stay for a moment, king of the masters of magic.'

The sky-traveler obeyed, and the god began to speak: 11.170
'Mádana·manjúsha, good lady, listen with attention:

You have a younger sister who absolutely hates men. She is to be married to Ámara·ketu, her husband in her former life.'

She said, 'Will you relate where he is, and how he became her husband in her former life, and for what reason?' The god said, 'Listen, good lady:

Now, in the Airávata region of Rose-apple Tree Island, there is a city, truly named Chandra·pura, Moon-city, illuminated all about by the faces of its moon-faced ladies. And in it lived a brahmin named Soma·datta, skilled in the six duties, knowing the essence of the fourteen branches
of knowledge as if he were their author. His wife was So- 11.175
ma·bhadra. Somáditya was their son. His father taught him everything, and he became respected for omniscience.

The brahmin Brahma·deva had a daughter, Sudarshaná, the vision of his soul. Somáditya's parents joyfully married him to her.

And then:

A rain cloud for the growth of creepers of right knowledge, a mine of the jewels of right insight, a season of spring for the ascetic life as one's wife, devoted to the prosperity of unending austerity, master of the ocean of manifold attainment, a treasury of his own merits, steadfast Dridha·dharman, the forehead ornament of reverend doctors, arrived at that place in the grove of the thousand mango trees.

kalpa|drumam iv' ôdītaṃ śrutv" âgāt taṃ namasyitum,
s'|ântaḥ|pura|parīvāro Jitāri|vasudhā|dhavaḥ.
pradakṣiṇayya natvā ca yiyāciṣur iv' ēpsitam
kṛt'|âñjaliḥ sa urv"|īśo nyavikṣata guroḥ puraḥ.
II.180 sad|deśanā|setu|bandhaḥ prabandhena garīyasā
bhav'|âmbhodhiṃ laṅghayituṃ babandhe sūriṇā tataḥ.
Somādityo 'śṛṇod, rājā sūri|pārśve yayāv iti,
tato 'haṃ|mānī, sāmarṣaḥ sa cintāṃ cakṛvān iti:
«tatra gatvā rāṭ|samakṣaṃ, taṃ jitvā ca sit'|âmbaram,
nṛpaṃ vipariṇamayya svaṃ yajamānam ādadhe.»
vicinty' êti so 'bhimānī tatr' āgaty' âbhyadhād gurum:
«kim evam aty|ucca|girā virasaṃ rāraṭīṣi, bhoḥ?»

guruḥ:

«sarva|jñ'|ôpajña|dharm'|ôktau
virasaṃ, mūḍha, kiṃ nanu?
a|jīrṇa|doṣiṇo yad vā
yāti pathya|mathyatām.»

dvijaḥ:

II.185 «bho bho, a|sati sarva|jñe, tad|ukta|dharma|saṃkathā
gagan'|âmbhoja|saurabhya|kīrtanām anudhāvati.»

Having heard that he, like a wishing-tree, had appeared, King Jitári, accompanied by the ladies of the royal women's quarters, went to pay his respects to him. Having circumambulated and bowed to him, with his hand folded in salutation as if craving a boon, the king sat in front of the teacher. Then the reverend doctor constructed a bridge of 11.180
the teaching of truth for crossing the ocean of existence by means of a serious story.

When Somáditya heard that the king had gone to the presence of the reverend doctor, full of pride, he became angry and thought:

"I'll go there and before the king's eyes refute that wearer of the white robe. I'll convert the king and make him my patron."

Having determined thus, full of self-pride, he went there and addressed the teacher, "Why are you screaming nonsense in a loud voice like this, good sir?"

Teacher:

"How can there be nonsense in proclaiming the religion taught by the omniscient one, you silly? For those whose faults have not been worn away travel the path of distress."

Brahmin:

"Good sir, good sir, since he is not truly omniscient, the 11.185
preaching of the religion taught by him is running after the rumor of the scent of a lotus in the sky."

guruḥ:
«aihik'|āmuṣmik'|ânek'|ânuṣṭhān'|ādi|nibandhanam
kiṃ n' âsty eva hi sarva|jñaḥ, sarva|bhāv'|avabhāsa|kṛt?»

dvijaḥ:
«sarva|jño n' âsti, sad|grā-
haka|sakala|samakṣ'|ādi|mān'|âti|gatvād.
yat syād evaṃ, tad evaṃ
kha|sumam iva tathā c' âiṣa, tasmāt sa n' âsti.
hetur: n' â|san parātm" â-
pi hi na kha|viṣayo 'bhraṃ ca rūp'|ādy a|bhāvāt.
taj|jñānaṃ tac ca sarv'|âr-
tha|gatam iti kathaṃ nāma vidyāt samakṣam?
pratyakṣe 'sati, n' ânumānam api taṃ
gṛhṇāti, tad|visphuṭam.
vyāpti|jñapti|bhavā na s" âniśa|paro-
kṣe liṅga|liṅgi|dvaye.
taj|jñaptāv anum"|ântarāt punar ava-
sthā n' âiva tat|kāraṇ'|â|
bhāvān n' âsty anumānam. atra samayo 'py
etasya na jñāpakaḥ.
tathā hi:
kiñcij|jña|pūrve 'tra na hi pramāṇatā,
sarva|jña|pūrvas tad|a|siddhito 'sti na.
a|pauruṣeye 'tra ca sarva|vid vṛthā,
tan n' āgamaḥ sarva|vidaḥ prasādhakaḥ.

Teacher:

"The origin of manifold religious practices and suchlike in this world and the next, isn't he surely omniscient, the one who creates light for all beings?"

Brahmin:

"The omniscient one does not exist. Having passed the proof of the true perception of all senses, sight, et cetera, he would be so. Accordingly, since he is like a flower in the sky, he therefore does not exist. The reason: although the supreme being certainly exists, he is not a cloud in the sphere of the sky, and because of the nonexistence of his body and so on. And since knowledge of him has altogether disappeared, how indeed could one perceive it actually manifest?

If there is no sense perception, inference too is unable to grasp that object — that is clear. As it originates from cognition of invariable concomitance, it cannot take place when the pair, middle term and major term, are forever beyond perception. However, in cognizing that object from another inference there is no new condition, so no inference takes place because a cause for it is absent. In this case scriptural authority also cannot cause its cognition.*

Just like so:

For in this matter a person of limited knowledge is not a valid source of knowledge. An omniscient person does not exist because that existence is not proved. And here an omniscient person is useless with regard to what is of non-human origin, so religious tradition does not guarantee an omniscient being.*

11.190 tasy' â|dṛṣṭe n' âiva sādṛśya|bodhas,
tasy' â|bhāvāt tatra n' âiv' ôpamānam.
dṛṣṭ'|ādyaṃ — kiṃ tad vinā? — durghaṭaṃ!, tan
n' ârthāpatter apy amuṣy'|ôpapattiḥ.
tataḥ pramāṇa|pañcakaṃ na yatra vṛttim aśnute,
bhavati bhāva|gocaraḥ sa sarva|vit kha|puṣpavat.»

guruḥ:

«yat proktaṃ bhavato, na sarva|vidur adh-
yakṣ'|ādi|dṛśyaḥ, sa kiṃ
dṛśyo n' âsti tav' âiva sarva|jagato
vāstavya|lokasya vā.
ādye niścita|sādhane na bhagavad|
vīkṣā|suyogyo bhavān.
pratyakṣ|ôparamo niṣedhati na ca
tvan|mātṛ|janm'|ādikam.
sarve 'pi paśyanti na hī tam ity ado
jānāti sarva|jñam ṛte na kaś cana.
tvaṃ ced vijānāsi tad" âsi sarva|vit.
taṃ tvaṃ niṣedhat svam, aho, niṣedhasi.
tathā yo yatr' ârthe niyatam a|visaṃvādi|vacanaḥ,
sa tat|samyag|jñātā tvam iva nija|geha|prabhṛtiṣu,
tathā cintālūkā|śaśa|bhṛd uparāg'|ādiṣu Jinas
tatas tad|vijñātā kṛtibhir urarīkartum ucitaḥ.

There is no perception of similarity in that which is not seen, and so, because it is absent, there can be no cognition by analogy. What starts with sense perception — what is there without that? — it's difficult! So that person does not result from deduction either. II.190

So, in a case where the five means of valid knowledge cannot operate, that omniscient person becomes like a flower in the sky as far as direct perception goes."

Teacher:

"Sir, your statement that there is no omniscient person, who would have to be visible through sense perception. Why to you alone would he not be visible, when he is visible to all the world or inhabitable space? If you make an initial decision on means of knowledge you are not properly fitted to perceiving the Lord. The lack of direct perception does not invalidate such things as your mother's birth.*

Except for an omniscient person no one can know that which you claim, namely that no one sees him. If you know that fact, then you are omniscient. If you deny it, you are denying yourself your own capacity to make the claim.

Just as someone for some reason speaks what is constantly not to be contradicted among his own household servants, so it is right for the Jina, since he knows what is right for them, to spread it among those who are eclipses for the moon of clear thought.

11.195 ‹na c' êyan|mātre 'sy' â-
vagatir› iti vidvaj|jana|matam
paṭāy' âkṣi|sphāraṃ
ghaṭa|mukham iha|sthaṃ hi manute.
tatas tad|dṛṣṭ'|ântād
bhagavati samātyakṣam a|man'|â-
numānaṃ dṛśy'|âik'|â-
vagatir iva dṛśy'|ântara|gatau.

yataḥ:
ek'|âtyakṣā (- - - - - -
- - - - - - -)
sarv'|âtyakṣ'|āvaraṇa|vigame
sarva|vit tvaṃ na kiṃ tat?
kiṃ vā stheyo jagati bhavat" âp'
îndriy'|âtīta|darśī?
yāga|svarg'|ânvaya|gatir api
syāt kathaṃ hy anyathā te?

a|pauruṣey'|āgamato 'tha yāga|
svargā vayasy'|âvagatiḥ samasti
n' âivaṃ vacaḥ syāt puruṣaṃ vinā, no
śāly|aṅkuraḥ śālim ṛte syāt.

yata uktam:
tālv|ādi|janmā nanu varṇa|vargo,
varṇ'|ātmako Veda iti sphuṭaṃ ca.
puṃsaś ca tālv|ādir ataḥ kathaṃ syād?
a|pauruṣeyo 'yam iti pratītiḥ.

tataś ca:
yaḥ sarva|jño yath" âbhūt
sa ca Bharata iv' âdhyakṣa āsīt tadānīṃ,

'And he can't be imagined in such limitations'—the mouth of a pot designed by a wise man being looked at over again on a painted cloth is considered to be actually here. And so through this example, since the holy one is situated among what is visible, it is as if the imagining of him is the same, through the proof being the visible together. 11.195

Therefore:

Beyond the sight of one... In the removal of what is an obstruction to the sight of everyone—is not that omniscience? Or, rather, do you hold that the sight of the universe is beyond the senses? How else would even your situation be connected to sacrifice and the heavens?

Now, belief in the association of heaven and sacrifice rests on superhuman doctrine. We wouldn't have the teaching in that form without a human. Would there be a shoot of the *shala* tree when the *shala* tree is dead?

Therefore it is said:

And it is well known that the Veda is articulated sound, the system of vocal sounds with their origins in the palate, et cetera. And the palate, et cetera, are human. Therefore it is acknowledged that it couldn't be of divine origin.

And so:

Because he, omniscient like Bharata, was then plain to see, inferred by the removal of manifold doubts, illustrated by comparison with all previous omniscient beings, that is

nānā|saṃśīti|hṛty" â-
numita upamitaḥ prāg|bhavaiḥ sarva|vidbhiḥ,
arthād v" ât'|îndriy'|ârtha|
praṇayanata ih'|āpanna uktaḥ śrute c' êty
āste 'sau sarva|māna|
prathita itarathā sarva|lopa|prasaṅgaḥ.

11.200 Somāditya, tad asti sarva|viduro 'tr',
ânyatra vā, sarvathā.
tad|dharma|pratipādanaṃ na virasaṃ,
tat, saumya, viddhi svayam.»
ity evaṃ Dṛḍhadharma|sūri|tilakair
uktaḥ sa mukt'|âṃhasā
natvā pūjya|padau jagāda, «bhagavan,
suṣṭhu tvayā bodhitaḥ.»

cāritr'|āvaraṇa|karma|kṣay'|ôpaśamato 'tha saḥ
ūce, «pitr|ādy|anumatyā dīkṣiṣye 'haṃ tav' ântike.»
prabhur āh', «âstv avighnaṃ te,
mā sma, bhoḥ, pratibadhyathāḥ.»
gatvā gṛhe tataḥ so 'vak
pitarau dayitām api.

«ādya|śvet'|âmbar'|ācārya|pārśve dharmaḥ kṣam'|ādikaḥ
bhav'|âbdhi|setur nirvāṇa|hetus, tāta, śruto mayā.
tatas taṃ tvad|anujñātas, tāt', âṅgī|kartum utsahe.
sahed bhavad|avasthānaṃ kaḥ paśyan nirgamaṃ sudhīḥ?»

11.205 iti sva|putrasya vācaṃ manvānā vajra|niṣṭhurām
tato mātā s'|âśru|pātā jagād' êti sa|gadgadam:

to say, rather, intent on providing guidance lying beyond the normal range of the senses, having come into this world, and spoken for the ear, he remained thus, known by every proof, in an opposite manner to one intent on the destruction of all.

So, Somáditya, he is omniscient in this world and the next 11.200
world, or, rather, everywhere. So realize yourself, Brahmin, that his granting of true religion is not nonsense." Thus addressed by Dridha·dharman, the forehead ornament of reverend doctors, Somáditya, his cares released, bowed to his honored feet and said, "Reverend sir, I have been properly enlightened by you."

Then, his mind made tranquil by the destruction of the karma that obstructed right conduct, he said, "With the permission of my parents, I will receive initiation at your hands."

The reverend doctor said, "May you meet no obstacle, may you be unhindered, good sir." Then he went home and asked his parents and wife for their permission.

"Father, in the presence of the teacher of the excellent white-clad monks, I have heard religion, which is fitting and so on, a bridge for the ocean of existence, the cause of final liberation. So, granted permission by you, I wish to make it my own. What intelligent person would endure abiding in existence, once he sees a way out?"

Thereupon his mother, considering that her son's state- 11.205
ment was as hard as adamant, let fall her tears and said amid her sobs:

«vats', âsmāka|kul'|āditya, Somāditya, vidāṃ|vara,
śreṣṭha|varṇa, jyeṣṭha|putra, kim a|vācyam avocyathāḥ?
trayī|mukhāḥ kva bhū|devās tīrtha|snātra|pavitritāḥ,
śūdr'|âdhamāḥ śramaṇakāḥ kv' âmī mala|malīmasāḥ?
dharmasya vārttā dvijeṣu, na śvet'|âmbara|dhāriṣu
kastūry|āmodo mṛgeṣu, na garta|śūkar'|ādiṣu.
tad vatsa, śramaṇ'|ôpānte dīkṣ"|êcchāṃ mā kṛthāḥ kva cit,
cet kulasya pituḥ svasya mama c' êcchasi gauravam.»

II.210 pit" âpy ācaṣṭa, «te vākyaṃ
prāṅ me 'bhūc candanaṃ hṛdi,
adhunā tu tvad|ākhyātaṃ
tatra vajrāna|lāyate.
trayī|bāhyeṣu śūdreṣu dharmaḥ śramaṇakeṣu kaḥ?
trayī|bāhyaṃ hy anuṣṭhānaṃ kaṣṭaṃ kaṣṭāya kevalam.
tvay" âdhītā trayī, brahma ṣaṭ|kṛtvo 'ṣṭau samādhṛtam.
gṛh'|āśrame 'dhunā putrāñ janayitvā trayī|dharān,
adhyāpya bahuśaś chātr'|âniṣṭ'|āpūrtaṃ vidhāya ca,
bhojayitvā dvijān, vāna|prastho bhūyāḥ, kul'|ôttama.
śūdr'|âdhamānāṃ tu dharmaṃ na cakruḥ, kurvate na ca,
kariṣyanti na ca kv' âpi sarva|varṇ|ôttamā dvijāḥ.
II.215 tatas tad aty|a|saṃbaddham, a|śraddheyaṃ, na sūnṛtam,
svacch'|āśaya, kādā cit te na vaktum api kalpate.»

"My son, sun for our entire family, Somáditya, most excellent of the learned, you whose appearance is excellent, my eldest son, why have you spoken what is not to be spoken? Where stand brahmins, gods on earth, reciters of the three Vedas, purified by bathing in holy places, and where on the other hand stand those Jain monks, the lowest of servants, befouled with filth? The business of religion is found among brahmin priests, not among the wearers of white robes. The fragrance of musk is found among musk deer, not among crows, hogs and such. So, my son, have no desire at all for initiation among the Jain monks, if you desire the respect of your family, your father and me."

His father said, "Your previous statements were moon- 11.210
light in my heart, but what you said just now caused thunderbolts to settle there. What righteousness is there among Jain monks, servants forbidden the three Vedas? Indeed, the task of those forbidden the Vedas is only hardship for the sake of hardship. You have learned the three Vedas and the sacred knowledge collected together in forty-eight books. So now, having given birth to sons while in the state of householders, teach them the Vedas, and having divided your unwanted excess belongings among many recipients, and having fed brahmins, become then a dweller in the forest, you finest of our family. But brahmins, the highest of all the ranks, have not performed, don't perform and never will perform the task of the lowest of servants.

So your mind is very clear. It is never right for you to 11.215
say that which is highly incoherent, unbelievable and not pleasant and true."

Somādityo 'tha guru|rāṭ|pradatta|jñāna|śeva|dhiḥ
vāg|vaibhavaṃ kuṭumbasya vyatanīd dur|gati|cchide.

«he tāt', ân|ādy|â|vidy"|ākhya|ṭhakena ṭhakit'|ātmanaḥ.
mati|moho 'n|ādir āsīn mam' âp' îyac|ciraṃ hṛdi.
samyag|guru|girā tattva|jñānen' âbhāti so 'dhunā,
tattvasya sākṣāt|kāro hi dhiyāṃ syāt paramaṃ balam.
tat, tāta, tattva|viduṣām a|vidyā|śilpi|kalpitam
n' ālambanaṃ bhavaty etad, yat tātena prajalpitam.

tatas ca:

11.220 vedā adhītā na trāṇaṃ, na trāṇaṃ bhojitā dvijāḥ,
na trāṇaṃ janitāḥ putrā, iti vetti na kaḥ su|dhīḥ?

yataḥ:

sarve vedās tan na kuryuḥ, sarve yajñāś ca, Bhārata,
sarva|tīrth'|âbhiṣekāṃś ca, yat kuryāt prāṇināṃ dayā.
dayā ca dharmasya mūlaṃ, sā ca pūrṇ" Ârhatāṃ mate.
ek'|êndriy'|ādikān jīvān n' âiv' ânye jānate 'pi hi.
yac ca śūdr'|âdhamā ity|ādy uktaṃ tan n' âiva yuktimat.
ke śūdrā, brāhmaṇāḥ ke v", êty api jñātavyam asti yat.

Then Somáditya, a treasury of the knowledge taught by the king of teachers, extended the power of his statements over his household in order to separate it from a bad destination.

"Oh, Father, my soul was deluded by the swindler named 'beginningless ignorance.' The delusion of my understanding was without beginning, so long did it abide in my mind. He who is resplendent with the knowledge of reality taught by the true teacher, since he is the one who makes truth evident to the senses, should be the supreme force in the intellect. So, Father, your statement, that it is made by a craftsman in ignorance of those who know the truth, is without support.

And so:

He who is wise certainly knows that having learned the 11.220
Vedas is no protection, feeding brahmins is no protection, and giving birth to sons is no protection.

Since:

All the Vedas, all the sacrifices, you descendant of Bháratas, all the bathing in sacred places, will not effect that which compassion for beings effects. Compassion is the root of religion and it is fulfilled in the doctrine of the Worthies. For certainly no others consider one-sensed beings and such to be fraught with souls. And your statement that they are the lowest of servants has not been properly proved, either. Who are the servants or who are the brahmins remains to be determined.

himṣ"|āsaktā, a|viratā, brahmacarya|vivarjitāḥ,
pāpmi|cāṭu|kṛto, veśy'|ādi|pratigraha|dhāriṇaḥ,
II.225 yāga|cchāg'|ādi|pañc'|âkṣa|ghāta|nirghṛṇa|mānasā ḥ
kathaṃ vayaṃ brāhmaṇāḥ smaḥ, śūdrā ev' êti lakṣaṇaiḥ?

śramaṇā bhagavantas tu hiṃs"|ādy|agha|parāṅ|mukhāḥ,
samiti|gupti|guptāś ca, sv|âdhyāya|dhyāna|lālasāḥ,
pratibandha|pratikarma|paratapti|vinā|kṛtāḥ,
śatru|mitra|tṛṇa|straiṇa|svarṇa|parṇa|samāśayāḥ,
dāntāḥ, śāntāḥ, tapo|līnā, nirīhās, tyakta|matsarāḥ,
kathaṃ śūdrā adhamā vā, kin tu te brāhmaṇ'|ôttamāḥ?

kiñ ca yajñ'|ôpavītena brāhmaṇaḥ syād, guṇena vā?
yady ādyas, tad brāhmaṇaḥ syāt tad|vṛttau yo 'pi so 'pi hi.
II.230 guṇena cet, sa hiṃs"|ādir a|hiṃs"|ādir atho mataḥ.
ādye vyādh'|ādayo viprā, dvitīye sādhavaḥ param.

yataḥ:

satyaṃ brahma, tapo brahma,
brahma c' êndriya|nigrahaḥ,
sarva|bhūta|dayā brahm', êty
etad brāhmaṇa|lakṣaṇam.

brāhmaṇo brahma|caryeṇa, yathā śilpena śilpikaḥ
anyathā nāma|mātraṃ syād indra|gopaka|kīṭavat.

Addicted to violence, unrestrained, devoid of chastity, makers of flattering words to sinners, bearers of gifts received from prostitutes and such, with minds lacking compassion 11.225
for the slaughter of five-sensed beings, goats, et cetera, at the sacrifice, how are we brahmins, since we are actually slaves in our characteristics?

But the holy Jain monks, averse to the sin of harming, et cetera, and preserving self-regulation and restraint, intent on meditation on their studies, free from obstacles, requitals and anguish, their minds regarding alike friend or foe, a woman or a blade of grass, gold or a feather, patient, tranquil, devoted to asceticism, their thoughts of self abandoned—how can they be the lowest servants? Are they not rather the highest brahmins?

And does a man become a brahmin by investiture with the sacred thread and sacrifice or by moral excellence? If the former, then he who participates in the business of that is a brahmin.

If by moral excellence, then it depends on whose mind is 11.230
set on violence and suchlike or on nonviolence and suchlike. Brahmins, being slaughterers and such, belong in the first category, but Jain monks in the second.

Since:

Truth is sacred, asceticism is sacred, control of the senses is sacred and compassion for all beings is sacred, then this is the characteristic sign of a brahmin priest. The brahmin priest is defined by the conduct of priestly chastity, just as a craftsman is by his craft, otherwise it is merely an empty name, like an insect called Shepherd of Indra (firefly). So it is not enough for a brahmin to be born a brahmin. Since

atha dvija|dvijī|jāto brāhmaṇo, na tad apy alam.
strīṇāṃ cāpalato n' âiva samyaṅ niścīyate pitā.
kuś'|âvalamba|suhṛdā tad|anena na kiñ cana.
tan māṃ tāt', ânujānīhi, yen' āśu pravrajāmy aham.»

II.235 bhaṭṭo 'vādīd, «vatsa, gṛh'|āśrama|pālana|kātarāḥ
adātāraḥ kā|puruṣāḥ pāṣaṇḍam adhiśerate.

tad uktam:

gṛh'|āśrama|samo dharmo na bhūto, na bhaviṣyati.
pālayanti narāḥ śūrāḥ, klībāḥ pāṣaṇḍam āśritāḥ.»

putro jagāda, «kiṃ, tāta, ye ke cid vratam āśritāḥ,
sarve kā|puruṣās te 'tra, yadi vā ke cid eva hi?
ādye Jaimini|Manv|ādyāḥ sarve kā|puruṣās tava.
tad|bhāṣitaṃ tato mithyā n' ânuṣṭheyaṃ budhaiḥ kva cit.
siddha|sādhanam anyasmin, ke cid ājīvakāḥ kila.
tat kāśa|puṣpavad idam avakeśi vacas tava.»

II.240 punar janayit" ācaṣṭa, «vatsa, pṛccha sva|mātaram.»
«bavadbhiḥ samam ev' âsau praśnit" âtra, na vā, pitaḥ?»

tato māt" āha, «he vatsa, pravrajiṣyasi kiṃ|kṛte?»
so 'vag, «dharma|kṛte, mātas.» «tarhi, vatsa, niśāmaya:

mātrā|pitror a|samādhiṃ kṛtvā pravrajatas tava
a|dharmo niścitas, tāvad dharmaḥ saṃdigdha eva, bhoḥ!»

women are wanton, not even father is rightly categorized; not at all with that friend of his, dependence of sacrificial grass. So, Father, grant me your permission to take the vows of a wandering Jain monk right now."

The brahmin said, "My son, those who are scared to take 11.235
on the duties of a householder, misers and effeminates resort to religious hypocrisy.

Since it is said:

No duty has been or will be equal to the status of householder. Valiant men undertake it. Those who have resorted to religious hypocrisy are sissies."

The son said, "Various men have resorted to a religious vow. Are they all effeminate in regard to this, or rather is it just certain of them? If the first, then Jáimini, Manu and the others were all effeminate. Therefore, what they stated falsely should not be heeded by the wise at all. If the other, then it's already proven, since some of them are certainly fatalists. So your statement is bald, like a *kasha* flower."

His father replied, "Son, ask your mother. Have you asked 11.240
her about this?" "Actually, I asked her too when I asked you, didn't I, father?"

Then his mother said, "Now, son, for what purpose do you want to take the vows of a Jain monk?" He said, "For the purpose of religion." "Then listen carefully, son.

If you don't pay heed to your parents, then your becoming a Jain monk necessarily entails irreligion. You're so mistaken about religion, son!"

putro 'vādīd, «ata eva yuṣmān vijñāpayāmy aham,
yan me yuṣmat|samādhānāt puṇyam puṇyāya jāyate.»
bhakty" ânukūlitau tau ca, «patnīṃ pṛcch'» êty avocatām.
s" ākhyat, «paṭhita|mūrkhasya bravīmy etasya kiṃ, pitaḥ?»
II.245 Somādityas tataḥ smitvā preyasīṃ pratyavocata:
«jāḍya|jvara|hare, vācāṃ devi, sākṣāt Sarasvati,
prasadya sadyas tvam eva mām adhyāpaya bāliśam!
paṭhita|mūrkhe mayy evam upālambhas tav' âiva hi.»
parīhāsa|vilāsen' ânena Smara|śar'|āturam
taṃ matvā, s" âpāṅga|dṛśā paśyantī tam abhāṣata:
«bhavat" ânuraktāṃ tāruṇya|puṇyāṃ mām evam eva hi
muñcan, prāṇ'|ēśa, niḥkleśa|socyatām upayāsyasi.»
priyo 'tha, «he priye, n' âham a|parīkṣita|kārakaḥ.
su|parīkṣita|kārī tu kathaṃ yāsyāmi śocyatām?»
II.250 punaḥ priy" ākhyat, «prāṇ'|ēśa,
prekṣāvattāṃ pravedmi te
āsaṃgharṣāt tv a|yukt'|ôkti|
mantuṃ kṣantuṃ mam' ârhasi.
kiñ ca dīkṣiṣyase tvaṃ cet, tad dīkṣiṣye 'smy api dhruvam.
sadane, kānane v" âpi satyaḥ paty|anugāmukāḥ.»

Her son said, "That's the very reason I myself am informing you, so that if you become reconciled, merit upon merit will be produced."

Won over by his devotion, his parents said, "Ask your wife." She said, "What should I say to this dunce's lesson?"

Then Somáditya smiled and replied to his wife, "Remover 11.245
of the affliction of stupidity, goddess of eloquence, Sarásvati, goddess of learning, made manifest, be propitious now and teach me, a dunce, since you are finding such fault with me for reciting stupidity."

She, led to believe by this sportive jest that he was suffering from Love's arrow, glanced at him with a sidelong look and said:

"I am loved by you and lovely in the bloom of my youth. If you actually abandon me like this, lord of my life, you will certainly experience sorrow in your freedom from worldly cares."

Then her husband replied, "Come, my wife, I am not about to undertake that which is untested. But since I am about to undertake that which has been very well tested, how will I feel sorrow?"

His wife replied, "Lord of my life, I understand full well 11.250
that you are acting with deliberation. Please forgive my offense of speaking unseasonably through my envy. And besides, if you take the vows of a Jain monk, I shall certainly take the vows of a Jain nun. In the home and in the forest, too, true wives are certainly the followers of their husbands."

Somādityo mud" ācaṣṭa, «sādhu sādhu, pati|vrate!
idaṃ te bhāṣitaṃ, kānte, prema|hema|kāṣ'|ôpalaḥ.»
ūce pitṛbhyāṃ, «yaḥ panthā yūnas tava vivekinaḥ,
sa āvayor viśeṣeṇa, su|kule hy eka|mārgatā.»
tataś ca sva|janān sarvān sukhā|kṛtya sa kṛtya|vit
patnyā pitṛbhyāṃ sa saha dīkṣāyai gurum āśrayat.
11.255 Somadattaṃ, Somabhadrāṃ, Somādityaṃ, Sudarśanām
caturo 'py adidīkṣat tān Dṛḍhadharma|yat'|īśvaraḥ.
abhyāsyatāṃ guroḥ pārśve saṃyatau tau śruta|kriye,
śrī|Suvrat"|âbhidha|mahattarā|pārśve ca saṃyate.
saṃvegāt te ca cāritraṃ ciram ācerur ujjvalam,
tapo 'gninā c' ātma|hemam adhik'|âdhika|nirmalam.
bhīṣme grīṣme 'nyadā bhīmair a|snān'|ādi|parīṣahaiḥ
brāhmaṇya|bandhubhir iva Somādityo jito 'vadat:
«kīdṛg dharmo vinā śaucaṃ? śaucaṃ na mala|dhāraṇe.
tataḥ prāsuka|nīreṇa snānaṃ n' ân|ucitaṃ khalu.»
11.260 ā|janma|lagnā brāhmaṇya|vāsanā yā tiras|kṛtā,
sā vahantī ca tad|vairaṃ vyalagat Somadatta|je.
tato 'nuśāsyamāno 'pi guruṇā janakena ca,
bakuśatvaṃ prapede sa gātra|prakṣālan'|ādibhiḥ.
vāryamāṇo, nindyamāno gītā|gīta|mumukṣubhiḥ
sa manāṅ malin'|ācāras tasthau pṛthag|upāśraye.

Somáditya joyfully exclaimed, "Excellent, excellent, you wife devoted to her husband! This statement of yours, my dear, is the touchstone of the gold of affection."

His parents said, "That path which is bound by you, discriminating one, will be the one path followed by us because it is certainly excellent for a good family."

And then he, knowing the right thing to do, treated his servants handsomely, and with his wife and parents went to the teacher to receive initiation.

And Dridha·dharman, the chief of the monks, initiated 11.255
the four of them, Soma·datta, Soma·bhadra, Somáditya and Sudarshaná. The two male initiates studied scripture and right activity in the presence of the teacher, and the two female in the presence of the superior nun named reverend Súvrata. And they very soon began to practice ascetic conduct blazing with long-lasting austerities, and with its fire the gold of their souls became ever more purified.

One day in the terrible hot season, overcome by the fearful resisters of going without baths, et cetera, like the kinsmen of Saturn, Somáditya said:

"What kind of religion is there without purity? And what purity is there in being clothed with filth? Therefore it is certainly not improper to bathe in filtered water."

And that false desire of the Brahmins' state that had clung 11.260
to him from birth, but had been set aside, bringing what was inimical to him, attached herself to Soma·datta's son. Then, despite being corrected by the teacher and his father, he entered the state of religious hypocrisy through his washing of his limbs, et cetera. Avoided, and taunted by those

tādṛg|jñāna|ram'|āvāsas, tādṛg|vairāgya|śeva|dhiḥ,
svair'|ācāraḥ so 'pi jajñe. mare karma|ripor balam!

sa|khedaṃ Somadatto 'tha
gurūn natvā vyajijñapat:
«bhav'|âbdher evam unmagno 'py
asmi maṅkṣyāmi, su|prabho.

yataḥ:

II.265 pṛthak|sthito 'sau svairitvād viruddhaṃ kiñ cid ācāran.
mā bhūd bhava|bhram" îty asya dvitīyaḥ syām ahaṃ yadi,
tad" ājñā|bāhyo 'ham api bhaviṣyāmi bhav'|āspadam.
tat prasady' âiṣo 'pi, vibho, kathañ cid anuvartyatām!

gurutve saṃgato 'sy' ânye 'py evaṃ syur vrat'|âlasāḥ.»
jagau muniḥ, «sādhavas taṃ hīn'|ācāraṃ hi jānate.
tato n' ālambanaṃ sa syāt teṣāṃ. yuṣmad|gir" âpi ca
Somādityas tad prasady' āhūyatāṃ sva|pad'|ântike.»

sūribhiḥ sādhavaḥ pṛṣṭās, tad|vacas taiḥ pramāṇitam.
jagade gurubhir, «bhūyo n' ânuśiṣyaḥ sa kena cit.»
II.270 Somādityas tato hūto gacche 'py asthād yadṛcchayā.
evaṃ śuddha|vratas tātaḥ, putras tu śabala|vrataḥ.
prānte 'n|aśanam ādhāya, samādhāya ca mānasam
Saudharme śrī|prabhe tau ca vimāne jajñatuḥ surau.

who were seeking release by chanting a song, he, since his ascetic conduct was somewhat defiled, remained in a separate lodging place. Although an abode of the fortune of such knowledge and a treasury of such aversion to the world, he nevertheless became one of unrestrained behavior. The power of the enemy karma in the world of mortals!

Then, full of care, Soma·datta bowed to the teacher and said, "Although I have emerged from the ocean of existence, I am going to sink again, good master.

Since:

Living on his own, he is producing some obstacle to his 11.265
ascetic activity because of his self-will. If I were to become his companion, with the idea of preventing his wandering in existence, then, having transgressed proper authority, I too shall become an abode of existence. So please, my lord, let him somehow be brought to compliance.

If he is allowed to associate with the holder of the office of teacher, then the others will likewise become negligent with regard to their vows." The monk said, "They know that his conduct is certainly inferior. So he would not be a model for them. So please let Somáditya be summoned by your own voice to your presence."

The teacher asked the monks and they approved Soma·datta's request. The teacher said, "No one is to correct him anymore."

Thereupon Somáditya was summoned, but he continued 11.270
to act willfully even among the monastic congregation. The father kept his vows pure, but the son defiled his vows. In the end, having fasted until death and having stilled their minds in meditation, the two became gods in a heavenly

pit" âbhavad vimān'|ēśaḥ, putras tasy' âiva kiṅ|karaḥ,
etāvad antaraṃ hi syāc chuddh'|â|śuddha|caritrayoḥ.

kiñ cic chabala|cāritre Somabhadrā|Sudarśane
prāgvat tayor eva patnyau devyau tatr' âiva jajñatuḥ.

te prāk|śabala|cāritrād alp'|āyuṣkatayā cyute.
Somabhadrā tvam abhavaḥ, Sudarśanā tu te svasā.

II.275 Somadattaḥ punar ahaṃ, sāgar'|āyur vimāna|rāṭ.
niṣkalaṅk'|â|khaṇḍa|puṇya|vilāsaḥ syād amūdṛśaḥ.›

iti dev'|ôkta|vṛttāntāj jāti|smṛty|eka|bījakāt
prāpan Madanamañjūṣā jāti|smṛti|mahā|nidhim.

iyaṃ devam ath' âvocad, ‹evam ev', êti niścitam!
tad ahaṃ pravrajiṣyāmi, vrajiṣyāmi tav' ântikaṃ.›

jagāda devo, ‹'dy' âpy asti karma|bhoga|phalaṃ tava.›
ūce Madanamañjūṣā, ‹sa putraḥ kv' âsti me 'dhunā?›

nirjaro vyājahār' âtha, ‹bhadre 'sty atr' âiva Bhārate
Kaccho nāma janapadaḥ, padam āścarya|sampadām.

II.280 tatr' âsti ratna|khacitaṃ rucitaṃ mahas" āñjasā
medinyās tilakam iva Medinītilakaṃ puraṃ.

tatr' ôttar'|āś"|adhipatiḥ sphuran nava|nidh'|īśvaraḥ
Alakāyām iv' ârājad rājā śrī|Naravāhanaḥ.

mansion in the Good Works heaven. The father became the king of the mansion and his son became his servant, for such was the difference between the pure and impure ascetic conduct of the two. Their ascetic conduct having been slightly defective, Soma·bhadra and Sudarshaná became goddesses in that very place, the wives of those two as before.

Those two, because of the shortness of their life spans due to their former defective ascetic conduct, fell from heaven. Soma·bhadra became you, and Sudarshaná your sister. But 11.275
I am Soma·datta, king of the heavenly mansion, with a life span of an aeon. He who is radiant with stainless and unbroken merit becomes such a one as this.'

Through the story, a unique source of the memory of former lives, related in this way by the god, Mádana·manjúsha attained the great treasure of the memory of her former lives.

Thereupon she addressed the god, 'It is so! There's no doubt about it! So I shall become a Jain nun. I shall take the vows in your presence.'

The god said, 'You still have to experience the fruit of the karma you have enjoyed.' Mádana·manjúsha asked, 'Where is that son of mine now?'

Then the immortal said, 'Good lady, here in this very continent of Bhárata is a country named Kaccha, a place of wonderful prosperity. In it there is a city, studded with gems, 11.280
shining with true glory, Médini·tílaka, like the forehead ornament of the earth. And there ruled His Majesty King Nara·váhana, lord of the new moon, like the god of wealth ruling the northern quarters of the heavens, in Álaka, his

«Arhan devo, guruḥ sādhur, dharmaḥ sarva|jña|bhāṣitaḥ,»
iti tattvaṃ sattvam iva yasy' âdhyātmaṃ vyajṛmbhata.

tasya prāṇa|priyā jajñe devī śrī|Kamalāvatī,
niḥsīma|rūpa|kamalā Kamalā Śrī|pater iva.
sa ca tvadīya|tanaya|deva|jīvas tata|cyutaḥ,
tasyāḥ kukṣāv avātārīt sarasyām aravindavat.

II.285 samaye 'jāyat' âitasyās tanayo 'dbhuta|rūpavān,
nāmnā śrī|Amaraketur mīna|ketur iva śriyaḥ.
krameṇa taṃ kalā|pātraṃ kal"|ācāryo vinirmame,
yuva|rāja|ramā|pātraṃ punaḥ śrī|Naravāhanaḥ.

tam anyadā rājya|pade 'bhiṣicya Naravāhanaḥ
Dharmaratna|gur'|ûpānte pravrajyā|rājyam ādade.

sa ca rāj" Âmaraketur, dhūma|ketuḥ pratāpataḥ,
indriy'|ârtheṣu śabdasya sāmrājya|padavīm adāt.

tataś ca:

madhu|matt'|âṅgan"|gīta|gīta|pīyūṣa|vāhinīm
sad" âvagāhate sm' âsau rājya|cintā|parāṅmukhaḥ.
II.290 gīta|vidyā|kovidānāṃ strīṇāṃ puṃsāṃ ca bhūriśaḥ
suvarṇa|ratn'|âlaṅkārān sa dadau ṭhakitaḥ kila.
cāraṇ'|ādyaiḥ śruti|sukham aty|uccaiḥ kṛtya|varṇitaḥ
a|tādṛśo 'pi tādṛkṣaṃ manyas teṣu dyu|vṛkṣati.

capital. "The Worthy is a god, the teacher is excellent, true religion has been expounded by the omniscient ones"—this truth, as if his essence, spread through his soul.

Her Highness Queen Kamalávati was his wife, as dear as his life, the lotus of her beauty was unbounded, a lotus for the husband of Prosperity. And the soul of that god who was your son fell from heaven and descended into her womb like a lotus in a lake.

In due course a son was born to her, possessed of remark- 11.285
able beauty. His name was His Highness Ámara·ketu. He was like the god of Love who bears the insignia of the fishes on his banner. In due course, a master of arts made him a receptacle of the arts, and moreover His Majesty Nara·váhana made him a receptacle of the rank of crown prince.

One day, Nara·váhana consecrated him to the rank of king and received the kingdom of wandering asceticism in the presence of the teacher Dharma·ratna.

Now, King Ámara·ketu, with haze as his banner on account of his splendor, among the objects of the senses gave the path of sovereignty to sound.

And so:

He became continually absorbed in the river of the nectar of songs performed by women drunk with wine, averse to the cares of government. And he gave ornaments of gold and 11.290
jewels in large amounts to women and men skilled in the knowledge of music, absolutely deluded by them. He was eulogized very highly for his deeds by wandering minstrels and suchlike in a manner pleasing to the ear, although he was not actually like that. Among them he was considered like a heavenly wishing-tree.

gāndharva|sat|kalā|gehaṃ gāndharvam iva devavat
tasya rājñaḥ puro v" āgāt pāna|gāyana|peṭakam.
rājñā sa|parivāreṇa sadyo 'sy' âvasaro dade,
yad iṣṭaṃ yasya, tatr' âsau vilambaṃ n' âvalambate.

tathā gītaṃ, tathā nṛttaṃ, tathā c' ântaḥ|su|bhāṣitaṃ
pāna|patnyā, yathā tasyāṃ rājā tan|mayatām agāt.
II.295 svarṇam, ratnāni, vastrāṇi, grām'|ākara|purāṇi ca
dattāny asyai bahv amaṃsta su|tīrtha|vyayitād api.
ahar|niśam upa|talpaṃ sthitāṃ tāṃ pāna|vallabhām
sv'|êcchay" âgāpayac. chāsti kaḥ sva|cchandaṃ nṛpa|dvipam?

ity a|sthāna|māna|dānāt kośasya vimṛśan kṣayam
mantrī Vimalamaty|ākhyo rahasy urv"|īśam abhyadhāt:

«rājya|śriyo mūla|pīṭhaṃ pūrva|jair vaḥ pratiṣṭhitam.
kośam a|sthāna|dānena kim eva khanasi, prabho?
svāmin, dattena vīrebhyo 'munā hi vijigīṣu|rāṭ
rājy'|ântaraṃ līlay" âiva duḥsādham api sādhayet.
II.300 vṛthā kṣīṇe punaḥ kośe prārabdho ripubhir nṛpaḥ,
rājya|bhraṣṭo, niḥsahāyaḥ, saha yāti vane|caraiḥ.

koś'|ādyakā mayā pṛṣṭā, śiṣṭam etair yathā|sthitaṃ:
‹bhāsvān iv' âsta|samaye, rāṭ|kośo 'jani nirvasuḥ.›

Now, a company of minstrels belonging to a low-caste musician, a household of the true art of music, like a heavenly consort, came before that king. The King, in company with his entourage, gave him as long an audience as they desired, and he made no delay about it.

As the wife of the low-caste musician performed songs and dances interspersed with poetic recitations, the King took great delight in her. Gold, jewels, garments, villages, 11.295 mines and towns were given to her. He regarded her more highly than even a proper object of veneration. Day and night he had the low-caste musician's wife stand by his couch singing at his desire. Who censures a king or an elephant when acting at will?

Noticing that the treasury was depleted through his immeasurable gifts to an unworthy object, a minister named Vímala·mati said to the King in private:

"The root basis of the royal wealth was established by your ancestors. So why are you uprooting it by presenting gifts to an unworthy object, sire? Your Majesty, by making gifts to eminent men and with relaxation among the cares of government, that's the way a king desirous of victory accomplishes what is difficult to be accomplished. But the 11.300 treasury is expended in vain, if the king, apprehended by his enemies and deprived of the kingdom, wanders devoid of help in the company of forest-dwellers.

I asked the superintendents of the treasury, and they informed me of the actual situation: 'Like the sun at the time of its setting, the King's treasury is devoid of its property.'

anyac ca kiñ cid devasya vacmi, cen n' âparādhy aham.»
rāj" ākhyan, «n' âparādhas te bruvāṇasya hit'|ôcitam.»
«dev'|â|samīkṣy' âbhidhāyī yat kiñ cid bhāṣate janaḥ,
gāyakīṃ pāna|patnīṃ tat saudhe vyāsedha yatnataḥ.»
posphuryamāṇ'|âdharo 'tha, kopāt pāṭala|locanaḥ,
rāj" ōce, «rājato 'mātyā vijñāḥ, kiṃ yena śāsti re!
II.305 rājñā bhṛtyā amāty'|ādyāḥ kriyante yadi kalpataḥ,
etāvat" âpi kiṃ te syuḥ śikṣakāḥ svāminaḥ pituḥ?
tathā sāmanta|mantry|ādeḥ kośāḥ sarve mam' âiva hi.
samudravat tataḥ kośaḥ, kalp'|ânte 'pi mam' â|kṣayaḥ.»
a|prasannaṃ prabhuṃ buddhvā
mantry avocat kṛt'|âñjaliḥ:
«evam etat, prabho, paura|
pravṛttiḥ kīrtitā mayā.
vetti sarvaṃ deva eva. pāmaro vetti kiṃ janaḥ?
vayaṃ prabhor apatyāni, śikṣaṇīyāḥ samantataḥ.
santu sāmant'|ādi|kośāḥ. kośā ye 'nya|mahī|bhujām,
svādhīnāḥ svāminas te 'ti|caṇḍa|dor|daṇḍa|śālinaḥ.»
II.310 sāntvayitv" êti nṛpatiṃ tad|ahar|jāta|māny asau
gṛhe 'gād, rāja|vijñapti|hevākas tu bahir yayau.

And if I say something further to Your Majesty, I mean no offense." The king said, "There will be no offense taken with you, if you say what is fitting and proper."

He said, "Your Majesty has not considered that the people are saying that you should detain the wife of the low-caste musician in the palace by force."

Then, his lips throbbing with fury, his eyes red with anger, the King said, "Ministers get their orders from the king, so
why is he giving the orders, then! If a king appoints servants, II.305
ministers and so on, according to precept, how can they become the instructors of the king, their father? And thus all the wealth of the barons, ministers and such is certainly mine. So, like the ocean, my wealth is inexhaustible even to the end of time."

Realizing that the King was displeased, the minister folded his hands in supplication and said, "This is just the talk of the people I've related, Your Majesty. Your Majesty understands everything, absolutely. What do the idiot people understand? We are Your Majesty's children, to be instructed on all points. Let the treasure of the barons and the others form the treasury. Those kings who are independent of other kings are possessed of a means of punishment consisting of a very fearful arm."

Having thus pacified the King, feigning the innocence II.310
of a newborn babe, he returned to his own home, but news of the King's capricious order wandered abroad.

sāmantasy' Ârisiṃhasy' ânyadā mantuṃ vin" âiva hi
deśaś ca rāja|dhānī c' âpahṛty' Âmaraketunā,
tebhyo vilebhe ḍumbebhyaḥ kuṭumbebhya iv' ātmanaḥ.
kva vā viveko viṣay'|āsakta|śravaṇa|saṅginām?
tatas ten' Ârisiṃhena s'|âbhimānena siṃhavat
sāmantā mantriṇaḥ sarve 'py evaṃ rahasi bhāṣitāḥ:
«yā me gatir abhūt, sā vo 'py adya śvo vā bhaviṣyati.
tac cintayata yat kṛtyaṃ, yad bhaviṣyā vinaṃkṣyathaḥ.
11.315 yato 'yaṃ gīta|vātūlo n' âpavādaṃ samīkṣate,
rājyaṃ na cintayaty ev', ādhatte kośa|kṣayaṃ bhṛśam.
kala|kaṇṭhīḥ pāna|patnīḥ kṣepsyaty antaḥ|pure 'cirāt,
tato ḍumbamayaṃ sarvam ayam ekī|kariṣyati.
ato 'dya sthāpyate rājā pratisphurann idaṃ samaiḥ.»
tato vimātṛ|jaṃ rājño bhayam iha samāhvayat.
ten' āgatya gīt'|āsakto (- - - -) rasajyata.
mantri|sāmanta|śaktyā ca rājyaṃ dvayam adhiṣṭhitam.
pravāhito 'maraketur nadyām ady' âiva, sundari.
vyasanaṃ n' âtra, n' âmutra kasy' âpi syāc chubh'|āvaham.›
11.320 ūce Mandanamañjūṣā, ‹tat kiṃ kāryaṃ may" âdhunā?›
‹bhadre, gaccha vane 'mutra drutaṃ, drakṣyasi tatra tam.
taṃ ca nītv" āśu Vaitāḍhye, Nabha|ābharaṇe pure,
bhaginīṃ svasya Madanaśalākāṃ tvaṃ vivāhaya.

One day, Ámara·ketu confiscated the land and residence of the baron Ari·simha, without his having committed any fault at all, and bestowed it on those minstrels, as if they were his own family. Where is the judgment of those attached to music because of their addiction to sensual pleasures?

Thereupon that Ari·simha, with threatening intent, like a lion, thus addressed the barons and ministers in secret:

"This fate of mine will be yours, too, either today or tomorrow. So consider what must be done to avert your fate. Since he, completely mad on music, heeds no contradiction, 11.315
pays no attention to the government and creates a huge loss to the treasury. Soon he will place the sweet-voiced wives of the low-caste musicians in the royal women's quarters and then he will associate himself with every kind of business.

So today a king will be established by the just who will put a stop to that." Therefore the son of the King's stepmother, a cause of fear to the King, was summoned here.

While he was absorbed in music, he approached the King ... And the twofold government was superintended by the ministers and barons.

And this very day, noble lady, Ámara·ketu was borne away in the current of a river. Attachment brings prosperity to no one at all, either here or in the next world.'

Mádana·manjúsha said, 'So what should I do now?' 'Good 11.320
lady, go into yonder forest and you will find him there. And, having quickly brought him to the city of Nabhábharana on Mount Vaitádhya, marry him to your sister, Mádana·shaláka.

tato yuvāṃ bhukta|bhoge, Dharmamatyāḥ pad'|âmbuje
pravrajya, kevalaṃ prānte prāpy' âtr' âiva hi setsyatha.
sa ca te prāg|janma|putro 'maraketur ito bhavāt
ṣaṣṭhe bhave setsyat', îti Dharma|svāmī mam' ādiśat.
tat, saumye, vraja tatra tvaṃ, yath"|ādiṣṭaṃ samācara.›
ākhyān Madanamañjūṣā, ‹tvaṃ tam ānīya me 'rpaya.›
II.325 devo 'vag, ‹me sah'|āyātā devāś celur divaṃ prati.
paścād ekākinaḥ sthātuṃ na ca, bhadre, mam' ôcitam.›
‹bho bho, Mahāśanijava, mad|uktam kurvatī sakhe,
tvayā n' êyaṃ niṣeddhavy"› êty uktvā divam agāt suraḥ.
s" âpi Madanamañjūṣ" âlpīyastara|paricchadā
patim āpṛcchya vegena dev'|ādiṣṭe vane yayau.
dadarśa ca tamālasya pādapasya tale sthitam
a|mar'|ākāram Amaraketuṃ, drutam upāsṛpat.
ucchoṭya tad|bandhanāni tay" âsau madhuraṃ jage:
‹bho bhadra, tvaṃ su|puruṣa|lakṣan'|āḍhyo nirīkṣyase.
II.330 viṣamāṃ duḥ|sahām etāṃ daśāṃ prāptaś ca lakṣyase.
mitho viruddhād etasmān manaś citrīyate mama.›
vyājahāra nṛpo, 'kasmāt tāṃ dṛṣṭvā vismit'|āśayaḥ:
‹he sundar', îdaṃ kiṃ citraṃ citra|citr'|ârṇave bhave?

Then you two, having enjoyed worldly enjoyments, will become Jain nuns at the lotus-feet of Dharma·mati, and in the end, having gained omniscience, will attain final liberation in this very place. And Lord Dharma has informed me that your son from your former birth, Ámara·ketu, will attain final liberation in his sixth existence after this one.

So, good lady, hurry there, and do as you've been directed.' Mádana·manjúsha said, 'You bring him and present him to me.'

The god said, 'My companion gods have set off for 11.325
heaven. It isn't right for me to remain alone any longer, good lady.'

Having said, 'Maha·shani·java, your wife is performing my command. She is not to be hindered by you,' the god went to heaven.

And Mádana·manjúsha, with the smallest number of companions, took leave of her husband, and hurried to the forest that had been indicated by the god. And she saw Ámara·ketu, having a god-like appearance, standing under a *tamála* tree and quickly hurried toward him.

She cut off his bonds and said to him sweetly, 'Good sir, you appear richly endowed with the characteristics of a fine man. Yet you appear to have reached an adverse condi- 11.330
tion, difficult to endure. My mind wonders at this mutual incongruity.'

The King, his mind amazed at having seen her unexpectedly, said, 'Noble lady, what is wonderful in the extreme agitation of the sea of existence?

yataḥ:

jagad vinaṭayaty eṣa nirnimitta|ripur vidhiḥ
nṛ|tiryaṅ|nāraka|sura|rūpair naikair an|antaśaḥ.
dhig, dhig bhavo yatra rājā raṅko, raṅkas tu bhū|patiḥ
pattiḥ patiḥ, patiḥ pattir, dāyako 'rthī, sa dāyakaḥ!›

tataḥ smitv" āha Madanā, ‹satyaṃ sat|puruṣo bhavān,
īdṛśyā yady api na hi viṣādī, katham anyathā?
11.335 kin tu yat te vidhatte sma daśā|veśmam amūdṛśam,
tat kāraṇam ahaṃ śrotum icchāmi svaccha|mānasā.›

rāj" âvadat, ‹Kaccha|deśe Medinītilakaṃ puram.
tatr' âham Amaraketur gīt'|āsakto 'bhavaṃ nṛpaḥ.
gīt'|āsakter mayā grāma|sahasraṃ dattam anyadā
ḍumbānām. atha mantry ūce, «dev', êdaṃ yujyate na hi.»
may" âpamānitaś c' âiṣa, dāyādaiḥ kṛta|melakaḥ,
māṃ gṛhītvā, saṃyamayya nimnagāyām acikṣipat.
bāhu|bandhanato n' âsmi tarituṃ saritaṃ kṣamaḥ.
a|sphurat pauruṣo, naṣṭa|jīvit'|āśaḥ sthitaḥ kṣaṇam.
11.340 atr' ântare mahā|nadyās tasyā uparigāmiṇā
bhāruṇḍa|pakṣiṇ" ātto 'haṃ bubhukṣā kṣāma|kukṣiṇā.
māṃ gṛhītvā gacchato 'sya
pradeśe 'tra nabhas|tale
bhāruṇḍen' ânyena lagnaṃ
yuddhaṃ bhakṣya|nibandhanam.

Since:

This is the movement of fate which causes eternal trouble with many forms of human beings, animals, hell-beings and gods. Alas, alas, for existence in which a king becomes a poor man, a poor man a king, a general a foot soldier, a foot soldier a general, a donor becomes a beggar and that one becomes a donor!'

Then Mádana·manjúsha smiled and said, 'You are truly a fine man, seeing that you are not at all cast down by such
an existence. How could it be otherwise! But I desire with II.335
a pure heart to hear the reason that apportioned you to be an abode of such a state as this.'

The King said, 'In the country of Kaccha is a city, Médini·tílaka. There I, Ámara·ketu, devoted to music, was king. Because of my devotion to music, one day I gave a thousand villages to wandering minstrels. Thereupon a minister said, "Your Majesty, this is not at all fitting." I treated him with contempt. Then he held a meeting with my kinsmen. They seized and bound me and threw me into a deep river. Because of my many bonds I was not able to swim across the river. For a moment courage failed me in the expectation that my life was lost.

At that moment I was plucked up by a *bharúnda* bird that II.340
was flying above that mighty river, its stomach wracked by hunger. It took me, and as it was flying in that region of the sky a fight over the meal broke out with another *bharúnda* bird.

yuddh'|ākulasya tasy' âhaṃ chuṭitaś caraṇa|grahāt,
vallī|vaṇe 'tra patito, dadṛśe, sundari, tvayā.›

tato Madanamañjūṣā sa|viṣādam ado 'vadat:
«aho mahā|dhīra, daśā viṣam" ôpasthitā tava!
hā hā, dhig dhig vidher astu para|vyasana|kāriṇaḥ!
parān vināśayann eṣa svayaṃ kiṃ na vinaśyati?
II.345 vidher ajananir v" âstu vicāra|vimukh'|ātmanaḥ,
sv|āpatyānāṃ mahā|puṃsāṃ yo datte sampad|āpadau!
sampattiś ca vipattiś ca dve priye vā mahīyasaḥ
vārakeṇa tato bhuṅkte bhoktā yuktam asāv ubhe.›

tay" êty ukte sa bhū|pālo vikasan|netra|paṅkajaḥ
vyājahāra hāra|suhṛd|daśan'|âbhīśu|dhoraṇiḥ.

‹pratyupakāram arhanti śatravas, te 'thavā vidhiḥ,
rājya|śrī|tyājanen' âpi yais tvaṃ me melitāś ca te.

dhana|devy asi kiṃ saumye, kiṃ vā vyom'|âdhidevatā,
yad vā Tilottamā|Rambh"|Ôrvaśīṣv anyatar" âpsarāḥ?
II.350 Smaraṃ vinā Ratir v" âsi, kiṃ vā pātāla|sundarī,
trailokya|Lakṣmīr yad v" âsi? satyaṃ brūhi, priyaṃ|vade.›

jagāda sā, ‹kim anayā kathayā, pṛthivī|pate.
ath' âtra tava nirbandhas, tad ākarṇaya, sattama.

I escaped by seizing its feet while it was fully engaged with fighting. I fell into this forest of creepers, where I was seen by you, noble lady.'

Then Mádana·manjúsha, full of dejection, said, 'Ah, you man of great fortitude, what a harsh condition has befallen you! Oh, oh, shame, shame on fate, the cause of the destruction of others! He destroys others; why doesn't he destroy himself? May fate cease to exist, who, himself averse to re- 11.345
flection, inflicts success and disaster on great men and their offspring! And success and disaster are his two wives, or even greater. Therefore the consumer is in turn consumed. Fate is conformable to both.'

Upon her speaking thus, the King, the lotuses of his eyes beaming as a continual series of flashes came from his teeth, which were very like pearls, replied:

'My enemies, or rather this fate of yours, are worthy of gratitude, who, even by causing me to abandon wealth and kingdom, caused me to meet you and them.

Are you the goddess of wealth, good lady, or are you rather the queen of heaven, or else are you one of the nymphs Tilóttama, Rámbha and Úrvashi?

Are you the goddess of sexual passion, her without love, 11.350
or are you a beautiful lady of the underworld, or are you rather the Fortune of the threefold universe? Speak truly, you lady who speak pleasantly.'

She said, 'Enough of this talk, Your Majesty. You are insistent on this matter, so pay attention, Your Excellency.

Bharate 'tr' âiva Vaitāḍhye, Nabhaābharaṇe pure
śrīmān Kamalavego 'sti mahā|vidyā|dhar'|ēśvaraḥ,
devy asya Madanarekhā, tayor asmy asmi nandanā
nāmnā Madanamañjūṣ"› êty|ādi vyatikaro nijaḥ
samasto 'pi vistareṇ' Âmaraketos tay" âucyata.
‹yāvad devena tena tvat|pitrā prāg|bhava|bhāvinā
II.355 bhaginyās te 'maraketur ayaṃ bhāvī manaḥ|priyaḥ.
ity uditvā preṣit" âhaṃ tvat|kṛte 'tr' āgat" êti, bhoḥ.
tad alaṅ|kuru Vaitāḍhyam svasāraṃ me sukhā|kuru.›
iti tad|vācam ākarṇya prativācaṃ nṛpo 'grahīt:
‹taḍil|latābhyas tarale strīṇāṃ vāṅ|manase sadā,
kas tad|vacasi viśvāsyād, viśvasy' âpi bhayaṅ|kare?
a|jānānas tvat|sva|rūpaṃ, saṃśayānas tvad|īrite,
bāhu|mātra|sahāyo 'haṃ nirmāmi tvad|vacaḥ katham?›
smitvā Madanamañjūṣā sudh"|āyuṣ'|ābham ākhyata:
‹mayi ko 'yam a|viśvāsas tava, prāg|janma|mātari?
kiñ ca:
II.360 tādṛg|vyasana|tīrṇasy' âpy āptasy' âtra ghane vane,
śīta|vāt'|ātapa|kṣut|tṛṭ|siṃh'|ādi|śvāpad'|āspade,
kim ūnam asti te duḥkhaṃ, yato 'bhyadhika|śaṅkayā
mayy apy evam a|viśvāsī, viśvāsī dīna|cetasi?
vaimānika|vimānānāṃ māna|śrī|paśyato|hare
tad āroha vimāne 'tra, n' âtra bhītiḥ kuto 'pi te.›

In this very continent of Bhárata, in the city of Nabhá-bharana, His Majesty Kámala·vega is king of the masters of magic. His queen is Mádana·rekha, and I am their daughter named Mádana·manjúsha.' Then she related to Ámara·ketu in detail their entire relationship. 'Since I have been sent by that god who is to become your father of the former life to tell you that you, Ámara·ketu, are to become the loving 11.355
husband of my sister, I have come here to expedite that for you, sir.

So ornament Mount Vaitádhya and marry my sister.' Having listened to her statement, the King replied:

'The mind and speech of women constantly waver about with forked lightning. So who, despite feeling confidence, would place confidence in their statements, the cause of fear? Not knowing your true nature, feeling uncertainty about your utterance, with only my arms as a companion, how can I perform your command?'

Mádana·manjúsha smiled and spoke as if with the efficacy of nectar. 'Who is this who does not trust in me, the mother of your former life?

And besides:

What hardship is wanting you, that you, having passed 11.360
through disaster and arrived at this fearful forest, the abode of cold, wind, heat, thirst, hunger, wild beasts, lions and suchlike, because of your over-apprehension, thus lack confidence even in me, trusting rather in a depressed spirit? So ascend this vehicle that steals away the wealth that is the pride of the vehicle-dwelling gods. There's no reason for you to have any concern at all about it.'

nṛpo daivam ath' ālambya tad|vimānam aśiśriyat,
kṣaṇāt prāpac ca Kamalavega|vidyā|dhar'|ântikam.
tato Madanamañjūṣā 'dhyāsya taṃ nṛpam āsane
namasyāmāsa janaka|pādau pādāta|dāravat.
11.365 ‹nirnimittaṃ kim atr' āgāḥ? kaś c' âyaṃ su|bhag'|ākṛtiḥ?›
iti pṛṣṭā s" âtha mūlāt pituḥ sarvaṃ vyajijñapat.
‹eṣa c' âivaṃ, mahā|rāja, īdṛg devena darśitaḥ,
ito bhavāt tṛtīyasmin bhave mama tan'|ûdbhavaḥ.
Madana|mūrtir Madanaśalākāyāḥ kṛte varaḥ
mayā, tāta, samānītas. tat tasyā darśyatām ayam.›
tataḥ Kamalavegena vegena parirabhya saḥ
priy'|ālāpair gauraveṇ' Âmaraketur abhāṣyata.
pitṛ|ādeśena Madanaśalākā tatra c' āyatī
Jayantīm api jayantī dṛṣṭ" êty Amaraketunā.
11.370 kara|krama|mukh'|âmbujā,
vikaca|locan'|êndīvarā,
kaṭ'|âkṣa|laharī|bharā,
sphurad|uroja|cakr'|ôddharā,
kac'|ôccaya|madhu|vratā,
Rati|Rat'|īśa|kelī|padaṃ
samujjvala|ras'|āpagā nv
iyam upaiti līlā|gatiḥ.
tāṃ dṛṣṭvā nayan'|ānanda|dāyinīṃ kaumudīṃ iva,
babhār' Âmaraketv|abdhiḥ pramod'|ôtkalikā iti.

Then the King entrusted himself to fate and entered her vehicle, and in a moment arrived in the presence of Káma-la·vega, the master of magic.

Thereupon Mádana·manjúsha sat the King in a chair and bowed to her father's feet like the wife of a foot soldier.

Asked by him, 'Why have you come here unexpectedly, 11.365
and who is this man of handsome appearance?,' she then related all to her father from the beginning.

'And, Your Majesty, he is the very one who was shown by the god to have been my son in the third existence from this. An image of Love, I have brought him here, father, so that he can become the husband of Mádana·shaláka. So let him be revealed to her.'

Thereupon Kámala·vega immediately embraced him and respectfully addressed him with endearing words.

At her father's command, Mádana·shaláka came there and was seen by Ámara·ketu, who thought that she surpassed even Jayánti, the daughter of Indra.

The lotus of her face continually beaming, the blue lo- 11.370
tuses of her eyes shining, bearing billows of side glances, with heavy orbs quivering on her chest, with bees devoted to the sweetness of her masses of hair, an abode of the amorous play of Sexual Passion and her husband, Love, assuredly a river of shining nectar, she stepped forward, charming in her gait.

When he saw her producing joy for the eyes like moonlight, the ocean that was Ámara·ketu became full of waves of joy.

‹aye ’tisāro ’pi pathyaṃ jāyate ’nuguṇe vidhau
rājya|bhraṃśo ’pi yad ayam iti lābhāya me ’bhavat.

kiñ ca:

kim udanvan|navanīta|nirmitatayā
mṛdvī su|mādhurya|bhāk?
śarad|indu|dyuti|sambhṛter nu paritaḥ
saundarya|rocir|mayī?
kim u puṣpeṣu śilīmukhā|hitatayā
saurabhya|bhṛt sad|guṇā?
mama bhāgyair niyataṃ kṛt” êyam anaghā
dūrāc ca mām ākṛṣat.›

s” âtha tāta|padau natv” ôtthitā yāmyā gariṣṭhayā
śliṣṭā, kalpa|lat”|āśliṣṭa|pārijāta|latāyitā.
II.375 tāt’|āsann’|āsan’|āsīnā s” âtha taṃ kṣitip’|âtithim
apāṅga|prekṣaṇa|sudhā|rasair muhur asisnapat.

tato Madanamañjūṣā tām ākhyat khalv, «imā dṛśaḥ
jāti|smṛteḥ priye puṣyanty, a|priye saṅkucanti yat.»

laghvyā pṛṣṭe, ‹katham?› iti jyeṣṭhay” ôkte sur’|ôdite
īh’|ādi|pūrv’|Ámara|śrī|Madanaśalākayoḥ
a|cintya|vīry’|ôllāsena, karma|lāghavatas tathā
udaij jāti|smṛti|dīpaḥ, prāg|bhava|prema|dīpakaḥ.

śrī|tātam atha Madanaśalāk” êti vyajijñapat:
‹dev’ âham asmai nṛpāya sampradey” â|vilambitam!›

'Come, dysentery would be fitting, or even loss of the kingdom, given the congenial fate that she become mine for the taking.

And besides:

Is the gentle woman so lovely because she has been created by the churned butter of the ocean? Or is she made up of a luminosity of beauty because she is surrounded by a rich splendor of autumnal moonlight? Or is the virtuous lady fragrant because she has been deposited by bees in flowers? This faultless woman has decidedly been created by my lucky fate, for she attracts me from afar.'

Then she bowed to her father's feet, stood and was embraced by her elder sister, made to resemble a coral tree of
paradise embraced by a wishing-creeper. Then she sat on 11.375
a seat close by her father, continually desiring to bathe the royal guest with drops of nectar from her side glances.

Then Mádana·manjúsha said to her, 'These glances certainly thrive on the one beloved in the memory of your existence, since they shrink from the one not beloved.'

On the younger sister's asking, 'How?,' the older sister repeated what had been said by the god. Then Ámara·ketu and respected Mádana·shaláka first made due consideration of what was for and against. Then, with inconceivable brilliance because of the lightening of their karma, the lamp of the memory of their former lives was produced, illuminating the affection of their former existence.

Thereupon Mádana·shaláka said to her respected father, 'Your Majesty, I must be married to that king without delay!'

11.380 tataḥ pitṛbhyāṃ su|lagne nānā|kautuka|maṅgalaiḥ
pāṇi|graha|mahaś cakre tayoḥ Śrī|Kṛṣṇayor iva.

khe|car'|ēśvara|datte 'tha prāsāde priya|melakaḥ
tayor ajani dam|patyor Gaṅgā|sāgarayor iva.

atho Madanamañjūṣā diṣṭyā pitaram abhyadhāt:
‹tāta, vidy"|ânugraho 'sya prasadya pravidhīyatām!›

tataḥ śrī|Kamalavego vinītaṃ tam yathā|vidhi,
vidyay" âpi pariṇāyya vitene khe|caraṃ varam.

kṛta|kṛty" âtha Madanamañjūṣā pitṛ|anujñayā
Mahāśanijavaṃ bheje. kula|vadhvāḥ patiḥ patiḥ.

11.385 ūce 'nyad" Âmaraketuḥ, ‹priye, yāmaḥ sva|pattanam.
vaimātreyam ahiṃ hatvā svī|kurmo rājya|śeva|dhim.›

tato jagāda Madanaśalākā, ‹deva, gamyate,
kula|devy|uktavac cet tvaṃ mad|uktam anuvartase.›

rāj" âkhyat sa|parīhāsaṃ sa|patnīṃ, ‹tvaṃ karoṣi kim?›
‹ārya|putr', êti mā vādīr. mad|uktam avadhāraya.

cir'|âparādhy|amāty'|ādīn sadyaś cen nijighṛkṣasi,
tan na yāmo. mad|uktyā cet, tadā yāmo 'dhun" âiva hi.

yata eka|mukhaṃ kena jigye 'māty'|ādi|maṇḍalam?
puṇy'|ôdayo 'pi hi prāyaḥ san|nyāyam anudhāvati.›

Then, at an auspicious moment, her parents celebrated their marriage ceremony with various auspicious festivities. It was like the marriage of Prosperity and Krishna. 11.380

Then, in a palace given by the king of the sky-travelers, the husband and wife's conjunction of love took place, like that of the Ganges and the ocean.

Then, at a good moment, Mádana·manjúsha asked her father, 'Please, father, let the benefit of magic power be conferred upon him!'

Thereupon His Majesty Kámala·vega, having had him educated according to precept and joined too with the magic power, made him an excellent sky-traveler.

Then Mádana·manjúsha, her business accomplished, took leave of her father, and returned to Maha·shani·java. The husband of a good wife is her master.

One day Ámara·ketu said, 'My dear, let's go to my capital. 11.385
Having killed that snake, my stepmother's son, we'll be masters of the wealth of the kingdom.'

Then Mádana·shaláka said, 'Your Majesty, it will turn out well if you follow my advice as if it were the advice of the family goddess.'

The King laughed and asked his wife, 'What would you do?' 'Noble sir, don't argue. Heed my advice.

If you want to suddenly destroy the ministers and suchlike for their previous offense, then we shouldn't go. But if with my advice, we should go this very moment.

For who has overcome a body of ministers and suchlike acting with one mind? And the success of good fortune certainly usually follows proper judgment.'

II.390 priy”|ôktam āśrutaṃ rājñā, baddhaḥ prasthāna|niścayaḥ.
vijñaptaḥ khe|car'|ēśaś c' âvocat, ‹kiṃ vaḥ pradīyate?›
‹putrī|vidyā|pradānena sarvam eva vyatāri me,
yac c' ânyad vo jñapayāmi, tad vidheyaṃ prasadya me.›
prapede tena tat sarvaṃ, visṛṣṭau tau ca dam|patī,
kṛtvā vimānam āruhya sva|pure niśi jagmatuḥ.
vimātṛjo Jayasiṃhaḥ prasupto jagṛhe 'munā,
kṣiptaś ca tasyāṃ sariti kṛta|pratikṛtaṃ kṛtam.
bhūyo devyā tayā sārdhaṃ tac|chayyām adhyaśeta saḥ.
maṅgala|pāṭhako 'pāṭhīd atha praty|ūṣa|maṅgalam:
II.395 ‹nihaty' Âmaraketuṃ taṃ mātaṅgam iva kaśmalam,
satyaṃ, deva, jagat|siṃhas tvaṃ jayī, vijayasy api.›
tat|pāṭhitam ath' ākarṇya nṛpaḥ kop'|āruṇ'|ēkṣaṇaḥ
devyā nivāryamāṇo 'pi sayy'|ôtth” âyam ado 'vadat:
‹are, kva Jayasiṃho 'sti, nāma brūṣe nirarthakam?
tad|vijet” Âmaraketur aṣṭā|pada udaid ayam!›
‹tat kañ cic charaṇaṃ gacch', Âmaraketus tav' ânta|kṛt!›
ity uktvā tam asau cchury” âvadhīt, praiṣīd Yam'|âukasi.
tato hā|h”|ārava|garbhas tatra kolāhalo 'jani.
tac chrutvā mantri|sāmantāḥ sarve mimelur ekataḥ.
II.400 a|sambhāvyam idaṃ satyam a|satyaṃ c' êti bodhitum
rājño saudhe samastais taiḥ prahitaḥ Sunareśvaraḥ.

Having assented to his wife's advice, the King's determi- 11.390
nation to set out became fixed. He informed the king of the sky-travelers, who asked, 'What can I give you?'

'By the gift of your daughter's magic power, everything has actually been bestowed upon me, but please let what I shall ask you for besides be given me.'

He gave him it all, and then the couple, man and wife, having constructed a celestial vehicle, ascended it, and arrived at his city during the night. He seized Jaya·simha, his stepmother's son, and cast him into that river, making requital for what he had done.

Then, together with his queen, he slept in his bed. Then a minstrel began to recite the dawn blessing:

'Having slain Ámara·ketu as if he were a foul barbarian, 11.395
Your Majesty, you are truly a lion conquering the universe. May you continue to conquer.'

Upon hearing his recital, the King, his eyes red with anger, despite being restrained by the Queen, rose from the bed and said this:

'Hey, where is this Jaya·simha you are praising in vain? Here comes his conqueror, the spider Ámara·ketu, come without a war chariot!'

Exclaiming, 'Now flee to some refuge! Ámara·ketu is making an end of you!,' he struck him with his dagger and sent him to the abode of Death.

Thereupon a hubbub filled with cries of 'Ah, Ah!' arose there. Having heard it the ministers and barons gathered
together in a body. Together they sent Sunaréshvara to the 11.400
King's palace to find out if this unbelievable thing was true or false.

itaś ca nām'|âvaśeṣe tathā maṅgala|pāṭhake
bhīta|bhītaḥ parijanaḥ sarvo nṛpam upasthitaḥ.
‹svaṃ svāmī, jīvitaṃ ca tvam, a|nāthānām asi prabhuḥ.›
ity ākhyān dhīrito rājñā sva|sva|sthāne nyayoji saḥ.
prātar|maṅgalyam ādhāy' āsthāne siṃh'|āsane sthitaḥ
sa nṛpaḥ saudha|pādātam ava (- - -) samūhavat.
niśāta|śarvalā|kuṃbha|śakti|paṭṭiśa|pāṇayaḥ,
bhindimāla|karavāla|cakra|daṇḍa|dhanur|dharāḥ,
11.405 rājā|saudh'|ântaḥ|pur'|âṅgan'|âṅga|rakṣā mahā|bhaṭāḥ
taṃ parivārayāmāsur bhāskaraṃ tat|karā iva.
saciv'|ādiṣu s'|āṭopaṃ bhūpaṃ vijñāya devy avak:
‹deva, sāma prayuñjīthās. tad|a|sādhye hi nigrahaḥ.›
rāj" ōce, ‹vidyā|bhṛto me n' âiṣu sām'|ādi yujyate.
kiṃ tv eteṣām aparādha|viṣa|droḥ phalam arpyate?›
devy ākhyad, ‹yujyate n' âiv' â-
dhun" âiv' â|kāṇḍa|viḍvaraḥ.
doṣ'|ântareṇ' ânyad" âmūn
nigṛhṇīyāḥ kadā cana,
deve virajyate yena na jano 'ti|bhay'|āturaḥ.
jan'|ânurāga ev' âyaṃ prabhavaḥ sarva|sampadām.›

Now, at the minstrel's leaving just his name behind him, all the attendants were extremely frightened and went over to that King.

They said, 'You are our wealth, master and life. You are the king of those lacking defense.' The King reassured them and sent them back to their respective posts.

After receiving the morning blessing, the King sat on the lion-throne in the audience chamber and summoned the palace bodyguard. Mighty warriors, the guardians of the inner chambers of the palace, carrying sharp weapons, clubs, pots, spears and tridents, bearing javelins, swords,
discuses, sticks and bows, surrounded him, like his rays 11.405
surrounding the sun.

Realizing that the King was angry with the ministers and the others, the Queen said, 'Your Majesty, you should act in a conciliatory manner. For fighting is only necessary when that conciliation is unsuccessful.'

The King said, 'Since I bear magic power, it is not fitting for me to show conciliation and such toward them. Why shouldn't they reap the fruit of the poisonous tree of their wrongdoing?'

The Queen said, 'It is not a good idea to start an unnecessary conflagration right this moment. You should arrest them on another charge some other time, lest the people, suffering from extreme fear, change their disposition toward the King. When the people are devoted such as this, kings meet with every success.'

11.410 ‹devi, kva yāsyanti janā viraktā mayi vairiṇi?
kiñ ca kiṃ na śrutaṃ, devi, «roṣe ghātaḥ, priyaṃ mudi»?›
‹cedd haniṣyasi, dev', âmūn, keṣāṃ svāmī bhaviṣyasi?
ko c' âikākī jayī, svāmin, vṛndam eva narendrati?
tad, deva, sāmanta|mantri|prajān v" â|varjanaṃ varam.›
tath" âpi rājā krodh'|ândho dhūpaṃ pātrīṃ na manyate.
sarvam etat su|vijñāya tena praṇidhinā kṣaṇāt
sāmant'|âmātya|cakrasya cakre hṛdaya|śāyakam.
taiś ca samyak sampradhārya vaco|yukti|paṭuḥ pumān
prahitaḥ praṇato baddh'|âñjalir bhūpaṃ vyajijñapat:
11.415 ‹prasādān nu prabhor bhuktvā
syur daivāt ke 'pi tad|druhaḥ.
daivaṃ hi duṣṭaṃ no datte
capeṭām kin tu dur|matim.
apakīrti|phalaṃ janm'|ântar'|ôpāttaṃ ku|karmataḥ
svāmya|karm'|âpekṣam evam aparādhaṃ vyadhāt prabhoḥ.
uditaḥ puṇyataś candras tārakaiḥ parivāryate.
tat|kṣayād bhāsvad|udaye sa tair eva vimucyate.
su|din'|ôdayato bhāsvāṃs tathā pratapati, prabho.
tat|kṣaye so 'pi rakto 'pi sandhyā|tad|dhvāntam āpyate.
paśyatām, udayaty arkaḥ, paśyatām, astam īyate,
sampadāṃ vipadāṃ prāptau vidan sv|alpam iv' ântaram.

'My Queen, where will the people, changed in affection, go, if I am hostile? And besides, haven't you heard the saying "Blows in anger, favor in pleasure"?' 11.410

'If you kill them, Your Majesty, of whom will you be master? Who indeed can rule alone, Your Majesty? For the multitude actually lords it. So, Your Majesty, it is better not to injure the ministers, barons and the subjects.' Nevertheless, the King, blind with anger, did not perceive smoke or vessel.

That messenger understood all this very well, and immediately allayed the curiosity of the minds of the circle of ministers and barons. Having given proper deliberation, they sent a man who was skilled in speaking the appropriate thing. He bowed, folded his hands in respectful salutation, and addressed the King:

'Despite having enjoyed His Majesty's favor, some people are fated to become hostile to him. However, our hostile fate is certainly giving a slap to disaffected thought. The reward of infamy is obtained in another birth, through the action of bad karma. Thus Your Majesty's karma entailed the consequent offense on Your Majesty. 11.415

When the moon rises because of its merit, it is attended by stars. But at its going at the rising of the sun it is abandoned even by them. In the same way the risen sun shines in the morning, Your Majesty. But, at its setting, despite being reddened, it too attains its juncture with night. Look at the sun rising and look at it setting, judging that just as small is the interval in the attainment of success and disaster.

kiñ ca:

11.420 eka ev' āyāti garbhe, jāyate 'py ekakaḥ sphuṭam
hasty|aśva|ratha|pādāta|śriyo 'bhyāyānti puṇyataḥ.
puṇya|kṣaye sa ev' ânyair jito 'ṭati nag'|ântare.
svāmin, Soma|kath" âtr'|ârthe prasadya śrūyatāṃ kṣaṇam.

Somo nāma nṛpo nityaṃ sammānayati sevakān.
duṣ|karmato 'tha dāyādaiḥ prārabdho 'tyāti sevakaiḥ.
dāyāda|militais taiḥ so rājyān nirghāṭito haṭhāt.
puṇy'|ôdaye 'tha tair eva sa rājā vidadhe punaḥ.

tuṣṭaḥ sa rājā teṣv ādhāt prasādam, iti hi, prabho,
asmad|duṣ|karma|nirmitaṃ mantuṃ kṣantvā prasīda tat.
11.425 tvat|pāda|sevā|hevākaḥ parisphūrjati ko 'pi naḥ,
lajjaya n' ēśmahe 'bhyetuṃ. pramāṇaṃ deva eva naḥ.›

atha devy avadad, ‹bhadra, n' âparādho 'tra ko 'pi vaḥ
karm' âiva sarva|sattvānāṃ vitanoti śubh'|â|śubhe.
tad atr' āyāta|nirbhākāḥ prabhuṃ praṇamat' âñjasā,
vardhāpanāni kurvīdhvaṃ, rāṭ|prasādān pratīcchata.›

atr' ântare 'maraketur dhūma|ketur iva jvalan
prāha, ‹priye, m" êti vādīr eṣām āgaḥ|phalaṃ dade.
are puṇyaiś cet kṛto 'haṃ bhavadbhiḥ kiṃ phalaṃ mama?
kurvīdhvaṃ śaraṇaṃ kañ cid; avaśyaṃ mārayāmi vaḥ!›

And besides:

A man is conceived alone in the womb, and also born alone when developed. Elephants, horses, chariots, foot soldiers and wealth accrue to him through his merit. But at the waning of his merit the same one is conquered by others and wanders among mountains. Your Majesty, on this point please listen for a moment to the story of Soma. 11.420

There was a King named Soma who always paid high regard to his attendants. One day, because of his bad karma, he was seized by his kinsmen and abandoned by his servants. His kinsmen gathered together and expelled him by force from the kingdom. Then, his merit having increased, the same ones appointed him King again.

Delighted, that King distributed favor among them, Your Majesty. Having forgiven our offense, which was created by our bad karma, please grant the same. Each of us is bursting 11.425
with devotion to serve Your Majesty's feet, but because of our shame were are unable to approach. Your Majesty, you are the one who is our judge.'

Then the Queen said, 'Good sir, none of you are to blame in this matter. Karma certainly distributes good and bad to all beings. So, having attained freedom from fear in this matter, bow immediately to the King, celebrate your second birthdays and accept the King's favor.'

At that moment, Ámara·ketu, blazing like the sun whose banner is smoke, said, 'My dear, don't speak thus. I will give them the reward of their transgression. Come, then: if I was made king by you because of my meritorious actions, what is my reward? Seek some refuge; I shall assuredly kill you!'

II.430 tac ca śiṣṭaṃ tena gatvā pradhānānāṃ, tataś ca te
niścikyur, mriyate kṣatr'|ācāreṇa na punar mudhā.
aika|matyena taiḥ sevyaṃ sarvaṃ svasya nṛpasya ca
sadyaḥ saṃvarmayāñ cakre tad|adhīnaṃ hy ado 'khilam.

tataḥ punaḥ śakti|bhakti|yuktaṃ bhāṇayituṃ vacaḥ,
prahitas tair jagau bhūpaṃ pracuraś Caturānanaḥ:

‹phalito 'pi tila|staṃbho niṣpatro 'tra yad aśnute,
tad asmābhir vin" âvaśyaṃ vidyā|baly api lapsyase.

kiñ ca:

tamo vigṛhya raviṇā prāptaṃ tejo vin" âpi kim
pṛṣṭha|lagnasy' âsya bhiyā kil' âikaḥ paryaṭaty ayam?
II.435 tejasvibhir yuto dhvānta|jay" îndu śobhate yathā,
tath" âsmābhiḥ kṛta|kośa|pānaḥ śobhiṣyase dhruvaṃ.
atha vidyā|madād yoddhum asmābhir abhilaṣyasi,
tad āgacch' āśu, yan nadyaṃ sa|vidyo 'pi pravāhyase.›

posphūryamāṇ'|âdhareṇa kopin" Âmaraketunā
tataḥ sva|vīrā aucyanta, ‹yudhyadhvaṃ tair yut" âthavā.›

vīrā udīrayāmāsur, ‹n' âiṣā nītiḥ, kṣit'|īśvara,
pradhāneṣ' ûpasthiteṣu vaimukhyam adhipasya yat.

anyac ca:

kop'|āṭopo yad apy eṣu svāmino n' ôpaśāmyati,
tath" âpy a|lakṣya|bhāvo 'dya devo vyāharatām amūn.
II.440 kāl'|ântare punar doṣ'|ântareṇ' âmūn yath"|ôcitam
nigṛhṇīthāḥ, saṃpradhāry' ânugṛhṇīyāḥ prasadya vā.

So the messenger then returned to the remainder of the 11.430
leading men, and they determined to die in the field of battle rather than in acting to no purpose. With one mind, they guarded all that was theirs and the King's and prepared to defend all that which had been left by him.

Then once more they sent shrewd Chaturánana to speak words mixed with devotion and threat. He said to the King:

'Without us, although you have magic power, you will certainly obtain what a sesamum bush, despite being fruit-bearing, obtains without leaves.

And besides:

And doesn't he, the moon, when his brilliance has been taken by the sun spreading darkness, wander alone with fear at his back? Just as the moon when joined with the 11.435
brilliant stars appears brilliant as it vanquishes darkness, so you will constantly appear brilliant, made by us a receptacle of treasure. But if you are eager to fight with us because of pride in your magic power, then come quickly, since you'll be carried away in the river, magic power and all.'

Then Ámara·ketu, his lip throbbing and trembling with anger, ordered his warriors to go fight with them, or else.

The warriors said, 'The moral principle here, Your Majesty, is contrary to Your Majesty, since the leading men have offered conciliation.

And besides:

Although Your Majesty's swelling with anger against them has not subsided, nevertheless Your Majesty should negotiate with them without showing his anger. Let Your Majesty parley with them today. But at another time you should 11.440

kiñ ca:

bāl'|âṅgan"|ādi|loko 'tra sarvo 'py eka|mukhaḥ, prabho,
etaṃ c' âika|mukhaṃ jetuṃ Śakro 'pi hi na śaknuyāt.
tat prasīda, prabho, sammānaya sāmanta|mantriṇaḥ,
hasty|aśva|koś'|ādy|adhyakṣān svasāt kuru yathā tathā.›

tān pratyūce tato rājā guru|huṅkāra|pūrvakam:
‹na vartadhve mam' ājñāyāṃ ced, yūyaṃ yāta tad drutam.
teṣāṃ sahāyā bhavata. tān yuṣmāṃś c' âika|helayā
pātāla|gān apy avaśyaṃ hanmy ev' âhīn Suparṇavat.›

11.445 punaḥ pravīrais tair ūce, ‹bhagna|bhāgyo 'si, bhū|dhava,
tath" âpi pratyāvṛttyā te 'smākaṃ citrīyate manaḥ.
yadvā phala'|rddhayaḥ kāś cit pāpa|spṛk|puṇya|sambhavāḥ
vaṃśasy' êva prapātāya jāyante pātak'|ôdaye.
puṇya|śūnyasya vidy" âpi sphuriṣyati na te dhruvam,
sneha|hīnasya vīrasya kiyat tejo vijṛmbhate?
dur|vacāṃsi na h' īdṛṃśi saṃsyuḥ puṇyavataḥ kva cit,
karpūra|pātrād udgāro n' âmedhyasya kadā cana.

yad" âsmābhir api tyaktas, tadā tyakto 'subhir dhruvam.
jalais tyaktā jala|carāḥ prāṇanti prāṇinaḥ kiyat?
11.450 rāja|siṃh'|āsanam idaṃ, manda|buddhe, tyaja drutam.
sūryasy' āsanam adhyāste na suto 'pi Śanaiś|caraḥ.

duly arrest them on another charge, or, having deliberated graciously, show them favor.

What's more:

The whole world, children, women, et cetera, is unanimous on this matter, and not even the god Shakra is able to overcome this unanimity. So be gracious and treat with respect the barons and ministers, and by all means make mastery of the elephants, horses and treasure, et cetera, here at hand.'

Then the King said to them with a deep groan, 'If you won't carry out my orders, then go quickly. Join with them. I will certainly destroy you and them, even if you go to the underworld, like Suparna destroying snakes.'

The men addressed the King once more: 'Your fortune is 11.445
shattered, Your Majesty, notwithstanding our minds wonder at your return. However, there are certain plants flourishing with fruit, which, because their goodness has come into contact with badness, when full grown make their actual stock fall, at the spreading of the decay. And since you are devoid of goodness, your magic power will not manifest itself firmly. How far does the splendor of a man devoid of merit extend? Harsh speech is never produced from one possessed of goodness. A discharge of excrement is never produced from a meal of camphor.

And when you are abandoned by us, you will certainly be abandoned by your vital spirits. How long do aquatic animals continue to breathe once abandoned by their waters? Slow of understanding, abandon this lion-throne of 11.450
kingship forthwith. Slow-moving Saturn, despite being the sun's son, does not sit on his throne.

yac ca vidyā|balaṃ, bāhu|balaṃ yac ca bal'|ântaram,
tad eva saṃsmar' êdānīṃ nedīyāṃs tava Daṇḍa|bhṛt.›

devy" âtha punar apy ūce, ‹pṛṇa, deva, paricchadam.
akāṇḍe m" âiva sarveṣām apakāra|paro bhava.

kiñ ca:

param'|ârthena na, svāmin, ko 'pi kasy' âpi sevakaḥ.
prajvalantīṃ diśaṃ sarvaḥ samāśrayati n' êtarām.
api tādṛg|balā vīrāś, cakra|bhṛc, cakra|pāṇayaḥ
sāmant'|âmātya|janatāḥ prīṇate janakā iva.
II.455 tad deva|rājya|prāsāda|mūla|stambhān imān dhinu,
m" âkāṇḍa|viḍvaraṃ kṛtvā svaṃ paraṃ ca vināśaya.›

tato devī su|vacanaiś candanād api śītalaiḥ
prāvṛḍ|jalair iva giraḥ kopa|tāpaṃ nṛpo 'mucat.

vyāharac ca, ‹kathaṃ, devi,
prīṇe 'mūn yoddhum utthitān?›
devy ākhyat, ‹tvat|pador etān
pātayāmy.› ‹astu, devy, adaḥ.›

devī cakre tato vyomni tat|pur'|āvārikāṃ śilām,
vyoma|sth" ākhyac ca, ‹re duṣṭā, upādhvaṃ nṛpam ādarāt.
na ced, vaś cūrayiṣyāmi prakṣipya tāṃ mahā|śilām.›
tatas tādṛg|a|sambhāvya|darśanāt te bhiy" âbhyadhuḥ:
II.460 ‹yadi rājā śaraṇyaḥ syāt, kurmas taṃ śaraṇaṃ tadā,
paraṃ rāj" âpi no hantā, varaṃ hiṃddhi tvam eva tat.›

Consider both magic power and the other power, the power of arms; Death is nearer you now.'

The Queen spoke once more, 'Your Majesty, be bounteous to your followers. Don't be intent on causing needless offense to all.

What's more:

In reality, Your Majesty, no one is servant to another. Each resorts to the bright part of the sky, not to any other. And, bearer of the scepter, men of such power, the ones who bear the scepter in their hands, the barons, minister
and people, should be propitiated like fathers. So show favor 11.455
to these foundation pillars of Your Majesty's kingdom, and don't, having ignited a needless conflagration, destroy both yourself and the others.'

Then the Queen emitted pleasant words, more soothing than sandalwood ointment, like showers of autumn rain, as the King emitted the heat of anger.

He said, 'My Queen, how can I show them favor, standing here ready to fight?' The Queen said, 'I shall make them fall at your feet.' 'Let it be done, my Queen.'

Thereupon the Queen created a rock in the sky directly above their citadel. And rising in the sky she said, 'Hey, you villains, pay respectful homage to the King. If you don't, I shall destroy you by hurling down this huge stone.' Then they spoke in fear because of this display of the impossible:

'If the King becomes our protector, then we will resort 11.460
to his protection, but if he is our destroyer it's better if you yourself cast it down.'

devy avādīd, ‹a|bhayaṃ vo nṛpaṃ śaraṇam īyuṣām.›
te skandha|parśvadhāḥ sarve tam ūrv"|īśam ath' āśrayan.
śilām saṃhṛtya devy ākhyat,
‹prabhau yuktaṃ vyadhatta na.›
te 'py ūcuḥ, ‹pāpino 'py asmān
pṛṣṭha|hastaya, su|prabho.›
śrī|devy|ukty|anurodhena madhur'|ālāpa|pūrvakam
te pṛṣṭha|hastitā rājñ". Âmaraketur nṛpo 'bhavat.
tat tad āgaḥ smaran bhūpo mantry|ādi|cchidram īkṣate,
tad|ājñā|devatām ete samyag ārādhayanti tu.
11.465 yad doṣāt tāṃ daśāṃ prāptā bhūyas te pāna|gāyanāḥ
punas taṃ kṣmā|patiṃ śrutvā bhejuḥ, prāgvad amaṃsta saḥ.
tad|gīta|pāna|malina|śruti|grahilito nṛpaḥ
vyasmarat tad|dur|antatvam anubhūtam ih' âiva hi.
itthaṃ vrajati kāle c' ânyadā su|svapna|sūcitam
devī prāsūta tanayaṃ prāc" îva hima|rociṣam.
taj|janm'|ôtsavam ādhāya bhū|bhuj" Âmaraketunā
Amarasena ity asya nāma|dheyaṃ vyadhīyata.
sa ca kramāt kalā|pātraṃ, vikrānto, vinayī, nayī,
tyāgī, priyaṃ|vado, mūrtaḥ kṣātro dharma iv' âśubhat.
11.470 prāg|mantu|doṣeṇa doṣ'|ântar'|āropān nṛpo 'nyadā
sāmantān mantriṇo hantum ārebhe. vyasadann amī.

The Queen said, 'You need have no fear if you go over to the King.' They shouldered their battle-axes and all surrendered to the King.

The Queen destroyed the rock and said, 'You did what was not fitting for the King,' and they said, 'Give a supporting hand to us wrongdoers, good master.'

In compliance with what Her Highness the Queen had said, they were offered support by the King, along with pleasant words. Ámara·ketu became king. But, mindful of their offense, the King looked out for faults on the part of the ministers and the others, but they duly propitiated the goddess that was his command.

Once more, low-caste musicians, who had attained that 11.465
condition through some fault, having heard that he was king again, came to wait upon him, and he remained in the same state as before. Maddened by his sense of hearing being defiled by drafts of their music, the King forgot about his bad end, which had occurred right in that very place.

Thus time passed. Now, one day the Queen gave birth to a son, foretold in an auspicious dream, like the east giving to the sun. King Ámara·ketu held a festival to celebrate his birth and gave him the name Ámara·sena.

And in course of time, he, a receptacle of the arts, courageous, well mannered, prudent, liberal and kindly-spoken, seemed like righteousness personified.

One day, the King, charging them with other offenses, 11.470
but by reason of their former offense, began to put to death the barons and ministers. They became sunk in despair.

Subuddhinā dhīritās te, ‹mā bhaiṣṭa, sth'|â|pramadvarāḥ
yato 'bhyasta|bhujaṅgasya santi nigraha|hetavaḥ.
tathā hi:
gīt'|āsaktaś Candralekhāṃ ḍumbinīṃ naktam ekikām
śayy"|ânte gāpayaty eṣa, ekam āgaḥ|padaṃ sphuṭam.
na datte 'marasenāya kumārāya mahīyase
vidyāṃ ca yauva|rājyaṃ ca, dvitīyam iti ca dhruvam.
Sulakṣaṇaḥ sutaś Catamañjaryā bhū|bhujā bhṛśam
sammānyate kumārasya pura, etat tṛtīyakam.
11.475 tad amībhiḥ padair devy|ādayo bhedyāḥ sukhād api,
sukhād api tato 'smākaṃ setsyaty eva manīṣitam.›
anye|dyuś ca śrī|Madanaśalākāṃ rahasi sthitām
mantrī Subuddhir ācaṣṭ', ‹â|cchalaṃ kiñ cin nivedaye.›
devy ūce, ‹brūhi niḥśaṅkaṃ.›
mantry ākhyad, ‹devi, bhū|patiḥ
tav' ânumatyā kiṃ bhuṅkte
ḍumbinīṃ Candralekhikām?›
rājñy avādīd, ‹a|sambhāvyaṃ sarvathā bhaṇitaṃ tvayā,
yato rāj" ânya|devībhiḥ saha śete div" âiva hi,
may" âiva saha rātrau tu.
tataḥ kiṃ n' âiva vedmy aham,
yady evaṃ syān?› mantry ady' ākhyad,
‹upayuṅkṣv' âtra sādaram.›
11.480 paredyur Amarasena|kumāro 'bhāṇi mantriṇā:
‹yathā Sulakṣaṇo rājño vallabhas, tvaṃ tathā na hi.

Subúddhi encouraged them, 'Don't be afraid. Those who are careful about the ground are the cause of destruction to many a snake.

Like so:

Mad on singing, at night he has the low-caste songstress Chandra·lekha sing to him at the edge of his bed. That's one manifest object of offense. And he does not give to Prince Ámara·sena, the elder, magic power or the rank of crown prince. That is certainly a second. Sulákshana, his son by Chata·mánjari, is given the place of honor by the King instead of the Prince. This is the third.

By means of these objects of offense the Queen and the 11.475
others will easily be set at variance with him, and then we will easily attain our desire.'

And on the following day the minister Subúddhi spoke to her highness Mádana·shaláka while she was in private, saying, 'I'm going to say something without pretence.'

The Queen said, 'Speak without fear.' The minister said, 'Your Highness, is the King enjoying the low-caste songstress Chandra·lekha with your consent?'

The Queen replied, 'What you've said is absolutely impossible, since the King lies with the other queens during the day, yes, of course, but at night with me only. So wouldn't I know if he was acting thus?' The minister now said, 'Apply yourself to this carefully.'

On the following day, the minister said to Prince Ámara· 11.480
sena, 'Just as Sulákshana is dear to the King, so you are indeed not.

kiñ ca:

kiṃ na hi sthāpyase yauva|rājye, vidyāṃ na pāṭhyase?
kumāre vayam icchāmo rājya|sarva|dhurīṇatām.
m" âivaṃ tiṣṭha nirudyogo, mā sm' âsmān upekṣathāḥ.
Sulakṣaṇ'|ādayo 'dhīta|vidyā yāsyanti jaitratām.›

tato 'bhāṇi kumāreṇa, ‹Subuddhe, 'nyā|dṛśaṃ manaḥ.
n' âiv' âsti. deva|pādānāṃ mā viṣādaṃ vṛthā kṛthāḥ.›

sacivo 'vocata, ‹svāminn, evam eva bhavatv iti
kin tu su|matyā mad|uktaṃ kumāraḥ paśyatu svayam.›

11.485 devī|kumārayor evaṃ śaṅkā|bījaṃ mano|bhuvi
nikṣipya kṣipram ādhatte śemuṣīr mati|vṛṣṭivat.

upacary' âbhyadhāc chayyā|pālikām abhyadh'| ādhy asau
‹rātry|ālāpo, hale, rājñor mama kathyo yathā|śrutaḥ.›

anyedyur avadac cchayyā|pālikā mantriṇaṃ prati:
‹mantrinn, adya raho rātrau rājñī rājānam abravīt:

«pūrvaṃ māṃ ghanam āślikṣaḥ proṣita|prāptavat, priya.
mand'|ādaraṃ, prāṇa|nātha, kim ady' âivaṃ viraktavat?»

sa|sambhramam ath' ôrv"|īśas tāṃ prati pratyapādayat:
«idānīṃ śithil" āśleṣe gharma ev' âparādhyati.»›

What's more:

Why haven't you been appointed crown prince and instructed in magic power? We desire for you the whole burden of government. Don't remain like this, not taking any action. Don't continue to disregard us. Sulákshana and the others, having gained magic power, will attain victory.'

Then the Prince said, 'Subúddhi, my mind is of a different view. It's not that way at all. Don't cause needless grief for His Majesty.'

The minister said, 'Your Highness, I hope it turns out like that, but let Your Highness consider what I've said with a keen mind.'

The seeds of doubt having thus been sown in the minds 11.485
of the Queen and the Prince, thought quickly instilled understanding like a shower of rain.

Careful of address, the minister approached the maid of the bedchamber and said, 'Relate to me what is said at night in argument between the King and Queen, just as you hear it.'

On the following morning the maid of the bedchamber said to the minister, 'Minister, last night, in private, the Queen said to the King:

"Previously, you embraced me tightly, as if you'd reached me after an absence from home, my dear. But why are you now doing it without enthusiasm, lord of my life, as if you were indifferent?"

The King retorted to her with a frown, "I made love sluggishly just now. The heat is what's bothering me."'

II.490 iti rājñor mitho vārttāṃ śrutv" âmātyo 'bhyadhād imām:
‹iyaṃ hale raho|vārttā pratipādyā na kasya cit.›
mantriṇ" ōce 'nyadā devī tatra kiñ cana niścitam
devy" ôktaṃ, ‹n' âsti śaṅkā me.› tatas tāṃ sacivo 'vadat:
‹pūrvavat s'|ādaro rāṭ cen, na śaṅkā, tvaṃ ca vetsi tat.›
dadhye devy", ‹ân|ādaro rāṭ.› tataḥ śaṅkā manāg abhūt.
pradviṣṭā Candralekhāyāṃ tato devy avadan nṛpam:
‹n' āney" âiṣā vāsa|gṛhe. chuptyā sarvaṃ hi dahyate.›
smitv" âth' ācaṣṭa pṛthv"|īśo, ‹mā bhaiṣīr, devi, kiñ cana.›
sā ca bāḍham a|śaṅkiṣṭ" âmucat tad|bījam aṅkuram.
II.495 anyadā c' Âmarasena|kumāreṇa pit" âucyata:
‹deva, vidyāṃ dehi mahyaṃ.› sa ca maunam aśiśriyat.
tan|mātr" âpy anyad" ōce, ‹'sau kumārāya pradīyatām
vidyā ca yauva|rājyaṃ ca.› so 'vag ,‹yogyo 'dhun" âpi na.›
kaṣāyitā devy avādīn, ‹nūnaṃ yogyaḥ Sulakṣaṇaḥ.
asmai ca ditsus tvaṃ sarvaṃ.› rājā joṣaṃ tad" âpy adhāt.
tac ca devyā kumārāya śiṣṭaṃ, sa ca kaṣāyitaḥ,
sadyo 'milad amāty'|ādyais. tad|bījam iti puṣpitam.
tataḥ Subuddhy|amātyena kumāro vyajñapi, ‹prabho,
militaṃ mad|vacaḥ, svāmi|bhṛtyā n' â|dṛṣṭa|vādinaḥ.

Having heard what had passed between the King and the Queen, the minister said to her, 'Tell no one at all about this matter of a private quarrel.' 11.490

One day, the minister said to the Queen something with a slight bearing on the matter. The Queen said, 'I have no doubt about it.' The minister said to her:

'If the King was devoted as before, there would be no doubt, and you know that.' Then the Queen thought, 'The King is not devoted.' Consequently a slight doubt arose.

Then the Queen, full of hatred for Chandra·lekha, said to the King, 'She should not be introduced into the bed-chamber. She defiles everything with her touch.'

Then the King smiled and said, 'Have no worry about it at all, my Queen,' and she, completely free from doubt, let go of its seedling.

Now, one day Prince Ámara·sena said to his father, 'Your Majesty, grant me magic power,' but he remained silent. 11.495

And one day the Prince's mother too said to him, 'Let him be granted magic power and the rank of crown prince,' but the King said, 'He's not yet ready for it.'

The Queen became embittered and said, 'But of course Sulákshana is ready. You want to give him everything.' Then, too, the King remained silent.

And then the Queen informed the Prince, and he, too, was embittered and came to terms with the ministers and the others. Thus his seed burst into flower.

Then the minister Subúddhi said to the Prince, 'My lord, the King's servants have concurred in my plan, since I have stated what is apparent.

kiñ ca:

11.500 caṇḍālī|saṅgāc caṇḍālī|cakre rājyam ado 'munā.
na c' âiṣa jīvaṃś caṇḍālīṃ caṇḍāla iva bhokṣyati.
tad ayaṃ pāpman" ânena vadh'|ākhyaṃ daṇḍam arhati.
tat, kumāra, vilambo 'tra śivatātir na te dhruvam.›

kumāro 'mātya|sāmantais tataś cakre mitho grahaḥ,
rājā tu mātaṅga|gīt'|ādy|āsakto n' âiva veda tat.
kumāreṇa tataḥ pṛṣṭā mātā, ‹tātasya vidyayā
sannidhiḥ sarvad" âpi syād, yad vā na syāt kadā cana.›

tad|āśayam a|jānatyā tay" ōce ‹dāra|saṅgame
vidyā sannihitā n' âsya, sapatnī|matsarād iva.›

11.505 mātaṅgī |saṅgato rājñi dviṣṭaḥ sarvaḥ paricchadaḥ.
vibhedy' âtha kumāreṇa cakre sv'|ādeśa|tat|paraḥ.
kumāra|saṅketitaiś ca vetri|mukhy'|â|nivāritaiḥ
ghātukaiś Cūtamañjary" āśliṣṭo 'ghāti nṛpo 'nyadā.

tad|bījaṃ phalitaṃ c' êti satyaṃ c' âitad ajāyata,
māhā|jana|virodhena kuñjaraḥ pralayaṃ gataḥ.

And besides:

By sexual contact with an outcaste woman he is making the kingdom outcaste. And he shall not while living enjoy an outcaste woman, like an outcaste himself. So because of this crime he is worthy of the punishment named capital. Therefore, my Prince, procrastination in this matter is certainly not propitious for you.' 11.500

Then the Prince, the ministers and the barons came to a mutual understanding, but the King was so engrossed in the singing, et cetera, of the untouchable woman that he didn't even notice it. Then the Prince asked his mother whether, although his father was always endowed with magic power, there were certain times when it wasn't present.

Not aware of his intention, she told him, 'When he's making love with a wife, his magic power is not close at hand, as if through jealousy of a co-wife.'

Because of his sexual association with an untouchable 11.505
woman, all his attendants had become hostile to the King. Then the Prince seduced them from their duty and made them obedient to his command. And one day, while he was making love with Chuta·mánjari, he was murdered by assassins appointed by the Prince, who were not prevented by the doorkeepers and the others.

Thus his seed bore fruit, and it truly came about that an eminent king attained destruction through the opposition of the people.

kumāro 'maraseno 'tha jajñe vasumatī|patiḥ,
krama|vikrama|rociṣṇū Rāma|rājyam apālayat.
sa ca raudra|dhyāna|bhūt'|âdhiṣṭhito 'maraketu|rāṭ
gharmāyāṃ bhīṣma|gharmāyām abdhy|āyur nārako 'bhavat.
II.510 tatra soḍhvā mahā|duḥkhaṃ
duḥkha|vyāpāra|sambhavam
kathañ cit tata udvṛttaḥ
sa prāg|duṣ|karma|śeṣataḥ
dṛṣad|dṛḍha|kaṭhorāyāṃ duṣ|prāpa|tṛṇa|pāthasi
śamī|karīra|babbūla|badarī|kaṇṭak'|âukasi
Vindhy'|âcala|mah"|âṭavyāṃ kṛṣṇa|sāra|mṛgo 'jani.
lūkā|jhalakkitaḥ kṛcchrāt pāda|cārī sa c' âbhavat.
saha mātr" âṭāṭyamānaḥ sa kramād yauvan'|ônmadaḥ
yūthena saha babhrāma vane vana|gaj'|êndravat.
gori|gāna|pravīṇen' ākarṇam ākṛṣṭa|dhanvanā
tad|gīta|lubdha|śrutiḥ sa vyādhena nihato 'nyadā.
II.515 a|kāma|nirjar'|â|jīrṇa|duṣ|karmā madhyam'|āśayāt
nibadhya ca manuṣy'|āyuḥ kṛṣṇa|sāra|mṛgo 'tha saḥ
ih' âiva puri Kauśāmbyāṃ
Śūradeva|dvi|janmanaḥ
Śūr"|ākhyāyāṃ dharma|patnyāṃ,
Śūra, tvaṃ nandano 'bhavaḥ.»

Then Prince Ámara·sena became king, and, brilliant with successive victories, ruled Rama's kingdom. And King Ámara·ketu, inhabited by the spooks of meditation on dreadful matters, became a hell-being with a life span of an aeon in the fearful heat of the cauldron hell.

And having there suffered great pain produced from his occupation with painful matters, he then somehow ascended, and because of his remaining bad karma he was reborn as a dappled black antelope in the wilderness of the Vindhya mountain, rugged with hard rocks, its paths of grass difficult to find, the abode of spikes of *shami*, bamboo, acacia and jujube. Scorched by the heat of summer, he found walking on foot very difficult. 11.510

He wandered with his mother and in time he became riotous with youth. He wandered in the forest with his herd like a king elephant in his forest.

One day he was slain by a hunter who was skilled in imitating the songs of female antelopes, and who had drawn his bowstring to his ear, since his hearing had been seduced by the hunter's singing.

Through his middling disposition, which had arisen as a result of unintentionally wearing away his undecomposed bad karma, that dappled black antelope, having attained human form, right here in this very city of Kaushámbi, was conceived as you, Shura, within a lady named Shurá, the lawful wife of the brahmin Shura·deva." 11.515

tad anuvahata īh'|ādy|
ātmake rāja|mārge
kila kim api hi mūrcch'|âik'|
âgryataḥ paśyataś ca
su|guru|taraṇi|dhāmnā
tasya Śūrasya jāti|
smaraṇa|rucita|cintā|
ratna|lābho babhūva.
so 'tha vyajñapayad guruṃ gurutamaṃ,
«saṃsāra|vārāṃ|nidhiṃ
tīrtvā yāmi yathā, prabho, śiva|pada|
dvīpe, prasīdes tathā.»
so 'py ākhyaj, «Jina|vallabha|prakaṭitaṃ
sāvadya|yog'|ôttama|
śrī|potaṃ śraya, bhoḥ, samīhita|padaṃ
prāpnoṣi yena drutam.»

iti śrī|nirvāṇa|Līlāvatī|mahā|kath"|êti|vṛtt'|ôddhāre Līlāvatī|sāre Jin'|âṅke śravaṇ'|êndriya|vipāka|vyāvarṇano nāma ekādaśa utsāhaḥ.

Then, as he began to travel along the sure royal highway that consists of proper consideration of what is for and against, and swooning for a moment as he considered single-mindedly, Shura, through the saving power of the true teacher, became possessed of the brilliant wishing-jewel of memory of his former lives.

Then he addressed the most venerable teacher: "Having helped me to cross the ocean of the waters of existence, grant, Lord, that I may arrive at the island of final liberation." And he replied, "Good sir, resort to the boat, most excellent for success against sinful activity, which is proclaimed by those dear to the Jina, and by its means you will quickly reach the desired place."

Here ends the eleventh canto, entitled "The Consequences of the Sense of Hearing," of the Jain epic *The Epitome of Queen Lilávati*, an abridgment of the events of *The Epic Story of the Auspicious Final Emancipation of Lilávati.*

CANTO 12
THE TAKING OF THE VOW OF THE FIVE GREAT MEN, HIS MAJESTY VÍJAYA·SENA AND THE OTHERS, THE GOING TO HEAVEN OF THE TEN GREAT SAGES, AND THE TAKING OF THE VOW AND APPOINTMENT TO THE RANK OF TEACHER OF HIS HIGHNESS SÁMARA·SENA, THE SOUL OF JAYA·SHÁSANA

12.1 ATHA ŚRĪ|VIJAYASENA|mukhyāḥ pañc' âpi sad|dhiyaḥ
Sudharma|svāminaṃ vijñāpayāmāsuḥ kṛt'|âñjali:
«svāmiṃś, catur|gati|vyūhaiḥ, su|dur|bhedyāt sur'|âsuraiḥ,
rāga|dveṣa|mahā|moha|daṇḍ'|âdhipati|bhīṣaṇāt,
hiṃs"|ādy|atirathāt, kāma|krodha|mukhya|mahā|rathāt,
hṛṣīka|varga|nāsīra|mahā|vīra|bhayaṅkarāt,
asmād bhava|ripor bhītāḥ, śritā yuṣmat|pad'|âmbujam.
śīlena saṃvarmay' âsmān yen' âitaṃ vijayāmahe.»
12.5 bhagavān āha, «yuktaṃ vaḥ śrī|śīlaṃ varma, kin tv iha
mahā|vratāḥ pañca pañca|māruto 'pi hi dur|vahāḥ.
sv'|âṅge 'pi mūrcchā|vicchedo, rātri|bhukti|vivarjanam,
dvi|catvāriṃśi|doṣa|tyag, bhojyam āhāryam ahny api,
gupti|samity|âṣṭakaṃ ca dhāryaṃ nity'|â|pramādibhiḥ,
dravy'|ādy|abhigrahā nānā pratimā dvā|daś' âpi hi,
keśa|loco, bhūmi|śayyā, yāvaj|jīvam a|majjanam
nityaṃ guru|kule vāsas, tanau niṣpratikarmatā,
bhava|pratyarthy|abhimara|sodar'|ākāra|dhāriṇām
parīṣah"|ôpasargāṇāṃ, jayanaṃ c' âvadhānataḥ,
12.10 aṣṭādaśa|śrī|śīl'|âṅga|sahasra|vyūha|madhyataḥ chinna ahar|
niśam avasthānaṃ, chidra|bhaṅga|vivarjanam,
vikathā|gaurava|tyāgāt svādhyāya|dhyāna|pūraṇam,
vaiyāvṛttya|tapo|maitry'|ādi|pūta|muni|darśanam,
prapālyam icch"|ākār'|ādi, pratilekh'|ādikaṃ tathā,

THEN THE FIVE friends, with His Majesty Víjaya·sena at 12.1
their head, addressed reverend Sudhárman with their
hands folded in respectful salutation:

"Reverend master, we have resorted to your lotus-feet,
frightened of the enemy, existence, because with his four
squadrons of birth destinations he is difficult to be torn
apart by gods and demons; he is frightening with his staff
generals of passion, hatred and major delusion; with his
mighty warriors, violence and the others; causing terror with
his great heroes, the fighters in the forefront, the company
of the senses. Gird us with moral conduct so that we may
overcome him."

The reverend doctor said, "You are capable of auspicious 12.5
moral conduct, but at this point the five great vows, like
the five winds, are difficult to master. Cutting away delu-
sion even in one's own body, giving up eating food at night,
abandoning the forty-two imperfections, eating what is fit
to be eaten even in the day, practicing the eightfold restraints
and rules of conduct with continual vigilance, placing lim-
its on what is to be done, et cetera, the various vows of
the twelve-stepped ladder of spiritual progress, plucking out
one's hair, sleeping on the ground, not bathing for as long as
one lives, staying among the teacher's household, not having
any grooming or decoration on one's body, having victory
by means of careful attention over the symptoms of hunger
and such, which bear the appearance of kin of the murder-
ous enemy, existence, day and night avoiding a fragment of 12.10
imperfection in the midst of a multitude of a thousand, by
means of the eighteen limbs of holy morality, after aban-
doning vain talk and prolixity, being engaged in meditation

samācāryaṃ sadā dhāryaṃ dhairyam āpatsu sarvataḥ,
hīn'|ācāra|parīhāraḥ, pravar'|ācāra|sevanam,
uttar'|ôttara|nirmera|guṇa|śraddhānam anvaham.
iti śīla|mahā|varma|varmitāḥ, sattva|śālinaḥ
amuṃ bhava|pratyanīkaṃ mah"|ânīkaṃ jayanty aho!»
12.15 tataḥ śrī|Vijayasena|rāja|mukhyaiḥ śiv'|ônmukhaiḥ
gurur vijñāpayāñcakre cakr'|ēśaḥ śīla|śālinām:
«bhagavan, sarvam etan no bhāti yuṣmat|prasādataḥ.
prabho, prasanna|dṛṣṭīnāṃ guṇā anucarāḥ khalu.
iyad vidma vayaṃ, tāvad asmākam adhunā, prabho,
mahā|puruṣa|dṛṣṭ'|ântair vratāy' ôttiṣṭhate manaḥ.
kāl'|ântare tu yat kiñ cid bhāvi, tad vidma no vayam.
kiñ ca yogy'|â|yogyatāṃ no budhyadhve yūyam eva hi.»
vyājahre bhagavān, «saumyāḥ, kalpa ity evam īritam.
jāgarti yogyat" âvaśyaṃ bhavatāṃ bhava|tānti|hṛt.»
12.20 pramoda|medurai rāj'|ādibhir vyajñapyata prabhuḥ:
«siddhy" âika|lagnaṃ kiṃ lagnaṃ prasādaya, dayā|nidhe.»

and the recitation of scripture, displaying oneself a monk purified by respectful service, asceticism and benevolence, putting to flight the forms of desire, purifying one's implements also, always practicing asceticism, displaying fortitude in all kinds of misfortunes, shunning infringements of ascetic conduct, honoring excellence of ascetic conduct, each day making an offering of ever-increasing transcendent merit—thus, armed with the mighty army of moral conduct, possessed of courage they conquer that enemy, existence, and his great army—bravo!"

Then His Majesty King Víjaya·sena and the others, eager 12.15
for liberation, addressed the teacher, the emperor of those possessed of moral conduct:

"Reverend sir, all this is clear to us, thanks to your grace. Excellences are the constant companion of those of right view. We have learned so much, reverend Lord, through the examples of great heroes that our minds are ready to take the vow of asceticism. But that will be after some interval, we don't know when. Besides, you're the one who knows whether we are suitable or not."

The reverend doctor said, "The manner of acting has been thus pronounced, good sirs. Your suitability is certainly awakened, you whose hearts are weary of existence."

Full of joy, the King and the others requested the holy 12.20
lord, "Declare when will be the auspicious moment, the one auspicious moment that leads to perfection, you ocean of compassion."

pratyuvāca prabhur, «ih'|āgāminyāṃ pañcamī|tithau
Vaiśākha|śukla|pakṣasya vilāsa|sarasī|śriyi.»

«prabho, 'stv evam.» iti procya
prabhuṃ natvā ca bhaktitaḥ
śrīmad|Vijayasen'|ādyāḥ
sarve praviviśuḥ purīm.

sāmant'|âmātya|sammatyā Jayasiṃhaṃ sva|nandanam
nandanaṃ sad|guṇa|drūṇāṃ rājā rājye 'bhyaṣicata.

rāj'|ādiṣṭāś ca mantry|ādyāḥ
svaṃ svaṃ dhaureyam aṅgajaṃ
sva|kuṭumba|dhurā|sarva|
dhurīṇaṃ srāg atiṣṭhipan.

12.25 rājā Vijayaseno 'tha pratīhārair ajūhavat
sāmantān mantriṇaḥ sarvān paurān jānapadān api.
samaiyarur marud|vegāt te ca prābhṛta|pāṇayaḥ
muktv" ôpadāṃ nṛpaṃ natvā sanniṣedur yath"|āuciti.

jagāda nṛpatir, «bho bhoḥ, sāmant'|ādyā mah"|āśayāḥ,
ayaṃ śrīmān Jayasiṃhaḥ su|svāmī vaḥ pratiṣṭhitaḥ.
vayaṃ punar niravadyāṃ padyāṃ śrī|mukti|pattane
pratipatsyāmahe dīkṣāṃ Sudharma|svāmino 'ntike.
yuṣman|madhye 'pi yaḥ ko 'pi didīkṣiṣur, upaitu saḥ.
yad|gṛhe tu na nirvāhas, tasya dadmo manīṣitam.»

12.30 śrī|Jayasiṃhas t' ūce 'tha,
«he vatsa, tvam iyac|ciram
para|skandh'|âdhirūḍho 'sthās,
tvat|skandhe 'ropyath" âkhilam.

The reverend lord replied, "On the fifth day from now, in the auspicious lake of beauty of the bright fortnight of April."

His Majesty Víjaya·sena and the others replied, "May it be so, Lord," and having bowed to the lord with devotion all returned to the city.

With the approval of the barons and ministers, the King appointed to the kingship Jaya·simha, his son, a grove of the trees of true virtue.

Ordered by the King, the ministers and such each quickly appointed their own sons who were fit for the burden chief bearers of all the burdens of their households.

And the King, by means of doorkeepers, summoned 12.25
the barons, ministers and all the townspeople and countrypeople. And as swift as the wind they assembled, bearing presents. They deposited the presents, bowed to the King, and sat in their appropriate places.

The King declared, "Good sirs, barons and others, noble sirs, here is His Majesty Jaya·simha, appointed to be your good lord. But we shall take initiation, the faultless path to the city of blessed liberation, in the presence of reverend Sudhárman. And if there is any here among you who desires to take initiation, but wouldn't be leaving sufficient means of support in his household, let him come forward. We will grant his desire."

Then he said to His Majesty Jaya·simha, "For as long 12.30
as you remain mounted on another's shoulders, you cause everything to rest on your shoulders. So you should day and night subdue the gang of the six internal enemies. For when

tad antar'|âri|ṣaḍ|vargaṃ vijayethā divā|niśam.
gṛhe hi vaśye bāhyānāṃ sambhāvyet' âpy vaśyatā.
  vijaya|śrī|parīrambha|hetūn setūn raṇ'|ârṇave
sāmantān a|mit'|âujaskān manyasv' âmūn sva|bāhuvat.
caturdhā dhiṣaṇ'|ādhārān, sad|ācāra|dhuran|dharān,
sva|svāntavad amātyāṃś ca manyethāḥ sarva|karmasu.
rājyasya s'|âṅg'|ôpāṅgasya sarva|sampan|nibandhanam,
sva|kukṣim iva rakṣes tvaṃ paurīr jānapadīḥ prajāḥ.»
12.35 śrī|Jayasiṃha|rājo 'tha vinayī nṛpam abravīt:
«yad ādiśati tātas, tat tīrtha|śeṣ" êva mūrdhni me.»
  atha śrī|Vijayasenaḥ sāmant'|ādyān upādiśat:
«nidhānam iva, kalpa|drur iva, cintā|maṇ' îva vā
param'|āptavat, parama|tattvavat param'|ātmavat
Jayasiṃha|mahā|rājaḥ samārādhyo divā|niśam.»
  te 'pi vijñāpayāmāsuḥ, «svāmy|ādiṣṭam idaṃ hi naḥ
hṛt|padma|kośe kiñjalka|kamalāṃ kalayiṣyati.»
  iti nirbhāti|niḥśeṣ'|āihika|kṛtya|kadambakaḥ
ath' âmuṣmika|kṛtyeṣu mano vyāpārayan nṛpaḥ.
12.40 rāj'|ādeśād vrat'|ārambhe prācīnam iva maṅgalam
caityeṣv aṣṭ'|âhnikāṃ cakruḥ śrī|Jayaśāsan'|ādayaḥ.
svasya prāduḥ|kartum uccair atha niṣkramaṇ'|ôtsavam
Kośāmby|ante 'bhitas tenur atha niṣkramaṇ'|ôtsavam.

the home is subdued, subjugation of the external enemies follows.

The causes of the embrace of the goddess of victory, bulwarks in the sea of battle, the barons of boundless vigor—honor them, they are like your arms. You should honor the ministers in every action. Reservoirs of fourfold intelligence, engaged in the business of right conduct, they are like your heart. You should protect the subjects, the townspeople and the countrypeople, the effecters of every support for the limbs and body of the kingdom. They are like your stomach."

Then His Majesty Jaya·simha, full of modesty, said to 12.35
the King, "What you are advising, Father, is like a stream of holy water poured upon my head."

Then his Majesty Víjaya·sena addressed the barons and the others, "You should cherish King Jaya·simha day and night like a treasure, like a wishing-tree, like a wishing-jewel, or like a supreme friend, like the supreme truth, like a supreme soul."

And they replied, "This advice of Your Majesty is assuredly causing a lotus bloom to manifest in the surrounding outer petals of our hearts."

Looking like a fragrant tree blossoming with the accomplishment of his worldly tasks, the King set his mind on the
task of the other world. On the King's orders, His Honor 12.40
Jaya·shásana and the others celebrated an eight-day festival in the temples, like a morning blessing for the undertaking of their vow. Then, to make manifest their intense joy at his departure, on the outskirts of Koshámbi they held a festival to celebrate his departure. In order to make known

viśve 'py a|bhaya|dānasy' ārambhaṃ jñāpayituṃ kila
viṣvak pravartayāmāsur a|bhī|dānaṃ pradānataḥ.

atha dāna|pravāheṇa pradānam iva śikṣayan
paścād deśāt kram'|ôccaistvād yath" ôttara|guṇa|sthitim;
an|ulvaṇ'|âkṣatāṃ śaṃsan stimit'|âkṣatayā dhruvam
sa|līla|gati|gāmitvād adbhut'|ācaritāni vā;
12.45 saṅkocita|kar'|âgratvāt khyān saṅkocaṃ parigrahe
cal'|â|calaiḥ karṇa|tālair viśva|cañcalatām iva;
khaṭikā|śvetitatvāc ca śukla|dhyānam iv' âdiśat
āvedayan maṅgalāni manye gulu|gul'|āravaiḥ;
śṛṅgāritaḥ śaila|tuṅgo jaya|maṅgala|kuñjaraḥ
bhūpāya sajjayāñcakre śrī|saṃyama|kar'|îndravat.

snāt'|ālipto deva|dūṣya|mālya|bhūṣaṇa|bhūṣitaḥ
tam adhyāsāmāsa rāja|kuñjaro rāja|kuñjaram.
mūrdh'|ôpari|carad|bhāgya|su|bhag'|ātapa|vāraṇaḥ, chinna
dina|cār'|ârtha|sevi|dvi|pakṣī|jyotsn"|ābha|cāmaraḥ,
12.50 Bharat'|ēś'|ādi|vairāgya|bhaṅgya|bhaṅgura|pāṭhakaiḥ chinna
utkīryamān'|â|samāna|kīrtir maṅgala|pāṭhakaiḥ,
purataḥ|pravādyamāna|nāndī|nādita|diṅ|mukhaḥ, chinna
tāra|tārair dvija|mantrais trāsit'|âmitra|mantritaḥ,
catur|dig|ant'|â|bhaya|kṛc catur|aṅga|varūthinīm
parīta|śrī|Jayasiṃha|sāmant'|âmātya|sevitaḥ,
prekṣā|pratīkṣyair vidvadbhiḥ ślāghyamāno muhur|muhuḥ,

throughout the world the assurance of freedom from fear, they caused a proclamation of freedom to be recited in all quarters.

Then, as if teaching generosity by his pouring forth of rut-fluid and, through the power of his course from the previous place, the condition of future excellence; commending the moderation of sensual perception by keeping his eyes firmly fixed and the wonderful procedures by his proceeding with
a playful gait; making known through the shrinking back 12.45
of the tip of his trunk the shrinking from possession and by the flapping to and fro of his ears the inconstancy of all; as if indicating meditation on pure matters by the whiteness of his chalk decoration; teaching auspicious blessings, I suppose, by means of the roars of his trumpeting; decorated with red marks, as high as a mountain, the state elephant auspicious with victory was prepared for the King, like the auspicious state elephant of self-restraint.

Bathed and anointed, decorated with ornaments, garlands and divine fabrics, that king of elephants was brought before that elephant of kings. A beautiful parasol like spreading good fortune above his head; fly whisks whose brilliance was like the light of two moons standing at each side of him
whose business is the course of day, the sun; with reciters 12.50
telling of the overcoming of perishability by means of the disgust for the world felt by Lord Bharata and others; with reciters praising the glory of different praiseworthy actions; as all quarters of the heavens reverberated with the eulogies being sounded before him; protected with a charm to frighten away hostility by means of the shrill spells of learned priestly ministers; creating freedom from fear to the end of

saudhāt pure paripāṭhyai pratasthe pṛthivī|patiḥ.
tataḥ prati|padaṃ svarṇam arthibhyaḥ puṇyavad dadat,
prati|haṭṭaṃ, prati|gṛhaṃ pratīcchan nāgar'|ârcanām;
12.55 prati|tīrthaṃ prati|catur|haṭṭaṃ saṅgītika|kṣaṇe
kalpa|druma iv' âbhīṣṭaṃ yacchan saṅgīta|kāriṇām;
pade pade kautukibhir darśit'|âneka|kautukaḥ
puraḥ|paṭhad bhaṭṭa|thaṭṭaiḥ prodghuṣṭa|birud'|āvaliḥ;
Jayaśāsana|mantry|ādyaiḥ dīkṣā|sa|rabhas'|āśayaiḥ,
vaśā|matallik'|ārūḍhaiḥ svarṇa|dhār'|ādharaiḥ saha;
dharm'|ântarebhyo 'rhad|dharmasy'
âtyant'|ôtkarṣa|siddhaye,
apareṣāṃ ca bhavyānāṃ
dīkṣ"|ākāṅkṣ"|âbhivṛddhaye;
Rādhe śukla|caturthyāṃ śrī|Kauśāmbyāṃ puri sarvataḥ
rājā śrī|Vijayasenaḥ paribambhramyate sma saḥ.
12.60 moh'|âri|saṃhāra|yuddhe kila vīra|jayantikām
pañc' âpi te sva|sva|dhāmni vīra|rātriṃ jajāgaruḥ.
snātv" ālipya prage kṣauma|mukt"|âlaṅkāra|bhāsurāḥ,
śveta|puṣpaiḥ sragviṇaś ca mūrta|dharma|mayā iva;
anuttara|vimānānām iv' âvatara|darśikāḥ,
śibikāḥ puṃ|sahasreṇa vāhyāḥ pañca samāśritāḥ;
chatra|cchal'|ādavāḍ|siddhi|śilyā tvarayā rayāt

the four quarters to be his army of four divisions, attended by His Majesty Jaya·simha, the barons and ministers all around him, again and again applauded by the wise and respectable spectators, the King left the palace to process through the city.

Then, at every step distributing gold, like his merit, to the needy; at every shop, at every home receiving the homage of the citizens; at the festive concerts in every holy place, in 12.55
every market square, presenting himself a wishing-tree to the performers of the concerts; at every step presented with festive shows performed by the festive people and preceded by a series of eulogies resoundingly recited by bards and minstrels; accompanied by the minister Jaya·shásana and the others mounted on excellent cows, their minds eager with the desire for initiation, vessels pouring streams of gold, in order to effect the ever-lasting superiority of the Jain religion over the other religions and to make the desire for initiation more desirable than further existences, on the fourth day of the bright fortnight of April, His Majesty King Víjaya·sena was paraded all around the lovely city of Kaushámbi.

The five had each remained awake in their respective 12.60
homes in an ascetic posture, a victory dance in the battle for the destruction of the enemy delusion. Bathed and anointed at daybreak, radiant in linen garments, pearls and ornaments, wearing garlands of white flowers, looking like images of righteousness made corporeal; the five of them mounted together on a palanquin, looking like the descent of a vehicle of the vehicle-dwelling gods, drawn by

cāmarābhyāṃ pratna|nūtna|puṇyābhyāṃ ca kil' ânvitāḥ;
puṣpa|vṛṣṭīr, lāja|vṛṣṭīr, āśīr|vṛṣṭīś ca sarvataḥ
sādaraṃ pratigṛhṇānāḥ paura|nārī|samīritāḥ;
12.65 «dīkṣayā vayam apy evaṃ syām',» êty ārya|kṛta|spṛhāḥ
dānaṃ dadānāḥ pūrṇ'|āśaṃ puṣkar'|āvartta|meghavad;
marut|preṅkholita|latā|pallavair bhṛṅga|guñjitaiḥ,
kokilā|komal'|āravaiḥ kil' āhvātuṃ samudyate;
vasanta|ṛtu|rājasya līlā|siṃh'|āsane vane
nandane te kramāt prāpuḥ śrī|Sudharma|pad'|ântikam.

Vijayasena|Jayaśāsana|Śūra|
dvija|Purandara|su|dhī|Dhanadevāḥ
prabhu|Sudharma|gaṇa|bhṛt|pada|mūle
su|vidhin" âtha parivavrajur ete.

guru|krama|mahā|tīrtha|sevā|hevāka|śālinaḥ,
samyag|jñāna|kriy"|âbhyāsa|saṃnaddha|karaṇa|trayāḥ,
12.70 muni|pravīra|tilakair maitrī|pāvitrya|dhāriṇaḥ,
viśeṣād Rāmadev'|ādyais tad|eka|kṣetra|dīkṣitaiḥ,
Vijayasena|rāja'|rṣi|mukhā muni|mataṅgajāḥ
pracakruḥ saṃyam'|ôdyogam. udyogaṃ tv antarā|ripuḥ.

a thousand men; and, yes!, instantly accompanied by a pillar of success quickly revolving a shimmering parasol and by two fly whisks, auspicious for the fresh undertaking; being respectfully presented with showers of flowers, showers of parched grain and showers of praises tossed up by
the townswomen; coveted by the respectable classes wish- 12.65
ing, "May we too thus meet with initiation!"; giving wish-fulling gifts like rain clouds nourishing lotuses; in the divine grove, which had the appearance of the lion-throne of the king of seasons, spring, and which was actually engaged in summoning them with buds on the creepers swayed by the wind, with the humming of bees, and with the sweet song of the cuckoo, in due course they reached the presence of reverend Sudhárman.

Then Víjaya·sena, Jaya·shásana, Shura the priest, wise Puran·dara and Dhana all received initiation as ascetics according to proper precept at the soles of the feet of Lord Sudhárman, the leader of the congregation.

With the King-monk Víjaya·sena at their head, those elephants of monks, possessed of the desire to serve the eminent holy place of the teacher's steps, armed with the protection of the three helpers, right knowledge, action and concen-
tration, wearing the sacred thread of benevolence, along 12.70
with the forehead ornaments of the surpassing heroism of monkhood, most notably Rama·deva and the others, who had been initiated by that unique field of merit, undertook the strenuous activity of self-restraint. But strenuous activity itself is an internal enemy.

Jayasiṃha|mahā|rājaṃ s'|ântaḥpura|paricchadam
ath' ābhāṣya vijahre śrī|gurur, bhāsvān iv' ânyataḥ.
bhavair Vijayasen'|ādyaiḥ prājyaiś c' âgryair maha"|rṣibhiḥ
bāla|khilyair iva pariṣevyamāṇa|kramaḥ sa ca
nān"|ākara|grāma|vara|purīṣu, sarasīṣv iva
prabodhayan bhavya|padma|khaṇḍān visphūrjitair gavām
12.75 sa|romāl'|astaṃ|papāyāṃ śrī|Campāyāṃ mahā|pure
sahasr'|āmra|vane prādur āsīj jñāna|divā|karaḥ.

udyāna|pālaken' âtha tat|purī|svaḥ|purī|hariḥ
rājā śrī|Vimalasena itthaṃ vyajñapyata kṣaṇāt:

«deva vardhāpyase yasmāt sahasr'|āmra|vaṇe vane
aneka|sādhu|śākhāvān śrī|Sudharmā gaṇ'|ēśvaraḥ
dharma|kalpa|drumo dharmaṃ dadāno 'sti sabhā|sadām
sur'|âsura|nṛṇāṃ. svāmin, devo jānāty ataḥ param.»

ghoṣayitvā tataḥ puryāṃ śrī|sad|guru|samāgamam
sah'|ântaḥpura|sāmant'|âmātya|paura|paricchadaḥ
12.80 rājā tatra mah"|ôdyāne gatvā, natvā ca sad|gurum
munīn namasyan Vijayasena|rāja'|rṣim aikṣata.

tataś ca tasya sarv'|âṅg'|ôpāṅga|santāpa|kārakaḥ
sahas" âiva prajajvāla hṛdi krodha|dav'|ânalaḥ.
dadhyau ca, «s' âiṣa me vairī yena nām' âsmy upadrutaḥ.
śīrṣa|cchedyas tad astv eṣa, prakaṭaṃ channam eva vā.»

Then, having addressed King Jaya·simha together with his court, the venerable teacher, like the sun, began to wander elsewhere. And, his steps constantly attended by the novices, Víjaya·sena and the others, and by the many senior sages, as if by the sages who attend on the chariot of the sun; awakening, with his bull-like roaring, in various villages and big cities, as if in lakes, the masses of lotuses that
are existences; in the great city of Champa, thrilling with 12.75
the setting of the sun, that sun of knowledge appeared in the grove of the thousand mango trees.

Thereupon the gardener of that grove immediately addressed the king of the city, His Majesty Vímala·sena, like the lord of the heavenly city, thus:

"Your Majesty, you will be made to prosper, since in the grove of the thousand mango trees the venerable Sudhárman, the lord of the congregation, like a wishing-tree of religion possessed of many branches that are his monks, is preaching religion to the gods, demigods and human beings seated in assembly. Sire, Your Majesty knows what follows."

Then, having caused the arrival of the venerable holy teacher to be announced in the city, attended by his
courtiers, barons, ministers and the citizens, the King ar- 12.80
rived at the extensive garden, and, having bowed to the teacher, as he was bowing to the monks, noticed the royal sage, Víjaya·sena.

And then all at once, making his limbs and body glow red, a forest fire of anger blazed up in his heart. And he thought, "Here is that enemy of mine by whom I was actually attacked. Let his head be cut off, either openly or secretly."

iti dur|dhyānam etasya manaḥ|paryava|saṃvidā
gur or nivedayāñ cakre, guruś c' âivaṃ tam abravīt:
«api dharm'|ârtham ārambhe pāpā valganti pāpmani.
daurgaty'|ādhi|vyādhi|pātraṃ te syur atra paratra ca.»
12.85 guruṇ" êty upadiṣṭo 'pi rājā n' ābuddha roṣaṇaḥ.
tato Vijayasena'|rṣir gurūn evaṃ vyajijñapat.
«asy' ôpakāram īkṣadhve cet, tad brūta viśeṣataḥ.»
iti tasya girā rājñaḥ krodh'|âgniḥ śata|hety abhūt.
prabhur Bhādra|pad'|âmbhodo vavarṣa vacan'|âmṛtam
rājño Vimalasenasya krodh'|ôṣar|budha|śāntaye:
«sāhasrāṇāṃ sahasraṃ yaḥ saṅgrāme dur|jayaṃ jayet,
sa jayatv ekam ātmānam, eṣo 'sya paramo jayaḥ.
kiñ ca:
sur'|âsura|śiro|ratna|cumbit'|âṃhri|saro|ruhām
sādhūnām apakār'|êcchur narak'|ândhau patet dhruvam.
12.90 sur'|êndra|kṛta|sānnidhyān sādhūn drogdhuṃ kṣameta kaḥ?
pāpas tu tat|parīṇāmād bhav'|âmbhodhau nimajjati.
bhū|pāla, tad alaṃ kṛtvā krodham atra mah"|ātmani.
rajaḥ kṣiptaṃ lagen n' êndau kin tu kṣeptari niścitam.»

His ability to apprehend the thoughts of others informed the teacher of that one's wicked thoughts, and the teacher spoke to him thus:

"Even when it has been undertaken for the sake of religion, evils spring upon one who commits evil. They become vessels of a bad destination, pain and disease both in this world and the next."

Even being thus advised by the teacher, the King was 12.85
not checked but remained angry. Then the sage Víjaya·sena sopke to the teacher:

"If you have regard for his favor, then speak to him individually." But at the sound of his voice the fire of the King's anger became fraught with a hundred weapons.

The venerable lord, a rain cloud for the rainy season, poured forth a shower of words of nectar to quench the fire of King Vímala·sena's anger.

"He who conquers thousands of thousands in battle has a poor victory, but if he overcomes his single self his victory is supreme.

And besides:

He who wishes ill for the monks, whose lotus-feet are kissed by the crest-jewels of gods and demigods, falls into the pit of hell without fail. He who permits to be injured 12.90
the monks to whom the king of the gods is brought in attendance, as a consequence of his action drowns in the ocean of existence.

Your Majesty, enough of this. Have done with your anger against this magnanimous one. When dust is thrown up, it doesn't hit the moon but the one who threw it. That's for sure."

«aho! bhagavatā jñātaṃ, hahā duṣ|cintitaṃ mama!»
iti bhūpas trapā|bhārād veṣṭuṃ bhuvi kil' âihata.

punar bhagavat" ōce 'sau, «saumy', anen' âiva hetunā
ih' āyāma. tan maha'|rṣim amuṃ kṣamaya tātavat.»

etad gur'|ûktam ākarṇya sa sa|karṇa|śiro|maṇiḥ,
hṛt paścāt|tāpa|taptaṃ nu siñcan bāṣpa|bharair nṛpaḥ,
12.95 Vijayasena|rāja'|rṣer nipatya pada|padmayoḥ
kṣamayitvā hṛd|anta|sthaṃ ninind' êti su|duṣ|kṛtam:

«hā! hā! dhig! dhig! mama mano
tvayy adhyāyad a|maṅgalam!
ahah", âham a|dhanyo 'tra!
kalaṅkaḥ sva|kule 'bhavam.

śrutiḥ, smṛtī, rāja|nītiḥ sarvaṃ vā vismṛtaṃ mama,
yatas tvāṃ sva|gṛh'|āyātaṃ nyajighāṃsam an|aṃhasam.
pūrve pumāṃso me 'kārṣur vairiṇo 'py eyuṣo gṛham
āpad|ambhodhi|magnasy' âpy uddhāraṃ paramaṃ khalu.

mayā nu tava rāja'|rṣer deva|sevya|pada|śriyaḥ
pāpaṃ tac cintayāñcakre, yena syād dur|gatiḥ svasāt.
12.100 tat prasīda, prasīd' āśu, puṃs|pāśe mayi, puṃs|pate.
tvat|prasatti|sudhābhir me pāpa|tāpaḥ praśāmyatu.»

Thinking, "Ah! The reverend doctor knew my wicked intention. Shame on me!," the King, because of the burden of his shame, actually wished to disappear into the ground.

The reverend doctor addressed him once more, "Good sir, it's for this very reason that we came here. So ask pardon of this mighty sage as if he were your father."

Having heard that statement of the teacher, the King, the crest-jewel of those with ears, sprinkling with copious tears his heart, which was heated with his regret, fell at the 12.95
lotus-feet of Víjaya·sena, the royal sage, and having begged his forgiveness, bitterly reviled the extremely wicked action that had been situated in his mind:

"Ah! Ah! Shame, shame! My mind intended disaster for you! Oh, I am unhappy about it! I have become a stain on my own family.

Sacred knowledge, law and the duties of kings, or, rather, all has been forgotten by me, since I wished to kill you, the sinless one, who had come to my house. No god smiles on me. The man who attacked me before, although an enemy, came to my house, certainly a supreme deliverance for one sunk in an ocean of disaster.

But I intended to harm you, royal sage, possessed of the rank of one to be attended by the gods, with the result that I will certainly have a bad rebirth. So please, quickly show 12.100
favor to me, a worthless man, an insect of a man. Let the heat of my wickedness be soothed by the nectars of your graciousness."

ath' âvocata rāja'|rṣir marṣit'|âri|parīṣahaḥ,
«saṃyama|pratipatty" âiva prasanno 'haṃ jagaty api,
viśeṣatas tu bhavati bhagavad|vacan'|ôdyate.
tac cintitam idaṃ ninda, prāyaś|cittam urīkuru.»
gur'|ûpānte ca tac cakre sarvaṃ sarvaṃ|sahā|patiḥ.
prasanno 'smai guruḥ śrāddha|dharma|cintā|maṇiṃ dadau.
Vijayasenam anu rāja|maha"|rṣiṃ,
Vimalasena|nṛpater durit'|âgnim
upaśamayya vijahāra Sudharm" âpy
amṛta|daḥ pura|var'|ântaram ārāt.
12.105 te sūtrato 'rthataś c' âpy ekādaś'|âṅgyām adhītinaḥ
tapo|'rṇavasya pārīṇāḥ sarve gīt'|ârthatām aguḥ.
itthaṃ varaṃ caritr'|âbdhim, amṛta|śrī|nibandhanam,
jñān'|êndu|kaumudī|bhārair bhṛśam ullāsya sarvataḥ
gurūn vijñāpayāmāsur, «āśu gatvaram eva naḥ
vapus tasmād an|aśanaṃ pratipadyemahi, prabho.»
vyājahāra guruḥ, «saumyāḥ,
samyak saṃlikhyatāṃ vapuḥ.»
tataḥ saṃlekhanāṃ gāḍhāṃ
te daś' âpi vitenire.
ath' â|mamatvāḥ sv'|âṅge 'pi, sarva|bhāveṣu niḥspṛhāḥ,
kṣamit'|âśeṣa|sattvāś ca prāg|duṣ|kṛte vigarhiṇaḥ,
12.110 guru|datt'|ālocanāś ca su|kṛtasy' ânumodakāḥ,
catuḥ|śaraṇa|yuktāś c' ân|aśanaṃ pratipedire.

The royal sage, patient with the forgiveness of enemies, replied, "I am indeed pleased with your gaining of restraint, even in the world, but especially with your beginning to undertake what was said by the reverend doctor. So curse that thought of yours and make extensive atonement."

And the king of the earth performed all in the presence of the teacher. The teacher was pleased with him and gave him the wishing-jewel of religious faith.

Having quenched King Vímala·sena's fire of evil regarding the royal sage Víjaya·sena, Sudhárman, the granter of immortality, began to wander in regions far from big cities.
Well read in the limb texts both by verse and by meaning, 12.105
receptacles of the ocean of asceticism, they attained the state of being ascetics who had completed their studies.

Having thus illuminated all around the excellent foundation of immortal prosperity, the ocean of asceticism, by means of copious amounts of the intense autumn moonlight of their knowledge, they requested the teacher, "Our bodies are soon perishable. Therefore we wish to undergo the fast until death, reverend lord."

The teacher said, "Your bodies should undergo true purging away in the proper manner." Thereupon those ten began to undertake strict purging away.

Then, with indifference to their own bodies, free from desire for all substances, having forgiveness for all beings,
despising their former bad actions, practicing self-censure 12.110
under the supervision of the teacher, feeling sympathetic joy in their good action, joined with the four refuges, they undertook the fast until death.

parameṣṭhi|namaskāra|dhyāna|dhārā|dhi|rohiṇaḥ chinna
sarve māsika|bhaktena vidhinā te vipedire.
tataś ca muni|rājās te mahā|puṇya|ratha|sthitāḥ
Saudharma|kalpe praty|ekaṃ vimāneṣu kṣaṇād aguḥ.
tataḥ sva|sva|vimāneṣ' ûpapāda śayan'|ântare
utpedire dyu|Gaṅgāyāṃ suvarṇa|kamalā iva.
samāna|catur|asr'|âṅgāḥ, sapta|dhātu|mal'|ôjjhitāḥ,
navanīta|mṛdu|sparśāḥ, prabhā|pūrita|diṅ|mukhāḥ,
12.115 vijñāna|pāra|dṛśvānaś c' âvadhi|jñāna|śālinaḥ,
mahā|vīryā, vajra|kāyāḥ, sampūrṇa|śubha|lakṣaṇāḥ,
aṇim'|ādi|maha"|rddhy|āḍhyā, a|cintya|mahi|mālayāḥ,
vimān'|ēśā Indra|sāmānikās te jajñire surāḥ.

antar|muhūrtās tri|daśī|bhāvam āsādya te surāḥ
deva|dūṣyaṃ c' âpanīy' ôpaviṣṭā dadṛśur mudā.
vimānam a|pratimānaṃ svarṇa|ratna|maṇī|mayam,
itas|tataḥ sampatataḥ santataṃ ca div'|âukasaḥ
tad|vibhūtiṃ c' ânubhūt'|êtarāṃ vīkṣy' âti|vismayāt,
sphār'|âkṣās te «kim idam?» ity antaḥ sambhramam ūhire.
12.120 asminn avasare tat|tat|
kiṅkarās tri|div'|âukasaḥ
svaṃ svaṃ svāminam utpannaṃ
vīkṣy' ôdyat|pramad'|ōrmayaḥ,
pratinādena kakubhaḥ kurvataḥ pratidundubhīn,
dundubhīn vādayāmāsuḥ prātas|tūrya|sah'|ôdarān.

Swelling with oceans of meditation on the prayer in praise of the supreme beings, by means of a monthlong fast according to precept, they passed away. And then, in a moment, those kings of monks, mounted in the chariots of excellent merit, one by one arrived in the Good Works heaven, among the gods who dwell in celestial vehicles. Then they became gods on couches each in their own heavenly vehicle, like golden lotuses in the heavenly Ganges. Their limbs regular and equal; free from the impurity of the seven elements; as soft to the touch as butter, their facing direction filled with light; completely versed in the subjects of 12.115
knowledge; possessed of the ability to perceive beyond the normal range of the senses; extremely strong; with bodies of adamant; their bodily signs of prosperity fulfilled; richly endowed with great powers, such as the ability to become as small as an atom, et cetera; garlanded with inconceivable glory; they became gods, lords of the celestial vehicles, with the rank of kings of the gods.

Having attained the rank of divine beings within a moment, those gods, having put on their divine garments, were seen to have attained a state of joy. When they saw the incomparable celestial vehicles formed of gold, diamonds and rubies, flying here and there in dense formation, the abodes of the gods, their eyes remained open in extreme astonishment as they wondered, "What is this?," and they rode inside them with eager excitement.

At that moment the servants, whose abode was the 12.120
heaven, having seen that their respective masters had arisen, sounded drums, akin to a morning concert, which with their echoing made the heavens answering drums.

«prabho jaya, jaya svāmin, nanda, nanda kṣat'|âvadhi!
tvam asmākam a|nāthānāṃ nāthaḥ samudagāś cirāt.
trāyasva vijitaṃ sarvaṃ, vijayasv' â|jitaṃ punaḥ!
rājyam eka|cchatram atra, svāmin, kuru sur'|ālaye!»

ity ucchitya karān uccair, mādyad|dantāvalā iva,
garjanto 'lam anuttālaṃ peṭhur vaitālik'|âmarāḥ.

12.125 «kalpaḥ Saudharma|nām' âyaṃ, kalpānām ādya udyate.
vimānam etad devasya rāja|dhānī|pur'|ôpamam.
amī puṇya|dhana|krītā, vayam ājñā|karāḥ surāḥ,
ete ca ratna|prāsādā, vilāsa|sadan'|ôpamāḥ.
nitya|puṣpa|phalāś c' ême, līl"|ārāma|mano|ramāḥ,
imāḥ kelī|ratna|vāpyaḥ svarṇ'|âmbho|ruha|bhāsvarāḥ,
amī krīḍ'|âcalā ratna|cūlāḥ, kāñcana|sānavaḥ,
amūḥ sudhā|taraṅgiṇyo jala|kelī|nibandhanaṃ.
āgāmi|bhava|kalyāṇa|sārva|kāmika|tīrtha|bham chinna sid-
dh'|āyatanam etac ca, dev'|ālaya iv' âukasi.
12.130 mahā|sabhā su|dharm" êyaṃ, divya|bhog'|âika|raṅga|bhūḥ.»
iti vyajijñapan sve sve tān kṛt'|âñjalayaḥ surāḥ.

iti tad|vācam ākarṇya vimāna'|rddhiṃ vilokya ca,
dadhyus te vismayāt, «prāptam asmābhiḥ su|kṛtāt kutaḥ?»

"Victory, victory, my lord, rejoice, rejoice, master you whose limits are unbounded! You, the master of us who lacked a master, have appeared at last. Protect all the conquered, but conquer the unconquered! Create a realm under the rule of one king in this abode of the gods, master!"

Raising their hands on high like rutting elephants raising their trunks, the immortal minstrels thus recited, thundering a very melodious note .

"This is the heaven called the Good Works heaven, in the 12.125
first level of the heavens. This is a celestial vehicle, like the capital city of the gods. And we are those gods, bought with the wealth of your merit, who will perform your orders, and those are palaces of jewels, like abodes of pleasure. These are ever-flowering plants and fruit, pleasing the mind with pleasure and delight. These are jeweled play ponds shining with golden lotuses. These are pleasure mountains with jeweled peaks and ridges of gold. These are rivers of nectar, the source of frolicking in their waters. And this is a miraculous abode, like a holy place granting all wishes for a
prosperous future existence, as if in a heavenly abode. And 12.130
this is the large dining hall, the assembly hall of the gods, a single place of assembly for the gods' enjoyment." Thus each of the gods informed them respectively, their hands folded in respectful salutation.

Upon hearing their description and seeing the prosperity of the celestial vehicles, they wondered in amazement, "Through what auspicious deed have we arrived at this?"

tato datt'|âvadhānās te sadyo 'py avadhi|dīpataḥ,
bhūmī|gṛham iva svaṃ svaṃ dadṛśuḥ prāktanaṃ bhavam.
«bat', Ârhad|dharma|mahimā mitair varṣaiḥ parāpi yat,
svaḥ|śrīr a|saṅkhya|varṣāṇy asmābhir evaṃ!» tv acintayan.
«abhiṣeka|gṛhaṃ, svāmin, prasādaṃ kurv, alaṅkuru,
kurmo 'bhiṣekaṃ yen'.» êti vyajñāpyanta surair ime.

12.135 samutthāya tato datta|hastikāḥ sva|sva|vetriṇā,
te 'lañcakruḥ siṃha|pīṭhaṃ samaṃ jaya|jay'|āravaiḥ.
tataḥ puṣp'|ôdakair, gandh'|ôdakaiḥ, śuddh'|ôdakais tathā
abhyaṣiñcanta tān vṛndārakā Jinam iv' ādarāt.

saṃmṛṣṭā gandha|kāṣāyyā, liptā go|śīrṣa|candanaiḥ,
saṃvastritā deva|dūṣyair, bhūṣitā mālya|bhūṣaṇaiḥ,
pārśvayoś cāmarābhyāṃ te bhāntaś chatreṇa mūrdhani,
mūrta|jñāna|trayeṇ' êva vyavasāya|sabhām aguḥ.

tatr' âvācyata taiḥ su|pustaka|varaṃ
siṃh'|āsan'|ôtsaṅga|gam,
yasmin rājata eva patra|nicayo
raiṣṭī ca varṇ'|āvalī,
jāti|svarṇa|mayo 'ntarā davarako,
nānā|maṇī|vastikā,

Then they, being furnished with the power to perceive beyond the normal range of the senses, by means of the light of that knowledge, each saw their former existence, like a chamber under the ground.

They thought, "Oh, the power of the Jain religion, with its gentle showers, which has caused us to obtain the countless showers of the prosperity of heaven!"

They were requested by the gods, "Graciously adorn the house of consecration, so that we may consecrate you, Your Majesty."

They were raised up together, their hands supported by 12.135
their respective chamberlains, and they each ornamented their lion-throne to shouts of "Victory, victory!" Then, with showers of flowers, showers of perfumes and pure water, the eminent gods consecrated them with as much respect as if consecrating a Jina.

Patted with a perfumed towel, anointed with the finest sandalwood ointment, dressed in divine garments, adorned with garlands and ornaments, they, resplendent with a fly whisk at each side and a parasol at their head as if with the embodiments of the three knowledges, entered the hall of assembly.

And there they had recited a book placed on a lectern of a lion-throne in which many leaves and series of jeweled pictures were resplendent, between which passed a string
of genuine gold with various kinds of jewels at its ends. Its 12.140
back covers were made of jewels flashing all around. There was a large inkpot made of flashing cat's-eye with dense ink made from jewels. Attached to a golden chain was a large, very hard writing stilus made from diamond. In it all the

bhāsvad|riṣṭa|maṇī|maye ca parito
bhātastarāṃ pṛṣṭhake.
12.140 yasy' ôddīpra|viḍūra|bhū|maṇi|mayaṃ
sphāraṃ maṣī|bhājanaṃ,
sāndro riṣṭa|maṇīmayo maṣi|raso,
raiṣṭaṃ pidhānaṃ ghanaṃ,
haimī śṛṅkhalikā draḍhīyasitarā,
vajrī mahā|lekhinī,
janm'|ânt'|âvadhi deva|kṛtyam akhilaṃ
lekhyaṃ tathā dhārmikam.

tataḥ sarva|śriyā, sarva|dyutyā, sarva|balena ca,
puro maṅgala|tūryeṇa pūryamāṇe kakum|mukhe,
sphurat|parimal'|ôddāma|puṣpa|dām'|ādi bhūriśaḥ
pūjā|vastu gṛhītvā te siddh'|āyatanam īyire.

tatra c' âṣṭ'|ôttara|śataṃ pratimānāṃ pramṛjyate
snāpayanti sma tair divy'|ôdakair bhakti|rasair iva.
divy'|âṅgarāgair, bhaṅgībhiḥ, sva|pratāpair nu piñjaraiḥ
vilipy' ānarcuḥ kusumair yaśaḥ|surabhi|nirmalaiḥ.
12.145 kṛtvā prasūna|prakaraṃ tat|phalair iva tandulaiḥ,
te mudā lilikhur lekhāḥ purastād aṣṭa|maṅgalīm.
pratimās triḥ praṇamy' âtha, nyañcy' ēṣaj jānu vāmakam,
dakṣiṇaṃ bhū|tale nyasya, viracayy' âlike 'ñjalim.

ṣaḍja|madhyama|gāndhāra|grām'|ôdgāra|mano|ramam
gandharva|vargeṇ' ārabdhe cāru|saṅgītak'|âmṛte,
aṣṭ'|ôttara|śata|śloka|mayair nava|navaiḥ stavaiḥ
te bhakti|vallī|prasavair gambhīrais tāram astuvan.

tad anv ime stūpa|caitya iva Māṇava|nāmani
stambhe Tīrthaṅkar'|âsthīni sthitāny ānarcur añjasā.

gods' commands for the terms of their lives and their just decisions were to be written.

Then, as the vault of heaven was filled with every prosperity, every splendor and every power, with an auspicious consort preceding, they took hold of various substances for ritual worship such as chaplets and garlands of riotous flowers spreading their fragrance, and entered their miraculous abodes.

And there the ablution of the hundred and eight finest images of the Jina took place. They bathed them with those divine waters as if with the essence of their devotion. And having anointed them with various kinds of divine unguent, they worshipped them with flowers, resplendent with the
fragrance of glory. Having made a pile of flowers, with grains 12.145
of rice, as if with their fruit, they joyfully traced patterns before making the offering of the eight auspicious things. They bowed three times before the images, bent their left knee slightly and placed their right one on the ground, raising their hands in reverent salutation to their foreheads.

As the nectar of a heavenly concert was played by heavenly musicians, delighting the mind with its sounding of scales and varied modulations, they praised the savior with ever-renewed hymns consisting of one hundred and eight excellent verses, deep shoots of the creeper of their devotion.

After that, they straightaway worshipped the relics of the Fordmaker situated at the pillar named Mánava, as if it were a holy burial mound.

12.150 Sudharma|nāma|dheyāyāṃ sabhāyāṃ sa|paricchadāḥ
«jaya, vardhasva, jīv'» êty āśāsyamānāḥ puraḥ suraiḥ,
gatvā sarv'|êndriya|grāma|sukhaṃ pratyūṣa|vātavat,
te nānā|bhaṅgi saṅgītaṃ cira|kālam acīkaran.
anyadā deva|rājasya sarv'|âvasara|saṃsadi
militānāṃ daśānām apy eṣāṃ tri|diva|vāsinām
mitho|darśanato jajñe 'nurāgo nirupādhikaḥ
prayukt'|âvadhitaś c' âbhūt pūrvavan maitryam uttamam.
tataḥ sabhāyā utthāy' âmilann ekatra te same,
mithas tulya'|rddhi|dṛṣṭyā ca paraṃ santoṣam ūhire.
12.155 tataḥ kadā cid vāpīṣu te 'krīḍan kala|haṃsavat,
udyāneṣv alivat puṣpa|kelīṃ tenuḥ kadā cana.
kadā can' âdri|śṛṅgeṣu vilesus te mṛgā iva,
saritsu pūrṇa|padmāsu kadā cic cakravākavat.
kadā can' âpi śrī|Nandīśvara|yātrāṃ vitenire,
Jina|janm'|ādi|kalyāṇa|mahāṃsi ca kadā cana.
ity|ādi|līlāṃ su|kṛta|phala|bīj'|ôpamāṃ muhuḥ
militās te sma kurvanti kil' âik'|ātmyam iv' āśritāḥ.
yaḥ śrī|Śauryapure 'vatāra|januṣī,
śrī|Raivat'|âdrau punar
dīkṣā|kevala|nirvṛtiḥ samagamat
tasy' âsya Nemi|prabhoḥ
vyākhyāyāṃ tri|daśāḥ pramoda|viviśā,
ete daś' âpy anyadā,
vanditvā bhagavantam ukta|vidhinā,
cyuty'|âvadhiṃ tuṣṭuvuḥ.

In the assembly hall named Good Law, attended by their courtiers, blessed by preceding gods shouting, "Victory, prosperity, long life!," having attained complete pleasure in every organ of sense, as if their wishes had been granted, they passed a long time desiring to have performed all manner of concerts. 12.150

One day, in the annual assembly of the king of the gods, those ten dwellers among the gods met, and at the sight of each other a pure affection was born. Through the employment of their ability to perceive beyond the normal range of the senses, as before they became the finest friends.

Then, after leaving the assembly, they continued to meet in the same place, and at the sight of their equal mutual prosperity they shared equal contentment. Then sometimes, 12.155
like swans, they played in pools, and sometimes in gardens, like bees, they played games with flowers. Sometimes they played on the peaks of mountains, like deer, sometimes in lakes filled with lotuses like chakra birds. Sometimes, too, they made pilgrimages to the Island of Rejoicing and sometimes celebrated the auspicious occasions of the Jina's birth, et cetera. They enjoyed these and other enjoyments, like the seeds of the fruit of their good actions, in company together as if subject to a single mind.

One day, at a sermon of Lord Nemi, whose descent from heaven and birth were in lovely Shaurya·pura, and whose renunciation, attainment of omniscience and final dissolution were on Mount Ráivata, those gods, full of spontaneous joy, and those ten, too, bowed to the lord and praised his attainments of omniscience with a spoken recitation.

12.160 «jaya, jagat|traya|kalpa|mahī|ruha,
tri|jagad|arcita|pāda|payo|ruha,
bhava|dav'|ânala|nirdalan'|âmbuda,
pramada|mandira Nemi|Jin'|ēśvara!
dhuri kuraṅga|mad'|āvila|vakṣasā
su|parirabhya vṛto 'si śiva|śriyā,
iti kil' âmbu|da|sodara|dīdhitis
tvam asi Rājamatī|vimukhas tathā.
prati|dinaṃ viṣam'|āyudha|saṃkathā|
prathana|hetutayā narak'|āvahā,
samucitaṃ khalu rājya|matis tvayā
samam amucyata Rājamatī ca sā.
gatavat" ā|yudha|dhāmani vādite
kutukato bhavatā Hari|vāri|je,
yad abhavat kila śabda|mayaṃ jagad,
bhuvana|śabda|mayatva|gatis tataḥ.
vitata|mūla|kadambaka|moha|saṃ-
jñita|mahattama|tāla|mahī|ruhaḥ,
madana|mastaka|sūci|visūtraṇāj,
Jina|pate, bhavat" âiva viśoṣitaḥ.
12.165 Jina|śiv'|âṅgaja|śakti|dharaṃ sphuṭaṃ
ghana|suhṛt|kamanīya|mahā|ruce,
nanu kumāra|vareṇa su|tejasā
yadi paraṃ, bhavatā vyatatāra kaḥ.
śiva|purī|patha|sṛṣṭi|karo bhavāṃs
tri|jagatī|jana|rakṣṇa|vicakṣaṇaḥ
sakala|duṣ|kṛta|saṃhṛti|kṛc ca tan,
nahi paraṃ puruṣ'|ântaram iṣyate.

"Hail, you earth-based wishing-tree for the threefold universe, you whose lotus-feet are worshipped by the triple universe, you rain cloud for the extinguishing of the forest fire of existence, you temple of joy, you lord of Jinas, Nemi. 12.160

Because you have been tightly embraced at the head by the breast of an antelope flurried with musk, and you are endowed with the good fortune of final emancipation, your splendor is indeed akin to a cloud and you are averse to Raja·mati.*

Since your purpose is every day to expound in sermons rugged nonviolence, your intelligence, which leads away from hell, is rightly royal, and you rightly gave up Raja·mati. You reached the abode of nonviolence, and caused it to resound with eagerness, you yellow lotus born in the lineage of Krishna, so that the universe was actually made to consist of sound, and then, through the world's consisting of sound, its destination.

You are the one, Lord Jina, who made the mighty palm tree known as delusion, a *kadámba* tree with spreading roots, wither, by throwing into confusion the sharp points of the leaves of passion at its crest.

You who have the radiance of a longed-for friendly cloud made manifest, bearing the power born of the final emancipation of the Jina, who passed over, if not by means of you, excellent prince of mighty splendor. 12.165

You are the creator of the path to the city of final emancipation, the visible protector of the people of the threefold universe. You are the destroyer of all bad actions. Consequently nothing further is desired among mankind.

namad|amartya|śiro|maṇi|mālikā|
dyuti|taraṅgavatī|vimala|kramaḥ,
su|bhaga|sīmatayā kila nirvṛti|
priyatam' âika|pate bhavate namaḥ.»
iti nava|stavan'|ôpaday" ânayā
yad u nar'|êndra|kul'|âmbara|bhāsvataḥ
Jina|pater amṛt'|ēśitur āmṛtīṃ
śriyamitā iva te dyu|sado 'bhavat.

bhagavantam anujñāpy', āsitvā siṃh'|āsaneṣu te,
ek'|âika|bāhoḥ praty|ekaṃ dvā|triṃśat pātrikā vyadhuḥ.

tataś ca:

12.170 vīṇā|veṇu|mṛdaṅga|śaṅkha|tilimā|
ḍakkā|huḍukk'|ādikān
bibhrāṇaiś catur|aṣṭabhiḥ su|ruciraiḥ
strī|puṃsa|pātraiḥ pṛthak,
śrī|Nemeḥ puratas tri|loka|janatā|
cetaś|camat|kārakam
kṛtvā nāṭya|vidhiṃ, praṇamya ca punaḥ,
papracchur ete prabhum:

«prabho, kadā naś cyavanaṃ, kṣetre 'vataraṇaṃ kva ca,
kutaḥ sambodhanaṃ, siddhiḥ kad" êti pratipādaya.»

«mayi siddhe, mama tīrthe divaś cyutv" âtra Bhārate
Sūr'|ātma|devāt sambuddhāḥ setsyath',» êty avadat prabhuḥ.

tatas tuṣṭāḥ samutthāya Sūra|dev'|âmaraṃ pare
nav' âpi vinayād ūcur, «vayaṃ bodhyās tvay", ânagha.

Your course is purified by an ocean of splendor of garlands, the crest-jewels of bowing gods, as you assuredly proceed in a straight line of good fortune. Reverence to you, unique lord, most beloved in restraint."

Thus, with this respectful gift of a hymn of praise, those gods were like brilliant suns in the sky of the families of kings, as they honored the immortality of the Lord Jina, the lord of immortals. Having asked the reverend lord's permission, they sat in their lion-thrones, and one by one they created thirty-two actresses from each of their arms.

And then:

Having put on a show of music and dancing before the 12.170
Lord Jina, the cause of astonishment to the inhabitants of the triple universe by means of each of the troops of male and female actors of brilliant appearance and bearing lutes, flutes, conches, trumpets, bass drums, tamborines and such, they bowed to the lord and asked once more:

"Lord, inform us when our falling away from heaven will occur, in what land we will descend, in what manner we will be enlightened, and when we will achieve final liberation."

The lord said, "At the time of my final liberation in my holy place of passing over, you will fall from heaven. There in Bhárata, enlightened by the god Sura himself, you will achieve final liberation."

Then, delighted, the other nine stood up together and respectfully addressed the god Sura, "We are to be enlightened by you, stainless one.

kuru pratijñām atr'|ârthe, yena syān no mano|dhṛtiḥ.»

so 'vag, «dhruvaṃ kariṣye 'do, m" âiv' âtr'|ârthe viṣīdata.»

12.175 āsannasya ca n' āsanna|siddhī|saṅg'|ôtsava|śruteḥ

viṣād'|ānandau bibhrāṇā vārdhivad garal'|âmṛte

daś' âpi devās te prāptāḥ sva|vimāneṣu vegataḥ,

vimāna|devī|ratn'|ādi śocanti sma muhur|muhuḥ.

cint"|ācāntāḥ kara|talpa|śāyi|mukh'|âmbujāḥ

kṣaṇaṃ kṣaṇaṃ varṣam iva yāvan nirvāhayanti te,

tāvad vāt'|āhata|dīpa iva, yad v" êndra|jālavat,

Jayaśāsana'|rṣi|devo dadhe 'kasmād a|darśanam.

itaś c' âtr' âiva Bharate manīṣita|sura|drumaḥ

samudra|vel"|ôpanīta|ratna|rocir|vibhās|varaḥ,

12.180 uddaṇḍa|padma|ṣaṇḍ'|āḍhya|sarasī|kula|saṅkulaḥ ,

campak'|âśoka|mākanda|puṃnāg'|ôdyāna|mālitaḥ,

nālikerī|nāga|vallī|drākṣā|maṇḍapa|maṇḍitaḥ, chinna elā|lavaṅga|kakkola|karpūra|vana|bandhuraḥ,

candan'|ônmedur'|āmod'|āmodit'|âśeṣa|diṅ|mukhaḥ chinna nāmnā Malaya|viṣayo deśo deś'|ôttamo 'sti, bhoḥ.

Make a promise, so that our minds be assured about this matter." He said, "I will certainly do it. By no means be dejected about this matter."

And on hearing of their end they were borne along in 12.175
despair and happiness, like the ocean in poison and nectar, not celebrating their assured association with final liberation. And the ten gods quickly returned to their celestial vehicles, and every moment felt regret for their celestial vehicles, goddesses and jewels, et cetera.

Sipping cares, the lotuses of their faces rested on the beds of their hands, and every moment they waited seemed like a year, when the god-sage Jaya·shásana, like a torch blown out by the wind, or, rather, like a magic illusion, suddenly disappeared.

Now, here in this very continent of Bhárata, a longed-for wishing-tree, its splendor made brilliant by the rays from
the jewels brought up by the current of the ocean; filled 12.180
with many lakes abounding in clumps of lotuses with upraised stalks; garlanded with gardens of fragrant *chámpaka* trees, *ashóka* trees, mango trees and white lotuses: ornamented with arbors of coconut trees, snake creepers, and vines; beatified with groves of cardamom trees, cloves, aromatic *kakkóla* plants and camphor plants; its every direction perfumed by the diffused fragrance of dense sandalwood, there is a country named the Málaya region, the finest country, sirs.

yatra grāmaḥ sa no, yatra nipānāḥ pañca|sapta na
na tan nipānaṃ, yat pañca|sapta|deva|kula|śri na.
na tad deva|kulaṃ, yatra vyākhy"|ôrvyaḥ pañca|sapta na.
vyākhy"|ôrvī sā, na yā pañca|sapta|cchātra|śat'|ânvitā.
12.185 na sac|chātro 'sti, yaḥ pañca|sapta|śāstrāṇi n' âbudhat
na tac chāstraṃ, yatra petuḥ śakalāḥ pañca|sapta na.
tatra cchatram iv' ônnamraṃ,
kamraṃ sarva|kakup|śriyām,
datt'|âr'|îbh'|âṅkuś'|āvartaṃ
Kuśāvartam abhūt puram.
mudryante sarasāṃ padmāḥ paurāṇāṃ yatra, no punaḥ
daṇḍo vijṛmbhate rājñāṃ nāgarāṇāṃ na jātu cit.
tac chaśāsa viśām īśo nāmnā śrī|Jayaśekharaḥ,
mah"|āhave mahā|bāhor yasy' êva jaya|śekharaḥ.
pratāpa|tapano yasya cakre para|mahaḥ kṣitau,
nirācakre ca yad asau tad aho kautukaṃ mahat.
12.190 devī|madhu|vratī|vrāta|kāmya|saubhāgya|mañjarī
babhūva tasya devasya devī Bhuvanamañjarī.
lajj" âti|sajjā sadhrīcī pronmīlac|chīla|kelibhiḥ
yasyāḥ prasādhayāñcakre 'lañcakre ca vapur|latām.
sukh'|âmbhodhi|vigāhinyās tasyāḥ śukter iv' ôdare
Jayaśāsana|dev'|ātmā mukt"|ābhaḥ so 'vatāram ait.
tadā ca Kārttika|jyautsnī|śeṣe 'śeṣe hit'|āvaham
mukhe viśantaṃ bhāsvantaṃ vīkṣya bhūpasya devy avak.
rājñā ca svapna|vijñaiś ca tat|sv|apnā|svapna|bhūruhaḥ

In which there is indeed that village, in which there are thirty-five lakes; there is indeed that lake which has the luster of thirty-five temples. There is indeed that temple in which there are thirty-five extensive lecture rooms. There is indeed that extensive lecture room which is endowed with thirty-five hundred students. There is indeed that good student 12.185
who knows thirty-five texts. There is indeed that text in which thirty-five sections occur.

In that country, like a lofty parasol desirous of the wealth of heaven, guided by the elephant hook of the gift of the faithful, was the city of Kushavárta. In which millions had been coined for the lakes of its citizens, but in which the punishment of the King was not at all extended over the citizens.

A king of the people named His Majesty Jaya·shékhara ruled over it, whose mighty arms had seen the summit of victory in great battles. The sun of his majesty created another splendor for the world. If he was opposed in anything, that was indeed a great wonder.

The blossom of his beauty longed for by the swarm of 12.190
bees that were queens, that King's queen was Bhúvana·mánjari. Modesty, her firmly attached constant companion, had beautified and adorned the creeper of her body with the signs of manifest morality.

The soul of the god Jaya·shásana descended, like a pearl in an oyster shell, into the womb of the Queen, who had plunged into the ocean of prosperity. And then, at the end of a full-moon night in autumn, she dreamed that the sun was entering her mouth, bringing what is salutary to all. She told the King. The King told interpreters of dreams, phalaṃ nyavedi mārtaṇḍa|pracaṇḍa|tanay'|ôdayaḥ.

12.195 sampūrṇ'|âṅgeṣv aśeṣeṣu māseṣu ca nirāmayā
tanayaṃ suṣuve devī prāc" îv' â|hima|rociṣam.
mahī|bhuj" âtha sva|rājy'|âbhiṣek'|ôtsavato 'dhikaḥ
pure viracayāñcakre putra|janma|mah"|ôtsavaḥ.

janm'|ôtsav'|âty|utsavena pitṛ|ṣvasrā Jayaśriyā
putrasya Samarasena iti nāma vinirmame.
dhātribhir iva rājñībhir nṛpair bāla|dharair iva
kumāraḥ śiśriye rūpa|śriy" êva vinaya|śriyā.
krameṇa ca kal"|ācāryas taṃ kalābhir apūrayat,
niṣkal'|ābha|gauraveṇa kal"|ācāryaṃ tv, aho, nṛpaḥ.

12.200 tri|loka|straiṇa|saundarya|sāram ādāya yatnataḥ
yāsāṃ sṛṣṭiḥ sṛṣṭi|kṛtā, manye, nirupamā kṛtā,
mahā|sāmanta|kanyās tāḥ catur|aṣṭ" âpi c' âikadā
vivāhayan kumāreṇa vicchardeṇa mahīyasā,
kal"|ācāryeṇa pariṇāyitaṃ dvā|saptatiṃ kalāḥ
taṃ dṛṣṭvā kṛpaṇaṃ|manyo, manye, 'bhūj Jayaśekharaḥ.

śrī|kumār'|âvataṃsāya śrī|prāsād'|âvataṃsakam
dvā|triṃśad|vallabhā|vāsa|parikṣiptaṃ pitā dadau.
tatra dvā|triṃśatā dārair udārair vilasann asau
tārābhiḥ sapta|viṃśatyā śliṣṭaṃ tār'|ēśam atyagāt.

who informed him that the fruit of the tree of the dream of that very fortunate woman was her pregnancy with a son as fiery as the sun.

Having fulfilled her days and months in good health, the 12.195
Queen gave birth to a son, like the east giving birth to the radiant sun. Then the King caused to be celebrated in the city a great festival for the birth of his son, greater than the festival at his coronation.

Full of great joy at the birth celebration, his father's sister Jaya·shri gave the boy the name Sámara·sena. The Prince was resorted to by queens like nurses and kings like child carriers, the radiance of his good behavior like that radiance of his body. And in due course a master of arts enriched him with all the arts, but, oh!, the King enriched the master of arts with a respectful gift of unbroken splendor.

Created without rivals by the creative goddess, I suppose, 12.200
who created them with great effort by taking the essence of the beauty of the women of the triple universe, they, the thirty-two maiden daughters of eminent barons, were married to the Prince with huge expenditures. Jaya·shékhara, having seen him married to the seventy-two arts by the master of arts, was considered stingy, I suppose.

His father gave that garland of a radiant prince a garland of a radiant palace encircled by the dwellings of his thirty-two wives. Appearing brilliant as he sported there with his thirty-two exalted wives, he surpassed the moon, the lord of the stars, united with his twenty-seven stars.

12.205 yauvanena vayo|rājñā yuva|rājaṃ kṛtaṃ purā
tam mṛṣṭvā yauva|rājye 'pi sthāpayan n' â|tuṣan nṛpaḥ.
kumāraḥ Samaraseno rāja|pāṭyāṃ kutūhalī
mahīyas" âśva|thaṭṭena jagām' ôdyānam anyadā.
tatr' âśva|khura|śabdena bhīta|bhīto 'tha jambukaḥ
palāyamāno dadṛśe kumāreṇ' â|vidūrataḥ.
tataś ca yauvan'|ônmādān nirvivekatayā hṛdaḥ
tad|vadhāya kumāreṇa mumuce 'śvo 'ti|vegataḥ.
sa ciraṃ khedito mṛtyu|bhītyā naśyan van'|ântare
nṛ|siṃhena, hahā, tena śalyen' âghāni jambukaḥ.
12.210 praśaṃsitaḥ pāpa|mitraiḥ kumāro 'tha praharṣulaḥ
yadā tadā ku|mitr'|ôktyā krīḍay" ākheṭakaṃ vyadhāt.
dṛṣṭvā varāham anyedyur dur|dharaṃ siṃha|potavat
kumāraḥ prerayāmāsa turaṅgam amum prati.
palāyate 'bhyeti v" ôccair bibhety udbheṣayaty api,
kātaraś ca pravīraś ca mlecchavac chū|karo 'bhavat.
kumāras tu tasya pṛṣṭhaṃ kathañ cana mumoca na,
prajahāra ca taṃ kolaṃ. ko 'laṃ tiryaṅ naraṃ prati?
prahaten' âpi ten' âśva|pad" ôcchedyata daṃṣṭriṇā,
mriyamāṇo mārayate kātaro 'pi hi śūravat.
12.215 chinn'|âṃhris turago vegān nipapāta mahī|tale,
kumāras tata utphalya turaṅg'|ântaram āśrayat.
niruñchitaḥ kumāro 'tha pāpa|mitrair muhur|muhuḥ
stutaś ca śū|kar'|ākheṭaṃ mene śaurya|kaṣ'|ôpalam.

Having discerned that he had already been made a crown 12.205
prince by the aged King that was his youth, the King was delighted to appoint him to the rank of crown prince.

One day, Prince Sámara·sena, intent on a royal progress, with a great troop of horses, arrived at a park. And there the Prince saw a jackal, extremely frightened by the sound of the horses' hooves, fleeing in the near distance.

Then, his mind lacking discrimination in the madness of his youth, he let his horse fly at a gallop in order to kill it. For a long time the jackal tried to hide in the wood, afflicted with the fear of death, but, shame!, that lion of a prince pierced it with his spear.

Then, since he was praised by his wicked friends, the 12.210
Prince was elated, and he then took up the amusement of hunting at the behest of his bad friends.

The next day, he saw a boar, difficult to withstand, and like a young lion urged on his horse toward it. Running away and charging forward, extremely frightened, but still the cause of fear, the boar, making a *shu* sound like a foreigner, became both cowardly and heroic.

But the Prince somehow managed to stick to its back and, less than a man, struck the boar, a man of a beast. As it died, it struck the foot of the horse with a blow from its
tusk. Although cowardly, it certainly died like a hero. Its 12.215
foot wounded, the horse immediately fell to the ground. Then the Prince jumped up and mounted another horse.

Then, continually thronged and praised by his wicked friends, he considered that boar hunting was the touchstone of heroism.

tataś ca:

pitṛ|vākyaṃ rājya|kāryaṃ puram antaḥ|puraṃ tathā
kumāro gaṇayāmāsa sva|śarīra|sukhaṃ ca na.
divā|niśam asau kin tu prāṇi|saṃhāra|kāriṇīm
mṛgayāṃ racayāmās' ājanm' âpy ākheṭikaḥ kila.

yataḥ:

krīḍ" êti prathamaṃ kutūhala|rasair
badhnāti mūlaṃ manāg.
utkarṣād apakarṣataś ca tad anu
prauḍhiṃ parāṃ gacchati.
ākramya kramataḥ kriy"|ântaram atha
prāpt'|ôdayaṃ bādhate.
vṛddhaṃ hi vyasanaṃ śanaiḥ su|manasām
apy eka|kāry'|āyate.

12.220 kṣaṇe 'tra, bhoḥ, siṃha|rāja|pratibodha|kṣaṇo 'dhunā
vimṛśy' êti Śūra|sādhu|devas tatra samāyayau.
prātar maṅgala|velāyām a|dṛśyam ca pur|ambare
Bhādr'|âbda|sodara|ravaḥ prārebhe paṭhituṃ yathā:

«hanti yaḥ śaraṇ'|āyātāṃs, tasya kā, deva, śūratā?
kathaṃ na śaraṇ'|āyātā ye tava kṣmā|talaṃ śritāḥ?
nirāyudhān kṣmā|tala|sthān varma|hīnān nihanti yaḥ
ghor'|āyudho hay'|ārūḍho varmito vīrat" âsya kā?
dhik pauruṣaṃ, vikramaṃ dhig,
dākṣyaṃ dhig, dhik ca śemuṣīm,
kāndiśīkān sṛgāl'|ādīn
nara|kesariṇāṃ ghnatām!

And then:

The Prince paid no heed to his parents' advice, the duties of government, the city, the court alike; not even to the comfort of his own body. But day and night he was intent on hunting, the cause of the destruction of living beings. Indeed, he was a hunter even from his birth.

Since:

Amusement first fixes its root with the waters of curiosity, with slight increase and attraction. After that it attains full growth. In due course interruption of business steps forth and troubles prosperity that has been gained, bringing the gradual destruction of the wealth even of the wise, in their devotion to only one thing.

At that moment, good sirs, the sage-god Shura, consid- 12.220
ering that it was now time for the enlightenment of the lion-king, arrived at that place. And at the time of morning blessing, on the outskirts of the city, with a sound like a rain cloud of autumn, he, invisible, recited thus:

"What heroism has he, Your Highness, who slaughters those who are seeking protection? Are not those who resort to the surface of your land seekers of protection? What heroism has he who, possessed of fearsome weapons, mounted on a horse and armored, slaughters those without weapons, situated on the ground, and devoid of armor? Shame on the manly bravery, shame on the cleverness, shame on the wisdom of those lions of men who slaughter fleeing jackals and suchlike!

12.225 tiraścā śū|kareṇ' âpi śastra|hīnena bhīruṇā
yuddhe palāyate yas tu, bhaṭa|vādo 'sya kīdṛśaḥ?
nṛ|siṃha, pūrva|puṃbhis te n' êdam ācaritaṃ kva cit,
pāpāt tad asmād virama, ramasva Jina|saṃyame.
sva|kṛtaṃ duṣ|kṛtaṃ bhogyaṃ n' âtra raṅko, na bhū|patiḥ.
viram' âsmāt tataḥ pāpāt, kiṃ bah'|ûktaiḥ, kṛt'|īśvara?»
niśamy' êti kumāreṇa proce, «'pāṭhy adya kena bhoḥ?»
maṅgala|pāṭhakair ūce, «ken' âpy a|prekṣya|varṣmaṇā.»
tataḥ kumāraḥ prage 'pi mṛgayāyāṃ gato rayāt.
samāyātaś ca madhy'|âhne, majjito bubhuje ca saḥ.
12.230 vilipya c' ânta|tāmbūla āsthāne tasthivān mudā
kṣaṇe 'tra sa punar devaḥ samāgān naṭa|peṭakī.
dṛṣṭvā kumāro vijñaptas tena prastāva|vedinā
«prekṣasva prekṣaṇaṃ, deva.» kumāreṇ' âpy urīkṛtam.
tataś ca:
raṅga|bhūḥ sajjayāñcakre gṛhītā varṇak'|ādayaḥ
ātody'|ādy|upakaraṇaṃ sarvaṃ ca praguṇīkṛtaṃ.
pratiṣṭhitaḥ pūrva|raṅgo, nṛtyaṃ gītaṃ ca nirmitaṃ,
Śūra|deva|naṭo raṅgād gātum evaṃ pracakrame:
«yāvan na cakre mṛgayā muni|kevali|nirmitā,
tāvan na prāpyate, svāmin, śarma duḥkh'|ôrmi|varjitam.
12.235 tad, deva, tan manībhūy' ântar|aṅgāṃ mṛgayāṃ śṛṇu,
hṛd|vṛttir ity aṭavy asti vikalp'|ôru|tar'|ûnnatā.

But he who flees from a fight with an animal, even a boar, 12.225
unarmed and timid, what heroic praises are due to him! Lion of a man, this conduct of yours was never undertaken by your ancestors, so desist from this wickedness and delight in the restraint of the Jina. Your behavior is very wicked, to be endured in neither a beggar nor a King. So desist from this wickedness. What need of more words, you lord of creation?"

He became silent. The Prince asked, "Who recited the morning blessing today, sirs?" The reciters of blessings replied, "Someone whose body couldn't be seen."

Then the Prince, as soon as it was daybreak, went on a hunt. He returned at midday, then bathed and dined.
Anointed with unguent, and having finished chewing betel, 12.230
the Prince remained making merry in the hall. At that moment that god returned once more in the guise of a strolling actor. He looked at the Prince, and, knowing that the moment was favorable, requested him, "Watch my show, Your Highness." The Prince assented.

And then:

Putting on the show, he got himself ready, taking the costumes and preparing his paraphernalia of bongos and such. When the prologue was over, and there had been a performance of dancing and music, the actor-god Shura proceeded to recite from the stage thus:

"As long as that hunting is not undertaken which is aimed at the omniscience of an ascetic, no happiness can be obtained, only waves of unhappiness. So, Your Highness, take 12.235
this to heart and learn about internal hunting. The activity

mithyātv'|ādyā nivasanti kirayas tatra bhūrayaḥ,
darśana|jñān'|āvaraṇa|moh'|ântarāyakā mṛgāḥ.
vedanīya|nāma|gotr'|āyūṃṣi go|māyavas tathā,
kārmaṇa|vargaṇā|śaṣpa|carvaṇ'|ânarva|vigrahāḥ.
nānā|vikalpa|dru|ṣaṇḍa|cchāyāsv ābaddha|goṣṭhayaḥ
nirītayaś cir'|āyuṣkā nityam ev' â|kuto|bhayāḥ.

tatra yāhi tvam ādāya jīva|vīryaṃ mahā|dhanuḥ,
paridhāya ca cāritr'|âḍḍanaṃ sarv'|âṅga|maṇḍanam.
12.240 pṛṣṭhe baddhvā su|leśeṣu dharma|dhyāna|niṣaṅgakam,
śīl'|âṅga|sahasra|vyādhair hṛd|vṛttiṃ pariveṣṭya ca,
tasyā madhye 'py udīry'|ākhyāṃ
śakaṭ'|ôrvy|ābha|saṃsthitim
kṛtvā niṣeddhuṃ taj|jīvān
kṣapaka|śreṇi|sad|vṛtim,
a|pūrva|karaṇe sthitvā gupty" âdhijyaṃ vidhāya ca
vīrya|cāpaṃ suleśyeṣvā ghātayāṇa|kuraṅgakān.

kṣipa krameṇa mithyātva|miśra|samyaktva|śūkarān,
pratyākhyān'|â|pratyākhyān'|âināṃś ca ten' êṣuṇ" âikadā.
gatī tiryaṅ|nārakayor ānupūrvyau tathā tayoḥ,
a|paryāptam eka|dvi|tri|catur|indriya|jātikāḥ.
12.245 sthāvar'|ātapa|mu|dyota|sūkṣma|sādhāraṇāni ca
styāna'|rddhi|trikam aṣṭānāṃ śeṣaṃ c' âik'|êṣuṇā kṣipa.

of the mind is a forest, lofty with the trees of mental imaginings. Mistaken views and suchlike are the hogs that live there in great numbers; obstacles to insight, to knowledge and to the prevention of delusion are the deer. Karmas that pertain to feelings, birth destination, family and life span are jackals, likewise. Feelings of possessiveness are the irresistible ruminating animals of the divisions of karma. Their pens are enclosed in the shade of groves of trees of various imaginings, free from affliction and long lived, yes, always causing sudden fear.

So go there, with your mighty sword, and undertake the heroism of the soul. Gird yourself around with the shield of asceticism, an ornament for every body. Bind to your back 12.240
the quiver of religious meditation on very brilliant matters, and wrap a fence around your heart with the thousand stakes of the constituents of morality, having made in the midst of it the defensive formation with the axle of a cart called 'standing in a upright defensive posture,' which, to settle their souls, is the true fence of the rows of the ascetics. Stand with restraint in the stage of previously unrealized thought, and, having fitted the taut bowstring to the bow of heroism, in pure contemplation slaughter the antelopes.

At the same time with that arrow kill the boar of false, mixed and blurred belief and also the deer of the obstacles to partial renunciation and complete renunciation. Destroy with one arrow the future succession of the birth destinations of animal and hell-being, and the boundless births of creatures with one, two, three and four senses, and the 12.245

tato napuṃsakaṃ vedaṃ, strī|vedaṃ ca mṛgāvatha,
hāsy'|ādīn mṛga|dārāṃś ca ṣaḍ eken' êṣuṇā kṣiṇu.
tataḥ puruṣa|vedaṃ ca kuraṅgaṃ hindhi patriṇā,
tataḥ saṃjvalana|krodha|māna|māyā|mṛgān kramāt.

tri|khaṇḍaṃ lobha|sāraṅgaṃ kṛtvā dve śakale dale,
khaṇḍaṃ tṛtīyaṃ saṃkhyātān khaṇḍān kṛtvā kṣaṇāt kṣipa.

dvābhyāṃ kṣaṇābhyām a|prāptaḥ
kevalaṃ prathame kṣaṇe
ghātaya pracalā|nidre
deva|gaty" ânupūrvike

12.250 vaikriyaṃ tīrtham āhārān'|ādi|saṃhananāni ca
saṃsthānakaṃ c' ânyatarad yauga|padyāt trayo|daśa.

kṣaṇe 'ntime jñāna|vighna|daśakaṃ dṛk|catuṣkakam
hatv" âika|bāṇena bhaja kevalaṃ vijaya|śriyam!

bhav'|āupagrāhi|karmāṇi pherūn duḥ|śakun'|ôpamān
tiraskṛty" â|kṣaya|sukhaṃ mokṣam āpnuhi, dhī|nidhe.

iti hatvā matyā nirdaya|vṛttyā c' ântar'|âri|paśu|vṛndam iti
śiva|padam a|cirād api gaccha sukhād api hitvā mala|mayam
aṅgam iti.»

iti s'|âbhinayaṃ tena naṭen' ākheṭa āntare
gīte pramuditā saṃsat sarva|svaṃ dātum aihata.

minute collective forms, in the heat of the pyre of constant asceticism, and the remnants of the thirty-two dense prosperities.

Next, hunt the desire for a hermaphrodite and the desire for a woman, kill with one arrow the six wild beasts of laughter, et cetera. Then kill with your arrow the antelope of desire for a man and in turn the deer of smoldering passion, anger, pride and deceit.

Having divided the antelope of greed into three pieces, two fragmented pieces and the third, having reckoned up the pieces, destroy them in the moment.

Unobtained in two moments, only in one moment, slaughter in the sleep of confusion, with the birth destination of a god, and the holy place subject to change, and 12.250
the destruction of taking food, et cetera, the other end simultaneously, thirteen.

At the final moment, kill with one arrow the tenfold obstacles to knowledge with foursquare eyes, and enjoy the glory of victory, omniscience!

Having removed the jackals of the karmas that entail existence, like birds of ill omen, attain the imperishable bliss, final liberation, you ocean of intelligence.

Thus having slaughtered, with deliberation and in a pitiless manner, that herd of animals of your internal enemies, go instantaneously to the abode of final liberation, having gladly abandoned your body, formed from impurity."

Delighted by the actor's singing of internal hunting, which he had accompanied with dramatic gestures, the assembly desired to give him all its wealth.

12.255 atha cintayāñcakāra kumāraḥ sthira|dhāraṇaḥ:
«aye prābhātika|pāṭhi|prāyaḥ ko 'py eṣa no pumān?»
vyājahāra kumāro 'tha, «bho bhoḥ, su|kṛti|śekhara,
naṭa|rūpeṇ' âmunā kiṃ? svaṃ rūpaṃ prakaṭī|kuru!»
prādur|āsīt tato divy'|âlaṅkārair bhāsuraḥ suraḥ,
jagāda ca śrī|kumāraṃ, «s'|âvadhānaṃ niśāmaya!
rantvā ratna|vimāneṣu kiṃ rajasya|śma|veśmaṣu?
tyaktvā ca tān ratna|rāśīn kā saktir maline dhane?
bhuktvā taruṇīr divyā rāgo '|śucya|balāsu kaḥ?
bhuktvā c' âṃśuka|bhūṣās tāḥ kutsit'|â|svāsu kā ratiḥ?
12.260 divy'|âṅga|rāgair ālipy' âṅga|rāgeṣv eṣu kā spṛhā?
sthitvā tādṛk|parīvāre kā khale 'tra jane sthitiḥ?»
kumāro vyāharat, «suṣṭhu! tvay" âśikṣ' îndra|jālakam.
tato 'smi tuṣṭo, yācasva sv'|êcchayā sva|manīṣitam.»
suro 'tha cintayāmāsa, «hā kim evaṃ lapaty asau?
dur|labha|bodhiko 'yaṃ kiṃ, yad ity ukto na budhyate?»
prayukt'|âvadhinā tena jñātaṃ, n' êty eṣa bhotsyate,
tat prāpy' âvasaraṃ kiñ cid bodhyo 'yam, iti cetasā
suro dṛśy'|êtaro jajñe peṭakaṃ c' âsya dhāmavat
smitvā kumāro 'vak, «ko 'pi mohayiṣyati mām api!»

Then the Prince, firm of understanding, thought, "Now, reciters usually come in the morning, so what kind of a man have we here?" 12.255

Then the Prince exclaimed, "Good sir, good sir, you peak of benevolence, what need of acting of this nature? Make manifest your true nature!"

Then the radiant god made himself visible wearing his divine ornaments and said to His Highness the Prince, "Listen with attention.

Having delighted in jeweled celestial vehicles, what delight in the dwellings of bodies of dust? And, having abandoned those heaps of jewels, why addiction to impure treasure? Having enjoyed the young women of heaven, what delight in the daughters of the impure? And, having enjoyed those ornamented garments, what delight in those
whose poverty is despised? Having been anointed with di- 12.260
vine unguents, what desire for these unguents? Having stayed among such a retinue, what desire to remain among earthly subjects?"

The Prince said, "Well done! You've taught me a magic trick, so I'm pleased. Ask for whatever you desire."

Then the god thought, "Ah, why is he babbling like this? He is difficult to enlighten. Why doesn't he become enlightened after being spoken to like this?"

Having realized by employing his supernatural powers of perception that he would not be enlightened like that but that he would be enlightened if he took some favorable opportunity, the god disappeared, and his powerful company also. The Prince smiled and said, "Some people can delude even me!"

12.265 dvitīye 'hni namaskṛtya pitaraṃ Jayaśekharam
tad|āsthāna|sarasy asthāt kumāro rāja|haṃsavat.
anye 'pi mantri|sāmanta|pramukhā rāja|pauruṣāḥ
cakravāk'|ādaya iva niṣedus tatra sarvataḥ.

atr' ântare Candrapurāc Candraśekhara|bhū|pateḥ
dūtas tatr' āgato natv" ôpaviṣṭo, 'pracchi bhū|bhujā.

«kac cit Candraśekharasya, mat|svasuś ca Jayaśriyaḥ
tat|putra|Haricandrasya kuśalaṃ?» «sarvato 'pi hi.
deva|dev'|âtivātsalyāc chreyo 'sty ev' âsya, kiṃ punaḥ,
yakṣiṇī|dhātuvād'|ādau Haricandrasya kautukam.
12.270 anyadā yogin" âikena yakṣiṇī|mantra īritaḥ,
kumāro 'pṛcchat tac|chaktiṃ, yogy uvāca, ‹śṛṇu, prabho.
yady eṣā yakṣiṇī sidhyet, tadā vaśyaṃ jagad bhavet,
kośo '|kṣayo, vyomni gatis, tad ārādhaya yakṣiṇīm.›

kumāreṇ' âiṣa papracche, ‹ko nv asyāḥ sādhanā|vidhiḥ?›
so 'vak, ‹kṛṣṇa|caturdaśyāṃ śmaśāne 'yuta|jāpataḥ.
nṛ|māṃsa|pala|sāhasra|homāt sidhyati yakṣiṇī,
uttara|sādhako 'smy eko 'nye catvāraś catur|diśi.
bibhīṣikās' ûtthitāsu jāp'|âik'|âgryaṃ viśeṣataḥ
mad|uktaṃ c' ādarāt kāryaṃ.› kumāreṇa pratiśrutam.

On the following day, the Prince bowed to his father, 12.265
Jaya·shékhara, and took his place in the lake of his assembly like a regal swan. And the other of the King's followers, too, the ministers and barons at their head, like chakra-cawers and other kinds of bird, settled all around in it.

At that moment a messenger from King Chandra·shé-khara in Chandra·pura arrived at that assembly, bowed, sat down and was asked by the King:

"Are Chandra·shékhara, my sister Jaya·shri and their son, Hari·chandra, well?" "They are absolutely fine. However, although he is wealthy because of the great affection felt for him by the king of kings, Hari·chandra has become inter-
ested in demigoddess alchemy. One day a magician recited 12.270
the demigoddess spell, and the Prince asked about its power. The magician said, 'Listen, my lord. If the demigoddess manifests, then the universe is at your control: imperishable treasure and traveling through the sky. So propitiate the demigoddess.'

The Prince asked, 'When, then, should one propitiate her?' He replied, 'On the fourteenth day of the dark fortnight, in a cemetery, with a myriad of murmured invocations. The demigoddess becomes manifest by means of a thousand oblations of human flesh. I am one of her chief devotees; there are four others for the four cardinal points. When the terrible demigoddess arises, carefully perform my commands, above all pay attention to the invocations.'

12.275 tataḥ kṛṣṇa|caturdaśyām an|āpṛcchy' âiva bhū|bhujam
kumāraḥ sarva|sāmagryā śmaśāne yogi|yug yayau.
dig|rakṣake puṃś|catuṣke yoginy|uttara|sādhake
mantra|jāpaḥ samārebhe kumāreṇ' âika|cetasā.
ardha|rātraṃ kṛte home, vijity' ôgrā vibhīṣikāḥ,
pañca|māṃsa|pala|śatī juhuve nṛpa|sūnunā.

ath' âgni|kuṇḍād uttasthau vetālo vibruvann iti:
‹vidyā|sādhakam admy anuttara|sādhakam admi vā?›

bhīto yogī tato hantum ārebhe tena sa drutam.
pāpminā yogin" âth' ôce, ‹pāhi, pāhi, kumāra, mām!›

12.280 ‹mad|uktaṃ kāryam!› ity etad
vacaḥ saṃsmṛtya bhūpa|sūḥ
muktvā homaṃ, khaḍga|pāṇir
vetālaṃ pratyadhāvata.
vetālo yoginaṃ lātvā diśam ekām adhāvata,
kumāraś ca tan anveva. mah"|âraṇye gatāv ubhau.

sa vetālaḥ prage yogi|śiraś chitv" âviśad darīm.
kumāras tāṃ darīṃ roṣād ārabdha khanituṃ balāt.
vetālen' âtha huñ|cakre, patito rāja|sūr bhuvi
dāha|jvareṇa jagṛhe, patitaṃ duṣkṛtaṃ tayoḥ.

Then, on the fourteenth day of the dark fortnight, without even taking leave of the King, the Prince with all his implements went to the cremation-ground in company with the magician. As the chief devotees of the goddess formed a human square guarding the four cardinal points, the Prince began to recite the invocations with single-minded concentration. Having made the sacrifice at midnight, the Prince began to overpower and summon the cruel, fearful demigoddess by means of a hundredfold oblation of the five meats. 12.275

But then a goblin sprang out from the brazier of the fire, saying, 'Shall I eat the devotee of magic or shall I eat the chief devotee?'

Then he started to kill the terrified magician. Then the wretched magician immediately cried, 'Protect, protect me, Prince!'

Remembering what he had said—'Carry out my orders!' 12.280
—the Prince abandoned the oblation, and ran toward the goblin, carving knife in hand. The goblin snatched up the magician and ran straight ahead in the other direction, and the Prince followed behind him. They both entered a big forest.

In the morning the goblin cut off the magician's head and entered a hole in the ground. His anger forced the Prince to begin digging out the hole. Then the goblin made a loud humming sound, and the Prince fell unconscious to the ground, overpowered by a burning fever. Their criminal action had rebounded on them both.

te ca dig|rakṣiṇo martyā rāṭ|sūn'|ûkt'|ânusārataḥ
kramāt tatr' āpur, adrākṣus taṃ kumāraṃ tathā|sthitam.
12.285 tato daṇḍikayā taiḥ sa ninye Candrapuraṃ puram,
rājñaś ca darśayāñcakre tad|vṛttānt'|ôkti|pūrvakam.
tato rājā viṣaṇṇo 'pi sadyo vaidyān ajūhavat,
taiś c' ārebhe kumārasya kriyā dāha|jvar'|ôcitā.
rājñā ca yakṣiṇī śānti|karmaṇā mānitā bhṛśam
prāsīdat, svastho 'bhūt putro, jajñe vardhāpanaṃ mahat.
pitr" ânyadā sa|puruṣaṃ
śikṣāyai bhāṣitaḥ sutaḥ
‹dhig, dhig dhiyaṃ te kiṃ nyūnaṃ,
yad evaṃ kliśyase mudhā?›
etāvat" âpy âpamānam a|mānaṃ dhṛtavān hṛdi
kumāro 'lpa|parīvāraś channaṃ niśi gṛhān nirait.
12.290 nirgamāt turyam udyāhas, tad rājñā samadeśi vaḥ,
sa ced vaḥ sannidhāveti, tadā dhāryo 'tra sarvathā.»
iti yāvad asau vakti tāvad anyaḥ pumān jagau:
«āgād, deva, dvi|yojanyāṃ kumāro, vardhyase tataḥ!»
tataḥ sadyaḥ pramudito rājā vetriṇam ādiśat:
«pūḥ|śobhā kāryatāṃ vegāt, śrī|kumāro 'bhigaṃsyate.»
tataś ca sajjitāḥ sarve hasty|aśva|ratha|pattayaḥ,
rājā jay'|êbham ārohat s'|ântaraṅga|paricchadaḥ.
kumāraḥ Samarasenaḥ paṭṭa|hastinam āśrayat,
sāmantās turagān, mantri|mukhāś c' āruruhū rathān.
12.295 tataḥ sarv'|âugheṇa Haricandrasy' âbhigamaṃ prati,

Those men who had guarded the four directions, following the sound of the Prince's voice, eventually arrived there and saw the Prince in that situation. Then they took him 12.285
on a stretcher to the city of Chandra·pura and showed him to the King, explaining what had happened to him. Thereupon the King was downcast and straightaway summoned doctors, and they began to apply the treatment appropriate for a burning fever. The demigoddess, having been given great honor by the King by means of a propitiatory sacrifice, became well disposed, and the Prince became healthy. The celebration was huge.

One day, his father, in order to instruct him and his companions, said to his son, 'Alas, alas, where is your intelligence when you let yourself be tormented like that to no avail?'

So much so that the Prince, taking it to heart that his disgrace was boundless, with a small number of followers at night quietly left home. Four days and nights have passed 12.290
since he left. The King requests you, that, if he should come and attend on you, you keep him here by all means."

As he was speaking, another man said, "Your Majesty, the Prince is within two leagues, so you may cheer up!"

Thereupon the King was overjoyed and immediately ordered the chamberlain, "See that the city is beautified quickly. His Highness the Prince is approaching."

Then all the elephants, horses, carriages and footmen were prepared. The King mounted the state elephant, attended by his kinsmen. Prince Sámara·sena resorted to his elephant of rank, and the barons mounted their horses and the ministers their carriages. Then, with all his multitude, 12.295

Jayaśekhara|rāj'|êndraś cacāla calayann ilām.
krośa|mātre Haricandro nṛpam abhyetya nemivān
rājā tam aṅgam āropy' âcalan nija|puraṃ prati.
atr' ântare gaja|ghaṭā|gala|garji|śruter iva
daivād ghana|ghaṭā|garjir ujjajṛmbhe 'lpa|vṛṣṭi|kṛt.
tato 'bda|dhārā|vāhābhiḥ śliṣṭ'|ôtkṛṣṭā babhūva bhūḥ,
gandha|sār'|ôdāra|gandhān gandha|vart" îva c' âmucat.
tataḥ Samarsenasya karī Vindhy'|âṭavīṃ smaran
smar'|ātura iv' âdhāvīd, anvadhāvīd varūthinī.
12.300 dhāvamāno vāyu|vegād gajo gambhīra|vedy asau
sainya|pramuktān nārācān na mene maśakān api.
niṣādi|sādināṃ vegād gajaṃ tam anudhāvatām
tadīya|bhāgyam iva h" âstam iyāya divā|karaḥ.
tato 'ndha|kāre prasṛte tad|a|bhāgya iv' âbhitaḥ
yo yatr' âbhūt, sa tatr' âsthāt tamasā stambhitaḥ kila.
kumār'|êbhas tu tarasā gacchan nikhilayā niśā
Vindhy'|âṭavyāṃ pūrva|bhuktāṃ nadīṃ prāpa priyām iva.
atha krīḍati tatr' êbhe tata uttīrya vegataḥ
tasyās tīre payaḥ pātum upaviṣṭo nar'|êndra|sūḥ.
12.305 kṣaṇe 'tra pracchanna|cārī dadhyau Sūra|suraḥ sa ca,
«prastāvo vartate 'muṣya pratibodhāya sāmpratam.

King Jaya·shékhara moved off to meet Hari·chandra, causing the earth to move.

When they were within the range of a shout, Hari·chandra, like a wheel, ran toward the King. The King took him by his side and set off toward his city. At that moment, suddenly the rumbling of a flock of clouds broke forth, to the ear like the rumbling of a herd of rutting elephants, producing a small shower. Then the earth became tightly embraced by the currents of water streaming from the clouds, and it released the perfume of vapors of sandalwood, like a perfume merchant.

Thereupon Sámara·sena's elephant, remembering the forest of the Vindhya mountain as if lovesick, ran away, and the rest of the troop followed it. Running as fast as the wind, 12.300
the restive elephant paid no regard to the arrows shot by the army, not even as much as to gnats.

Hey! The sun suddenly set, like the good fortune of the elephant drivers and horsemen who were swiftly pursuing that elephant. Then the darkness spread around like their misfortune, and whoever entered it, there he remained, actually held fast by the gloom.

But the Prince's elephant, traveling swiftly all through the night, reached the river in the Vindhya mountain he had previously enjoyed like his beloved. Then, as his elephant sported in it, the King's son quickly dismounted and sat on its bank in order to drink water.

At that moment, the god Sura, who was traveling invisi- 12.305
ble, thought, "The right opportunity for his enlightenment is now at hand.

yataḥ:
yāvan na duḥkhaṃ saṃprāptā,
viyuktā n' êṣṭa|bāndhavaiḥ,
tāvan na prāṇinaḥ prāyo
dharmaṃ gṛhṇanti bhāvataḥ.»

tataḥ puṃ|rūpeṇa ten' âgrāhi bāhau sa rāja|sūḥ,
sa ca taṃ prāharat kṣuryā prahāro 'muṣya n' âlagat.
puṃs" ânyena tato 'muṣya churīm uddāya hastataḥ
nadyāṃ nimajjayāñcakre bhūpa|bhūr jala|kumbhavat.
kumāraḥ kṣaṇa|mātreṇa dadarśa narak'|ālayān,
param'|âdhārmik'|āhanyamāna|nānā|jan'|ôccayān.
12.310 pṛṣṭaḥ kumāreṇa pumān,
«bhoḥ, ke 'mī ghnanti nirghṛṇāḥ?
ke vā raṭanto virasaṃ
nihanyante varākakāḥ?»

pumān āha, «n' âham api samyag jāne, tataḥ, sakhe,
gatvā dvāv api pṛcchāvo.» 'tha gatvā tāv apṛcchatām.
«ke yūyam?» iti te 'py ūcuḥ «param'|â|dhārmikā vayam.»
pumān ūce «ka ime ca, kiṃ v" êmān hatha cauravat?»
param'|â|dharmiko 'vādīd «ete te nārakāḥ, sakhe,
ayaṃ ca narako. yen' âmī hanyante ca tac chṛṇu.
etena jagdhaṃ deva|svaṃ, taj|jihvā chidyate 'sya, bhoḥ.
caity'|ārcā|vighna|kṛc c' âiṣa kumbhī|pākena pacyate.
12.315 bimbā|śātanayā pāpa udbaddhaḥ śālmalī|tarau,
utsūtra|bhāṣiṇo 'sy' āsyaṃ sīvyate, nṛpa|nandana.
sādhu|dāna|niṣeddh" âyaṃ kṣudh|ārtaḥ sv'|âṅgam ādyate,
saṅghasya pratyanīko 'sāv ayo|bhrāṣṭreṣu pacyate.
sādhvī|gantā jvalad|ayaḥ|putrīm āliṅgyate balāt,

Since:

For as long as they don't meet with misfortune apart from their unwanted kinsmen, for so long embodied beings generally do not accept religion naturally."

Then, in the form of a man, he grabbed the Prince by the arm, and he struck at him with his knife, but the blow missed him. Then another man took away his knife from his hand, and submerged him in the river, like a water pot.

In the passing of a moment the Prince saw the series of hells with various heaps of people being tortured by the extremely unjust ones.

The Prince asked the man, "Sir, who are these merciless 12.310
torturers and who are these wretches who are screaming in pain as they are being tortured?"

The man said, "I don't rightly know, so, my friend, why don't the two of us go and ask?" Then they went and asked, "Who are you?," and they replied, "We are the extremely unjust ones." The man said, "Who are these, and why are you beating them like thieves?"

The extremely unjust one said, "These are the hell-beings, my friend, and this is a hell. Listen to why they are being tortured. This one who consumed a sacrifice to a god is having his tongue cut, sir. This one who made an obstacle to worship in the temple is being cooked in a cooking pot.
For plucking *bimba* fruit, that criminal has been bound 12.315
to a thorn tree. For stringing together untruths, that one's mouth has been sewn up, Prince. This opponent of making donations to Jain monks, wracked with hunger, is having his body eaten. That enemy of the Jain congregation is being roasted on iron griddles. That one who had sex with

nirmantu|jantu|hant” âyaṃ pāṭyate krakacena, bhoḥ.
mṛṣā|vādy eṣa piśunaḥ pāṭit’|āsyo raṭaty alam,
stainya|kāry eṣa chinn’|âṅga udbaddhaḥ kaṇṭaki|drume.
ayaṃ para|strī|bhoktā c’ āśleṣyate śālmalī|latām,
mahā|parigrahī tv eṣa tapt’|âyo nasi yojyate.
12.320 rātrī|bhojī, kumār’, âyaṃ bhojyate ’|śuci|piṇḍakān,
madhu|madya|pibo ’sau ca prataptaṃ pāyate trapu.»
iti śrutvā ca dṛṣṭvā ca cintayaty eṣa rāja|sūḥ:
«ke ’py ete puruṣāḥ prātaḥ|pāṭha|kṛn|naṭa|bāndhavāḥ.»
punaḥ sa puruṣaḥ prāha, «dṛṣṭaṃ pāpa|phalaṃ, sakhe.
su|kṛtasya phalaṃ samyak, kumār’, ēkṣasva samprati.»
ity uktvā bhuvana|pati|gṛheṣv etaṃ sa nītavān.
tatra devāṃś ca devīś ca kumāro vīkṣya taṃ jagau:
«ke ’mī?» pumān ākhyad, «amī śabala|vrata|pālanāt
a|kāma|nirjar’|â|bāla|tapasaś ca purā|kṛtāt
12.325 jaghanya|madhyam’|ôtkṛṣṭāj jātā bhuvana|vāsinaḥ.»
rāja|putras tato dadhyāu, «jñāyate satya|vādy asau.»
atha nīto vyantareṣu tena puṃsā narendra|ṣūḥ
vyantara’|rddhiṃ darśayitvā tat|kāraṇam ath’ ādiśat.

Jain nuns is being forced to have sexual intercourse with a doll made of red-hot iron. Here is a slaughterer of innocent creatures being rent by a saw, sir. Here is a slanderous speaker of falsehood who, even with his mouth rent, is still able to scream. Here is a committer of theft, his body pierced by being bound to a thorn tree. This enjoyer of others' wives is being made to embrace a creeper of thorns, and here is an extremely covetous one having a hot iron pincer applied to his nose. This eater at night, Prince, is being fed lumps of 12.320
shit, and that is a drinker of intoxicating liquor being made to drink molten tin."

Having heard and seen, the Prince thought, "These men are some kinsmen of the reciter of the morning blessing and of the actor."

Then the man said, "You have seen the reward of wickedness, my friend. Now in the same manner, Prince, see the reward of good actions."

Having said this, he led him among the dwellings of the lords of the world, and upon seeing the gods and goddesses there, the Prince said to him: "Who are these?" The man said, "These, through their former protection of their vows of asceticism from pollution, their disinterested wearing away of their karma and through their strenuous asceticism, have risen from the lower and middle ranks and become 12.325
gods who dwell in earth." The Prince thought, "This man is definitely speaking the truth."

Then the man took the Prince among the dwellings of the interstitial gods. He showed him the prosperity of the interstitial gods and then explained the reason for it.

«rajj'|ûdbandh'|āditaḥ ke cit kiñ|cic|chobana|cetasā,
a|kāma|nirjar'|â|bāla|tapobhyāṃ vyantarā amī.»

ity ado darśayitv" âiṣa gṛhītvā taṃ nṛp'|ātmajam
vyomni jyotiś|cakra|ṛddhiṃ darśayāmāsa sarvataḥ.

«karmaṇ" âmī kena jātā,» ity ukte rāja|sūnunā
sa pumān āha, «śabala|viraty" â|jña|tapasyayā.»

12.330 taṃ gṛhītvā ca Saudharme vimāne 'gāj jaghanyake.
kumāras tatra deva'|rddhiṃ vīkṣya vismita ūcivān:

«ken' êyaṃ karmaṇā jajñe?» «'jña|tapasy'|ādinā, sakhe.»
atr' ântare kumāreṇa pṛṣṭo 'yaṃ, «kaḥ punar bhavān?»

pumān ūce «'haṃ vayasyas tava prāg|bhava|saṃstutaḥ,»
tataḥ Kauśāmby|ādi vṛttaṃ spaṣṭam ācaṣṭa tasya saḥ.

yāvac|chrī|Nemi|tīrth'|ēśaṃ. «Sūra|devas tv ahaṃ sa ca,
yad atra tava sandehaḥ, sva'|rddhiṃ tad darśayāmi te.»

ity ākhyāya sva|vimāne taṃ ināya sa nirjaraḥ,
svaḥ|śriyaṃ vismaya|karīṃ tasya c' âsāv adīḍṛśat.

12.335 tam āyāy' âtha Śakrasya sabhāyāṃ so 'nayat kṣaṇāt,
aty|āścarya|karīm Indra|vibhūtiṃ dṛṣṭavān ayam.

Indra|sāmānikaḥ so 'pi Sūra|devaḥ kṛt'|ānatiḥ
upa|Śakraṃ niṣasāda, kumāras tasya pārśvataḥ.

Śakra ākhyad, «bhoḥ, ko 'yam ih' ānīto manuṣyakaḥ?»

"Certain people, with their minds attached from the start with a cord to whatever is auspicious, through their disinterested wearing away of karma and strenuous asceticism, become interstitial gods. Here they are."

After showing him that, he took the Prince in the sky and showed him all around the prosperity of the spheres of the stellar gods.

Upon the Prince's asking for what reason they became thus, the man said, "Through aversion to pollution and through the mortification of ignorance."

And he took him and went to the first celestial vehicle 12.330
of the Good Works heaven. When he saw the prosperity of the god in it, the Prince was amazed and said:

"For what reason did he become like this?" "Through mortification of ignorance, et cetera, my friend." Thereupon the Prince asked him, "But who are you, sir?"

The man said, "I am your companion, the intimate friend of you former life," and he made clear to him what had happened at Kaushámbi, et cetera, as far as their attendance on holy Lord of the Ford Nemi. "I am he, the god Sura. If you have any doubt about it, then I'll show you my prosperity."

Upon saying that, the god took him in the celestial vehicle and showed him the astonishing prosperity of heaven.

Then he took him and brought him into the assembly 12.335
of Shakra, the king of the gods, and showed the majesty of Shakra, which surpassed amazement. Then, although he was of equal rank to Shakra, the god Sura bowed and sat by Shakra with the Prince by his side. Shakra said, "Good sir,

devo 'vag, «deva|pādānāṃ bhṛtyo 'yaṃ me punaḥ suḥṛt.»
Indraḥ kumāram ācakhyau, «parijānāsi mām aho?»
kumāraḥ prāha, «dev'|êndra, na jānāmi kim apy aham.»
Harir vyāharad, «āsīs tvam Indra|sāmāniko mama,
Jayaśāsana|sādhv|indra|tapo|lakṣmī|latā|phalam!»

12.340 rāṭ|putro 'tha bhṛśaṃ dadhyau,
«kiṃ satyaṃ sarvam apy adaḥ?
kiñ c' êndra|jālaṃ? kiṃ svapna?
āho mama mati|bhramaḥ!»
taṃ sandihānam ity eṣa deva utpāṭya raṃhasā
Mahāvidehe ninye śrī|Sīmandhara|vibhoḥ puraḥ.
tataś ca:
śrī|indra|dhvaja|dharma|cakra|camara|
cchatra|tray'|âśoka|yuṅ
marty'|â|martya|jala|sthal'|âmbara|carat|
tiryak|su|paryañcitam
prākāra|tritayaṃ maṇī|caya|maya|
sphāra|sphurat|toraṇaṃ
śrī|Sīmandhara|tīrtha|pasya jagatāṃ
sāraṃ kil' āikṣiṣṭa saḥ.
kiñ ca:
durvarṇa|svarṇa|ratn'|ôc-
caya|maya|varaṇair moha|rāḍ|duḥ|praveśaṃ
śrī|yakṣ'|âdh'|īśa|dauvā-
rika|rucita|catur|gopura|dvāra|sāram
ākīrṇaṃ bhūr|bhuvaḥ|svas|
tritaya|janatayā Tīrtha|rājā sa|nāthaṃ

who is this mortal you have brought here?" The god said, "He is Your Majesty's servant, but also my friend."

Shakra asked the Prince, "Do you recognize me, then?" The Prince said, "King of the gods, I don't recognize anything."

Shakra said, "You were a king of the gods, of equal rank to me, the reward of the fortune of the asceticism of the king of monks, Jaya·shásana!"

Then the Prince thought hard, "Is all this indeed true? Is it 12.340
a conjuring trick? Is it a dream? Oh, my mind is wandering!"

As he was thus perplexed, the god suddenly picked him up and with great speed took him to Maha·vidéha, to the presence of the majesty of holy Siman·dhara.

And then:

He saw the triple rampart of the preaching enclosure of the holy Lord Siman·dhara, which had been well circumambulated by animals, the denizens of air, land and water, gods and mortals; which was possessed of an ashóka tree, a triple parasol, fly whisks, a wheel of law and a lovely banner of Indra; and which had gateways glittering with an extensive inlay of pearls and jewels; indeed, it was the epitome of the triple universe.

And besides:

He himself saw the preaching assembly filled with the divisions of the island of the wealth of Prosperity, very difficult to enter by the king of the earth's delusion because of its rampart made from masses of jewels, gold and silver; with doors in its four gateways resplendent with majestic kings of the demigods, obstructors of bad; filled with the threefold

śrī|śreyo|dvīpa|śākh"|ā-
puram avasaraṇaṃ s' âiṣa vīkṣāṃbabhūva.

api ca:

āgneyyāṃ gaṇa|bhṛd|vimāna|vanitā
sādhvyas tathā nairṛte
jyotir|vyantara|bhāvan'|ēśa|dayitā
vāyavya|gās tat|priyāḥ
aiśānyāṃ ca vimāna|vāsi|vara|nār-
yaḥ saṃśritā yatra tat
Jain'|āsthānam idaṃ catus|tri|pariṣat|
sevyaṃ kumāro 'viśat.

12.345 tataḥ kumāraṃ devo 'sau jagāda, «su|dhiyām nidhe,
puṇya|prakarṣam adrākṣīr, vandasva śrī|jagat|prabhum!»
prabhoḥ purastād īh"|ādi kurvāṇo 'tha nṛp'|âṅgajaḥ
mumūrccha, sa ca devena siṣice gandha|vāribhiḥ.
tālavṛnt'|ânila|hṛta|tuccha|mūrcchaḥ parāpa ca
jāti|smṛtiṃ jagan|nātha|kevalasy' êva varṇikām.
prabuddhaḥ śrī|kumāro 'tha tam uvāca sur'|ôttamam:
«tav' ânuśāstim icchāmi, sādhu, sādhv asmi bodhitaḥ!
aho te satya|saṃdhatvam! aho te 'ny'|ôpakāritā!
aho sv'|ârtha|na|prekṣitvaṃ! tav' âho sādhu|sauhṛdam!
12.350 yan na śrutaṃ, yan na dṛṣṭaṃ,
yan narāṇāṃ na gocaraḥ,

peoples of the earth, sky and heaven; together with its lord, the Lord of the Ford.

And what's more:

The Prince entered that assembly of the Jina, which was attended by the twelvefold audience, in the southeastern part of which had gathered the leaders of the troops, the gods of the celestial vehicles and their wives, and the Jain nuns; in the southwestern part of which had gathered the stellar, interstitial and mansion-dwelling gods and their wives and the travelers in the wind and their wives; and in the northeastern part of which the excellent the most eminent of the celestial vehicle-dwelling gods and their wives had assembled.

Then that god said to the Prince, "You ocean of intelli- 12.345
gence, you have beheld preeminent merit; pay your respects to the holy lord of the universe!"

Then, as the Prince was making due consideration of what was for and against in the presence of the lord, he swooned, and the god sprinkled him with perfumed water. Revived from his swoon by the breeze from a palm-leaf fan, he attained memory of his former lives, a sample of the actual omniscience of the lord of the universe.

Then the Prince, enlightened, said to that most excellent of religious teachers, "I desire your instruction. Excellent, excellent, I've been enlightened! Oh, your union with the truth! Oh, your benevolence to others! Oh, your disregard for your own interest! Oh, the excellence of your affection!
That which has not been heard, that which has not been 12.350
seen, that which is not in the range of senses of men, made

bhūr bhuvaḥ svas trayaṃ tan me 'dhy-
akṣaṃ tvan|niśray" âbhavat.»

tataḥ sura|kumārau tau namaskṛtya jagat|prabhum
vaco 'pātāṃ sudhā|pāyam. aho, puṇy'|ôdayas tayoḥ!

Jina|vyākhy"|âvasāne ca gatau tau taṃ nadī|hradam
śāntayitvā hastinaṃ tam, āropya nṛpa|nandanam,

«nirvighnam astu te vīra, pratibadhyasva mā kva cit,
kārye smaryo 'sm'» îti c' ôktvā Śūra|devo divaṃ yayau.

dvip'|ārūḍhaḥ kumāras tu prasthitaḥ sva|puraṃ prati,
pade pade sva|śibiraṃ cint"|āturam avaikṣata.

12.355 kumāraṃ ca tathā yāntaṃ prekṣya sarve 'pi sainikāḥ
marālā Mānasam iva prahṛṣṭāḥ paryavārayan.

śrutvā sva|putr'|âbhyudayaṃ samudro 'bhyāgaman nṛpo,
tama|stomaḥ kṣayam agān mud|advaitaṃ vyajṛmbhata.

bhukty|uttaraṃ śrī|Samarasenaḥ satvaram abhyadhāt
Jayaśekhara|Bhuvanamañjaryau pitarāv iti:

«amba, tāta, mayā jñātā viṣayā viṣa|sannibhāḥ,
āpāta|mātra|madhurāḥ pariṇāme 'ti|dāruṇāḥ.
tad alaṃ, tāta, bhogair me kin tu cāritra|senayā
mukti|rājyam arjayāmi, jayāmi bhava|vairiṇam!»

12.360 tato māt" âvadad, «vatsa, tvad|dīkṣā|vacana|śruteḥ
hṛdayaṃ me sphuṭat' îva, mā vādīs tad idaṃ punaḥ.»

evident before me, the triad of earth, sky and heaven, by resorting to you!"

Then the god and the Prince both bowed to the lord of the universe and drank the liquid nectar of his sermon. Oh, the merit that was produced in them!

On the termination of the Jina's sermon, the two returned to that river, and the god Shura calmed the elephant, mounted the Prince on it, and saying, "May you be unhindered, may you meet with no obstruction. I am a reminder of what is to be done," returned to heaven.

Then, mounted on his elephant, the Prince set out for his city, at every step glancing toward his camp, which was
sick at heart. And when all the soldiers saw the Prince ap- 12.355
proaching like that, they delightedly flocked around him like swans on Lake Mánasa.

When the King heard that his son had arisen, he, like the ocean, went to meet him. The gloom disappeared from his face, and nothing but joy spread over it.

Immediately after eating, his highness Sámara·sena said to Jaya·shékhara and Bhúvana·mánjari, his parents:

"Mother, Father, I've learned that sensual pleasures are like poison, having only the appearance of sweetness, but extremely bitter in the digestion. So, Father, enough of sensual pleasures. With my army of asceticism I shall win the kingdom of final liberation and conquer the enemy of existence!"

Thereupon his mother said, "My heart seems to be break- 12.360
ing through hearing you talk about your initiation, so don't mention it again."

kumāro 'th' âbhyadhān, «mātaḥ,
ko 'yaṃ śok'|ôdayas tava?
jaya|śriyo hy āgame syāt
pratyuta pramad'|ôdayaḥ.»

mātā:

«svairaṃ vilasa sāmrājya|sampadā yauvan'|âvadhi,
bhukta|bhogas tato, vīra, ramethāḥ saṃyama|śriyā.»

putraḥ:

«yasy' âsti mṛtyunā sakhyaṃ, yaḥ śakto 'taḥ palāyitum,
yaś c' â|jarā|maro 'tr' âsti, mātar, bhog'|êcchur astu saḥ.»

mātā:

«ati|priyo 'si me, vatsa, jīvāmi tvāṃ vinā na hi.
yāvaj jīvāmi tad ahaṃ, tāvan mā, saumya, niṣkramīḥ.»

putraḥ:

12.365 «yathā pradīptāt sadanān nirgacchan vallabho janaḥ
na vāryate, vāryate na tath" âiva bhava|cārakāt.»

Then the Prince said, "Why is this sorrow swelling up in you? On the contrary, it's great joy that should swell up at the approach of the fortune of victory."

Mother:

"Enjoy at your own will the blessings of the whole kingdom during the time of your youth. Then, when you've enjoyed sensual pleasures, brave son, you may enjoy the fortune of ascetic restraint."

Son:

"Let he who is on good terms with Death, he who is able to escape from him, and he who is then ever youthful and immortal long for sensual pleasures, Mother."

Mother:

"You are very dear to me, my son. Without you, I shall not be able to live, for sure. So for as long as I am alive don't abandon worldly life, good sir."

Son:

"Just as you don't prevent a loved person from escaping 12.365
from a blazing dwelling, in just the same way you don't prevent him from escaping from wandering in existence."

mātā:

«nirāsvādā vālukāvad duś|carvā yā javā iva
dīkṣā jñeyā Jin'|êndrāṇām. atra bhagnā mahā|rathāḥ.»

putraḥ:

«niḥsattvānāṃ sarvam etat, kin tu sarve na tādṛśāḥ.
vinā sattvaṃ gṛham api dur|nirvāham a|saṃśayam.»
«dhanyo 'si sarvathā, vatsa, saṃyamaṃ yaḥ prapatsyase.
kin tv anujñāpya pitaraṃ duṣkaraṃ vratam āṣṛṇu!»
tataḥ kumāraḥ pitaraṃ sādaraṃ pratyapīpadat,
«tāta, tvay" âsmy anujñātaḥ, prapadye siddhi|paddhatim.»
12.370 tat putrasya vacaḥ śrutvā tapta|tomara|sodaram,
Jayaśekhara|rāj'|êndraḥ sa|gadgadam ado 'gadat:
«putr', â|nātha iv' âikākī dīkṣitas tvaṃ gṛhād gṛham
yad bhramiṣyasi, ten' êdaṃ hṛn me nu śatadhā sphuṭet.»
«tāt', â|nāthasy' âikakasya syātāṃ kiṃ mūrdhni śṛṅgake?
Jina|dharmaṃ vin" â|nāthā ekakāḥ sarva eva hi.
tathā hi:
prāg|duṣkṛt'|ôdaye, tāta, pitṝṇāṃ paśyatām api
putreṇa vedyate duḥkhaṃ nānā|roga|samudbhavam.
garbha|vāse, priyā|yoge, '|priya|yoge jar"|āgame,
vyaye, 'ntar|āle, dur|gatyāṃ anārth'|âiko vyathāṃ sahet.

Mother:

"You should know that the initiation of the Lord Jinas is like tasteless pulse, like gravel difficult to chew. Mighty warriors have been shattered in it."

Son:

"All this befalls those without strength of character, but all are not like that. Without strength of character even the life of a householder is difficult to accomplish, no doubt about it."

"My son, you will be blessed in every respect, you who are going to undertake asceticism. But without your father's leave your vow will be wrongly done; pay heed!"

Then the Prince respectfully addressed his father: "If you grant me your permission, I will set out on the path to final perfection."

On hearing this statement of his son, which was like a 12.370
heated lance, king of kings Jaya·shékhara managed to stammer this:

"My son, if you take initiation and wander alone from house to house like a helpless beggar, that would cause this heart of mine to break into a hundred pieces."

"Father, would a lonely helpless beggar have two horns on his head? Without the Jain religion, all are lonely helpless beggars.

Just like so:

At the working out of bad actions committed in former lives, although his parents are watching him, pain is experienced by their son in the form of various diseases. In the dwelling of the womb, in union with a dear wife, in

12.375 tan nātho vā, sahāyo vā, ko 'pi dharmaṃ vinā na hi.
sa|nāthaḥ sa|sahāyaś ca tad|dharmeṇa bhavāmy aham.»

ity asya vairāgya|siddha|rasair bhinna|manā nṛpaḥ
tan|mayatvam api prāptas tad|udgāram iv' âmucat.

«dhanyas tvam eva, yen' êyaṃ tṛṣṇā|vally udamūlyata,
dravya|kṣetr'|ādau ca yena pratibandho vyabādhyata!
mātā|pitṛ|priyā|bhrātṛ|sneho 'nartha|nibandhanam
tvayā yathāvad ajñāyi, su|labdhaṃ janma tat tava!
jānīma eva hi vayaṃ virasaṃ bhava|nāṭakam,
mahā|moha|naṭen' âiva param evaṃ vimohitāḥ.
12.380 jananī te kṛt'|ârth" êyam, pitā te jagad|uttamaḥ,
jagad|uttama|vairāgyo yat putras tvaṃ pavitra|dhīḥ.
āvayor api saṃsāra|vārdhi|potas tvam eva hi,
tat tvarasv'! âika|tūryeṇa pravrajāmo vayaṃ same.»

tato 'rikesarī putro laghū rājye 'bhyaṣicyata,
rājā, rājñī, kumāraś ca tvarante sma vrata|śriye.

tatr' âiv' âvasare śarac|chaśa|dhara|
jyotsnā|samucchālita|
kṣīr'|âmbho|nidhi|bhṛṅga|śṛṅga|vilasad|
ḍiṇḍīra|sadhryag|yaśaḥ

union with what is not dear, at the coming of old age, in dissolution, in the midst of bad rebirths, he, a lonely beg-
gar, endures pain. So without religion no one at all has a 12.375
protector or a helper. By means of this religion I will have a protector and a helper."

The King, his mind opened by the potions of his son's indifference to the world, as if he had attained the same state, seemed to repeat the same utterance.

"You are truly blessed, you who have uprooted the creeper of desire and have released one who was bound to possessions, property and suchlike! You have duly shown that attachment to mother, father, wife and brother is attachment to objects of no value. This your birth was advantageous! We have certainly learned that the drama of existence is in bad taste, but formerly we were truly deluded by the actor
of mighty delusion. Your mother here has achieved her pur- 12.380
pose, and your father, the greatest in the world, has become indifferent to the greatness of the world, since you are their son, whose understanding is a means of purification. You are truly a boat for us to cross the ocean of existence, so hurry!—we will renounce the world together at the same instant."

Then the King, who had consecrated his younger son Ari·késarin to the kingship, and the Queen and Prince hastened to the splendor of the vow.

At that very moment, with the area of the sky covered in fine garments issuing from the vault of the praise of the glory, the foam flashing on the peaks, bees for the ocean of milk attracted upward by the light of the autumn moon,

stom'|ôdāra|visāri|jādara|paṭa|
prāvārit'|āś"|âṅganaḥ
prodain nandana|kānane 'dbhuta|catur|
jñānī gurur Nandanaḥ.
udyāna|pālaken' âtha guru|kalpa|drum'|ôdayāt
vardhāpitaḥ svarṇa|lakṣaṃ nṛpo 'dāt pāritoṣikam.
12.385 jaya|kuñjaram āruhya rājā śrī|Jayaśekharaḥ
s'|ântaḥ|puraḥ sa|sāmant'|Ârikesari|nṛp'|ânvitaḥ
śrīmān Samarasenaś c' âdhirūḍho maṅgala|dvipam
pañca|śatyā rāṭ|kumārair vayasyaiḥ parivāritaḥ.
gatvā śrī|nandan'|ôdyāne triḥ|pradakṣiṇan'|âdbhutam
natvā guruṃ parīvāraṃ c' āsīnau tau yath"|āuciti.
tataś ca bhagavān Bhādr'|âmbho|dhara|dhvani|ḍambaraḥ
vistārayāmāsa dharma|deśanāṃ kleśa|nāśinīm.
tathā hi:
«a|sāraḥ s' âiṣa saṃsâraḥ kār'|āgāra|sah'|ôdaraḥ,
mūla|stambhau tasya parigrah'|ārambhau su|niścitaṃ.
12.390 tayoḥ punaḥ parīhāsas tat|pradhvaṃsa|nibandhanam
tataḥ parigrah'|ārambhau bhaṅktvā stha śiva|sadmani.»
rājñā vijñāpayāñcakre tataḥ śrī|Nandano guruḥ
«putraḥ Samaraseno 'yaṃ, prabho, dīkṣāṃ jighṛkṣati
vayaṃ c' ânuyiyāsānaḥ puṇyavantam amuṃ sutam.
prasadya sadyo, bhagavan, pūryatāṃ naḥ samīhitam.»

the teacher Nándana, possessed of the astonishing fourfold knowledge, appeared in the paradise park. Then the gardener congratulated the King on the appearance of the wishing-tree that was the teacher, and the King rewarded him with a gratuity of a hundred thousand gold pieces.

His Majesty King Jaya·shékhara, mounted on the state 12.385
elephant, accompanied by his court, his ministers and King Ari·késarin, and His Highness Sámara·sena, mounted on an elephant of good fortune, surrounded by five hundred royal princes of the same age as he, arrived in the lovely paradise garden, and, having made a remarkable threefold circumambulation, bowed to the teacher and his entourage, and sat in an appropriate place.

And then the reverend teacher, his voice reverberating like the thunder of a rain cloud in the rainy season, began to spread forth the teaching of religion, the cause of the destruction of distress.

Just like so:

"This here cycle of death and rebirth is worthless; it is just like a prison. Its two foundation pillars are greed and destruction of life; there's absolutely no doubt.

But their abandonment entails their utter destruction. 12.390
So, once you put them to flight, you will be in the abode of final emancipation."

Then the King addressed reverend Nándana the teacher: "This is my son, Sámara·sena, my lord. He wishes to take initiation. And we wish to follow this meritorious son of ours. So please be gracious, reverend sir, and fulfill our wish right now."

gurur ūce, «vayam ih' âitad|artham hi samāgatāḥ.
niṣpratyūhaṃ siddham eva bhavatāṃ vāñchitaṃ tataḥ.»
tato rājā ca rājñī ca kumārāṇāṃ ca pañcabhiḥ
śatair vṛtaḥ kumāraś ca dīkṣāmāsus tad|antike.
12.395 tato jñāna|kriy"|âbhyāsaṃ te samārebhire 'dhikam
catur|daś' âpi pūrv'|âbdhīn kumāras tv apiban mudā.
avadhiṃ manaḥ paryavaṃ ca sa puṇy'|ātmā parāpa ca
rājā rājñī c' ânta|kṛtau siddhi|saudham avāpatuḥ.
muniḥ Samarasenas tu guṇa|ratna|mahā|khaniḥ
sva|pade sthāpayāñcakre guruṇā guru|gauravāt.
śrī|sarva|saṅgha|pratyakṣaṃ śrī|Samarasena|sūraye
śrīmān Nandana|sūr'|îndro 'nuśāstim adadād iti:
«dhanyas tvaṃ, yena vijñātaḥ saṃsāra|giri|dārakaḥ
vajravad durbhidaś c' âyaṃ mahā|bhāga Jin'|āgamaḥ.
12.400 idaṃ c' āropitaṃ yat te padaṃ sat|sampadāṃ padam
aty|uttamam idaṃ loke mahā|sattva|niṣevitam.
dhanyebhyo dīyate tāvad, dhanyā ev' âsya pāragāḥ
gatv" âsya pāraṃ dhanyās tu pāraṃ gacchanti saṃsṛteḥ.
bhītaṃ saṃsāra|kāntārāt samarthasya vimocane
sādhu|vṛndam idaṃ sarvaṃ bhavataḥ śaraṇ'|āgatam.
samprāpya sa|guṇaṃ dharmaṃ nirmalaṃ pāramēśvaram
trāṇam saṃsāra|bhītānāṃ dhanyāḥ kurvanti dehinām.

The teacher said, "I came here for this very purpose. The accomplishment of your wish will be unimpeded."

Then the King, the Queen and the Prince, accompanied by the five hundred princes, received initiation in his presence.

Then they began an intense study of knowledge, ceremony and practice, and the Prince joyfully drank the oceans of the fourteen original scriptures. And he, pure of soul, attained the ability to see beyond the normal range of the senses and to read the thoughts of others. The King and Queen died and reached the palace of final liberation. 12.395

And with great respect the teacher appointed the monk Sámara·sena, a huge mine of the jewels of excellence, to his own position.

In the sight of the whole venerable congregation, Nándana, the venerable leader of the teachers, gave this advice to the venerable teacher Sámara·sena:

"You are blessed, since you have learned how to split the mountain of existence and that this Jain religion is as hard to split as diamond; you are very fortunate. And it has been determined that your position is the position of those possessed of true good fortune. This is the supreme position in the world, honored by the truly good. 12.400

While so much is given to the blessed, the blessed even pass beyond that, for having passed beyond that the blessed pass beyond the cycle of existence. This entire multitude of monks, frightened of the wilderness of existence, has come for your protection, since you are competent in providing liberation. Having attained the religion with excellent qualities, stainless, which comes from the supreme lord, the

tad ete bhāva|rog'|ārtās tvaṃ bhāva|bhiṣvag|varaḥ
atas tvay" âmī saj|jīvā mocanīyāḥ prayatnataḥ.

12.405 guruś ca mocayaty etān na pramatto hit'|ôdyataḥ
baddha|lakṣo dṛḍhaṃ mokṣe niḥspṛho bhava|cārake.

kalpo 'yam iti kṛtvā tvam īdṛśo 'pi praṇoditaḥ
Jin'|âvasthāna|rūpaṃ hi ceṣṭitavyaṃ sadā tvayā.

yuṣmābhir api n' âiv' âiṣa sustha|bohittha|sannibhaḥ
saṃsāra|sāgar'|ôttārī vimoktavyaḥ kad" âpi na.

pratikūlaṃ na kartavyam anukūla|rataiḥ sadā
bhāvyam asya gṛha|tyāgo yena vaḥ sa|phalo bhavet.

anyathā viśva|bandhūnām ājñā|lopaḥ kṛto bhavet,
tato viḍambanā sarvā bhaved atra paratra ca.

12.410 tataḥ kula|vadhūn yāyāt kārye nirbhartsitair api
yāvaj|jīvaṃ na moktavyaṃ pāda|mūlam amuṣya, bhoḥ.

te jñāna|bhājanaṃ dhanyās, te sad|darśana|nirmalāḥ,
te niṣprakampa|cāritrā, ye sadā guru|sevinaḥ.»

guravo 'n|aśanaṃ kṛtv" ântakṛtaḥ siddhim aiyaruḥ,
sūriḥ Samarasenas tu vijahāra mahī|tale.

blessed provide protection for embodied beings who are frightened of existence. So these monks are pained by the disease of existence and you are the best doctor for existence. Henceforth you are to endeavor to liberate these true souls.

Their teacher will without negligence cause them to be 12.405
liberated, intent on their good, attached to restraint, fixed on liberation and free from desire for the prison of existence.

This is your duty, which, having performed, you will be endowed with such qualities, for you are always to strive for the likeness of the condition of a Jina.

And you monks are not to abandon this one who is like an auspicious boat carrying you across the ocean of existence; never at all. You are not to oppose him but always perform what he wishes to be done very obediently, so that your abandonment of household life may be fruitful. Otherwise the orders of those who are kin to all would be neglected, and then there would be every disgrace both here and in
the next world. So, good sirs, in the manner of virtuous 12.410
wives, you should not abandon the soles of his feet for as long as you live, even though you are abused for doing it. They are blessed in their possession of knowledge, they are unblemished in their true insight, they are unshaken in their asceticism, who always attend on their teacher."

Then the teacher fasted until death, died and attained final liberation, and the teacher Sámara·sena wandered over the surface of the earth.

su|guru|Samarasenaḥ senay" êv' âti|mityā
parivṛta ṛṣitatyā pālit'|ājño jagatyā
catasṛbhir iha ridbhir dīpikābhiḥ samantāt
kim api hi Jina|datt'|âdhvānam āviścakāra.

iti śrī|nirvāṇa|Līlāvatī|mahā|kath"|êti|vṛtt'|ôddhāre Līlāvatī|sāre Jin'|âṅke śrī|Vijayasen'|ādi|mahā|puruṣa|pañcaka|vrata|grahaṇa|maha"|ṛṣi|daśaka|svar|gamana| Jayaśāsana|jīva|śrī|Samarasena|vrata|grahaṇ'|ācārya|pada|sthāpana|vyāvarṇano nāma dvādaśa utsāhaḥ

The true teacher Sámara·sena, defended by his army of firmly fixed asceticism, his commands obeyed by the universe, by means of the shining lamps of the fourfold congregation made visible absolutely everywhere in the world the way granted by the Jina.

Here ends the twelfth canto, entitled "The Taking of the Vow of the Five Great Men, His Majesty Víjaya·sena and the Others, the Going to Heaven of the Ten Great Sages, and the Taking of the Vow and Appointment to the Rank of Teacher of His Highness Sámara·sena, the Soul of Jaya·shásana," of the Jain epic *The Epitome of Queen Lilávati*, an abridgment of the events of *The Epic Story of the Auspicious Final Emancipation of Lilávati.*

CANTO 13
THE ENLIGHTENMENT AND INITIATION OF HIS HIGHNESS PRINCE VÍMALA·SENA, THE SOUL OF THE MIGHTY ASCETIC RAMA·DEVA

13.1 ITAŚ CA ŚRĪ|Nemi|nātha|vihāraḥ pūta|bhū|talaḥ
Surāṣṭr'|êty asti viṣayo viṣayo na hi vidviṣām.
bhāty atra Girinagaraṃ Girinārasya ḍimbhavat,
yat prakhelaty a|skhalitair akhilair dharma|khelanaiḥ.
rāṭ tatr' āsīd Vatsarājo vatsarā yasya ghasravat
niṣkaṇṭakita|viśvasya līlay" âiv' aticakramuḥ.
Jayaśrī devy abhāt tasya jaya|śrīr iva dehinī
bahubhiḥ prārthanīy" âpi y" āśrayan na nar'|ântaram.
13.5 tayoḥ paraspara|prema|pārā|vāra|samudbhavam
pibatoḥ śarma|pīyūṣam atr' âiva svar|avātarat.
tato Jayaśriyo devyāḥ kukṣau śukti|puṭ'|ôpame
mukt"|ôpamo Rāmadeva|deva|jīvaḥ samāgamat.
niś'|ânte sā sahasr'|âṃśuṃ tad|dev'|âṃśu|sahasravat
mukhe viśantam adrākṣīj, Jain'|āgāraṃ tad eva ca.
prahṛṣṭā bhūbhuje sā ca svapnam enam acīkathat,
patir eko guruḥ strīṇām iti khyāpayituṃ kila.
rāj" ācaṣṭa, «pratihat'|âśeṣa|tejasvi|maṇḍalaḥ,
ākhaṇḍalaḥ kṣmā|talasya bhavitā, devi, te 'ṅgajaḥ.»
13.10 vihār'|āhāra|vyāhāraiḥ sthāna|saṃveśan'|āsanaiḥ
hṛdyaiś ca dohadair devī garbhaṃ puṇyam iv' âidhayat.

NOW, ITS GROUND purified by the temple of holy Lord Nemi, there is a region named Suráshtra, by no means a region in the sphere of its enemies. And in it lies resplendent the city of Giri·nágara, like the child of Mount Giri·nara, which plays with continued and unfaltering pastimes of religion. And there reigned a king, Vatsa·raja. He was completely free from troubles and his years passed in pleasure just as easily as a day. 13.1

Jaya·shri was his queen, like the embodiment of the goddess of victory, who, despite being prayed for by many, had not resorted among men.

And to that very place they made fall from heaven the nectar of happiness, which was produced as they drank the water of the rivers of their mutual affection. 13.5

Then the soul of the god Rama·deva, like pearl, appeared in Queen Jaya·shri's womb, which was like the hollow of an oyster shell.

As the night came to an end, she dreamed that the thousand-rayed sun, as if with the thousand rays of that god, entered her mouth, and then a Jain temple, the one in that place. Delighted, she related her dream to her husband for his interpretation, for husbands are certainly the only teachers of their wives.

The King said, "My Queen, you will have a son, the sphere of whose majesty will dazzle all, a king of the gods for the surface of the world."

And the Queen bore her embryo like her merit along with heartfelt pregnancy longings to sit and lie in ascetic postures and to converse and eat in temples. 13.10

samaye 'sūta sā deva|kumāram iva dārakam
saubhāgya|su|bhag'|ākāraṃ saubhāgyam iva mūrtimat.
Vimalasena ity ākhyāṃ dvādaśe 'hni parāpa saḥ,
sphāyan śaś" îva sarvābhiḥ kalābhiḥ paryapūri ca.

kalā|pātrībhir urv"|īśa|putrībhir yuva|rāṭ|śriyā
samam eva kumāraṃ taṃ bhū|patiḥ paryaṇāyayat.

tato vibhinne bhavane tābhiḥ samam araṃsta saḥ
sūry'|ôday'|âsta|samayāv abudhat padma|ṣaṇḍataḥ.

13.15 kumārasya nij'|āsthāne sukh'|āsīnasya c' ânyadā
sāmantau Yaśodhavala|Jayasiṃhāv upeyatuḥ.
natvā yāthā|svam āsīnau prārebhe tair mithaḥ kathā.
prasaṅgād vismaya|karī dhātu|vāda|kath" âbhavat.

uvāca Jayasiṃho 'tha, «dhūrtair viracitāny, aho,
dhātu|vād'|ādi|śāstrāṇi. satyaṃ n' âtr' âikam akṣaram.»

kumāro 'tha nyaṣedhat taṃ, «m" êty āśātaya prāṅ|narān.
na sidhyati tad|uktaṃ ca satya|sāhasa|varjinaḥ.»

anyo 'vādīn, «mama saty'|ādi|bhāvān n' âiva sidhyati.
na sādhayati kiṃ nāma satya|sāhasavān bhavān.»

13.20 ākhyat kumāraḥ, «kiṃ ruṣṭaḥ ko vakti? mama sidhyati.»
ūce 'nyo, «yadi te sidhyet, kūrc'|ârdhaṃ muṇḍayer mama.»

And at the due time she gave birth to a son who was like a prince of the gods, his body lovely in its beauty, like beauty personified. On the twelfth day he was given the name Vímala·sena, and waxing like the moon he was filled with the digits of all the arts.

The King united the Prince with the daughters of kings of the earth, vessels of all the arts, and at the same time with the rank of crown prince.

Then, in a secluded palace, he enjoyed himself with them. He, like a clump of lotuses, was aware of two times: the rising and the setting of the sun.

One day, while the Prince was relaxing at ease in his own 13.15
place, two barons, Yasho·dhávala and Jaya·simha, came to visit him. The two bowed and sat in their respective places, and they all began to talk together. The conversation happened to turn to tales of the wonderful results of alchemy.

Then Jaya·simha said, "Bah! The manuals of alchemy and such are made up by swindlers. There's not a true syllable in them."

Thereupon the Prince warned him, "Don't denigrate the men of old like that. The word of one who lacks truth and boldness is not accomplished."

The other said, "Mine is certainly accomplished through my character of truth and boldness. Your Honor has accomplished nothing at all, even possessed of truth and boldness."

The Prince said, "Who is this angry man, what is he 13.20
saying? Mine is accomplished." The other said, "If yours is accomplished, you can shave off half my beard."

ūce kumāras, «trāt" âhaṃ, na kasy' âpi viḍambakaḥ.»
anyo 'vak, «kim ahas tat syād yatra trāsye 'smi kena cit.»

sa|roṣaṃ rāja|sūḥ prāha, «cec chaktaḥ, sevako 'si kim?»
ūce 'nyaś, «cen na sevāmi, kaḥ sevayati mām balāt?
tan, mitra, vyasanaṃ kiṃ te, sevā|kaṣṭaṃ karoṣi yat?»
Yaśodhavalo 'th' â|buddha jajñe vairasyam etayoḥ.

tataḥ kumāraṃ sa prāha, «tava tāta|prasādataḥ
a|samīkṣy'|âbhidhāne 'pi n' â|prasāda|padaṃ vayam.

api ca:

13.25 bhṛtyasy' āgo mṛṣyate yo, guṇān vakti ca ya prabhuḥ,
tasy' âri|varga|mathane bhṛtyāḥ prāṇān dadaty api.»

Jayasiṃho 'vadad atha, «Yaśodhavala, mā vada.
na so 'sti, yo 'parādhe 'p' īkṣiṣyate mama sammukham.

kiñ ca:

re, cāṭu|kāra! dhig, dhik te Yaśodhavala, pauruṣam,
yad vā dātā kumāras te deśaṃ, ten' âsi cāṭu|kṛt!»

Yaśodhavala āha sma, «maryād" âiva hi jīvitam.
tan|mukto mṛta ev' âsi. kiṃ śauryaṃ mṛta|māraṇe?
tvaṃ ca me pitṛṣvasrīyas, tat tav' âgre bhaṇāmi kim?
evaṃ hi bruvato 'nyasya jihvām apaharāmy aham.»

The Prince said, "I'm a protector. I'm not a swindler of anyone." The other said, "That will be the day on which I'm protected by anyone."

The Prince said angrily, "If you are powerful, why are you an attendant?" The other said, "If I weren't an attendant, no one would be forced to attend on me. So, my friend, what's your problem that you make attendance on you unpleasant?" Then Yasho·dhávala, the fool, became disgusted with them both.

So he said to the Prince, "Although the title may be disregarded, through your father's grace our position is not without honor.

What's more:

The King's the one who forgives the mistakes of his at- 13.25
tendant or praises his excellence. Attendants even give their lives in the struggle with the ranks of his enemies."

Jaya·simha said, "Shut up, Yasho·dhávala. The one who could confront me over a mistake doesn't exist.

What's more:

Hey, you flatterer! Shame, shame on your manliness, Yasho·dhávala, that the Prince is the one who gives you the orders for you to be his flatterer!"

Yasho·dhávala said, "There is certainly a contract for our livelihood. If he lets you go, you will certainly die. What heroism is there in death by starvation? And you are my nephew; I can speak this before you, can't I? But if another spoke like this I would cut out his tongue."

13.30 ath' âvadaj Jayasiṃho, «Yaśodhavala, cāṭubhiḥ
jīvaṃ rakṣan śūla|viṣādibhyas tatr' āsyase katham?»
kumāro 'vag, «Jayasiṃha, tav' âgre nanu ke vayam?
tvam eva vīra|tilakas, tvaṃ tilakayasi kṣamām.»
krodh'|āviṣṭo 'nya ūce 'tha,
«kas tvaṃ nāma? stanaṃ|dhayaḥ.
mam' âgre tava tāto 'pi
cañcāvat pauruṣ'|ôjjhitaḥ.»
tataḥ krodh'|âtirekeṇa kumāro 'jvalad agnivat.
jāt'|ākūtaiḥ kumārasy' âṅga|rakṣaiḥ sa hato 'sibhiḥ.
mahā|kalakalo 'th' âbhūd rodaḥ|kukṣiṃ|bharis tadā.
«kumāreṇa Jayasiṃho 'ghāt'!» îty ākhyaj jano 'bhitaḥ.
13.35 a|jñāta|tattvāḥ sāmantā mantriṇo 'tha padātayaḥ
sarve 'py eka|matī|bhūya mimilur dur|grahā iva.
tato rājā Vatsarājo 'cintayan mati|śeva|dhiḥ:
«ete sarve 'py a|viśvastāḥ kumāre mayi c' âbhavan.
vigrahe viḍvaraṃ kuryuḥ, sva|tantrasya kṣayas tataḥ,
druhyeyur vā kumārāy' âmī mileyur ath' âribhiḥ.
tataś c' âivam iha vihite na pratiyanty amī.
n' ânyath".» êti viniścitya kumāraṃ tad vibhodhya ca,
kop'|āṭopād dāru|gṛhe kumāraṃ nyasya sarvataḥ
āptān prāharikān kṛtvā sāmant'|ādīn nṛpo 'bhyadhāt:

Then Jaya·simha said, "Yasho·dhávala, protecting your 13.30
life with flattery, how can you stay there to receive poisoned darts?"

The Prince said, "Jaya·simha, who are we compared with you? You are the forehead ornament of heroes. You will ornament the earth."

Then, full of anger, the other said, "Who are you, then? You're a suckling. Compared with mine, your daddy is a man of straw, devoid of manliness."

Then the Prince, like a fire, blazed with an excess of anger. The Prince's bodyguards, made aware of his intention, killed Jaya·simha with their swords. Then a great commotion arose, filling the belly of the vault of heaven and earth. Everywhere the people cried, "The Prince has killed Jaya·simha!"

Then the barons, ministers and soldiers, despite not 13.35
knowing the true facts, all became of one mind and gathered in conjunction like inauspicious planets.

Then King Vatsa·raja, a treasury of intelligence, thought, "These have all become suspicious of the Prince and me. Set at variance, they will make a rebellion, and then their army will be destroyed, or they will seek to harm the Prince and join with my enemies. But if matters are arranged like so here, they will make no opposition. It won't be otherwise." Having thus determined, he informed the Prince of his plan. Glowing with anger, the King threw the Prince into a wooden cage and placed trustworthy guards all around it. He addressed the barons and the others:

13.40 «duṣṭaḥ putro ’pi nigrāhyaḥ, śiṣṭo ’nugrāhya ity asau.
rāṇ|nītiḥ kula|dev” îva samārādhyā sad” âiva naḥ.
iyaṃ kāṣṭh” âtra naḥ prayetavyaṃ yuṣmābhir añjasā.»
rāj” êty ādhād rājya|sausthyam aho matimatāṃ matiḥ!

tam kumāram atha jñānāj jñātvā tādṛg|vipad|gatam
dadhyau Samaraseno, ’muṣya bodha|kṣaṇo ’dhunā.
so ’th’ âsmarac Chūra|devam, āyātaṃ taṃ jagāda ca.
«kumāro ’yaṃ mad|ādeśa|yogyaḥ śīghraṃ vidhīyatām.»
tath” êty aṅgīkṛtya devas tatr’ āgāt pratyuṣaḥ|kṣaṇe,
uddiśya ca kumāraṃ taṃ papāṭh’ êti sphuṭ’|âkṣaraṃ:

13.45 «saṃsāram etaṃ dhig, dhig bho,
yatra mantu vin” âiva hi
priyo ’pi vipriyaṃ kuryāt
pit” âpi pratikūlati,
jāyeta rāj” âpi raṅkaḥ, pad|gaḥ syād gaja|gāmy api,
ājñā|dāyy api c’ ādeśyo gupto bhogy api saṃvaset.
tad bho, budhasva! budhasva! na ko ’pi svo ’tra tattvataḥ.
Vimalasena kumāra, mā rajya viṣay’|â|śucau!»
paṭhitv” êti suraḥ so ’gāt, kumāras tv ity acintayat:
«vairāgya|kṛn māṃ prat’ îdaṃ peṭhe kena su|bhāṣitam.»

"This criminal, even though my son, is to be arrested, 13.40
and, when he has learned his lesson, released. I must ever foster kingly policy as I would a family goddess. This is my intention in this matter. You must accede to it forthwith." Thus the King effected the King's welfare. Oh, the intelligence of the intelligent!

Sámara·sena, having perceived through the power of his knowledge that the Prince had fallen into such a bad situation, thought that the time for his enlightenment had now come.

Then he remembered the god Shura. When he came, Sámara·sena said to him, "The Prince is fit to receive my teaching. Let it be effected."

Having promised to do so, the god arrived at that place just before dawn. And he instructed the Prince, reciting this with clear enunciation:

"Alas, alas, sir, for this cycle of existence, in which a man 13.45
is absolutely alone, and a husband causes estrangement and a father acts contrarily,

and a king becomes a beggar, one who goes by foot becomes one who travels on an elephant, the giver of orders becomes one who takes orders, and the protected retainer leads a life of wealth. So, good sir, be enlightened, be enlightened! Truly there is no paradise here at all. Prince Vímala·sena, delight not in the impurity of sensual pleasures!"

The god recited that and left, and the Prince thought, "Someone has recited this verse, which creates disgust with the world, with regard to me."

dvitīye 'hni punar devo bhṛśaṃ vairāgya|kṛj jagau,
yath"|āgataṃ gataś c' âyaṃ. kumāraḥ pṛṣṭavān janān.

13.50 «bho bhoḥ, ken' âdya paṭhitaṃ?» jagaduḥ pāripārśvikāḥ:
«na vidmaḥ. ko 'py a|dṛśyo 'yaṃ, kevalaṃ śrūyate dhvaniḥ.»

punas tṛtīye 'hni suro 'pāṭhīd vairāgya|kṛd bahu:
«kiṃ bah'|ûkter? na saṃsāre sukhaṃ, vahnau saro|javat.
tat kumāra, muñca, muñca viṣay'|āśā|viḍambanām.
Jina|dharme samudyaccha, sāmagrī durlabhā punaḥ.»

tataḥ śrī|Vimalasenas tam ūce, «bhadra, ko 'si, bhoḥ?»
suro 'vocat «prasmṛto 'smi bhavataś cira|saṃstutaḥ.
Kauśāmbyāṃ śrī|Sudharm'|ântike prāvrajāma vayaṃ daśa,
Saudharme dyusado 'bhūmo, 'kārṣma bodhāya saṃśravam.

13.55 svargāt tvaṃ Rāmadeva'|ṛṣi|jīvo 'tr' âbhūr narendra|sūḥ.
tasya te bodhaye 'smy āgāṃ, tad budhyasva, mahā|mate!»

iti śrutv" ēh"|ādi kurvan jāti|smaraṇam ujjvalam
lebhe śrī|Vimalasenas tṛtīyam iva locanam.

On the second day, the god again recited a verse that aroused strong disgust with the world, and left by the way he had come. The Prince asked his attendants:

"Sirs, good sirs, who recited today?" The attendants re- 13.50
plied, "We don't know. It was someone invisible. Only his voice was heard."

Once more, on the third day, the god recited several times a verse arousing disgust with the world: "What need of many words? Like a lotus in a fire, happiness does not exist in the cycle of existence. So, Prince, give up, give up the disgrace of longing for sensual pleasures. Apply yourself to the Jain religion. The means here at your disposal will be difficult to find again."

Then His Highness Vímala·sena said to him, "Good sir, who are you?" The god said, "You've forgotten me, your long-time intimate friend. In Kaushámbi we ten took the vows of initiation in the presence of reverend Sudhárman. We became gods in the Good Works heaven and made a
mutual promise for our enlightenment. And from heaven, 13.55
you, the soul of Rama·deva, became the King's son in this place. I have come to enlighten him and you, so be enlightened; great is your understanding!"

On hearing this, His Highness Vímala·sena made due consideration of what was for and against, and attained luminous perception, like a third eye, producing memory of his former lives.

tataś ca prāpta|saṃvādaḥ kumāras taṃ suraṃ jagau:
«aho te satya|samdhatvam! aho saujanyam adbhutam!
nistārito bhav'|âmbhodher a|gādhād apy ahaṃ tvayā,
tad ādiś' âdhunā kāryaṃ yad vidhātuṃ mam' ôcitam.»
devo 'vadat «pravraj' āśu śrī|Jayaśāsan'|ātmanaḥ
pārśve Samarasenasya bodhitasya may" âiva hi.
13.60 sa ca prabhuś catur|jñānī sādhu|saṅgha|pariṣkṛtaḥ
tava pravrājana|kṛte svayam eva sameṣyati.»
«kār'|āgār'|ôdara|stho 'ham dīkṣiṣye 'smi kathaṃ, sakhe?»
ūce devo, «mā viṣīda, yat te bhavati, paśya tat!»
tataḥ pur'|ôpari vyomni vicakre 'sau mahā|śilām
ati|pracaṇḍa|malinaṃ su|ghanaṃ ghana|vārdalam.
vyoma|sthito 'vadad devo,
«bho bhoḥ, sāmanta|mantriṇaḥ
dur|ācārās, tathā rājan,
kañ cic ccharaṇam icchata?
devo vā dānavo vā yaḥ pāti yuṣmān ito bhayāt?
mā brūta yan na bhaṇitam, eṣa vaś cūrṇayāmy aham.
13.65 bhavadbhir yat kumāro 'sau nirmantuś cārake dhṛtaḥ,
tad asau mānyatām, svāmī kriyatāṃ, yena vaḥ śivam.»
tato rājā ca devī ca pramod'|â|dvaitam ūhatuḥ,
sāmant'|ādyāś ca bibhiyur, menire ca sur'|ôditam.

Then, having gained that information, the Prince said to the god, "Oh, your conjunction with the truth! Oh, your wonderful benevolence! You have rescued me from the ocean of existence, a receptacle of impurity. Tell me the duty that is right for me to undertake."

The god said, "Take initiation forthwith in the presence of Sámara·sena, the soul of the honorable Jaya·shásana. I'm
the one who enlightened him. And the reverend lord, pos- 13.60
sessed of the fourfold knowledge and surrounded by his congregation of monks, will come himself to initiate you."

"How will I be initiated, confined within a prison, my friend?" The god said, "Don't despair of this happening to you. Look at this!"

Thereupon he made appear in the sky, hanging over the city, a huge stone, very sharp and black, very solid, like a cloud bringing bad weather.

Standing in the sky, the god said, "Sirs, sirs, barons and ministers, you whose conduct is bad, Your Majesty likewise: what protection do you seek? A god or a demon that will protect you from this impending fear? Don't say what wasn't
said—I'm the one who is going to pulverize you. Since you 13.65
held the Prince in prison although he is innocent, you must treat him with respect and make him King in order for you to attain felicity."

Then the King and the Queen summoned him with nothing other than joy, and the barons and the others were frightened and paid regard to what the god had said.

atha śrī|Vimalaseno rājñā rājye 'bhiṣicyata
sarvaiś ca mānayāñcakre, cakre vardhāpanaṃ mahat.
kṣaṇe c' âtr' ôdyāna|pālaḥ sva|bhāla|ghaṭit'|âñjaliḥ
harṣa|prakarṣād uttālaḥ śrī|bhū|pālaṃ vyajijñapat:
«dev' âdya nandan'|ôdyāne nandan'|ôdyāna|tarjane
catur|jñānī śrī|Samarasena|sūrir upāgamat.»

13.70 sarvair ūce, «'bhavat kautūhale prati|kutūhalam.
kumāra|rājy'|âbhiṣeke yaj jajñe su|gur'|ûdayaḥ!»
śrī|Vatsarājo Vimalasen'|ādi|tanayair vṛtaḥ
sāmanta|mantri|pauraiś ca sarvaiḥ saha paricchadaiḥ
catur|aṅga|varūthinyā kiñ cin nyañcita|śeṣayā
nantuṃ yayau guru|tīrthaṃ nandan'|ôdyāna|maṇḍanam.
praṇamya vidhin" āsīnaṃ rājānaṃ sa|paricchadam
śrī|gurur bhojayāmāsa vyākhyā|rasavatīm iti:
«ā|janm'|ôpātta|sarvaṃ|
kaṣa|viṣama|kaṣāy'|âṭavī|vahni|bhīme
dur|dānt'|â|śrānta|matt'|ên-
driya|karaṭi|ghaṭ'|â|bhagna|sādhiṣṭha|ṣaṇḍe
rāga|pradveṣa|moha|
prakaṭa|caraṭakair luṇṭyamān'|â|khila|sve
saṃsār'|âraṇya|deśe
na khalu nivasatāṃ śarmaṇo 'bhyastir asti.

Then the King consecrated His Highness Vímala·sena to the kingship, and they all paid respect to him and held a great festival.

Now, at that moment the head gardener, his forehead touched by his hands folded in salutation, absolutely thrilled with joy, informed His Majesty the King:

"Your Majesty, the reverend doctor venerable Sámara·sena has just now arrived in the paradise garden, which puts to shame the garden of paradise."

They all said, "It is a cause for festivity on top of a cause for 13.70
festivity that the coming of the true teacher has been made known at the consecration of the Prince to the kingship!"

His Majesty Vatsa·raja accompanied by his sons, Vímala·sena and the others, the barons, ministers and citizens, and all his courtiers, and by his fourfold army, all bowing slightly, went to pay his respects to the worthy teacher who was adorning the paradise garden.

The King paid his respects according to the precept and then sat surrounded by his entourage, and the teacher fed him a meal of instruction, as follows:

"There is no experience of happiness at all for those who dwell in the wilderness country of the cycle of existence, which is fearful with the forest fires of impurity, a rough touchstone of hard knocks received from birth, with its very dense thickets unshattered by the troops of elephants that are the senses, deluded, intoxicated, unwearied and difficult to tame, its wealth plundered by the thieves of manifest desire, hatred and delusion.

13.75 abhyetuṃ tad imaṃ sarva|
darśi|sarva|jña|darśitam
dharma|vartma śrayadhvaṃ, bho.
labhadhvaṃ padam avyayam!»
śrī|deśanā|rasavatīm etām āsvādya jajñire
praśānta|tṛṣṇā bahuśo, 'tha vṛṣṭiṃ cātakā iva.
tataḥ kumāraḥ saṃsāra|kāntār'|ôttāra|hetave
gurūn vijñāpayāmāsa satat'|āsanna|sevivat.
gurur ūce, «dhīra, vayam upem' âitat|kṛte svayam,
yat tvaṃ naś cira|saṃsṛṣṭaḥ.» «prasādo, bhagavan, mahān.»
tataś ca:
sambodhya pitarau bhakti|nānā|yukty|udgirā girā
kārayitvā tīrtha|mah"|ādikaṃ Vijayasenavat
13.80 nṛpati|mantri|mah"|êbhya|su|sārthapa|
prabhṛti|putra|śataiḥ saha pañcabhiḥ
Vimalasena|kumāra upaid vrataṃ
Samarasena|guroḥ pada|padmataḥ.
puri puri Jina|candra|śrī|vilāsaṃ dadhānaḥ
su|guru|Samaraseno 'nyatra cakre vihāram.
su|muni|Vimalasen' âpi tat|pāda|padme
madhu|madhu|kara|līlā nirmame nirmameṇa.

iti śrī|nirvāṇa|Līlāvatī|mahā|kath"|êti|vṛtt'|ôddhāre Līlāvatī|sāre Jin'|âṅke Rāmadeva|maha"|rṣi|jīva|śrī|Vimalasena|kumāra|pratibodha|vyāvarṇano nāma trayodaśa utsāhaḥ.

So to approach the country revealed by the all-seeing and 13.75
all-knowing ones, sirs, resort to the path of religion. Attain the imperishable country!"

And, having eaten the meal of the holy teaching, their thirst became satiated; they were like *chátaka* birds that had fed on the rain.

Then the Prince, with great respect, requested the teacher to rescue him from the wilderness of existence.

The teacher said, "Resolute one, I came here myself for this very reason, since you are my longtime friend." "You are very gracious, reverend sir."

And then:

Having enlightened his parents with a voice emitting devotion and various proofs, and like Víjaya·sena having caused festivals and such to be performed at holy places,
Prince Vímala·sena, accompanied by five hundred, the sons 13.80
of kings, ministers, great men, wealthy merchants and suchlike, took the vow at the lotus-feet of the teacher Sámara·sena.

Spreading the lovely light of the moon of the Jina from city to city, the teacher Sámara·sena wandered elsewhere, and the good monk Vímala·sena in his selflessness took on the appearance of a bee for the honey of the lotus of teacher's feet.

Here ends the thirteenth canto, entitled "The Enlightenment and Initiation of His Highness Prince Vímala·sena, the Soul of the Mighty Ascetic Rama·deva," of the Jain epic *The Epitome of Queen Liláavati*, an abridgment of the events of *The Epic Story of the Auspicious Final Emancipation of Lilávati.*

CANTO 14
THE INITIATION FESTIVAL OF HIS HIGHNESS PRINCE SURAN·DHARA, THE SOUL OF THE MERCHANT PURAN·DARA, AND OF PRINCE KÚSUMA·SHÉKHARA, THE SOUL OF PRINCE SULÁKSHANA

14.1 ITAŚ CA: kṣoṇī|lalāṭa|deśo nu Lāṭa|deśe ’sti viśrutam
maṇī|tilaka|saṃkāśaṃ Bhṛgukacchaṃ mahā|puram.
rāj” âtra Kusumaketur mīna|ketur iv’ âparaḥ.
jagaj|jaitra|śaro reje bhava|sarvaṃ|kaṣaḥ param.
mangalyā vinay’|ôjjvālā mithyātva|viṣa|nāśinī
a|dāhyā gurvy|a|kutsyā ca śrī|śīlasya rasāyanam,
pradakṣiṇ’|āvarta|ramy” êty aṣṭa|spaṣṭa|guṇ’|ôlbaṇā
sthāne śrī|Kanakalatā nāmnā jāne ’sya devy abhūt.
14.5 bhuñjānayos tayor bhogān yath”|âvasaram adbhutān
Sulakṣaṇa|mahā|sādhu|jīvaḥ svargāt tataś cyutaḥ.
vapuṣmad|ānanda|piṇḍa|sama|piṇḍa|vapur|lataḥ chinna
kula|pradīpaḥ putro ’bhūn nāmnā Kusumaśekharaḥ.
so ’dhītī sarva|śāstreṣu sarva|śastreṣu kauśalī
patiḥ pāṇi|gṛhītīnāṃ yauva|rājya|śriyo ’py abhūt.
anyad” ôdyāna|pālena Datta|nāmnā sa bhūpa|bhūḥ
śrī|vasant’|âvatāreṇ’ âvardhāpyata kṛt’|âñjali:
sarv’|āśā|cakra|vicaran Malay’|ânila|śāsanaḥ
pragīto matta|madhupair vādyat|pika|jay’|ānakaḥ,
14.10 prati|dru|mūrdha|vismera|puṣpa|śṛṅgāra|bhāsuraḥ chinna
vasanta|rājo vilasaty udyāne deva|nandane.

Now, in the Lata country, indeed the forehead country of the world, like its forehead jewel, is a famous capital city, Bhrigu·kaccha. And there ruled Kúsuma·ketu, like another fish-bannered god of love, his arrow victorious over the universe, and a touchstone for every excellence. 14.1

Bestowing good fortune, splendid in her modesty, destroying the poison of falsehood, unflammable, unreproachable by her elders, an elixir of the fortune of morality, and, because she was lovely with her locks curling to the right, richly possessed of the eight evident excellences, in her posture a lovely golden creeper, so named at birth, Her Highness Kánaka·lata (Golden Creeper), was his queen.

And as they enjoyed wonderful pleasures as was seasonable, the soul of the great monk Sulákshana fell from heaven. And he, the creeper of his body put together with morsels of embodied joy, became their son, the light of his family, named Kúsuma·shékhara. 14.5

Well read among all textbooks, proficient among all weapons, he became the husband of young ladies of marriageable age and attained the rank of crown prince.

One day, the head gardener, Datta by name, with his hands folded in salutation, congratulated the Prince on the arrival of the lovely spring season:

"Spreading his dominion over all quarters; commanding the breezes of the Málaya mountains; hymned by intoxicated bees; his drums of victory, the cries of cuckoos; resplendent in the finery of blossoms blooming on the top 14.10
of every tree, the king of the spring is sporting in Your Highness's garden of delight."

hasty|aśva|ratha|pādāt'|ântaḥpureṇa vṛtas tataḥ
rantuṃ śrī|nandan'|ôdyāne yayau Kusumaśekharaḥ.
itaś c' âtīva|ramyatvāt tasy' ôdyānasya sarvataḥ
svaira|cāritayā deva|jāteḥ krīḍitum uttvaraṃ
kinnara|dvandvam atr' āgān mithaḥ|prem'|ōrmi|varmitam,
ramye ca kadalī|gṛhe rahasi praviveśa ca.
tatr' âiva rambhā|dhāmny āgāt kumāro 'pi riraṃsayā,
jñātvā ca mithunaṃ madhye kumāro 'pāsarad drutam.
14.15 tad|dvandva|niḥsāraṇāya naraṃ praiṣīn narendra|sūḥ.
tad dvandvaṃ tena puṃs" ōce, «re drutaṃ niḥsar' âmutaḥ!»
tayā khara|girā ruṣṭo devo 'vag, «darśayāmi te
phalaṃ dur|vinayasy' âsya! re, tiṣṭh' âtr' âiva, dur|mukha!»
tad|vaco rāja|sūḥ śrutvā puṃs" ânyena niṣevya tam
sv'|āgat'|ôkti|pūrvam etad dvandvam evam abībhaṇat:
«na kopitavyaṃ bhavadbhiḥ. kiñ cit praṣṭavyam asti me
tad āyāta dros tale 'sy'.» êty ukte puṃsā sa|gauravam,
suro jagāda, «na vayaṃ kumār'|ādeśa|gocarāḥ.
cet praṣṭavyaṃ kiñ cid asti, kiṃ n' âtr' āgatya pṛcchati?»
14.20 puṃs" ōce tat kumārasya, tat|pārśve 'gāt sa c' âikakaḥ.
abhyuttasthe sa yugmena premnā sv|āgata|vādinā.
datt'|āsano 'tha kinnary" āsīno 'vādīn nṛp'|âṅga|jaḥ:
«bhavadbhyām anvagṛhye 'haṃ, yad udyānam alaṅkṛtam.

Accompanied by elephants, horses, carriages, foot soldiers and his royal ladies, Kúsuma·shékhara went to make love in the lovely garden of delight. And then, because of the surpassing loveliness everywhere in that garden, a couple of heavenly musician gods, of the class of god that moves at will, enveloped by waves of mutual affection, came there to make passionate love, and entered the seclusion of a lovely plantain bower. The Prince, too, wishing to make love, entered that same plantain bower. When he saw the couple in the middle of it, the Prince immediately withdrew.

The Prince sent a servant to make the couple leave. That 14.15
man said to the couple, "Hey, get out of here right now!"

Angered by his rough speech, the god said, "I'll show you the reward of your bad manners! Hey, stay right here, bad-mouther!"

The Prince heard his statement, and sent another to ameliorate what the man he had sent before had said, and to speak to the couple on his behalf.

On the man's saying respectfully, "Please don't be angry. I have something to ask you. Just come to the foot of this tree," the god said, "We are not subject to the Prince's commands. If he has something to ask, why doesn't he come here and ask us?"

The man related that to the Prince. He went to their 14.20
presence, and the couple treated him respectfully with kind words of welcome.

Then the heavenly musician goddess presented him with a seat, and when he was seated the Prince said, "I am obliged to you, since you have adorned the garden.

kiṃ c' â|niyojyayor eva niyogaṃ yuvayor dade,
nityaṃ yuvābhyām udyānam idaṃ pāvyaṃ nija|kramaiḥ,
syātāṃ pavitre man|netra yad yuṣmad|darśan'|âmṛtaiḥ.
mahatāṃ darśanaṃ tīrtha|darśan'|âdhikam ucyate.»
tābhyām ath' ōce, «dhanye no netre śrotre ca, sattama,
pape yakābhyāṃ tvad|rūpaṃ tvad|vacaś ca sudh"|ôpamam.»
14.25 «kau yuvām?» iti tat|pṛṣṭe tau brūtaḥ, «kinnarāv» iti.
«kiṃ yair atr' ôpamīyante gāyānāḥ? sādhu vetsi, bhoḥ.»
«yuṣmad|gīte kautukaṃ me, gāyataṃ kṣaṇam atra tat.»
tābhyāṃ ca gātum ārebhe, camac|cakre ca rāja|sūḥ.
kinnaro 'vak, «kumāra, tvaṃ vādyaṃ kiñ cana vādaya.
vādya|tāl'|ânusāreṇa suṣamām gītam eti yat.»
kumāro 'vādayat paṭā|todyam, mithunakaṃ tu tat
jagau viṣama|tālena, kumāro 'vīvadat tathā
gīte viṣama|tāle 'pi na punaḥ kva can' âskhalat.
ath' ōcatur vismitau tau, «gāya tvam api, rāṭ|suta.»
14.30 jegīyamānaḥ kumāraḥ kinnarāv atyaśeta tau.
yathā|praśnaṃ sarva|kalāsv eṣa tāv atyarañjayat.
guṇaiḥ kalābhī rūpeṇa vinayena nayena ca
tasya tuṣṭaṃ mayu|yugam, «varaṃ vṛṇv!» ity abhāṣata.

And may I give a task to you who are certainly not to be given tasks? May you please ever continue to purify this garden with your footsteps. May my eyes be purified by the sight of beholding you. It is said that the sight of great ones is better than the sight of holy places."

Then they replied, "Our eyes and ears are blessed, you best of men, which have drunk your form and your words, like nectar."

On his asking who they were, the couple replied, "We 14.25
are heavenly musician gods. Who can compare with us in singing? You will know full well, good sir."

"I am longing to hear your singing, so sing for a moment right here." They began to sing and the Prince was amazed.

The heavenly musician god said, "Prince, play some instrument, since a song becomes very beautiful when it is performed to the beat of an instrument."

The Prince began to play a kettledrum, and the couple sang in a difficult rhythm as the Prince kept time. But even though the song was in a difficult rhythm, he didn't make a mistake in any place at all. Thereupon the couple were amazed and said, "Now you sing, Prince."

The Prince sang so well he surpassed the two heavenly 14.30
musician gods. According to their requests, he delighted them in all the arts.

And the heavenly musician couple, pleased with him because of his excellences, his skills in the arts, his beauty, his manners and his wisdom, said, "Choose a boon!"

«smṛtāv āgantavyam» iti kumār'|ôktaṃ prapadya tau
kinnarau sv'|āspadam itau, rantv" ôccai rāja|sūr api.

itaś ca Payasā|deśe śrīmaj|Jayapuraṃ puram,
jaya|śrī|vallabho Ratnavallabhas tatra bhū|patiḥ.
līlāvatī|śiro|ratnaṃ Ratnacūl" âsya devy abhūt,
yāṃ vīkṣy' âiva Ramā|Gauryau patyur aṅgaṃ na muñcataḥ.

14.35 tayoḥ prāk|puṇya|saṃsāra|sphurat|saundarya|sundarī
śrī|sura|sundarī|ślāghyā putry abhūt Surasundarī.

cañcac|campaka|hema|ketaka|nabho|
Gaṅgā|saroja|śriyāṃ
jyotsnā|mauktika|candra|kānta|mahasāṃ
sāraṃ śirīśa|śriyāṃ
yady ādāya vidhiḥ pramṛjya sudhayā
kāñ cit sṛjet sundarīṃ
tasyā apy upadāspadaṃ pratipadaṃ
manye yad|aṃhri|śriyaḥ.

itaś ca:

Varāṭā|nāma|deśo 'sti tatra Siṃhapuraṃ puram
siṃho 'ri|dantiṣu Nabhovāhano 'tra mahī|patiḥ.
tasya niḥsāmānya|rūpa|kamalā Kamalāvatī
antaḥpuram iv' âtyantaṃ vibhūṣayati hṛt|puram.

The two heavenly musician gods, having assented to the Prince's request that they should come whenever he thought of them, returned to their own abode, and the Prince was highly delighted.

Now, in the Páyasa country is a city, lovely Jaya·pura, and there was a king, Ratna·vállabha, beloved of the fortune of victory. The crest-jewel of beautiful women, Ratna·chula, was his wife. Once Lakshmi and Gauri had set eyes on her, they never left the side of their shared husband.

The loveliness of her beauty manifest because of her for- 14.35
mer merit in the cycle of existence, praised by the lovely beautiful goddess, their daughter was Sura·súndari (Beautiful Goddess).

If the creator, having taken the essence of the loveliness of lotuses on a Ganges formed by the perfumed vapor of swaying *chámpaka* and golden *kétaka* trees and of the loveliness of acacias whose lovely brilliance is like the moonlight of the pearl-moon, and having sprinkled it with nectar, had created some beautiful woman, the place given to her at every step, I suppose, would be the beauty of her foot.

And then:

There is a country named Varáta, and in it a city Simha·pura, in which was a king, Nabho·váhana, a lion among those who had subdued their enemies. His wife of extraordinary beauty was Kamalávati, who highly ornamented the city of his heart, like his married women's apartments.

sā c' ânyadā niśā|śeṣe svakīy'|ôtsaṅga|śṛṅga|gam
mṛga|puṅgavam adrākṣīt sākṣībhūtaṃ suta|śriyaḥ.
14.40 tataḥ Purandara|muni|jīvo jīvātur ojasām
tasyāḥ kukṣau ratna|khanyām ādya|svargād avātarat.
janm'|ôtsavo nāma|dhey'|ôtsavaś ca bhuvan'|ôtsavau
Surandhara iti nāma c' âsya karṇ'|ôtsavo 'bhavat.
kal"|ācāryo 'dhyāpayaṃs taṃ niṣprati|pratibhodayam
adhyāpak'|âdhyāpya|bhāva|viparyayam amanyata.
yauva|rājye tath" ôdāra|dāra|rājye 'bhyaṣicya tam
pṛthak|prāsāde sva|mūrta|prasāde nu nyadhān nṛpaḥ.
atha pratyantikāḥ ke cin Nabhovāhana|bhū|bhujaḥ
giri|durga|balāt siṃhā iva deśam upādravan.
14.45 tad|deśa|vāsibhiḥ siṃha|dvāre bhūpasya put|kṛtam
kṛtaṃ ca rājñā durdharṣ'|â|marṣād āsthāna|vīkṣitam.
tataḥ Surandharo rājñaḥ
pādau natvā vyajijñapat:
«kva devaḥ, kva ca te kṣudrāḥ?
kva mṛg'|êndro, mṛgāḥ kva ca?
deva|pādā dadātv ājñāṃ mam' âiv' ājñ"|âñujīvinaḥ
tac|chiraḥ|kamalair yen' âbhyarcāmi svāminaḥ padau.»
rājā tato vyājahāra, «vats', âsmaj|jīvitair api
su|ciraṃ nanda jaivātṛkatām āsedivān bhuvi.
asmadīyo daṇḍa eva daṇḍaṃ nirmāya vidviṣām.
tadīya|sarva|svam api kṣaṇād daṇḍaṃ grahīṣyati.»

One day at the end of the night, she dreamed that a stag entered the cusp of her lap, a witness of the fortune of a son. The soul of the monk Puran·dara, an elixir of vitality, 14.40
descended from the first heaven into the mine of jewels that was her womb.

The festival for his birth and the festival for his name-giving were two festivals for the world, and his name, Suran·dhara, was a festival for the ear.

As a master of arts educated this incomparable student, he considered that the roles of teacher and pupil had been reversed.

The King consecrated him to the junior kingship and to the kingship of noble wives and established him in a separate palace, the very image of his own.

Then certain borderers of King Nabho·váhana from their
mountain stronghold attacked that country like lions. The 14.45
inhabitants of that area made cries of complaint at the gates of the palace, and the King, his anger dreadful, held an audience in the assembly.

Then Suran·dhara bowed to His Majesty's feet and said, "What are those insignificants compared with Your Majesty? What are deer compared with the king of the animals? Let Your Majesty give the command to me, dependent on your commands, and I will reverence Your Majesty's feet with the lotuses of their heads."

Then the King declared, "My son, enjoy, even by means of my own life, a very long life span as you dwell on earth. Having meted out punished to enemies, punishment is indeed mine. He will take his punishment in an instant, even the confiscation of all his wealth."

14.50 mantry ūce Vimalamatir, «vicāro n' âiṣa sundaraḥ.
pratihastā hi kāryāṇi nāśayanti ku|mitravat.

yataḥ:

daṇḍ'|âdhipāḥ kūṭa|hṛdo lobhāt svāmy|artha|nāśakāḥ
ripu|lañcām upajīvya dīvyant' īśa|kriy"|âlasāḥ.

kumārasya prayāṇaṃ tu sarvathā na khal' ûcitam.
rājya|sāraṃ kumāro 'yaṃ jīvatāc candra|kālikam!
svāminaḥ svayam udyogo, deva, samprati sāmprataṃ
su|svāminaḥ puraḥ sarve yataḥ svāmy|artha|kāriṇaḥ.»

rāj" ākhyad, «yuktam ev' âitat.»
putras t' ūce, «'vadhāryatām.
sva|putre sva|pratāpasy' â-
vatāraṃ paśyatu prabhuḥ.»

14.55 kumāra|vāky'|ânurodhād anvamanyata tan nṛpaḥ,
ubhayor anurodhāt tu bahv amanyata mantry api.

tato 'nurakt'|âṅga|rakṣa|sāmant'|âmātya|varmitaḥ
catur|aṅga|camū|bhāraiḥ śeṣ'|â|śeṣa|phaṇā|rujam
prati|grāmaṃ prati|puraṃ sausthyam utpādayan nayam
Surandhara|kumāraḥ srāk pratasthe sthema|parvataḥ.

tathā camv" âti|bhūyasyā prayāṇair a|vilambitaiḥ
śrutvā yāntaṃ taṃ kumāraṃ dviṣo durgam aśiśriyan.

The minister Vímala·mati said, "This noble youth should 14.50
not go. Deputies, like bad friends, certainly cause the failure of necessary business.

Since:

Judges, their minds deceitful, destroy the King's wealth through their greed. Living on the bribes of his enemies, they spend their time gambling, neglectful of the King's business.

Now, it is not all right for the Prince to lead the expedition. The Prince is the essence of the kingdom; may he live for as long as the moon! But, sire, it is fitting for His Majesty to undertake this himself right now, since everyone, when in the presence of a good master, performs his master's business."

The King said, "This is certainly right." But his son said, "We should consider it. Let the King observe the descent of His Majesty into his son."

Through regard to the Prince's statement, the King gave 14.55
his approval, and through regard to them both the minister, too, gave his full approval.

Then, defended by a devoted bodyguard of barons and ministers, crushing all the serpents of the world through the weight of his army of four divisions, effecting welfare and prudent policy by village and by town, Prince Suran·dhara, a mountain of firmness, swiftly advanced.

Having heard that the Prince was thus advancing with unbroken marches of an extremely large army, the enemy withdrew within a fort.

kumāras tad|durga|saṃnidhāne sthāne varīyasi
dvipad|vīra|dur|nivāraṃ skandhāvāraṃ nyavīviśat.
14.60 taiḥ pratyanīkaiḥ sva|svāmī hūto Jayapur'|ēśvaraḥ
śrī|Ratnavallabho bhūpaḥ samāyāsīd a|lakṣitaḥ.

kumāro 'lpa|parīvāraḥ krīḍayā mṛgayāṃ gataḥ
tena dṛṣṭaḥ parijñāto jagṛhe helay" âiva hi.
puṇy'|ôdayāt tena putra|darśam dṛṣṭaḥ Surandharaḥ
sandhāya pratyanīkaiś ca svāmi|darśam adṛśyata.
sa ca rājā kumārāya mene tāṃ Surasundarīm,
tato jāmātaram amuṃ putr'|âdhikam amaṃsta ca.

itaś ca sā Jayapure rāṭ|putrī Surasundarī
sakhī|dāsī|kañcukibhir vṛtā su|bhaṭa|veṣṭitā.
14.65 yayau krīḍitum udyānam udyānasy' êva devatā.
sakhībhir ṛtu|devībhir iva sārdham araṃsta ca.
tatra c' âgre śrī|Kusumaśekharasy' âti|saṃstutam
svaira|cāri krīḍituṃ tat kinnara|dvandam āgamat.
rambhā|gṛhe ca Kusumaśekharasya guṇān jagau,
tac ca gītaṃ kuraṅg" îva papau sā Surasundarī.

jagāma ca tayoḥ pārśve, tau papraccha ca, «kau yuvām?
ka eṣa subhag'|āpīḍo gītaḥ Kusumaśekharaḥ?
sa kiṃ bhavati bhavatoḥ? kiñ ca vāṃ dattavān asau?»
tāv ūcatuḥ, «surāv āvāṃ, naraḥ Kusumaśekharaḥ.
14.70 Bhṛgukacche Puṣpaketu|Svarṇalatā|tan'|ûdbhavaḥ.

In a broad plain adjacent to the fort, the Prince besieged the royal headquarters, difficult to blockade by elephants and men.

Those rebels summoned their commander, who was the King of Jaya·pura. His Majesty King Ratna·vállabha arrived unobserved. 14.60

The Prince, accompanied by a small entourage, went to divert himself at hunting. The King saw and recognized him, and captured him quite easily. Because of the manifestation of his merit, the King saw that Suran·dhara had the appearance of a son, and, having come to terms, the rebels saw that he had the appearance of a king. And the King betrothed Sura·súndari to the Prince and then regarded his son-in-law more highly than a son.

Now, Princess Sura·súndari was in Jaya·pura, surrounded with her friends, maidservants and attendants, guarded by mighty warriors.

She went to play in the garden. She, like the goddess of the garden, played in the company of her friends, who were like goddesses of spring. And that couple of heavenly musician gods, the great friends of Kúsuma·shékhara, had just before come to play in that place. And in a plantain bower they sang of the excellencies of Kúsuma·shékhara, and Sura·súndari, like a female antelope, drank in that song. 14.65

She approached their presence and asked, "Who are you, and who is this chaplet of good fortune of whom you are singing, Kúsuma·shékhara? What is he to you, and what has he given you?" They said, "We are gods, Kúsuma·shékhara is a mortal. He is the son of Kúsuma·ketu and Kánaka·lata. 14.70
He is nothing to us, and we desire nothing from him. But,

tan na nau kiñ cid bhavat', îcchāvaḥ kiñ cin na c' âmutaḥ.
kin tu tasya guṇa|grāma|nikām'|ākṛṣṭa|mānasau
gāyāvas taṃ prati|padaṃ dhyāyāvaś ca prati|kṣaṇam.»

Surasundary ath' âbhūt s'|ôtsukā tat|saṅgam'|ôtsave,
ten' âiva hṛta|citt" êva śūnya|śūny" âbhavat kṣaṇāt.
nītā gṛhaṃ sakhībhiḥ sā jñāta|vṛttāntay" âmbayā
na jīvaty eṣ" ânyath" êti rājñi yātrāṃ gate 'pi ca
maha"|rddhyā praiṣi Kusumaśekharāya svayaṃvarā,
pariṇinye ca mahato vicchardād Bhṛgupattane.
14.75 sa ca pratyantika|pure sthitaḥ śrī|Ratnavallabhaḥ
Surandharam uvāc', «âihi tām udvaha mam' ātmajām.»

kumāro 'py āha, «sma pitṛ|anujñay" êdaṃ karomy aham.»
tat|siddhyai sa nṛpaḥ Siṃhapure praiṣīn narāṃs tataḥ.

āgatās te 'bhyadhur, «deva, Nabhovāhana|bhū|patiḥ
bhavad|uktaṃ bahu mene, saṃdideśa ca kiñ cana.
yuṣmat|kṛta|kumār'|âvagraha|śravaṇa|śālyitā
kumār'|â|darśane devī na bhuṅkte Kamalāvatī.
tat kumāro gṛham etu, natvā pitarau drutam
sameṣyati bhavat|pārśvē.» tan mene Ratnavallabhaḥ.
14.80 sambhāvit'|âdhika|kārya|siddhyā pramada|medurau
prāptau svaṃ svaṃ puraṃ Ratnavallabha|śrī|Surandharau.

atha bhūmī|bhujā jñātaṃ yathā devyā vyasṛjyata
Surasundarī Kusumaśekharāya svayaṃvarā.

our minds attracted by love of his multitude of excellences, we hymn him at every step and meditate on him at every moment."

Then Sura·súndari became intent on the celebration of union with him, and, as if her consciousness had been stolen away by that very one, in a trice became completely vacant. Her companions carried her home. Her mother, thinking that she would not otherwise live, and since the King was away, too, on his expedition, sent her with a large dowry as a self-betrothed bride to Kúsuma·shékhara, and she was married with great expenditure in Bhrigu·kaccha.

Now, His Majesty King Ratna·vállabha, while in that bor- 14.75
der town, asked Suran·dhara, "Come, marry my daughter."

The Prince said, "I will do it with my parents' permission." Thereupon the King sent men to Simha·pura to accomplish that.

On their return, they said, "Your Majesty, King Nabho·váhana pays high regard to your request but made a certain stipulation: Stung by hearing of her separation from the Prince that you have caused, Queen Kamalávati is pining in the Prince's absence. So let the Prince come home. Having paid his respects to his parents, he will quickly return to your presence." Ratna·vállabha agreed to that.

Full of joy at the accomplishment of a matter they both 14.80
attached great importance to, Ratna·vállabha and His Highness Suran·dhara each returned to his respective city.

Then the King learned how the Queen had sent Sura·súndari as self-betrothed bride to Kúsuma·shékhara.

«hā hā duṣṭhu|kṛtaṃ devyā, kṛtasya ca kṛtir na hi!»
prakhidy' êti ciraṃ Ratnavallabho maunam āśrayat.
Surandhara|kumāre ca sva|puraṃ drutam īyuṣi
ānanda|sāgaraḥ pitror abhraṃ|liha|lahary abhūt.
anyad" ādiṣṭaḥ pitṛbhyām udvoḍhuṃ Surasundarīm
Surandharaś cāru|camv" âcālīj Jayapuraṃ prati.
14.85 ath' âgrataḥ Siṃhāpurān Nabhovāhana|rāṭ|priyaḥ
Surandhara|kumārasya mitraṃ bhuvana|vatsalaḥ
dātā priyaṃ|vado bhogī dhanī nāmnā Dhanāvahaḥ
āghoṣya guru|sārthen' âcalaj Jayapuraṃ prati.
sa ca pratyanta|caraṭair grahītum upacakrame,
grahītuṃ śakyate n' âiva yoddhṛ|bāhulyataḥ param.
sauptikaṃ te vyadhuḥ sārthe yodhā naṣṭāḥ śṛgālavat
Dhanāvaho 'sinā yudhyamāno jarjarito 'sibhiḥ.
caraṭair jagṛhe so 'tha sārthaḥ sarvo vyaluṇṭyata
Dhanāvahaṃ sa|sarva|svaṃ gṛhītvā caraṭā yayuḥ.
14.90 tat|sārth'|ôdantam ajñāsīt prāptas tatra Surandharaḥ
tatr' āvāsya tatas tena caraṭā bhāṇitā iti:
«Dhanāvahaṃ sa|sarva|svaṃ drutam eva vimuñcata,
Dakṣiṇ'|ēśa|pure yad vā gṛhṇīt' âvakray'|āśrayaṃ.»
vicārya bahuśas te 'tha pradhāna|nara|pāṇinā
Dhanāvahaṃ kumārāya pradadur vyasta|vastuvat.

Dejectedly thinking, "Oh, the Queen has done wrong and there's nothing at all to be done about it!," Ratna·vállabha remained silent for a long time.

On Prince Suran·dhara's quickly reaching home, the ocean of his parents' joy swelled till it lapped the clouds.

One one day his parents ordered Suran·dhara to marry Sura·súndari and sent him to Jaya·pura with a handsome army.

Now, prior to that, a friend of King Nabho·váhana and a 14.85
friend of Prince Suran·dhara, affectionate to the world, generous, kindly-speaking, a wealthy merchant named Dhanávaha, made an announcement and from Simha·pura set out for Jaya·pura. And borderland bandits tried to capture him, but they were not able to capture him because of the size of his armed escort. They mounted a night attack on the caravan and the armed escort disappeared like jackals. Dhanávaha, fighting with a sword, was hacked by their swords. The bandits captured him and plundered the entire caravan. The bandits went, taking Dhanávaha and all his property.

When Suran·dhara arrived there he found out what had 14.90
happened to that caravan. He halted there and sent a message to the bandits:

"Release Dhanávaha together with all his property or else take a lodging in the city of the king of the dead."

And they, made to think very differently by him who was possessed of attendants and soldiers, returned Dhanávaha to the Prince as if returning lost property.

sādaraṃ sa kumāreṇ' ôpagūhya sthāpito rahaḥ
ādiṣṭā gauravād vaidyāḥ, «praguṇīkurut' āśv amum.»

caraṭānāṃ tat|pradhānaiḥ kumāreṇ' êty abhāṇyata:
«Dhanāvahasya sarva|svaṃ datta, mokṣo na vo 'nyathā!

14.95 yūyaṃ mitr'|ârpaṇān mitraṃ mam', êty ebhyo 'pasarpatha
anyeṣāṃ jīvitaṃ n' âiva sahāmy asmi kṛt'|ântavat.»

caraṭānāṃ ca taiḥ puṃbhiḥ kumār'|ôkte nivedite
sārtha|sarva|sva|dānāt taiḥ kumāraḥ prabhur ādadhe.

ath' â|sādhyatayā vaidyaiḥ vyamucyata Dhanāvahaḥ.
kumāra|suhṛd" ânūce Jinadāsena dhīmatā:

«bāḍhaṃ paricitān mṛtyor mā bhaiṣīr, dhīra|śekhara.
etasya jitvaraṃ śastraṃ hṛd" âvaha, Dhanāvaha.

tac c' Ârhan deva etasya bhāṣitaṃ brahmavān guruḥ
pramāṇam iti samyaktvaṃ pañc'|âṇuvrata|dhāraṇam

14.100 parameṣṭhi|namaskāro 'n|aśanaṃ kṣamaṇaṃ tathā
iti paṇḍita|maraṇaṃ sarva|mṛtyu|bhay'|âpaham.
sarvam anyad vimucy' êdaṃ, Dhanāvaha, dṛḍhīkuru
yen' âtr' âpi paratr' âpi vṛṇvate tvāṃ śiva|śriyaḥ.»

ten' âpy ūrīkṛtaṃ bhāvāt sarvam etat samādhinā,
vipadya sa ca Saudharme jajñe vaimānikaḥ suraḥ.

The Prince, having embraced him with devotions, placed him in seclusion and respectfully asked doctors to cure him quickly.

The Prince addressed the bandits through his attendants, "Return all Dhanávaha's property or else there will be no
deliverance for you! You, because you are my friends through 14.95
the returning of my friend, separate yourself from these; like the god of death, I will not suffer the others to live."

On being informed by his attendants of what the Prince had said, the bandits returned all the property from the caravan and accepted the Prince as their lord.

Now, because they were unable to accomplish anything, Dhanávaha was given up by his doctors. Jina·dasa, a wise friend of the Prince, addressed him:

"Because of what is certainly well known, you shouldn't fear death, you crown of fortitude. Bear in your mind the weapon that overcomes it, Dhanávaha.

Dying in the knowledge that the Worthy is a god, and 14.100
the teacher who expounds his teaching is the authority, and having understood about righteousness, the taking of the five subsidiary vows, the recitation of praise to the supreme beings, fasting and forbearance, takes away all fear of death. Abandoning all else, hold fast to this, Dhanávaha, so that both in this world and the next the riches of good fortune will surround you."

And therefore, having assented to all this in his mind, he died in meditation on it, and became a celestial vehicle-dwelling god in the Good Works heaven.

Surandhara|kumāreṇa prānte saṃdidiśe tv asau:
«smṛtaḥ saṃnidadhīthā me.» tat ten' âpi pratiśrutam.
tad|aurdhva|dehikaṃ kṛtvā krameṇ' âtha Surandharaḥ
kṣemāj Jayapuraṃ prāpa prāvikṣac ca mah"|ôtsavaiḥ.

14.105 śrī|Ratnavallabhen' âtha hṛtv" âmātyā it' īritāḥ:
«mayā yātrāṃ gaten' âsya manitā Surasundarī.
sā ca mātrā Bhṛgupure prahitā prāk svayaṃvarā,
prāpta|kālaṃ tad iha kiṃ vicārya brūta, mantriṇaḥ.»

śrī|Buddhisāgaro 'vocad, «dev', êyaṃ Priyadarśanā
Ratnamālā|kukṣi|ratnam etasmai dīyatām iti.
na punar jñāpyate 'muṣya, n' âiv' êyaṃ Surasundarī.»
tad abhyupetya rāṭ cakre vivāh'|ôtsavam etayoḥ.

līlā|gṛhe kumāro 'sthāt Priyadarśanayā saha,
tat|sakhībhis tad|ucita|parihāsaṃ vyadhatta ca.

14.110 priyāṃ c' ākhyat, «kiṃ na sakhyaḥ
preṣyante, Surasundari?»
tataḥ sa|tālaṃ sakhībhiḥ
smitaṃ, «kva Surasundarī?
deva, Priyadarśan" âsau n' âiv' êyaṃ Surasundarī.»
tataḥ Surandharo dadhyāv, «a|sambaddham idaṃ kim u?»

dhātry ūce, «'syā nāma cakre jananyā Priyadarśanā,
Surasundar" îti pitr" âmūr jānanty ekam eva hi.
tan n' âtra vismayaḥ kāryas.» tato reme mudā tayā,
tayā ca kamaliny" êva vāsitaṃ tasya *mānasam*.

Now, in Dhanávaha's final moments the Prince had asked him, "When I think of you, please appear before me," and he had promised to do it. Then, having performed his funeral rites, Suran·dhara in due course safely arrived at and entered Jaya·pura amid great festivities.

Then His Majesty Ratna·vállabha took his ministers aside 14.105
and said, "While I was away on my expedition I promised Sura·súndari to this man. Now, her mother had previously sent her to Bhrigu·kaccha as a self-betrothed bride. The time is at hand. So, ministers, consider and state what is to be done in this matter."

His Honor Buddhi·ságara said, "Here is Priya·dárshana, jewel of the womb of Ratna·mala. Let her be married to him. And afterward he is not to be informed that she is not Sura·súndari." The King agreed to this, and held the marriage festival for the couple.

And the Prince remained with Priya·dárshana in a pleasure house and devised amusements fitting for her with her female companions.

He called to his wife, "Why don't you send for your 14.110
companions, Sura·súndari?" Thereupon her companions clapped their hands and laughed, "Where is Sura·súndari? Your highness, this is Priya·dárshana; she isn't Sura·súndari." Then Sura·súndara thought, "What is this nonsense?"

Her nurse said, "Her mother gave her the name Priya·dárshana and her father the name Sura·súndari. They know it's one and the same. There's no need to be surprised about it." Then he joyfully made love with her, and his *mind* was filled with her, like *Lake Mánasa* filled with lotus plants.

dhātry" âtha nāma|vṛttānte kathite rāṭ saccakāra tām.
satkṛtya putryā sah' âmuṃ svaṃ puraṃ prāhiṇon nṛpaḥ.

14.115 pade pade prīṇyamānaḥ su|janaiḥ śakunair iva
sa ca Siṃhapuraṃ prāpa, prāvikṣac ca mah"|ôtsavaiḥ.

Priyadarśanayā sārdhaṃ Ramay" êva Ramā|patiḥ
saudhe dugdha|sindhu|bandhau sa vyalāsīd divā|niśam.

vāt'|âyana|sthito 'nye|dyus tayā saha Surandharaḥ
khar'|ārūḍhaṃ cauram ekaṃ nīyamānaṃ vyalokayat.
tataḥ sa|khedam ūce tāṃ, «paśyetaḥ, Surasundari,
ih' âiva sva|kṛta|karma vipākam ayam aśnute.»

Priyadarśanā:

«śata|khaṇḍaṃ hy ana iva syād gotra|skhalitena hṛt
yoṣitām iti yantr" êva bhartr" êdaṃ varjyam ādarāt.»

Surandhara:

14.120 «yadi brūvīta dayitāṃ dayit"|ântara|nāmataḥ
dayitaḥ syāt tadā gotra|skhalanaṃ na sva|nāmataḥ.»

Priyadarśanā:

«sva|nāmavan mama nāma ciraṃ ghoṣitam apy aho
mam' â|bhāgyena ken' êdam a|kasmāt, priya, vismṛtam?

The King gave the nurse a gift for telling the story about the names. Having given him gifts, the King sent Suran·dhara with his daughter back to his own city.

Blessed at every step by the good people, who were like birds of good omen, he arrived at and entered Simha·pura amid great festivities. 14.115

In a stuccoed palace resembling the ocean of milk, he sported day and night with Priya·dárshana like Vishnu with Lakshmi, the goddess of good fortune.

One day, while he was with her on the balcony, Suran·dhara saw a thief being paraded on a donkey. Thereupon he said to her with distress, "Look, Sura·súndari, even in this world he is obtaining the consequences of the actions he has committed."

Priya·dárshana:

"Making an error in my name would shatter my heart, like my life, in a hundred pieces. Husbands, who are like supports for their wives, should take care to avoid this."

Suran·dhara:

"If a husband addresses his wife by the name of another woman, then there would be a mistake in her name, but not by her own name." 14.120

Priya·dárshana:

"Like your own name, my name has been made known for a long time; through what misfortune of mine have you suddenly forgotten it, husband?

priya, Priyadarśan" âhaṃ, n' âiv' âhaṃ Surasundarī.
tad anya|nāmnā māṃ jalpan gotra|skhalitam āpitha.»

Surandhara:

«yady evaṃ, tava pitrā kiṃ kṛt" ākhyā Surasundarī?
pitṛ|kḷpt'|ākhyayā vaktur na mantur me manāg api.»

Priyadarśanā:

«yā Surasundarī nāmnā s" âmbayā Bhṛgupattane
pur" âiva praiṣi Kusumaśekharāya svayaṃvarā.»
14.125 Surandharas tato « (- - - - -) n' âsmi vañcitaḥ.
yadi vā kiṃ tay", âiṣ" âpi prāṇebhyo 'pi priyā mama.»

Surandhara:

«dvidhā priya|darśan" âsi, tat tvaṃ me sura|sundarī.
Surasundaryāḥ śirasi kiṃ viṣāṇaṃ vijṛmbhate?»

Priyadarśanā:

«mahā|prasādo 'yam adya, yady āropo yathā|tathaḥ
paraṃ na kāñcanāraṃ syād āropāc campakaṃ kva cit.
lāvaṇya|puṇyās taruṇyaḥ
santu, tattv'|ântaraṃ tu sā.
drākṣ"|ādyāḥ svādavaḥ santi
mudh" âiv' ândhaḥ sudh"|ândhasām.»
kumāro 'th' âbhajan maunam amarṣāt tv ity acintayat:
«surandharas tad" âhaṃ, yady ādāsye Surasundarī!»

Husband, I am Priya·dárshana; I am certainly not Sura·súndari. So by addressing me by the name of another you have committed a mistake in my name."

Suran·dhara:

"Even if it was your father who gave you the name Sura·súndari, by saying the name given by your father I'm not committing the slightest fault."

Priya·dárshana:

"The one named Sura·súndari has been sent previously to Bhrigu·kaccha to be the self-betrothed bride of Kúsuma·shékhara."

Then Suran·dhara thought, "I have been deceived by Ra- 14.125
tna·vállabha. Nevertheless, what is this to do with her? I love her more than my life."

Suran·dhara:

"You are twice as beautiful, so you are my goddess of beauty. Doesn't a horn grow on Sura·súndari's head?"

Priya·dárshana:

"This would be a great compliment if it were true now, but a mountain ebony can in no respect be compared to a *chámpaka* tree. Let there be young women, fair and beautiful; she surpasses them in her essence. Grapes and such are sweet in vain when there's the nectar of the gods."

Thereupon the Prince remained silent, but in a passion thought, "Then I will be blessed, if Sura·súndari is given to me!"

14.130 Dhanāvaham ath' ôddiśya
brahmaṇā so 'ṣṭamaṃ vyadhāt.
Dhanāvaha|suro 'th' āgāt,
«kiṃ karom'?» îti c' âbravīt.
Surandharo 'vak, «Kusumaśekharāt Surasundarīm
mam' ârpaya.» suro 'vādīt, «para|dārā|kath" âpi dhik.»
kumāro 'th' āha, «sā n' âiva para|dārā, mam' âiva sā
yato pitrā dade sā me, mātr" âiva kṛtam anyathā.»
«yā yen' ōḍhā, tasya s".» êti sureṇ' ôkte ca so 'vadat:
«na kart" âsi mad|iṣṭaṃ cet, tad vṛthā kim ih' āgamaḥ?»
«yady eṣa tava nirbandhas tad" ānīt" âiva sā, sakhe.»
ity uditvā satya|sandhaḥ suro dṛśy'|êtaro 'bhavat.
14.135 sa c' āgamad Bhṛgu|puraṃ, tatr" âpi nṛpa|mandiram,
tatr' âpi ca śrī|Kusumaśekharasya niketanam.
tatr' âpi candra|śālāyāṃ śayyāyāṃ sa vyalokayat
patyā saha rati|kal"|ântāṃ viśrāntāṃ Surasundarīm.
imām īdṛg|vidh'|âvasthām patyā saha viyojayan
niṣṭhyānām api c' â|spṛśyo «bhaviṣyāmy asmi pātakī.
yad vā bhavatu yat kiñ cit, kāryam ev' ôrarīkṛtam.
prāṇāt prāṇ'|âdhikaṃ Rāmaṃ hy asmai Daśaratho 'mucat.»
vicinty' êti suraḥ s' âiṣa jahāra Surasundarīm
sadyaḥ sā ca jajāgāra pūc|cakāra ca nirbharam.
14.140 «ārya|putr' ārya|putr', âsmi hriye ken' âpi pāpmanā!
dhāva dhāva, rakṣa rakṣa, kṣatriy'|ôttama, māṃ, priya!»

He summoned Dhanávaha, making an eightfold oblation with a priest. Then the god Dhanávaha appeared and asked, "What should I do?" 14.130

Suran·dhara said, "Take Sura·súndari from Kúsuma·shékhara and bring her to me." The god said, "It's a disgrace to even talk of another's wife."

Then the Prince said, "She's not another's wife. She is mine, since she was betrothed to me by her father; her mother's the one who acted otherwise."

And on the god's saying, "She is the wife of the one who married her," he replied, "If you're not going to do what I want, then why did you come here to no purpose?"

Saying, "If you insist, then she will certainly be brought here, my friend," the god, who was true to his word, became invisible. And he went to Bhrigu·kaccha, and there too went 14.135
to the King's palace, and there too went to the apartment of His Highness Kúsuma·shékhara. And there too in the rooftop chamber, on a couch, resting with her husband after making love, he saw Sura·súndari.

As she was in that position with her husband, he while invisible parted her from him, although she was clinging to him. "I will become a criminal. Nevertheless, let it be, since whatever is promised must be performed. Dasha·ratha banished Rama, dearer to him than life, for this reason."

Thinking thus, he, the god, suddenly seized Sura·súndari. She awoke and shouted loudly:

"My noble husband, I am being carried away by some 14.140
criminal! Run, run, husband, protect, protect me, you finest of warriors!"

tasyāḥ karuṇa|śabdena vibuddho nṛpa|nandanaḥ,
«dhīrā bhav'! âiṣa rakṣām'!» îty ākhyann asi|su|duḥ|sthitaḥ.
aṅga|rakṣa|sakho 'dhāvat tasyāḥ śabd'|ânusārataḥ,
vidyut|kṣipta|prakaraṇād api prākāram atyagāt.
«kva re yāsi? kva re yāsi priyāṃ hṛtvā mam', âsura?
mā bhaiṣīs tvaṃ, priye, tvāṃ hi vegāt pratyāharāmy aham!»
iti bruvann aikako 'pi dadhāva vāyu|vegataḥ.
śāla|ruddhais tv aṅga|rakṣaiś cikhide pūd|akāri ca.
14.145 any'|ânya|jana|pūt|kāraiḥ pūrṇā tat|pūt|kṛti|sarit
Bhṛgukaccham kaccham iva plāvayāmāsa sarvataḥ.
tat|taraṅgair abhihataḥ prabuddhaḥ Puṣpaketu|rāṭ
vijñāta|putra|vṛttāntaḥ sadyaḥ sarva|camū|vṛtaḥ
aṅga|rakṣ'|ādiṣṭa|diśā kumār'|ânveṣaṇa|vratī
prahiṇvann abhitaḥ sainyāṃs cacāl' âbdhi|pravāhavat.
praty|udyānaṃ prati|saraḥ praty|adri prati|vartma ca
kumāram anviṣya nṛpas tad|vārttām apy avāpa na.
try|ahaṃ paryaṭya Kusumaketur etu|manā na hi,
puraṃ mantri|gir" âiv' āgād gata|sarva|sva|māny asau.
14.150 a|putrasya gṛhaṃ śūnyam, ity uktaṃ tuccham eva hi;
a|putrasya jagac chūnyam, iti pūrṇam avain nṛpaḥ.
tath" âpi dhairyam ālambya devyāḥ sambodhanāya saḥ
antaḥpuram upaic chūnyaṃ śūny'|āgāra|sahodaram.

Awoken by her cries of distress, the Prince, shouting, "Be brave! I will protect you!," could scarcely stay for his sword. Accompanied by his bodyguard the Prince ran following the sound of the cries. Like a hurled thunderbolt, he surmounted the wall.

"Hey, where are you going, hey, where are you taking my wife, you demon! Don't be frightened, my dear. I'll rush and snatch you back!"

Thus he shouted, and, although he was alone, ran forward as fast as the wind. His bodyguard, held back by the wall, made a loud cry of distress. Their cries taken up by the peo- 14.145
ple, one after another, formed a stream of cries that flooded all over Bhrigu·kaccha, making it like a marsh. Struck by its waves, King Kúsuma·ketu awoke, and, informed of what had happened to his son, suddenly surrounded with his entire army, fully intent on searching for the Prince in the direction indicated by the bodyguards, arrayed his troops all around and ordered them to issue forth, like a stream of water from a cloud.

The King followed the Prince by park, by lake, by mountain and by road, but obtained no news of him. Having traveled for three days, Kúsuma·ketu decided to go no further, and on the advice of his ministers returned to the city, concerned about the loss of his wealth. The King fully con- 14.150
sidered it an absolute understatement to say that the house was empty without his son; rather, the universe was empty without his son. Nevertheless, the King took courage to inform the Queen. He entered the empty inner apartment, which was like a deserted house.

dṛgbhyāṃ prāvṛṣam āsyena rāhum āhūtavattamām
paśyantīṃ bhuvam asyāṃ nu veṣṭuṃ tāṃ vīkṣya rāṇ jagau.
«devi, nāṭakavan nānā|ras'|āveś'|ôdbhavo bhavaḥ,
tad ayam tattva|viduṣāṃ na viṣāda|mud|āspadam.»

devy uvāca, «svāmi|pāda|padma|nitya|vilāsy asau
kumāra|haṃso 'raṇyānyāṃ prāṇiti, prāṇit'|ēśa, kim?
14.155 tan na yāvat tat|pravṛttis tapta|śūcī śrutī mama,
bādhate tāvad ev' âgniṃ śraye tad|duḥkha|jitvaraṃ.»

atha rāj" âvadad, «devi, kumār'|âdhīna|jīvitaḥ
kim ih' âham avasthāsye? sārtha ekas tad āvayoḥ.»

atha mantrī Suragurur vijño vyajñāpayan nṛpam,
«pṛcchyantāṃ, deva, daivajñāḥ kumār'|āgaman'|ôtsavam.
kumār'|ôdantaṃ vadate lakṣa|dīnāra|dāpanam
udghoṣyatām ānakena, mānyantāṃ kula|devatāḥ.
catur|diśaṃ ca preṣyantāṃ kumār'|ânveṣakā narāḥ
a|kasmāt prāṇa|prahāṇaṃ kumār'|āloka|hṛt param.»

14.160 tato rāj" âvadan, «mantrin, kāray' âitad drutaṃ drutam.»
mantry ūce, «siddham ev' êdam, avadhārayatu prabhuḥ.»

The King beheld her as she summoned the monsoon rains with her eyes and the eclipse of the moon with her face and looked at the ground wishing to actually enter it. He said, "My Queen, worldly existence, like actors, is produced from infusing oneself in various sentiments. Therefore it should not be the cause of either dejection or happiness for those who know the truth."

The Queen said, "What, lord of my life, is the Prince, a royal swan who always played at the lotus of Your Majesty's foot, living in a wilderness? Since that which has happened 14.155
to him, causing my ears to burn with heat, cannot be prevented, for that very reason I shall enter fire, the vanquisher of this distress."

Then the King said, "My Queen, my life is not worth living without the Prince. Why should I remain here? You have the right purpose; let it be the same for us both."

Thereupon the wise minister Sura·guru addressed the King, "Your Majesty, let astrologers be asked about the festival for the Prince's return. Let a reward of a hundred thousand gold pieces be proclaimed at the beat of a drum for the one who brings news of the Prince, and let the family deities be worshipped. And let men be sent in all directions to search for the Prince. Abandonment of life will be needless if they bring sight of the Prince."

Then the King said, "See that this is accomplished as 14.160
quickly as possible, minister." The minister said, "Let Your Majesty consider that it is already accomplished."

atha nānā|kathā|mukhya|vinodaiḥ kovid'|ôcitaiḥ
prabhuṃ vinodayāmāsuḥ sāmant'|ādyā nirantaram.
śikṣayitv" ânyadā sarvaṃ mantriṇā jñāpitaḥ pumān:
«naimittiko 'yaṃ, tad, deva, pṛcchyatāṃ tanay'|āgamam.»
tataḥ sammānya rājñ" ōce, «priyaṃ|vada, vada priyam.
kumār'|ôdantam asmākam a|kasmāj jīvitā|mṛtam?»
sa māyayā samādāya praśna|varṇ'|āvalīm imām
tat|kāla|lagna|grahāṃś ca tathā vīkṣya svar'|ôdayam
14.165 rājānam avadad, «dev', ânubhūte 'rthe mam' ôditam.
cet saṃvadati tat satyaṃ mad|uktaṃ, n' ânyathā punaḥ.»
mantri|śikṣā|vidyay" âth' âbrūta, «deva, tvayā prage
mantriṇaḥ pura ity ukte, mantriṇā c' êdam aucyata.
kim etad asty, atha vā na?» mantry ūce, «na tav' ôpari
rājño '|pratītis, tad brūhi, kumārasy' āgamaḥ kadā?»
praṇidhāya nimitty ūce, «ṣaṇ|māsyā, deva, niścitam
prāpya rājya|śriyaṃ kṣemān śrī|kumāraḥ sameṣyati.»
mantry avādīd devam etan, «n' âtra naḥ saṃśay'|ôdayaḥ,
yat kumāro rāja|lakṣmīm arjat'» îty atuṣan nṛpaḥ.

Then the barons and the others continued to divert the King with diversions suitable for the learned, chief among them various stories.

One day, having previously instructed him in everything, the minister introduced a man, saying, "This man is an astrologer, so, Your Majesty, let's ask him about your son's return."

Then the King gave him a respectful gift and said, "Your countenance is pleasant; speak what is pleasant. Will news of the Prince render our departure from life needless?"

Having apprehended the series of syllables of the question 14.165
with his supernatural power, and having inspected how the planets were aligned at that time, he addressed the King with a reverberating voice, "Your Majesty, my business is finished. If what I am about to say is correct, then my utterance is true. If it is not, then it won't be."

Then, by means of the information given him by the minister, he said, "Your Majesty, you said this in the presence of the minister, and the minister said this. Is that what happened or not?" The minister said, "You have the King's full confidence, so state when the Prince will return."

The astrologer concentrated and said, "When six months have elapsed, His Highness the Prince will return in safety to the fortune of the kingdom."

The minister said to the King, "I have no doubt about it, that the Prince will attain the fortune of the kingdom." The King was delighted.

14.170 sammānya mantriṇā naimittika utthāpito drutam,
anyad rājñā praśnito 'sau n' âiva jñāsyaty a|śikṣitaḥ.
evaṃ kumār'|āgamana|mano|ratha|ratha|sthitāḥ
dinān nirgamayāmāsuḥ sukhena kṣitip'|ādayaḥ.
itaś ca, «dhīrā bhav'!» êti muhur jalpan sa rāja|sūḥ
prāpto 'ṭavyāṃ sureṇ' ōce, «kiṃ mudhā kliśyase, 'nagha?
tava sattva|parīkṣ"|ârtham agāṃ mandam iyac|ciram,
ath' âti|vegād yāsyāmi, n' āgantavyam atas tvayā.
anyac ca n' âhaṃ sva|kṛte 'paharāmi tava priyām,
kiṃ tu prāg|janma|suhṛdo nimittaṃ hṛdya|sauhṛdāt.
14.175 kiñ c' ânayā dayitayā na melas te 'dhun" âiva hi,
ṣaṇ|mās'|ântaraṃ hy eṣā satī saṅgamyate tvayā.»
ity uktvā sa tirobhūtaḥ, kumāras tu hṛta|priyaḥ
dūr'|âdhva|pāda|cārāto 'sthāt tamāla|taros tale.
sarvataḥ prekṣate yāvat, tāvad Yama|purīm iva
nirmānuṣatayā bhīmāṃ paśyaty eṣa mah"|âṭavīm.
priyā|hṛty" â|phal'|āyāsāt pitr|a|darśanataś ca saḥ
dūno 'pi vyaṣadan n' âiva bhava|sv'|â|bhāvya|bhāvanāt.
dadhyau c' ākāraṇa|kruddho, «'tiśete dur|janaṃ vidhiḥ.
sarvaṃ vighaṭayaty eṣa, yan nimeṣ'|ârdha|mātrataḥ.
14.180 mama sāhasam ekatr', ânyato vidhi|vidhānakam,
kāry'|ārambha|tul"|âgre drakṣyate yato vijitvaram.»

The minister gave the astrologer a gratuity and sent him 14.170
away immediately, lest, asked another question by the King, he would not know the answer, being unapprised of it.

In this way the King and the others passed their days agreeably, seated in the vehicle of their desire for the Prince's return.

Now, continually shouting, "Be brave!," the Prince came to a forest wilderness. The god said, "Why are you tormenting yourself to no purpose, stainless one? I've gone slowly for so long in order to see what you were made of, sinless one, but now I'm going to go very fast, and you will not be able to follow from now on. And besides, I'm not carrying away your wife on my own doing but for the sake of a friend of a former life, because of our heartfelt friendship.
What's more, you will not join with your wife right at this 14.175
very moment, but as soon as six months have elapsed your faithful wife will be reunited with you."

On saying that, he disappeared, but the Prince, deprived of his wife and having traveled by foot along distant roads, halted at the foot of a *tamála* tree. In every direction he looked, he saw nothing but a great forest wilderness, like the city of Death, fearful in its solitude. Although he was distressed by his fruitless effort of rescuing his wife and by the absence of his parents, he did not despair, because he meditated on his nonexistence in the world.

He thought, "Angered by their appearance, fate overcomes bad people. In the passing of half a moment he confounds them all. My rashness in one place has become a 14.180
punishment of fate in another, since before the scales of

iti dhyātv" ôttarīyaṃ c' āstīrya suṣvāpa bhuvy asau
yāvat, tāvat kuto 'py etya dandaśūko dadaṃśa tam.
tadīya|viṣama|viṣa|laharībhir asau kṣaṇāt
vidadhe sarva|deśīyaḥ. prātikūlyam, aho, vidheḥ!

itaś c' âsyām araṇyānyām asty Apratipathā purī,
tasyāṃ rājā Rāmacandro Rāmadevī ca tat|priyā.
tayoḥ putrī Ramaṇamatī rūpa|dheya|śriyo nidhiḥ.
sā ca tāruṇya|pūrṇ" âbhūt puruṣa|dveṣiṇī param.

14.185 rājñ" ânyadā śrutaṃ, «putryām
anūḍhāyāṃ dhruvaṃ pituḥ
tāvanto narakāḥ proktā,
yāvanto rakta|bindavaḥ.»

tataḥ khinnena bhūpen' âpracchi naimittiko 'nyadā:
«putrī me Ramaṇamatī varaṃ kañ cid variṣyati?»

sa jagāda, «mahā|puṃsaḥ preyas" îyaṃ bhaviṣyati.
sa c' âhi|daṣṭo 'tr' âṭavyām asti. praguṇay' āśu tam!»

tad" âiva Rāmacandreṇa narā praiṣyanta sarvataḥ,
dadṛśe taiḥ sa kumāro mṛta|kalpo 'hi|daṃśataḥ.
utpāṭya ninye sa puryāṃ, hūtā gāruḍikās tataḥ.
sammānya darśitas teṣāṃ rājñā sa nṛpa|nandanaḥ.

14.190 samyag|vibhāvya tair ūce, «vām'|âṅge strī, pare pumān
daṣṭo na jīvaty. ayaṃ tu vām'|âṅge, tena jīvati.
nās'|ādhara|cibukeṣu var'|âṃhri|tala|meḍhrayoḥ
na jīvaty ahinā daṣṭo, 'yaṃ c' ânyatr', êti jīvati.

what should be done and what is attempted fate appears victorious."

Having pondered thus, he spread his cloak and went to sleep on the ground, whereupon a snake came from somewhere and bit him. In a moment he was completely held fast by waves of venomous poison. Oh, the contrariety of fate!

Now, in that forest wilderness was a city called Áprati·patha, and there lived a king, Rama·chandra, and Rama·devi, his wife. They had a daughter, Rámana·mati, a treasury of the wealth of beauty. She became abundant in youth; however, she hated men.

One day the King heard someone say, "The father whose 14.185
daughter is unmarried is certainly condemned to as many hells as he has drops of blood."

The worried King one day asked an astrologer, "What sort of man will my daughter Rámana·mati marry?"

He replied, "She will be the beloved of a great man. And he is here in this forest, bitten by a snake. Go and attend to him immediately!"

That very moment, Rama·chandra sent out men in all directions, and they found the Prince lying unconscious because of the snakebite. They gathered him up and brought him to the city. Then the King, having summoned antidote-mongers, gave them gratuities and showed the Prince to them. Having made due consideration, they said, "If a 14.190
woman is bitten on the left of her body, or a man on the other side, they will not survive. But he has been bitten on his left-hand side; therefore he will survive. Bitten by a snake on the nose, neck or chin, on the ball of the foot, or

chinne 'ṅg'|âvayave yasya na niryāty asra|bindukaḥ
parāsuṃ taṃ vijānīyān, niryāty asy', êti jīvati.»
tataś ca caccarī gāna|pūrvaṃ tair upacakrame
krameṇ' ôtthāya so 'nartīd rājñaś ca pramado hṛdi.
vardhāpanakam ātene śrī|Ramaṇamatī vṛtā,
pariṇītā ca Kusumaśekhareṇa mah"|ôtsavaiḥ.
14.195 ath' ânyadā Rāmacandraḥ kumāraṃ pṛṣṭavān iti:
«dhīman, ka eṣa vṛttāntaḥ?» kumāraḥ pratyavocata:
«prāg dur|vahita|duṣ|karma|
tāṇḍavaṃ sarvam apy adaḥ.»
Rāmaḥ punaḥ prāha, «kas tvaṃ?
kutaḥ, katham ih' āgamaḥ?»
kumāreṇ' âtha s'|ādy|antaḥ sv'|ôdantaḥ pratyapādyata.
yāvat suptas tamāl'|âdho, jāne n' âtaḥ paraṃ punaḥ.
Rāmo 'vadan, «mahā|bhāga, pratīpen' âpi vedhasā
tvad|darśana|sut"|ôdvāhābhyām ati|prīṇitā vayam.
aye kumāra, saṃsāra|pārāvāro 'yam īdṛśaḥ.
na viṣādo vidhātavyas tad atra mati|śālinā.»
14.200 Surasundarī|viyoga|duḥkha|śaly'|ôddidhīrṣayā
patyuḥ pati|vrat" âbrūta pitre Ramaṇamaty atha:

on the penis, one will not survive, but since he has been bitten elsewhere, he will survive. The drops of venom will not leave that dying man whose bodily members have been perforated. Because of his being deprived of a wife, it is leaving him, so he will survive."

Then they started to sing and chant, and in due course he stood up and began to dance. The King's heart was filled with delight. He arranged the ceremony, and Princess Rámana·mati was betrothed and married to Kúsuma·shékhara amid great festivities.

Now, one day Rama·chandra asked the Prince, "Intelli- 14.195
gent one, what is your actual story?" The Prince replied,

"Formerly, a mad dance of bad karma, difficult to endure; that's all it was." Then Rama·chandra asked, "Who are you, where are you from and how did you come here?"

The Prince told his whole story from beginning to end as far as the time when he fell asleep below the *tamála* tree, but he was not able to say what happened after that.

Rama·chandra said, "Highly fortunate one, because of your adverse wound we had the great delight of both seeing you and marrying you to our daughter. Come, then, Prince. This is like the far shore of the ocean of existence, so one possessed of intelligence should not despair about this."

Then the faithful wife Rámana·mati, wishing to remove 14.200
from her husband the painful thorn of his distress at being separated from Sura·súndari, said to her father:

«tāta, śrutaṃ may" āptebhyaḥ,
samyuktānāṃ sura|drumaḥ
cintā|manir viyuktānāṃ
śailo 'sti Priyamelakaḥ.
nānā|nadī|vana|khaṇḍa|mekhalā|parimaṇḍitaḥ
asyām eva mah"|âṭavyām ito yojana|pañcake.
tato yas tatra gatvā ‹auṃ namo bhuyaṇa|bhūsaṇassa savva-
nnuṇo ihaṃ mīlaya mīlaya svāhā!›
mantrasy' âsya sad" āsanna|patnīko brahma|carya|bhṛt
prāṅ|māsaṃ kara|jāpena, māsaṃ puṣpa|japena ca,
māsaṃ ca madhu|homena, sarpir|homena māsakam,
upacāraṃ karoty asya turye mās' îṣṭa|melakaḥ.»
14.205 vyājahāra kumāro 'tha, «tena kānt"|âpahāriṇā
ṣaṇ|māsy ante prīyā|melo mam' ādiṣṭaḥ kil' âbhavat.
māsa|dvayam ati|krāntam etāvadbhiś ca vāsaraiḥ,
nayāmaś caturo māsān preyasy|ukta|vidhānataḥ.»
jñāt'|āśayo 'vadad Rāmaḥ, «kumāra, tvam idaṃ kuru
sah' âiva Ramaṇamatyā camvā ca catur|aṅgayā.»
tatas tad" âiva Kusumaśekharaḥ Priyamelakam
jagāma kara|jāp'|ādi|vidhiṃ prārabdhavān mudā.
varam āhuti|paryante kuṇḍikā|daṇḍa|dhāribhiḥ
skandha|nṛtyaj|jaṭair agre vṛtā muni|kumārakaiḥ,
14.210 paritaḥ prāvṛt'|âṅgībhir ghana|bh"|ūrja|taru|tvacā
nitamba|cumbaj|jaṭābhis tāpasībhiś ca pṛṣṭhataḥ,

"Father, I have heard it said by credible people that, a wishing-tree for the married and a wishing-jewel for the separated, there is a mountain called Union of the Beloved. Decorated all around with a girdle of various rivers, woods and chasms, it is five leagues from this very forest wilderness. So he who goes there and recites, 'Aum! Praise to the all-knowing one, the ornament of the universe! Make her come here, make her come! Blessings!,' always remaining close by his wife, but remaining chaste, and who makes attendance for the first month by praying with hand gesture, and then for a month by prayerful offerings of flowers, and then for a month with offerings of honey, and then for a month with offerings of clarified butter, at the end of the fourth month meets with his desire."

Then the Prince said, "The one who abducted my beloved 14.205
actually informed me that I would be reunited with my wife at the end of six months. Two months with so many days have elapsed. We will pass four months according to the precept stated by my beloved."

Informed of his wish, Rama·chandra said, "Undertake this, Prince, in company with Rámana·mati and with the army of four divisions."

So at that very moment Kúsuma·shékhara went to Mount Union with the Beloved and joyfully proceeded to perform the rite of the prayerful offering with hand, et cetera. When he had completed invoking the boon, attended in front by young ascetics bearing bowls and staves, their matted locks
dancing on their shoulders, and at her sides by beautiful 14.210
women dressed in bark from *lodhra* trees, and at her back by female ascetics, their matted locks kissing their buttocks,

aruṇ'|āsy'|âṃhriṇā nīla|pakṣeṇa vyoma|gāminā
śoṇa|nīl'|āśm'|ātman" êva śukena ca samanvitā,
tan|mantr'|ākṛṣṭa|dev" îva sadyaḥ sā Surasundarī
kuto 'py etya kumārasya pādayor nyapatad, bata.

prāṇ'|ēśa|virah'|âsaukhyam uṣṇ'|āsraiḥ kila muñcatī
sā tat|pada|sthit" ârodīd rodaḥ|kukṣiṃ|bhari|svaram.
ādāya bāhu|latayoḥ kumāraḥ prāṇa|vallabhām
sva|vām'|ôru|gadvikāyāṃ sa|romāñcaṃ nyaveśayat.
14.215 atho Ramaṇamaty" âmbu|pūrṇen' âiṣa sva|pāṇinā
rakt'|ôtpala|puṭ'|ābhena tasyāḥ prākṣālayan mukham.
sv'|ôttarīya|pallavena śirīṣa|mṛdun" ādarāt
svarṇ'|ādarśam iv' āmārjīd Rāmacandrī tad|ānanam.
pradatte ca tayā divye prāṇ'|ēśvara|niyogataḥ
āsane 'tyantam āsanne nyaṣadat Surasundarī.

te tāpas'|ādyāḥ kumāra|praṇatā īrit'|āśiṣaḥ
āsaneṣu pradhāneṣu niṣeduḥ kheditāḥ pathā.

asminn avasare rāja|kumār'|ôpāntam etya saḥ
rājakīraḥ kṣīra|pāṇaṃ śrutyos tanvan jagāv iti.
14.220 «kumāra, sad|guṇ'|āgāra, bhuvan'|ādhāra, sādaram
priy" êyaṃ te samāninye. 'dhunā yāmas tapo|vanam.»

so 'py avādīt, «parāṇinye yair eṣā mama vallabhā,
te gauravyās, tad ātithyam ādheyaṃ, sthīyatāṃ tataḥ.

accompanied by a flying parrot with crimson legs and face and blue wings, as if its essence were of blue and crimson sapphire, like a goddess attracted by his spell, Sura·súndari suddenly appeared from somewhere and fell at the Prince's feet.

Letting go her sorrow at her separation from the lord of her life with warm tears, she remained at his feet and emitted a cry that filled the circumference of the earth. Thrilled, the Prince raised with the creepers of his arms his wife as dear as life and sat her on a lovely cushion of honor. Then he cleansed her face with his hand, which Rá- 14.215
mana·mati had filled with water; it was like the hollow of a red water lotus. Rámana·mati carefully wiped her face, like a mirror of gold, with the fringe of her shawl, as soft as acacia. On her husband's command she brought very close a seat, and Sura·súndari sat in it.

The ascetics and the others were bowed before by the Prince, and, after uttering a benediction, sat in seats of honor.

At that moment when the Prince was raising her up, the parrot approached him, and, diffusing nectar for his ears, said:

"Prince, you abode of true virtue, you upholder of the 14.220
world, I have carefully brought back this your wife to you. Now we shall return to our hermitage grove."

Then he replied, "Those who brought back my beloved must be treated with respect, so let them abide for the pledge of hospitality.

ātithyaṃ c' ôcitaṃ yad vas, tad ākhyāhi.» śuko 'bhyadhāt,
«ādhatse yat tad iṣṭaṃ nas.» ten' ōce «'nugraho mahān.
kiñ ca pṛcchyā sva|vṛttāntam eṣā tat kṣaṇam āsyatām.
ayi priye, sva|vṛttāntaṃ yathā|sthitam udāhara.»

pade pade vahad bāṣp" âth' ācakhye Surasundarī:
«yadā te sa suro 'vādīt, ‹kīm mudhā kliśyase, 'nagha?›
14.225 tata ūrdhva|nimeṣeṇa sa māṃ Siṃhapure 'mucat
Priyadarśanā|pārśva|stha|Surandhara|mukh'|âgrataḥ.

tena c' ôktaṃ, ‹samānītā, mitr', êyaṃ Surasundarī.›
pratipādy' êti tarasā sa jagāma sur'|ālayam.

tato, ‹bagn'!› îti s'|ānandaṃ, ‹sa|patn'!› îti sa|matsaram
samutthāy' āsanasthāṃ mām ākhyat sā Priyadarśanā:

‹kutaḥ, katham ih' āyātā, he bhagni Surasundari?›
‹vidhir niṣkāranaṃ kruddho jānāt'.› îti may" āucyata.

ath' âpāṅga|dṛśā vīkṣya mām uvāca sa bhūpa|sūḥ,
‹priye, daivena n' ānītā, kin tu devena mat|kṛte.
14.230 tad ānanda|pade ko 'yaṃ viṣādas tava, su|smite?
svāminyās tava dāso 'smi, tvad|adhīnā mam' āsavaḥ.
tad viṣāda|viṣaṃ muñca, siñca māṃ karuṇ"|âmṛtaiḥ,
mahā|devī|pade tvāṃ c' âbhiṣiñcāmi, su|locane.›

tato may", ‹ārya|putr',› ōce, ‹mahā|bhāga Surandhara,
santo 'nya|dār"|ēkṣaṇe 'pi sa|celaṃ snānti śuddhaye.
tvaṃ tu mahā|kulīno 'pi katham evaṃ vibhāṣase?›
sa ūce, ‹tvāṃ pitā me 'dān. n' ânya|dārās tato 'si me.›

And since it is fitting for you to receive hospitality, please agree to it." The parrot said, "We will grant your desire." The Prince said, "You are very gracious. So stay for a moment while I ask her what befell her. Come, my dear, relate what befell you, with all the circumstances."

Then Sura·súndari, her tears spreading everywhere, said, "When the god said to you, 'Why are you tormenting yourself to no purpose, stainless one?,' then, in the twinkling of 14.225
an eye, the god set me down in Simha·pura, in front of Suran·dhara, Priya·dárshana standing by his side.

The god said, 'My friend, I have brought Sura·súndari. Here she is.' Having thus presented me, he sped to the abode of the gods.

Then, exclaiming with joy 'Sister!' and with envy 'Co-wife!,' Priya·dárshana raised me up and said to me:

'Where have you come from, Sura·súndari, my sister, and how did you come here?' I replied, 'When fate is angered he approves the requital.'

But the Prince looked at me with a sidelong glance and said, 'My dear, she wasn't brought here by fate but by a god at my doing. So why this dejection of yours at a joyful event, 14.230
pretty smiler? I am your slave, my mistress. Subjection to you is nectar for me. So give up the poison of depression and sprinkle me with the nectar of sympathy, and I will consecrate you to the rank of chief Queen, pretty eyes.'

Then I replied, 'Highly distinguished noble husband Suran·dhara, pure men bathe fully clothed in the sight of others' wives. But you are of noble family; how can you speak thus?' He said, 'Your father betrothed you to me; how can you be any other's wife but mine?'

may" ācakhye, ‹yadi pitrā dattā, n' ōḍhā katham tvayā?›
sa, ‹mūḍho.› 'brūt', ‹âdhun" âiv' ôdvahāmi nanu, Sundari.›
14.235 ūce mayā, ‹bhukta|bhogā para|strī pariṇīyate,
iti sthitis tvat|kule vā loke vā kim u vidyate?›
kaṣāyito 'tha so 'brūta, ‹śādh' îmāṃ, Priyadarśane.›
s" âvak, ‹s'|ērṣyaṃ manuṣyeṣu śikṣā dṛṣadi no punaḥ.
grāmīṇa|naṭa|mūrkhāṇāṃ yad vā yogaḥ khal' ûcitaḥ,
a|sthān'|âbhiniveśī tvaṃ, nūnam eṣ" âpi tādṛśī.›
evaṃ tayā bhagna|mukhaḥ sa|joṣaṃ jujuṣe kṣaṇam.
punar a|jñān'|âbhimānāt so 'vadan māṃ gata|trapaḥ:
‹mad|ukte 'ṅgīkṛte, subhru, tava śreyo, 'nyathā na hi.›
‹kim ito 'py adhikaṃ mūḍha|vidhiḥ kart"?› êty avādiṣam.
14.240 ‹vidhinā vihitaṃ kiṃ te?› ‹drakṣyasy etarhi mat|kṛtam!›
atho kumāraṃ kumār'|âmātyo 'brūta, ‹prabho, śṛṇu.
kādambaryāṃ mah"|âṭavyāṃ tāpaso 'bhūn mahā|tapāḥ,
sa c' ātapan niścal'|âṅgas tasthau sthāṇu|bhrama|pradaḥ.
balāk" âtr' âmucad viṣṭhām, etasyai kupyati sma saḥ.
gāḍhaṃ mumoca huṅ|kāraṃ, tataḥ sā bhasmy|abhūt kṣaṇāt.
«tena jñātaṃ tapaḥ|śaktir,» visphūrjati, «mam' ēdṛśī.
yaḥ kariṣyaty a|bhaktiṃ me, taṃ kariṣyāmi bhasmasāt!»

I said, 'If I was betrothed by my father, how come you didn't marry me?' He said, 'I was tricked. I'm going to marry you right this moment, Sura·súndari.'

I said, 'Another's wife can be enjoyed and married? Is that 14.235
an axiom known in your family or here on earth?'

Then he blushed and said, 'Correct her, Priya·dárshana.' She said, 'Correction causes resentment among mankind but is like a millstone for us. Since a magic trick is actually suitable for silly village pantomime players, you have certainly become attached to impermanent things; that's just what she is.'

His face dejected, he was thus reduced to silence by her for a moment. But then, because of his ignorant desire, his shame vanished, and he said to me:

'It will be better for you if you assent to what I say, lovely 14.240
brows; if not, it will be otherwise, for sure.' I said, 'What will happen later? Will deluded fate perform for you what is devoid of precept?' 'Pay regard to my object right now!' Then the Prince's minister said to the Prince, 'Listen, sir. In a large forest of *kadámbari* trees lived an ascetic of mighty austerities. And practicing his austerities he stood with such a motionless body that he was mistaken for a post.

A crane dropped its excrement on him, and he became angry with it. He let loose a deep roar, thereupon it was instantly burned to ashes.

He roared, "Such is the power of my asceticism, made evident by this. Whoever treats me with lack of devotion, him I will burn to a cinder!"

sa c' ânyadā Varāṇasyāṃ bhikṣāyāṃ kv' âpy agād gṛhe.
gṛhiṇī tatra ca patiṃ bhojayaty añjas" ādarāt.
14.245 tatra bhukte cirān ninye bhikṣā tasmai tapasvine,
sa ca kruddhas tad|upari mahā|huṅ|kāram ātanot.

s" âpy ūce, «n' âhaṃ balākā. bhikṣām ādatsva cet kṣudhā.»
nipatya tat|padoḥ so 'vak, «kuto vetsi balāhikām?»

jagāda sā, «yatas tvāṃ, bhoḥ, kariṣye bhasmasāt kṣaṇāt.»
so 'vag bhīto, «bhagavati, śaktis te kuta īdṛśī?»

s" âpy āha, «sva|prāṇa|nāthān manas" âp' îtaraḥ pumān
na mam' êṣṭas, tataḥ śaktir iyam āvirabhūn mama.»

dṛṣṭ'|ântasy' âsy' ôpanayaḥ svayaṃ, deva, prabudhyatām.›
itthaṃ kumār'|âmātyena prokte 'sthāt so 'vahitthayā.
14.250 tataḥ Priyadarśanāyā eten' âsmi samarpitā.
evaṃ vyatīyur ahāni hāyanān' îva katy api.

aśrauṣam anyadā, ‹tatr' ārya|putraḥ kv' âpi n' āpyata.
na jñāyate kva c' âst'› īty kṣāram āpaṃ kṣate tataḥ.

tatr' ânyad" âśva|vaṇij" âsy' âśva|ratnam aḍhaukyata
tad āruhya sa bāhy'|ālīm iyāya sa|paricchadaḥ.
dhārābhiḥ pañcabhis tatra vāhayitv" âtha taṃ hayam
carma|yaṣṭy" āhatya vegān mumuce sa nṛp'|âṅgajaḥ.
veg'|āvegād adhāvat prāg atha divy utpapāta saḥ
tato harṣa|viṣādābhyāṃ pūc|cakre tat|paricchadaḥ.

Now, one day in Varánasi, he went to a certain house to beg for food. And there the housewife continued to prepare food for the husband with continued attention. Later, after 14.245
he had been fed, she brought food for that ascetic, but he, angered because of this, emitted a mighty roar.

But she said, "I am not a crane. Take your food, if you are hungry." Then he fell at her feet and asked, "Why do you mention the crane?"

She said, "Because I will burn you to ashes in an instant." Then he became frightened and said, "Venerable lady, how did you gain such power?"

She replied, "I have never cherished another man, not even with my thought set on anyone other than the lord of my life. That is why this power became manifest in me."

My lord, you yourself may understand the application of this parable.' On his minister's speaking thus, the Prince continued to prevaricate. Then he handed me over to Pri- 14.250
ya·dárshana. Several days thus fled by like absconders.

Then, one day, I heard someone say, 'His Highness Kúsuma·shékhara cannot be found anywhere. No one knows where he is.' So that rubbed salt into my wound.

A dealer in horses came there one day to show a gem of a horse to Suran·dhara, who mounted it and went to the outdoor track accompanied by his entourage. There he made the horse go in the five paces. Striking it with his whip, the Prince let it go at a dash. First it galloped in a rush of speed, then it flew up into the sky. His entourage cried out in mingled delight and apprehension.

14.255 Nabhovāhana|rājo 'tha taj jñātvā haya|senayā
Surandhara|kumārasya sadyo 'dhāviṣṭa pṛṣṭhataḥ.
tadā Siṃhapurāt, kānta, sarvato 'py ākul'|ākulāt
mṛgīvad bandhanāt sadyaḥ śīlaṃ trātuṃ palāyiṣi.
prāpt'|ôdyāne na jāne tu tāta|pattana|paddhatim.
dṛṣṭ" âtha chinna|nās'|âuṣṭhā tatr' âikā carikā mayā.
uktā ca sā, ‹Jayapure mām, amba, nayase yadi,
tad" âvaśyaṃ survarṇasya śataṃ tubhyaṃ dadāmy aham.›
‹svarṇam ādāya hanmy enām atr' âiv',› êti vicintya sā
carik" ākhyat, ‹kva te svarṇam?› tataḥ, kānta, may" āucyata:
14.260 ‹pure tatra mama tāto Vāmadevo vaṇig|varaḥ.
sa dāsyate suvarṇaṃ te dṛṣṭvā māṃ kṣema|śālinīm.
na datte te svarṇam asau, mātar, yadi kathañ cana
kurvīthā māṃ tadā dāsīṃ, vikrīṇīthā dhanena vā.›
ity uktv" âhaṃ tayā sārdhaṃ prāsthiṣi sva|puraṃ prati,
yāvad dṛṣṭaḥ sārtha ekas. tay" âsmi jagade tataḥ:
‹sārthen' âiva samaṃ yāmo.› may" ôktam, ‹evam astv,› iti.
sārdhaṃ sārthena ten' āvāṃ dināni kati cid gate.
atha sā carikā pāpā sārtha|vāhaṃ raho 'bhyadhāt:
‹gṛhāṇ' âitāṃ mama sutāṃ, dehi svarṇa|sahasrakam.›
14.265 ‹evam astv,› iti sārth'|ēśaḥ pratyapadyata tad|vacaḥ.
tac ca, nātha, mayā jñātaṃ, dhyātaṃ ca, ‹mama karma dhik!›
atr' ântare mahā|sārthaḥ sa viveśa mah"|âṭavīm.
tābhyāṃ bhītā tv ahaṃ sārthān niśy anaśyam a|lakṣitā.
bhrāmyanty araṇye bhrāmyadbhir
dṛṣṭ" âhaṃ ghādi|vāhakaiḥ.
tad|darśanād asmi bhītā
taiḥ samāśvāsitā punaḥ.

When King Nabho·váhana perceived this, he began to race alongside the Prince on his thunderbolt of a horse. Then, my dear, in the flurry of the confusion everywhere, I suddenly escaped from Simha·pura, like a doe from confinement, in order to protect my virtue. I came to a garden, but I didn't know my way to my father's city. And there I was seen by a wandering nun, whose nose and lips were cut off. 14.255

And I said to her, 'If you take me to Jaya·pura, mother, I promise to give you a hundred gold pieces.'

Thinking, 'I'll take the gold and kill her right here,' the nun asked, 'Where is your gold?' Then, my dear, I said,

'My father, Vama·deva, is a leading merchant in that city. 14.260
He will give you the gold, once he sees me safe and sound. But he won't give you the gold, mother, if you do me any harm or if you sell me as a slave girl for money.'

After I had said that, I set off with her to go to my city, when we saw a caravan. Then she said to me, 'Let's travel with that caravan,' and I agreed. The two of us traveled with the caravan for several days.

Then that wicked nun said to the caravan-leader in secret, 'Take my daughter here and give me a thousand gold pieces.'

The caravan-leader said, 'All right,' and agreed to her 14.265
proposal. I found this out, husband, and thought, 'Alas for my karma!'

At that same time the large caravan entered a huge forest wilderness. But I, frightened of those two, ran away at night, unobserved. While wandering in the forest, I was seen by bearers of nets. Although I was frightened by their appearance, they reassured me.

pṛṣṭā ca, ‹saumye, k" âsi tvaṃ?›
may" ōce, ‹'smi vaṇig|vadhūḥ.
mahā|sārthena mad|bhartā
saha gacchan kil' âbhavat.
sārthaś ca luṇṭhitaś caurair. naṣṭ" âsmi patit" âṭave.
yūyaṃ tu prasthitāḥ kva stha?› tair uktaṃ, ‹Bhṛgupattane.›
14.270 may" ōce, «yadi māṃ tatra nayadhvaṃ naya|śālinaḥ,
tatra prāptā tadā svarṇa|śataṃ vo dāpayāmy aham.»
śīghram evaṃ hi tair ūce, taiḥ saha prasthit" âsmy atha.
tan|madhyād ekena yūnā prārthit" âhaṃ punaḥ punaḥ.
dadhye mayā, ‹na sārtho 'yaṃ śīla|kṣemaṅ|karo mama.›
tato niśy eṣu supteṣu diśy ekasyām acāliṣam.
vahner jayani madhy'|âhne kāñ cana prāpam āpagām.
prakṣālya tatra vadanaṃ, nātha, kṛcchrād apām apaḥ.
tasyās tīre tamāl'|âdho viśrāmyantī vyalokayam
śūnya|śūnyā diśaḥ sarvā, Yamasy' âpi bhayaṅ|karāḥ.
14.275 nāga|vallyā pūga|nagaṃ, kokyā kokaṃ ca saṅgatam
paśyanty a|kuṇṭhām utkaṇṭhām ārya|putre vyadhām aham.
a|nabhra|vṛṣṭivad daiv'|ânukūlyena kuto 'py upait
su|lakṣaṇā bhagavatī tatr' âsau saumanasya|bhāk.
pratyāyāta|jīvit'|āśā tatas tad|darśane 'bhavam.
abhyutthāya prahṛṣṭ" âsmi vismit" âitām avandiṣi.
tato 'ham etayā pṛṣṭā, ‹kutaḥ, putri, samāgamaḥ?›
ath' âsmi dīrghaṃ niḥśvasya sadyaḥ praruditā bhṛśam.

They asked, 'Who are you, good lady?,' and I replied, 'I am a merchant's wife. He was actually traveling with a large caravan.

But the caravan was plundered. I ran away and entered this wilderness. But where are you going?' They said, 'To the city of Bhrigu·kaccha.'

I said, 'If you take me there and act in a proper manner, 14.270
once I arrive there I will see that you are given a hundred gold pieces.'

They immediately agreed, so then I set off with them. I was repeatedly solicited by one of their young men.

I thought, 'This gang will not let my virtue remain secure,' so at night, when they were asleep, I ran straight ahead in a single direction. At midday, hotter than fire, I came to a river. I managed to wash my face in it, husband, and drink its water. Resting beneath a *tamála* tree on its bank, I looked around and saw that every direction was absolutely barren,
the cause of fear even to Death. As I beheld a betel tree 14.275
embraced by a betel creeper and a cuckoo by a cuckoo hen, I was in a state of continual longing for my noble husband.

By a stroke of unexpected good fortune, like a shower without a cloud, a nun of auspicious appearance arrived at that place, intent on benevolence. Then, at the sight of her, my hope for survival became certain. I rose and, thrilled with wonder, paid my respects to her.

Then she asked me, 'Where have you come from, my girl?' Thereupon I heaved a deep sigh and suddenly broke out in floods of tears.

ath' âitayā samāśvāsya nīt" âhaṃ tāpas'|āśramam,
tatr' ânamaṃ kula|patiṃ. tat|pṛṣṭā sarvam abhyadhām.
14.280 ten' ânuśiṣṭā saṃsār'|āgāra|vairasya|darśanaiḥ
tad|ādeśāt tāpasībhiḥ phal'|āhāram akāriṣi.
tāpasais tāpasībhiś ca Sudarśana|śukena ca
bāndhavair iva gauravyāt tatr' âsthāṃ kati cid dinān.

aparedyur guru|pārśve 'smāsu sarveṣu vartiṣu
kuto 'pi dvau narāv ety' âvandetāṃ tam ṛṣ'|īśvaram.
āsīnau guruṇā pṛṣṭau tau sv'|ôdantam avocatām:
‹āste Jayasthalaṃ nāma nagaraṃ naga|rañjitam.

vaṇik|Kalādhipas tatra, priyā tasya Naliny, aho,
tat|putrau Śaśi|Candr'|ākhyāv āvām ā|bālya|sauhṛdau.
14.285 yauvane 'neka|bhāṇḍ'|âughaiḥ prapūry' āvāṃ vahitrakam
vārdhau manīṣita|bhuvaṃ prāptau, lābho mahān abhūt.
gṛhītvā prati|bhāṇḍāni pratyāvṛttau gṛhaṃ prati
mahā|samudre dur|vāta|dur|din'|ādyā udaiyaruḥ.
prakṛteṣ' ûpakrameṣu bahuṣv api vahitrakam
āvayor hṛdayam iva sahasā śatadh" âsphuṭat.

sphuṭamāṇe tatra pote gṛhītvā phalakaṃ balāt
āvābhyāṃ mumuce sv'|ātmā sindhau nirvedataḥ kila.
tato 'par'|âpar'|ōrmībhiḥ preritaṃ phalakaṃ, prabho,
Śaśino me prāpa tīraṃ. prīṇito 'haṃ van'|ânilaiḥ.
14.290 samutthāya, phalair bhuktvā yāna|pāttra|vipattitaḥ

Then she reassured me and took me to her hermitage, where I paid my respects to the head of the order. On his asking, I related everything.

He instructed me in the teachings of aversion to existence, 14.280 and on his command I was fed on fruit by the nuns. I remained there for some days, being held in high regard by the monks, nuns and Sudárshana, a parrot, who were like my own kinsmen.

One day, when all were attending on the teacher, two men came from somewhere and bowed to the head of the order. They sat, and on being asked by the teacher related their story: 'There is a city named Jaya·sthala, the delight of a mountain in its situation.

There lived a merchant Kaládhipa and his wife Nálini. We two are their sons, named Shashin and Chandra, friends from boyhood.

On attaining youth, we loaded a ship with an abundance 14.285 of various kinds of merchandise. We arrived at the land we were making for over the ocean, and the profit was great. Taking goods received in exchange, we set sail for home. Bad winds, bad weather and such began to swell upon the mighty ocean. Although we attempted many expedients, the ship, like our heart, was violently shattered a hundred times.

When the boat was shattered we each grabbed hold of a plank and abandoned ourselves to the ocean, full of despair. Then the plank, impelled by wave after wave, cast me, Shashin, on the shore. I was revived by a breeze from the woods. I rose and, after eating fruit, lamented for a long time over 14.290

bhrātṛ|Candra|viyogāc ca mayā ciram aśucyata.
dhairya|vīryam ath' ālambya prasthitaḥ sva|puraṃ prati.
prāpto mah"|âṭavīṃ nānā|taru|ṣaṇḍa|vimaṇḍitām.
tatra ca śābarī|vidyā|sādhanīyaṃ maṇī|mayam
khe|caraiḥ kṛtam adrākṣaṃ yug'|ādi|Jina|mandiram
praviśy' âtra jagan|nātha|bimbam abhyarcya sādaram
tatr' âik'|ânte din'|ânte ca svāpa|sthānam aśiśriyam.
ath' ârko 'staṃ svavan me 'gād vistṛtaṃ śokavat tamaḥ
rajany upaid a|dhṛtivat tridoṣyā sannyapatyata.
14.295 ātmānaṃ bhrātaraṃ svaṃ ca śocan yāvat śaye 'smi na,
tāvad vidyā|bhṛt|kumārau tatr' āgātāṃ Jin'|ālaye.
dev'|âdhidevaṃ c' âbhyarcya vedikāyāṃ niṣedatuḥ,
mithaś ca vastu|sāmarthya|kathām iti vitenatuḥ.
eken' ôce, «'sya mantrasy', âsyā vidyāyās, tath" âśmanaḥ,
mūlasya, dhātor, deśasya prabhāvo 'yam ayaṃ sphuṭam.»
anyen' ôktaṃ, «kiṃ bah'|ûktaiḥ?
prabhāvo yādṛśo 'dhunā,
Priyamelaka|śailasya
tādṛṅ n' ânyasya kasya cit.»
ādya ākhyat, «kaḥ prabhāvo girer asya? kva c' âsty asau?»
anya ūce, «sa kalpa|dru|cintā|maṇi|vijitvaraḥ.
14.300 yath"|ârtha|nāmā kiñ c' âiṣa bahubhir bahudh" ēkṣitaḥ.
yatra c' âyaṃ giri|varas, tat samprati nigadyate.

the disaster to the ship and my separation from my brother, Chandra.

Then, taking hold of courage and manliness, I set out for my native city. I arrived at a big forest, adorned with groves of various trees. And there I saw a temple of the Jina Ríshabha, built by the sky-traveling masters of magic, made of jewels, effective against black magic. I entered it and reverently worshipped the image of the lord of the universe. And in that secluded spot at the end of day I found a place to sleep.

The sun, my protector, set, and darkness spread as if it were gloom. Night approached as if it were unhappiness.

While I was lying there awake worrying about myself 14.295
and my brother, two young masters of magic arrived at the temple. And after worshipping the Jina, the god over gods, they sat on a bench and began to talk together about ways of gaining wealth. One of them spoke of the various spells, charms, rocks, roots and places from which such power could be obtained.

The other said, "There's no need for long explanations. Such a power can be obtained immediately from Mount Union with the Beloved; such power can be obtained from nowhere else."

The first one said, "What is the power of that mountain and where is it?" The other replied, "Its power surpasses a
wishing-tree and a wishing-jewel. Has it not been seen to be 14.300
appropriately named Union with the Beloved by many people many times over? And I will declare where that excellent mountain is situated right now.

ito 'sti daśa|yojanyāṃ puṇyā Puṇyavatī nadī
tasyāḥ sahasra|pattr'|ādi lātv", âśoka|taros tale
maṇī|śilāṃ cāraṇa'|rṣy|ātāpan'|āspadam ārcya ca,
uttar'|âbhimukhaṃ, mitra, gamyate pañca|yojanīm.
tataḥ pratyakṣam ev' âiṣa dṛśyate giri|śekharaḥ.»
ity|ādi|saṃkathāṃ kṛtvā tau yathā|sthānam īyatuḥ.
maya dadhye, «Jina|yātrā mam' âtr' âiv' âphalat|tarām,
yato 'muṣmād upāyān me bhrātā saṅgamyate dhruvam.»
14.305 tato 'smi supto, buddhaś ca Jina|pūjā|puraḥsaram
khe|car'|ôkta|diśā yāvat prasthitas taṃ giriṃ prati.
tad" âiva dakṣiṇaṃ cakṣus triḥ prapusphora māmakam,
pūc|cakre vāmataḥ śyāmā, mṛgo 'dhāvat pradakṣiṇam.
ath' ôdyadd|hṛd|avaṣṭambhaś calito 'smi drutaṃ drutam
yathā|śruta|vidhānāc ca kṣemeṇa prāpa taṃ girim.
dināni kati cit tatra sthito 'smi giri|pūjakaḥ.
tan|nikuñje yayāv asmi puṣpāṇy uccetum anyadā.
vivarāt tatra niryātau tumba|hastau narāv ubhau.
pratyāsattau mayā Candraś, Candreṇ' âsmy upalakṣitaḥ.
14.310 tato mayā sasvaje 'sau, rurod' âiṣa, pade 'patat.
pṛṣṭo 'smy anena Candreṇ' ākhyāṃ sva|vartām aśeṣataḥ.

Ten leagues from here is an auspicious river, Púnyavati. Having taken from it lotuses and such, and, at the foot of the *ashóka* tree, having worshipped the jeweled slab, the place heated by the wandering sage, one should proceed, my friend, in a northerly direction for a distance of five leagues. Then the mountain peak will be clearly visible." After making further conversation, the two returned to their native place.

I thought that if I were to perform a Jain pilgrimage to that place, it would be very advantageous to me, since by that means my brother would certainly be reunited with me. Then I went to sleep, and when I awoke I first worshipped 14.305
the Jina and then set out for the mountain in the direction described by the master of magic.

At that very moment, my right eye throbbed three times, a cuckoo cried out on my left, and a deer ran toward the right. Then, with the confidence of an uplifted heart, I traveled extremely quickly, and, acting according to the instructions I had overheard, easily arrived at that mountain.

For several days I remained there, performing devotions on the mountain. One day I went to a mountain grove to pluck flowers. Two men carrying pails came out of a well-shaft in the grove. At close quarters, I recognized Chandra, and he me.

Then my brother and I wept at the sight of each other and 14.310
fell at each other's feet. Then, asked by Chandra, I related the full details of what had befallen me.

mayā pṛṣṭena Candreṇa sva|pravṛttir it' īritā:
«bhrātas, tadā pota|bhaṅge phalaken' ârṇave 'patam.
any'|âny'|ōrmi|preritaṃ ca phalakaṃ taṭam āsadat.
velā|van'|ânilaiḥ kiñ cit prīṇito 'smy ata utthitaḥ.
tvad|viyog'|ârditen' âpi prāṇa|vṛttiḥ phalaiḥ kṛtā,
pracele ca mayā vegāt sva|deś'|âbhimukhaṃ tataḥ.
kiyaty api gate mārge militau puruṣāv ubhau.
ekaḥ pustaka|bhṛt pṛṣṭo mayā, ‹ko 'si? kva yāsi ca?›
14.315 ‹dhātu|vādy asmi, kalpena yāsyāmi rasa|kūpikām.
lakṣa|vedhi|ras'|āptau ca prāpsyāmi svarṇam akṣayam.›
punar may" ōce, ‹kva punar, mitr', âsti rasa|kūpikā?›
ten' ôktaṃ, ‹Priyamel"|âdrau.› mayā dadhye 'tha, bāndhava:
‹Priyamelaka|śailaś cet satyam eva, tad" âsmy api
sva|bhrātṛ|Śaśi|mel"|ârthaṃ tatra yāmi. milatv asau!›
atha, ‹kva yās'?› iti pṛṣṭo 'nen' âhaṃ dhātu|vādinā
mayā yath"|ârtham ākhyāyi tato 'nen' âsmy abhāṣiṣi:
‹tvam apy ehi, rasa|tṛtīy'|âṃśaṃ dāsye tav' âpy aham.›
mayā dadhye, ‹ko 'tra doṣaḥ? Śaśi|prāptau mahā|gunaḥ.›
14.320 tato, ‹'stv evam,› iti prokte trayo 'pi calitā vayam.
gacchadbhir mahatī rajju srāg asmābhir avalyata.

Asked by me, Chandra related what had happened to him: "Brother, when the ship broke up I jumped into the ocean holding a plank. Impelled by wave after wave, the plank reached the shore. I was somewhat revived by breezes from the woods on the shore, so I stood up.

Although tormented by my separation from you, I reinvigorated myself on fruit and then speedily set out in the direction of my native city.

Having gone some way on my journey, I encountered two men. I asked the one who was carrying a book who he was and where he was going.

'I am an alchemist. I am duly going to a well of mercury, 14.315
and on obtaining that success-giving mercury I shall obtain inexhaustible gold.'

I replied, 'But where is the well of magic fluid, my friend?,' and he said, 'On Mount Union with the Beloved.' Then, brother, I thought:

'If Mount Union with the Beloved is real, then I, too, will go there to meet Shashin, my brother. May he meet me!'

So, when the alchemist asked me where I was going, I answered truly, and then he said to me:

'Come, too, and I'll give you a third share of the mercury.' I thought, 'What harm is there in this? In the finding of Shashin there will be great merit.'

Thereupon I agreed to that, and the three of us set off. 14.320
As we went, we quickly unrolled a long rope.

tataḥ prāptā iha girau vivara|dvāry anena ca,
asmi proktas, ‹tvam atr' âiva rajjum ādāya tiṣṭha, bhoḥ!
dvāv apy āvāṃ pravekṣyāvo vivaraṃ bibhratau kare,
ṣaṇ|māsī|ghṛta|saṃsikta|mahiṣī|puccha|dīpakam.›
pravіṣṭau tau, dvāra|deśe rajju|hastas tv ahaṃ sthitaḥ,
bhrātar, ekam aho|rātraṃ. prātar ady' âiṣa nirgataḥ
ekāky eva rasa|pūrṇaṃ gṛhītvā tumbaka|dvayam
mahā|rajjv|anusāreṇa. tato mām uktavān iti:
14.325 ‹vardhāpyase, Candra mitra, sampūrṇās te mano|rathāḥ.
tav' ôpabhuñjato 'pi śrīr na niṣṭhāsyati vārdhivat.
tat tumbakaṃ gṛhāṇ' âikaṃ, gacchāvaḥ sva|sva|veśmani.›
tata ūce mayā, ‹yas te dvitīyo 'bhūt, sakhe, kva saḥ?›
anen' ôktaṃ, ‹mayā, mitra, rasa|kūpyāṃ sa cikṣipe.
na vinā puṃ|baliṃ hi syād rasa|siddhiḥ kathañ cana.›
vivarāc calitau c' āvāṃ, militas tvaṃ, bāndhava.»
iti bhrātṛ|gir" âtuṣyaṃ, rasa|prāptyā viśeṣataḥ.
āvābhyāṃ dhātu|vādī sa praṇato 'gāt svam āspadam.
āvāṃ prāpta|rasau tatr' āgacchāvo, bhagavann, iti.›
14.330 Śaśy|uktam avadhāry', ārya|putra, cetasy ado 'dadhām:
‹Priyamelaka|śaile syād dhruvaṃ me priya|melakaḥ.›

Then, when we arrived at the mountain and the entrance to the well, he, the alchemist, said to me, 'You stay right here and hold the rope, good sir. We two shall enter the well, holding a torch made of a buffalo's tail impregnated with six-month-old cooking oil.'

They went in, and I stood at the entrance, holding the rope, for a day and a night, brother. Then, in the morning, the alchemist came out by means of the long rope, just on his own, carrying two pails full of mercury. Then he said to me:

'You're made rich, Chandra, my friend. Your heart's de- 14.325
sires are fulfilled. Even if you consume it, your wealth, like the ocean, will not be exhausted.

So take one of the pails, and we will return to our respective abodes.' Then I said, 'Where is the other one who was with you, my friend?'

He said, 'I threw him into the mercury well, my friend. Without a human sacrifice, the mercury would have no efficacy at all.'

We came from the well, and met you, brother." I was cheered by what my brother said, particularly by the acquisition of the mercury.

We gave our farewells to the alchemist, and he returned to his own abode. We two, bringing the mercury we had obtained, arrived here, reverend sir.'

Having heard what Shashin had said, in my mind I con- 14.330
sidered this: 'On Mount Union with the Beloved, I will certainly be united with my beloved.'

ākār'|ādyaiḥ kula|patir vijñāy' âtha mam' āśayam
tāpasa|tāpasī|kīrān etān drutam ado 'vadat:

‹bho bhoḥ, sambhūya yuṣmābhir netavyā Surasundarī
Priyamelaka|tīrthe, 'syā yena syāt priya|melakaḥ.›

tataḥ patra|puṣpa|madhya|kṛt" êv' âtīva|vatsalaiḥ
etair atr' âham āninye, satyo 'bhūt priya|melakaḥ.»

tato, bhoḥ, śrī|Siṃha|rāja,
kumāras tām avocata:
«priye 'nubhūtaṃ prabhūtaṃ
duḥkhaṃ duṣkarma|nirmitam.»

14.335 papraccha s" âpi, «prāṇ'|ēśa, mudhā kiṃ kliśyase, 'nagha?
iti deva|giraḥ paścāt kiṃ tvay" âpy anvabhūyata?»

sa ca sv'|ôdanta|pīyūṣaṃ tamāla|prāpti|mukhyakam,
tat|samāgama|paryantaṃ nyadhāt tat|karṇa|kūpayoḥ.

tato Ramaṇamaty|aṃhrī natv" ōce Surasundarī:
«tvaṃ mama svāminī, prāṇa|nātha|prāṇa|pradānataḥ.»

s" âpy abhyadhād atha Surasundarīṃ prīta|mānasā:
«tvam eva mama sarvatra praṣṭavyā jyeṣṭha|bhagny asi.»

kumāreṇ' âtha Ramaṇamaty ūce, «sajyatāṃ, priye,
śīghraṃ bhagavatām eṣāṃ bhojan'|ātithyam ādarāt.»

14.340 s" ākhyat, «siddhaṃ eva dev'|ārcām kuruta drutam.»
anu|dev'|ārcanaṃ bhaktyā bhojitās tāpas'|ādayaḥ.

Then, the head of the order, knowing my desire through my expression and suchlike, said this to the monks, nuns, and the parrot:

'Good people, gather together and take Sura·súndari to holy Union with the Beloved, so that there may be union with her beloved.'

Then they, treating me with great devotion, like a flower in the midst of leaves, brought me here. The union with the beloved was real."

Then, Your Majesty King Simha, sire, the Prince said to her, "My dear, pain results from and arises from bad karma."

She asked him, "Why are you needlessly tormenting 14.335
yourself, lord of my life? You are free from sin. What happened to you after the god spoke?"

And he deposited the nectar of his doings beginning with the finding of the *tamála* tree and finishing with his reunion with her into the hollows of her ears.

Sura·súndari bowed to Rámana·mati's feet and said, "You are my mistress because you saved the life of the lord of my life."

Thereupon she, pleased in mind, replied to Sura·súndari, "You, rather, are my eldest sister, to be placed foremost in every respect."

The Prince said to Rámana·mati, "My dear, let food and respectful hospitality be quickly prepared for these holy ones."

She said, "It's ready now. Quickly worship the gods." 14.340
After devotedly worshipping the gods, the ascetics and the others dined.

kīraḥ punaḥ pūta|bhūta|phal'|ādy alam abhojyata.
pūgī|phal'|ādi|satkāraḥ sarveṣām apy atanyata.

tena kāntā|yugalena Rati|Prīti|śriṇā saha
ath' âika|pātre bubhuje kumāraḥ Smara|sodaraḥ.

tatas te tāpas'|ôpānte niṣedur medurā mudā.
kumāro 'vag «bhagavadbhir anvagṛhe 'smi sarvathā.
manye yuṣmad|ānukūlyād viddhir apy anukūly abhūt.
a|sambhāvyam idaṃ sarvaṃ mama saṃjaghaṭe yataḥ.

14.345 kevalaṃ mad|viyogena pitarāv ati|tāmyataḥ,
prāptasy' Âpratipathāyāṃ vilambo bhavitā ca me.»

ity uktv" âiva kumāreṇa dṛgg|hṛdāv uttaraṅgitau.
tataḥ śuko 'vadat, «pitros tav' ôdantaṃ nayāmy aham.»

tataḥ kumāraḥ smer'|âkṣo 'vak, «tvam eva, Sudarśana,
īdṛg|duḥkh'|ânal'|āsāraḥ!» pratyāyady anujānate.

tāpasā vyāharan kīraṃ, «gacch', āgaccheḥ punar drutam.»
rāja|sūr abravīt, «pūjyā, anvagṛhy'|êtarām aham.»

atha prahṛṣṭa|vadanaḥ punar ūce Sudarśanaḥ:
«kumāra, māṃ praguṇaya!» sa vijñaptiṃ tato 'likhat.

yathā:

14.350 «sv|asti! śrī|Bhṛgupattane Kusumake-
tu|śrī|mahā|bhū|pater
devī|Svarṇalat"|āyutasya vimalaṃ
śrī|pāda|padma|dvayam
mūrdhn" ānamya muhur mud" Âpratipathā|

But the parrot just ate fruit that had become rotten and such. The respectful offering of betel nut was extended to all.

Now, the Prince ate from a single plate with his pair of beloveds, akin to Love with lovely Passion and Pleasure.

Then they, cloyed with joy, sat near to the ascetics. The Prince said, "I have been favored by you, blessed ones, in every respect. I suppose by means of your favor even fate became favorable, since it is inconceivable that I have met with all this.

Only my parents are perishing through separation from 14.345
me, and once I have arrived in Ápratipatha I will be delayed."

As soon as he said this, tears billowed from the center of the Prince's eyes. Then the parrot said, "I will go and take news of you to your parents."

Then the Prince, his eyes smiling, said, "You are really, Sudárshana, a hard rain for the fire of such a trouble!" The chief ascetic gave his permission.

The ascetics said to the parrot, "Go, but come back quickly." The Prince said, "Venerable ones, I am highly favored by you once more."

Then Sudárshana, his countenance cheerful, said, "Prepare me, Prince!," so the Prince wrote a letter.

Like so:

"Blessings! Having repeatedly bowed with joy his head 14.350
to the revered pair of lotus-feet, free from stain, of His Majesty King Kúsuma·ketu in company with Queen Kánaka·lata in the lovely city of Bhrigu·kaccha, and having folded his hands like buds in greeting, Kúsuma·shékhara,

puryāḥ karau kuḍmalī|
kṛty' âsau Kusumādiśekhara idaṃ
vijñāpayaty ādarāt:
kṣema|śrīr mama Rāmadeva|nṛpateḥ
putrī may" ôḍh" âpi ca
samprāptā Surasundarī drutam upe-
ṣyāmi pramodyaṃ tataḥ
yac c' âyam hi Sudarśanaḥ śuka|varo
vijñāpayaty etad apy
ākarṇyaṃ viśada|prasāda|sadanaiḥ
śrī|tāta|pādair mayi.»

kaṇṭh'|ābaddha|divya|lekhaḥ, saṃdiṣṭ'|âśeṣa|vācikaḥ,
Sudarśano div" ôtpatya kṣaṇen' âbhūd a|darśanaḥ.

sammānya tāpasān praiṣīt svayaṃ kāntā|dvayī|sakhaḥ
purīm aid Apratipathāṃ. Rāmadevas tam abhyagāt.
praveśakam aho jajñe, jajñe vardhāpanaṃ mahat!
evaṃ sukhena tatr' āsthād dinān katy api rāja|sūḥ.

14.355 itaś ca śrī|Bhṛgukacche prāsād'|ôpari|kuṭṭime
śrī|Kanakalatā|devī|ruddh'|ârdha|hari|viṣṭaraḥ
rājā śrī|Kusumaketur mitr'|âmātya|paricchadaḥ
lekha|graiveyakaṃ kīraṃ nabhasy āyāntam aikṣata.

kṣaṇān nipatya purato, vartma|śramam apāsya ca
camat|kṛt'|âśeṣa|sabhyaṃ kīro nara|gir" âpaṭhat:
«nar'|êndra|mauli|māṇikya|rocir|yāvakita|krama ,
putr'|ôdanta|vasantena, deva, vardhāpyase 'dhunā.

from the city of Ápratipatha, respectfully informs them of this:

I am healthy and prosperous. I have married the daughter of King Rama·deva and have found Sura·súndari, so rejoice! And let what this here excellent parrot Sudárshana shall relate in addition be heard by my respected father as he abides in the grace of tenderness for me."

The divine letter tied to his neck, and instructed with the remaining verbal message, Sudárshana flew up into the sky and vanished from view in an instant.

Having paid his respects to the ascetics, accompanied by his two wives, he himself departed and arrived at the city of Ápratipatha. Rama·deva met him. Oh, what a great entrance procession took place, what a great festival! Thus the Prince remained there for several days at his ease.

Now, in lovely Bhrigu·kaccha, on the mosaic terrace 14.355
above the palace, with the royal throne half taken by Her Highness Queen Kánaka·lata, surrounded by his companions and ministers, His Majesty King Kúsuma·ketu saw the parrot bearing the letter on a chain around his neck coming through the sky.

In an instant the parrot landed in front of him and, disregarding the fatigue of the journey, as the entire assembly cried out in astonishment, recited:

"You whose feet are reddened with the light from the crest-rubies of the lords of men, Your Majesty, you are now going to be made to flourish by the spring season of tidings of your son.

deva, devasya, devyāś ca śrīmān Kusumaśekharaḥ
Surasundarī|Ramaṇamatyau c' âṃhrī namanty amī.»
14.360 iti śrutv" âvadad bhūpo mudā vistārya dor|late:
«sv|āgataṃ te, svaccha. vats', āgacch', ôtsaṅgam alaṅkuru.»
atha tasya mahī|bhartur anujñāpya śuk'|âgraṇīḥ
utsaṅga|śṛṅgam ārohat kumārasy' êva nandanaḥ.
vyajijñapac ca rājānaṃ, «lekhaṃ vācāpaya, prabho.»
praty|akṣaraṃ kṣarad|vāṣpaṃ rāṭ svayaṃ tam avācayat.
lekhaṃ kumār'|āgamana|vardhāpakam avetya tau
rajā rājñī ca kim api pramod'|â|dvaitam ūhatuḥ!
teṣāṃ trayāṇāṃ vṛttāntaṃ kīraḥ kṣīra|kirā|girā
yathā|śrutaṃ nṛpasy' ākhyad eka|saṃstutikaḥ kila.
14.365 cumbaṃ cumbaṃ śukaṃ mūrdhni
nyāsaṃ nyāsaṃ sva|vakṣasi
bhūpo 'ti|harṣa|vātūlaḥ
kathañ cid api n' âtṛpat.
nṛpam aty|uparudhy' âtha
gṛhītvā taṃ tathā vyadhāt
devy" âth' âmātya|sāmantāḥ
kaumāraṃ bhāgyam adbhutaṃ.
drākṣā|dāḍima|kharjūra|sahakār'|ādibhiḥ phalaiḥ
taṃ prīṇayantī sā devī teṣv arocakinaṃ vyadhāt.
nṛpa|saudhe kṣaṇe 'tr' āgād vihartuṃ sādhu|yāmalam.
rājā tat praviśad vīkṣy' ājūhavat svasya sannidhau.

Your Majesty, His Highness Kúsuma·shékhara, Sura·súndari and Rámana·mati bow to the feet of the King and Queen."

On hearing that, the King joyfully bent down the creepers 14.360
of his arms and said, "Welcome to you, you pearl. Come and ornament my lap, my child."

Then the foremost of parrots obeyed the King and climbed into his lap as if he were the son of the Prince.

He said to the King, "Have the letter read, my lord." The King read it out himself, tears flowing at every syllable.

Since the couple considered the letter to be a birth ceremony for the arrival of the Prince, what joy did the King and Queen experience!

The parrot gave news of three according to his instructions in a voice pouring milk; he was certainly the King's chief panegyrist!

Pressing kiss after kiss on the parrot's head, and pressing 14.365
the parrot to his own chest, the King, mad with extreme joy, was not all satisfied. The Queen managed to restrain the King and took the parrot. Then, as was proper, the Queen informed the ministers and barons of the wonderful good fortune of the Prince. Refreshing him with fruit, grapes, pomegranates, dates, mangoes and such, the Queen satisfied his appetite with them.

At that moment a pair of Jain monks came to the royal palace in the course of their wanderings there. When the King entered and saw them, he summoned them to his presence.

kṣmā|patiḥ sa|parīvāro bhakty" âvandiṣṭa tau munī,
«niviśyatām āsanayor,» ity uvāca ca gauravāt.

14.370 «go|car'|âgra|praviṣṭena
n' āsitavyaṃ maha"|rṣiṇā.
dvi|trair vākyair dharma|kath" âpy
ādhey" âtra prabandhataḥ.
rājaṃs, tav' âtha sabhyānām upakāram avetya tu
sthāsyāvaḥ kṣaṇam.» ity uktv" ôpaviṣṭau tau mahā|munī.
bhūpo 'brūt' âtha, «bhagavan,
paśy' âmuṃ śukam uttamam.
etadīy'|ôkti|vaicitryād
bhṛśaṃ citrīyitā vayam.»
muninā jñāninā proce, «'yaṃ sa|pūrva iv' âsti naḥ.»
śuko 'vag, «n' âsmi yuṣmābhir dṛṣṭaḥ kv' âp' îti vedmy aham.
kin tu śrutaṃ mayā, santi kv' âpi śvetāmbara'|rṣayaḥ
kad" âpi na punar dṛṣṭāḥ. sa|pūrvo 'smi tataḥ katham?»

14.375 jñāny uvāc', «â|sannihitam api sannihitaṃ yathā
jñānena jñāyate, tasmād dṛṣṭa ev' âsi mūlataḥ.»
tato vijñāpayāñcakre rājā Kusumaketunā:
«bhagavan śuka|vṛttāntaṃ brūhi.» «rājan, niśāmaya.
purā hi puri Kauśāmbyāṃ Sudharma|svāmi|sannidhau
Rāmadeva|śrī|Vijayasen'|ādyā daśa dīkṣitāḥ.
bhagavantas tataḥ śrīmac Cāmpāpuryāṃ vijahrire.
tatra śrī|Vimalaseno rāj" âvandiṣṭa tān gurūn.
sādhūn namasyatā tena dadṛśe guru|sannidhau
śrīmān Vijayasena'|rṣir dadhye dur|manasā tataḥ.

The King, attended by his retinue, bowed with devotion to the two monks and with respect invited them to be seated.

"When a great ascetic has previously entered upon a field 14.370
of ascetic action, he should not be seated. We should here give a religious discourse of two or three sentences by means of a story. But, Your Majesty, having regard for your benefit and that of the assembly, we shall stay for a moment." After saying that, the two great ascetics sat down.

The King said, "Look at that excellent parrot, reverend sir. We are struck with wonder by the wonder of his speech."

The monk, who was possessed of knowledge, said, "We have indeed seen him before." The parrot said, "I know that you have never seen me before anywhere. But I have heard that somewhere there are white-clad monks, but I have never seen them before anywhere. How, then, have you seen me before?"

The one possessed of knowledge said, "Since what is not 14.375
present just as what is present is known by higher knowledge, so you were certainly seen right from the start."

Then King Kúsuma·ketu said, "Reverend sir, relate the story of the parrot." "Pay attention, Your Majesty.

Now, in the past, in the city of Kaushámbi, Rama·deva, His Majesty Víjaya·sena and the others, ten in all, were initiated in the presence of Lord Sudhárman. Then the reverend ones wandered in lovely Champa and there His Majesty King Vímala·sena came to pay his respects to the teacher. As he bowed to the monks he saw in the presence of the teacher the royal monk Víjaya·sena. Thereupon he malevolently thought:

14.380 ‹s' âiṣa me 'rir, yena purā parito 'smi vibādhitaḥ,
tad amuṃ vairiṇaṃ hasta|prāptaṃ hanmi sva|pāṇinā.›
tac|cintita|prakaṭanād guruṇā bodhito 'tha saḥ,
kṣamayāmāsa Vijayasena'|rṣiṃ, śrāvako 'py abhūt.
ath' ântar'|ântarā dadhyau, ‹na suṣṭhu vihitaṃ mayā,
yat tadā na hataḥ so 'riḥ.› punar nindati duṣ|kṛtam.
prānte c' âsau māsik'|ânaśanād bhavana|paty abhūt.
tato nṛ|tiryaṅ|naraka|bhaveṣu bahuśo 'bhramat.
punar nṛṣu śrāvako 'bhūd virādhya śrāvaka|vratān.
babhūva Camar'|êndrasy' êndra|sāmānika|nirjaraḥ.
14.385 prānte c' ārtta|dhyānato 'sau tiryag|āyur|nibandhanaḥ
atr' âiva Bharata|kṣetre Priyamelā|mah"|âṭavau
śālmalī|śālino nīḍē kil' āpīḍe śuko 'bhavat.
pitṛbhyām poṣyamāṇaś ca kiñ cit saṃjāta|pakṣy abhūt.
anyadā puṅkhita|śarā śavarā Yama|kiṅ|karāḥ
tatr' āyayuḥ pitṛbhyām so 'vāci, ‹mā cuṅ|kṛthā!› iti
teṣv āsanneṣv ati|bhayāc cuñ|cakāra śuk'|ârbhakaḥ.
tasya svar'|ânusāreṇa mumucuḥ śavarāḥ śarān.
mṛtyu|bhītyā śuk'|ârbhakasya pitarau jagmatuḥ kva cit.
śuk'|ârbhas tv a|prauḍha|pakṣo 'patad bhuvi bhay'|āturaḥ.
14.390 ninye lilye taru|gahane na dṛṣṭas taiḥ sa|pāpmabhiḥ,

'Here is that very enemy of mine who formerly used to harass me everywhere. So now that he has come to hand I will kill him with my own hand.' 14.380

Through revealing what he had thought, the teacher enlightened him, and he spared the monk Víjaya·sena. He even became a Jain layman. But from time to time he thought, 'I did not act well that time when I did not slay my enemy,' but blamed it as a bad action. And on his death, because of his monthly fasts, he became a lord-of-the-mansion god. After that, he wandered many times in human, animal and hell-being existences.

Again among human beings, he became a Jain layman. Because of his infringement of his vows as a Jain layman, he was reborn a god with the rank of a general of Lord Chámara. A powerful lord-of-the-mansion god. Through 14.385
meditating on painful matters at the time of his end, he was bound with an animal life. And here, in this very land of Bhárata, in the great forest Union with the Beloved, he was born as a parrot dwelling in a tree, in a confined nest, of course. Nourished by his parents, his wings became somewhat mature.

One day, savages armed with feathered arrows, the servants of Death, came there. His parents told him, 'Don't make a squeak!'

When they came nearby, the young parrot, because of his great fear, squawked. Aiming at his cry, the savages loosed their arrows. Fearful of dying, the parents of the young parrot flew away somewhere. But the young parrot, not yet fledged, fell to the ground, sick with fear. He fell into 14.390
and was hidden by a hollow of a tree, unobserved by those

kṣut|tṛṣ|ārttaḥ katham api tamāla|gahanaṃ yayau.

itaś ca daiva|yogena tatr' âgāt tāpas'|ēśvaraḥ.
ten' āśvāsya gṛhīto 'sau pāyitaś ca saraḥ|payaḥ.
bhojayitvā dāḍim'|ādi|phalāny ati|kalāni saḥ
vineya iva vātsalyād āninye tāpas'|āśramam.
taṃ dṛṣṭvā tāpasā ūcur, ‹aho, kīraḥ su|darśanaḥ!›
tataḥ kula|patin" âsau cakre nāmnā Sudarśanaḥ.

gur'|ûktyā muni|kumāraiḥ pālito 'dhyāpitas tathā,
yathā Vyāsa|vad'|ākhyātā vyākhyātā ca babhūva saḥ.
14.395 atha tatr' āśrame 'bhyāgād vadhūr vaḥ Surasundarī,
tayā sah' âit Priyamele kumār'|ôktyā tv ih' âyam ait.»

pratyakṣ'|ôdanta|saṃvādāt parokṣe 'numiti|sthiteḥ
pratyayaḥ «sādhu, sādh'!» ûkte 'tha jajñe tasya pakṣiṇaḥ.
īh'|âpohau kurvataś ca kṣaṇaṃ mūrcchām upeyuṣaḥ
navya|caitanyavaj jāti|smṛtir asy' ôdajṛmbhata.

tato natvā muni|rājaṃ so 'bhyadhāt patatāṃ varaḥ:
«mayā jāti|smṛter jñātaṃ tvad|vaco vajra|varmitam.
aho mahā|muner jñānam!,» iti tatra sabhā|sadaḥ,
«dhik saṃsāraṃ yatra devas tiryaṅ syād!» iti c' ūcire.

wrongdoers. Oppressed by hunger and thirst, he somehow arrived at a grove of *tamála* trees.

Now, by juncture of fate, the chief of the ascetics arrived there. Having revived the parrot, he took him and gave him water from the lake to drink. He fed him on grapes and such, very soft fruit, and with affection took him, as if he were a pupil, to the hermitage. On seeing him the monks cried, 'Oh, the parrot is good-looking!,' so the chief ascetic gave him the name Sudárshana, meaning 'good-looking.'

On the teacher's request the junior ascetics looked after the parrot and educated him to such an extent that he became a famed reciter of historical narratives and an expos-
itor. Then your daughter-in-law, Sura·súndari, came to that 14.395
hermitage, and the parrot went with her to Mount Union with the Beloved. But on the Prince's request he came here."

Through his agreement to his life story, which had been made manifest, the bird, in a state of assent to what was beyond the range of the senses, saying, "Excellent, excellent!," became possessed of firm conviction. While making consideration of what was for and against, the parrot fell into a swoon for a moment, and his memory of his former lives, like his renewed consciousness, unfolded.

Then the hero of parrots bowed to that king of a monk and said, "I have knowledge of my former lives, clad in the adamant of your discourse. Oh, the knowledge of the great monk!" Those sitting in assembly there said, "Alas for the cycle of existence in which a god becomes an animal!"

14.400 rājā tat|pāriṣadyāś ca samyaktv'|âlaṅkriy"|âdbhutāḥ
tatr' âho yugapad|deśa|viratyā pariṇinyire!
rājñ" âtha prāsuk'|āhārair gauravāt pratilābhitau
mahā|munī prasthitau tau. so 'vag vihaga|puṅgavaḥ:
«prabho, kim atha kāryaṃ me,
kiñ ca bhāvi bhav'|ântaram?»
ṛṣir babhāṣe, «sa|karṇa|
pūrṇam ākarṇay'. ôcyate:
‹Arhan devo, guruḥ sādhus, tad uktaṃ tattvam› ity adaḥ
samyaktvam aṇuvratāṃś ca pālayethāḥ, śuk'|ôttama.
tato Rājagṛhe Siṃha|rāj'|êndra|tanu|janmanaḥ
śrīmat|Padmakesarasya Dṛḍharath'|ākhya|sāratheḥ
14.405 putro bhaviṣyati bhavān Nāgaśarm' âbhidhānataḥ
tvay" āśrame dayālutvāt prâṇ|nar'|āyur abandhi yat.
tataḥ Padmakesar'|ôdbhū|Kārttavīrya|mahī|pateḥ
sārathī bhūya ten' âiva saha pravrajya setsyati.
tat saṃsār'|âpāra|pārād grāsas tvaṃ, kīra, mā sma bhūḥ!»
ity uktvā tau munī, kīraś c' âiṣa jagmur yath"|āgatam.
ath' ānanda|mah"|ōrmībhiḥ preritaḥ Puṣpaketu|rāṭ
prasthāne 'tāṇḍayad bherīṃ rodaḥ|kukṣiṃ|bhari|svarām.
tato nisvāna|nisvānair vācālita|kul'|âcalaḥ
calayann acalā|pīṭhaṃ catur|aṅga|camū|bharaiḥ
14.410 devyā Kanakalatayā saha sāmanta|mantribhiḥ
purīṃ praty Apratipathāṃ prati|panthī|kath"|âti|gām
sva|vaṃśa|śekharaṃ pratyānetuṃ Kusumaśekharam

The King and his assembly were wonderfully ornamented 14.400
by righteousness. Oh, they were joined with the self-restraint displayed by the pair of monks!

Then the King respectfully gave the monks food and water. As the two prepared to set out, that eminent bird said to them:

"Sir, what should I do now, and what will be my next existence?" The monk said, "Listen, with all your ears. It is said:

'The Worthy is a god, the teacher is excellent. This saying is the truth.' Therefore, you should follow righteousness and the subsidiary vows, you excellent parrot. After that, in Raja·griha, you will become the son, named Naga·sharman, of Dridha·ratha, the charioteer of His Highness Padma·késara,
the son of King Simha, since through your compassion in 14.405
the hermitage he had been previously enjoined with life as a man. Then, having become the charioteer of Padma·késara, in company with him, he will take initiation and gain final salvation. So don't be swallowed in the endless cycle of existence, parrot!" Having said that, the two monks and the parrot returned to the places from which they had come.

Then, impelled by huge waves of joy, King Kúsuma·ketu on their departure ordered a drum to be struck, its sound filling the hollow of the vault of heaven and earth. Then, the chief mountain range filled with the echoing sounds; making the base of the mountain shake with the masses of
his fourfold army; accompanied by Queen Kánaka·lata and 14.410
by his barons and ministers, Kúsuma·ketu set out for the city of Ápratipatha, which surpasses the stories of return

pratasthe Kusumaketuḥ ketu|danturit'|âmbaraḥ.
a|vilambita|prayāṇaiḥ prāptas tat|pura|sīmani.
mantriṇā jñāpayāmāsa sv'|āgamaṃ Rāma|bhū|pateḥ.
tataś ca śrī|Rāmacandraḥ sa|śrī|Kusumaśekharaḥ
tam abhyāgān maha"|rddhy" âbhūt sarveṣām priya|melakaḥ.
śrī|Puṣpaketu|kalpa|drū Rāmacandra|nṛp'|ârcitaḥ
saha|grāma|sahasreṇ' âphalat kari|hay'|ādibhiḥ.
14.415 kumāraṃ saha jāyābhyām ādāya Bhṛgu|pattanam
prāpa śrī|Kusumaketuḥ ketu|toraṇa|mālitam.
dīn'|â|nātha|vahad|dānaṃ nidānaṃ harṣa|sampadām
kumār'|āgamane rājā vardhāpanam acīkarat.
evaṃ ca medurā|mand'|ānanda|tundilit'|ātmanām
teṣāṃ dināny anekāni vyatijagmur nimeṣavat.
tataś ca, bhoḥ Siṃha|rāja, gurubhiḥ Śūra|nirjaraḥ
kumārasya caraṇa|śrī|varaṇāya nyadiśyata.
so 'tha devas tatra gatvā praty|uṣaḥ|pāṭhana|kṣaṇe
antarikṣe 'n|īkṣya|mūrtiḥ papāṭha prasphuṭ'|âkṣaram:
14.420 «dhig, dhig, viṣaya|manaso 'samprāpta|viṣayāḥ kṣaṇāt
viṣay'|â|vinivṛttatvād dur|gatiṃ yānti jantavaḥ.
tvayā kāma|kṛte, saumya, kiṃ na vyasanam āpyata
viyoge Surasundaryās? tat kāmebhyo namaskuru!
kām'|ārtena Daśāsyena lebhe 'tr' âmutra kiṃ nanu?
Subhūma|Brahmadattau ca kām'|āsaktau kim āpatuḥ?

travelers, to bring back Kúsuma·shékhara, the crest of his family, the sky filled with his brightness.

By means of unbroken advances he arrived at the border of that city. A minister announced his arrival to King Rama·chandra. Then His Majesty Rama·chandra, together with His Highness Kúsuma·shékhara, welcomed him with great abundance. There was a joyful union with all.

His Majesty Kúsuma·ketu, a wishing-tree honored by King Rama·chandra with a thousand villages, ripened with elephants, horses and suchlike.

Then His Majesty Kúsuma·ketu took the Prince, together 14.415
with his two wives, and arrived at the city of Bhrigu·kaccha, which had been festooned with brilliant archways. The King held a festival for the Prince's return; spreading gifts among the poor and those without protection, it was the essence of the wealth of joy.

Thus they passed many days like gods, their souls fattened with the clotted cream of their joy.

And then, King Simha, sire, the teacher ordered the god Shura to go and marry the Prince to the fortune of the ascetic life. So the god went there at the time of the recitation of the morning blessing, and in the sky, his form invisible, recited, with distinct pronunciation:

"Alas, alas, beings, their minds on sensual pleasures, in- 14.420
tent on what they have not got, in a moment, though their failure to abandon sensual pleasure, attain a bad rebirth. And when you had enjoyed sexual pleasure, good sir, didn't you meet with ruin in your separation from Sura·súndari? So pay your farewells to sexual pleasures! Sick with sexual passion, what didn't ten-faced Rávana meet with in this world

pumāṃso 'nye ca bahavaḥ
kāma|kimpāka|bhoginaḥ
su|dur|gāṃ dur|gatiṃ prāpur.
dhik, kāmān muñca muñca tat!»

ity|ādikaṃ paṭhitv" âsau suro 'yāsīd yath"|āgatam.
dvitīye 'hni punas tasya vairāgyāy' âpaṭhat|tarām.
14.425 punas tṛtīye 'hny apāṭhīt|tamāṃ vairāgya|kārmaṇam.
kumāro 'cintayad, «aye, vairāgyaṃ kaḥ paṭhaty ayam?»
tataḥ pṛṣṭāḥ kumāreṇa pārśva|sthāḥ, «kaḥ paṭhaty ayam?»
ta ūcur, «n' ēkṣyate kaś cit, kevalaṃ śrūyate dhvaniḥ.»
dadhyau kumāro, «yady eṣa punaḥ prātaḥ sameṣyati,
tadā prakṣyāmy asmy âvaśyaṃ.» so 'tha turya|dine 'paṭhat.
«kiṃ n' âvadhānaṃ mad|vākye, kumāra|vara, dīyate?»
iti yāvat paṭhaty eṣa, tāvat taṃ rāṭ|suto 'bhyadhāt:
«kas tvaṃ, bhoḥ? kiñ ca vairāgyaṃ
paṭhasy evaṃ dine dine?»
so 'vak, «kumāra, vismāri|
śīlatā te 'bhavat kutaḥ?
yataḥ:
14.430 Kauśāmbyāṃ śrī|Sudharm'|âgre pravavrāja Sulakṣaṇaḥ
nav'|ânye 'pi, daś' âpy āpur divi Śakra|samānatām.
śrī|Nemi|pṛcchayā sūra|mānanaṃ pretya bodhaye,
tad etat smara, kumāra, tvam eva hi Sulakṣaṇaḥ,
sthitvā divya|vimāneṣu tābhir adbhuta|mīrubhiḥ

and the next? And, addicted to sexual pleasure, what did Subhúma and Brahma·datta meet with? Many other men, too, enjoying the bitter fruit of sexual pleasure, have come to a bad rebirth, very difficult to endure, alas. So abandon, abandon sexual pleasure!"

Having recited that and other such, the god returned as he had come. On the next day, once more the god recited emphatically in order to arouse asceticism in him.

Again on the third day he recited most emphatically 14.425
about ascetic activity. The Prince thought, "Now, who is this reciting about asceticism?"

The Prince asked those standing by him, "Who is this who is reciting?" They said, "We can't see anyone. We can only hear the voice."

The Prince thought, "If he comes again in the morning, I'll certainly inquire myself." Then he came and recited once again on the fourth day.

As soon as he had recited, "Why aren't you paying attention to what I say, excellent Prince?," the Prince said to him:

"Who are you, sir? And why are you reciting asceticism like this, day after day?" He said, "Why has your character become forgetful, Prince?

Since:

In Kaushámbi, in the presence of Lord Sudhárman, Su- 14.430
lákshana and nine others, too, took initiation. And the ten attained the rank of kings of the gods in heaven. Asked by Lord Nemi, the teacher promised to come to enlighten you. So remember this, Prince: you are indeed that very Sulákshana, who lived in the celestial vehicles, with those

tayā ca sāmānika'|rddhyā parīvāreṇa tena ca.
kiṃ dārva|śmēṣṭakā|gehe yoṣābhir mala|khānibhiḥ
alpīyasyā śriy" ânena parivāreṇa muhyasi?»
iti śrutvā tato devād īh"|âpohād ito 'labhat
nyāsīkṛtam iva jāti|smaraṇaṃ Puṣpaśekharaḥ.
14.435 tataḥ kumāras tam ūce, «sv|āgataṃ, sv|āgataṃ tava,
mahā|bhāga! tathā dhehi, pravrajyā syād yathā mama!»
ath' ōce Śūra|devena, «bhos, tvāṃ bodhayituṃ dhruvam
śrī|Samarasena|sūri|sūraḥ prātar udaiṣyati.
gamyaṃ tvayā tasya pārśve, vidhātavyaṃ tad|īritam.»
ity āśrutaṃ kumāreṇa, devaḥ sva|sthānam aiyata.
tato yāvat kṛta|prābhātik'|āvaśyaka|maṅgalaḥ
mātā|pitror vandanāya prasthitaḥ Puṣpaśekharaḥ.
udyāna|pālako 'bhyetya tāvat priya|nivedakaḥ
praṇipatya kumār'|âṃhrī prāñjal" îti vyajijñapat.
14.440 «deva, śrī|su|manaḥ|śreṇi|sevye śrī|tilak'|âdbhute
spurat|puṃnāga|pūg'|āḍhye sarvato 'śoka|maṇḍite;
nānā|śākh"|āgata|vipra|sevite 'dbhuta|jātike
uccair|vaṃśe mah"|ôdyāne tvat|praticchandake kila;
sādhu|śākhā|virociṣṇur nān"|âtiśaya|puṣpitaḥ
sur'|âsura|nar'|āsevya|pāda|mūla|mahī|talaḥ;
catur|jñānī devatānāṃ līlā|vāsa|sah'|ôdaraḥ
śrī|Samarasena|sūriḥ kalpa|druḥ samavāsarat.»
(- - - - - - - - - - - - - - - - -)

wonderful goddesses, and with that wealth appropriate to your rank, and with that entourage. So why, in a house like a wooden coffin, are you beguiled by women who are mines of filth, by very scanty wealth, by this entourage?"

Having heard this, through the god's stating of what was for and against, Kúsuma·shékhara obtained memory of his former lives, like a hidden treasure.

Then the Prince said, "Welcome, welcome to you, illus- 14.435
trious one! Tell me when my initiation will take place!"

Then the god Shura said, "Good sir, the most reverend doctor Sámara·sena will certainly come in the morning to enlighten you. You must go to his presence and undertake what he declares." The Prince agreed to this, and the god returned to his own place.

Then, just as the daily blessing had been recited and Kúsuma·shékhara had paid his respects to his parents and set out, the park keeper came, a messenger of pleasing news. He fell at the Prince's feet, folded his hands in salutation and announced:

"Your Highness, in the great park, which is attended by 14.440
rows of well-disposed nobles in the form of rows of lovely flowers; which is wonderful with the ornaments of wealth in the form of lovely *tílaka* trees; which is opulent with masses of distinguished men bowing in the form of masses of waving *pun·naga* plants; which is everywhere adorned with freedom from sorrow in the form of *ashóka* trees; which is thronged by Brahmins fraught with various traditions of learning in the form of acacia trees fraught with many branches; which has a wonderful disposition in the form of wonderful jasmine trees; which has a lofty lineage

(- - - - - - - - - - - - - - - - -)

14.445 pāritoṣika|vṛṣṭyā samprīṇya priya|nivedakam
pramoda|bāṣpa|mudiraḥ sadyaḥ Kusumaśekharaḥ
gatvā praṇamya pitarau harṣa|romāñca|cañcuraḥ
guru|rāj'|āgam'|ôdanta|bhaṇityā srāg avīvṛdhat.
tataḥ śrī|Kusumaketus tathā Kusumaśekharaḥ
sāmant'|âmātya|paur'|ādyaiḥ sārdham, antaḥpureṇa ca,
tam sad|guruṃ namaskartuṃ jagām' ôdyānam utsukaḥ
triḥ pradakṣiṇa|n'|âpūrvaṃ namasyāmāsa c' ādarāt.

tau yathā|sthānam āsīnau jñāna|dharā|dharaḥ prabhuḥ
sad|deśanā|sudhā|vṛṣṭyā prīṇayāmāsa sarvataḥ:

tathā hi:

14.450 «rāga|dveṣa|kaṣāya|moha|mukharair
bhūtaiḥ sad" âdhiṣṭhite
saṃsār'|âvasathe catur|gati|catur|
bhūme nṛṇāṃ nyūṣuṣām
nān"|ôpadrava|vṛndam eva satataṃ
sā tasya vārtt" ân|ṛtā
tad bhūtai rahite nivastum ucitaṃ

in the form of tall bamboo canes; which is indeed the reflected image of yourself, the reverend doctor Sámara·sena, a wishing-tree, brilliant with the branches of his monks, blossoming with manifold excellences, the ground pressed by the soles of his feet attended by gods, demigods and human beings, possessed of fourfold knowledge, akin to the abode of the grace of the gods, is holding a preaching assembly."

Having gratified the messenger of pleasing news with 14.445
the shower of a gratuity, Kúsuma·shékhara, a rain cloud for tears of joy, immediately went and bowed to his parents. Trembling and thrilled with joy, he told them the news of the arrival of the king of teachers and instantly congratulated them. Then His Majesty Kúsuma·ketu and Kúsuma·shékhara likewise, together with the barons, ministers, citizens, et cetera, and the royal ladies, went to the park, eager to pay respects to the true teacher. Having first circumambulated him three times, they respectfully bowed to the teacher.

When the two had sat in appropriate places, the lord, a cloud for the rain of knowledge, filled them entirely with the shower of the nectar of his teaching of truth:

Like so:

"The multitude of various disasters that men encounter as 14.450
they are destroyed in the abode of existence, the four-square foundation of which is the four birth destinations and which is inhabited by beings who embody greed, hatred, passion and delusion, is everlasting. That way of life in it is unrighteous. So you should dwell in the lovely palace of final liberation, devoid of spooks, you awakening ones. The means of

śrī|siddhi|saudhe, budhāḥ.
jñāna|darśana|cāritra|pavitrāḥ
saṃnivastum iha, hanta, labhante
tad, budhās, tritayam etad avaśyaṃ
vaśyam ātanuta yāta ca siddhim!»

tad|deśanā|sudhā|svāda|parīṇāmasya mātrayā
ke 'py āpus tiryaṅ|nṛ|surā mithyātva|viṣa|saṃhṛtim.
apare tu nṛ|tiryañco deśa|santoṣam apy alam
sarva|santoṣa|sampattim apy anye nara|puṅgavāḥ.

atha sarvā sabh" ôttasthau, tasthau Kusumaśekharaḥ.
tato gurubhir ūce 'sau, «saumy', āgāma bhavat|kṛte.
14.455 yac ciraṃ naḥ saṃstuto 'si, kiṃ na smarasi, dhī|nidhe,
Kauśāmby|ādi Śūra|deva|prāntaṃ vṛttāntam ātmanaḥ?

yaḥ prābhātika|vairāgya|pāṭhī, Śūr'|âmaraḥ sa ca
tathā Jayaśāsana'|rṣi|devo Malaya|maṇḍale
Kuśāvartta|pure śrīmaj|Jayaśekhara|bhū|bhujaḥ
devyā tu Vanamañjaryāḥ putraḥ Śūra|prabodhitaḥ
Nandan'|ācārya|pād'|ânte dīkṣitas taiḥ pade nije.
sthāpitaś ca śrī|Samarasenaḥ, so 'haṃ nṛp'|âṅgajaḥ!

yo Rāmadeva'|rṣi|jīvaḥ Surāṣṭrā|viṣaye pure
Girinagare 'bhūt putro Vatsarāja|Jayaśriyoḥ,
14.460 kumāro Vimalasenas tena devena bodhitaḥ
mayā parivrājitaś ca, rāja'|rṣiḥ s' âiṣa vīkṣyatām!

purification—knowledge, insight and asceticism—are taking their abode here, see! So, awakening ones, extend daily obedience to this trio and go to final liberation!"

Some of the animals, humans and gods, by merely digesting the nectar of his teaching, attained the antidote for the poison of error. But other human beings and animals attained a good satisfaction from the teaching. Others, too, bulls among men, attained the prosperity resulting from complete satisfaction.

Then the entire assembly arose, but Kúsuma·shékhara remained. Then the teacher said to him, "Good sir, I came on your doing. Since for a long time you were my familiar 14.455
friend. Do you not remember, you ocean of intelligence, what happened to you in Kaushámbi and so on, finishing with the god Shura?

And that reciter of asceticism in the morning blessing is that god Shura. Likewise the regal ascetic Jaya·shásana, the son of His Majesty Jaya·shékhara, who ruled in the city of Kushávati in the Málaya country, and his queen, Bhúvana·mánjari, was enlightened by Shura, initiated at the feet of the teacher Nándana and appointed by him to his own position. I, reverend Sámara·sena, am he; I am that Prince!

And the soul of the monk Rama·deva became the son of Vatsa·raja and Jaya·shri in the city of Giri·nágara in the
Suráshtra region. The Prince, Vímala·sena, was enlightened 14.460
by that god and initiated by me. See, there he is, the royal monk!

Purandhara'|ṛṣi|devo 'pi Varāṭe Siṃhapattane
Nabhovāhana|Kamalāvatyoḥ sūnuḥ Surandharaḥ.
bodhitas tena devena, dīkṣitaś ca mayā tv asau.
Sulakṣaṇa'|ṛṣi|jīvas tu tvam eva, kṛtinām vara.

tatas tvad|bodha|vidhaye vayam atra samāgatāḥ.
prāñjaliḥ śrī|kumāro 'vak, «prabhūṇāṃ sv|āgataṃ khalu.
pūjyair anugṛhīto 'smi, tat kurve sa|phalaṃ januḥ.
āpṛcchya mātā|pitarau preyasyau ca drutaṃ drutam.»

14.465 Surasundarī|Ramaṇamatyau tat|pura ūcatuḥ:
«pṛcchye kim, ārya|putr', āvāṃ satyaḥ paty|anugāḥ khalu?»
ākhyat kumāraḥ, «sādh' ûktaṃ
yuvābhyāṃ sva|kul'|ôcitam.
rājye hi sarve sakhāyaḥ,
pravajyāyāṃ tu ke cana?»

atha karṇe praviśy' ōce kumāraṃ Surasundarī:
«yen' âpahārit" âsmy, eṣa maha"|ṛṣiḥ śrī|Surandharaḥ.»
kumāreṇ' âtha vanditvā smitvā c' āucyata muny asau:
«bhagavan, Surasundaryā yady artho, 'muṃ gṛhāṇa tat.»
munir ūce, «mahā|bhāga, sarv'|â|vidyā|bhidā|paṭuḥ
dīkṣā mayā kṛtā, kāntā mukti|kānt"|ôtsava|pradā.»

And the royal monk Puran·dara became Suran·dhara, the son of Nabho·váhana and Kamalávati in Simha·pura, in the Varáta country. And he was enlightened by that god but initiated by me. Now the soul of Sulákshana is you, really, most eminent among the good.

And I have come here to effect the accomplishment of your enlightenment." The Prince folded his hands in salutation and said, "Welcome to your lordship, indeed. I have been honored by your reverence, so I will render my birth fruitful immediately after I have asked permission from my parents and my two wives."

Before he could do that, Sura·súndari and Rámana·mati 14.465
said, "Why should we be asked, noble husband? True wives follow their husbands, for sure."

The Prince said, "This is excellently spoken by you and worthy of our family. In the possession of a kingdom, of course, all are companions, but in ascetic wanderings, who at all?"

Then Sura·súndari approached his ear and said to the Prince, "There is the one who carried me away, the great monk reverend Suran·dhara."

Then the Prince bowed and smiled and said to the monk, "Reverend sir, if your need is for Sura·súndari, then take it."

The monk said, "Illustrious one, I have taken initiation, intense in separation from all ignorance, the wife who will effect the festival for the wife who is final liberation."

14.470 kumāraḥ prāha, «dhanyo 'si. jīvitaṃ te phale|grahi.
kin tv aśv'|âpahṛteḥ paścān, maha"|rṣe, kiṃ kim anvabhūḥ?
kathaṃ mukti|purī|vrajyāṃ pravrajyāṃ pratyapadyathāḥ?
yadi kathyaṃ, tad idaṃ me prasadya pratipādaya.»

anujñāto 'tha guruṇā sva|vṛttāntam aśeṣataḥ
sa muniḥ śrī|kumārasya vaktum evaṃ pracakrame:

«tasminn utpatite vegād yāti c' âśve vihāyasā
may" êti cintayāñcakre, ‹n' âśva|mātram ayaṃ dhruvam.
tad ayaṃ haya|rūpeṇa ko 'py aho mama vairikaḥ
vairike dhīra|vīraiś ca prahartavyam a|śaṅkitam.›

14.475 tataś churyā turaṅgo 'sau kukṣi|deśe mayā hataḥ.
chinna|vidyaḥ kheṭa iva sa papāta mahī|tale.
tasmād a|patitād eva phālen' ôttīrṇa|vāhanam
ūrīkṛtya diśaṃ c' âikāṃ pratasthe sthemavāṃs tataḥ.

ath' âdrākṣaṃ vana|ṣaṇḍam ekaṃ pakṣi|kul'|ākulam,
sambhāvyamāna|salil'|āśayam āśaya|sausthya|kṛt.
tasmin viśann eva Jina|bhavanaṃ bhuvan'|âdbhutam
prekṣāmāsa, tad|āsannaṃ saraś ca bhuvan'|âdbhutam.
aṅg'|âvaholikāṃ tatr' ādhāy' ādāy' âmbujāni ca
yug'|ādi|Jina|mānañ ca prāñcad romāñca|kañcukaḥ

14.480 navaiḥ stavaiḥ prabhuṃ stutvā śuddha|rāgaiḥ pragāya ca
sthito bahir vedikāyāṃ yāvat paśyāmi sarvataḥ,
tāvad divyā nāyik" âikā niryayau sarasas tataḥ.
tad|anv anyā api ghanā niṣpuṇy'|ālabhya|darśanāḥ.

The Prince said, "You are blessed. Your life is successful. 14.470 But, great sage, what things did you experience after the horse carried you away? How did you meet with initiation, the wandering city of final liberation? If you are able to relate this, then please explain it to me."

Then, granted permission by the teacher, the monk proceeded to relate his whole story to His Highness the Prince.

"As that horse flew up and swiftly went through the sky, I thought, 'This is certainly no mere horse. Therefore it is some enemy of mine in the form of a horse, and true men should fearlessly slay their enemy.'

So I struck the horse with a dagger in the region of the 14.475 belly. Like a master of magic deprived of his magic power, he fell to the surface of the earth. After that, for he really hadn't fallen, the horse sprang up with a jump, chose a direction and set off straight ahead, full of strength.

Then I saw a forest of trees filled with families of birds, in which a water reservoir might be found, providing a resting place and comfort. On entering it I saw a Jain temple, a wondrous building, and nearby it a lake, wondrous with its water. I gave my body a shower in it and gathered lotuses. I faced the image of Ríshabha, the first Jina of the time cycle, worshipping him. I praised the lord with renewed hymns 14.480 and sang to him with pure melodies. As I stood outside on the balcony, looking all around, a divine maiden came out of the lake. Thereupon she was followed by many others, their appearance partaking of perfection.

tato dadhye may", ‹âśven' âpahāro 'pi mam' êṣṭa|kṛt,
yad īdṛg|divya|vanitā|darśanaṃ samapādi me.›
snātvā tataḥ sarasi tā, gṛhītvā kamalāni ca
samājagmus tatra caitye may" âbhyuttasthire ca tāḥ.
kara|saṃjñāya niveśya mām imā vīkṣya c' ârcitam
prabhuṃ mithaḥ procur, ‹ārcīd eṣa tat sama|dhārmikaḥ.›
14.485 tac ca śrutvā mayā dadhye, ‹prīṇayiṣyanti mām imāḥ.›
tato 'panīya mat|pūjām ānarcus tā jagat|prabhuṃ.
stutvā gītvā ca Tīrth'|ēśaṃ prasthitās tās tato mayā
praṇāma|pūrvaṃ bhaṇitāḥ, ‹kā yūyaṃ? kim ih' āgatāḥ?›
tābhir ūce, ‹yakṣa|kanyā Jin'|ârc'|ârtham ih' āgatāḥ.›
mayā pṛṣṭaṃ punaḥ, ‹ken' âkāryat' âitaj Jin'|āspadam?›
‹śrī|vidyā|dhara|rājen',› êty ukte tābhir may" āucyata:
‹kim ity asyāṃ mah"|âṭavyāṃ ten' êdam niramāpyata?›
ūcus tāḥ, ‹śābarī|vidy" âṭavyāṃ bhagavataḥ puraḥ
dīyate, gṛhyate c' âpi ten' âtr' êdaṃ nyadhāpy atha.›
14.490 may" ôktam, ‹āyāta yūyāṃ kim ity atr'?› êti tā jaguḥ,
‹sakhe, Varendro yakṣ'|êndrī|bhūtaḥ samprati vartate.
sa ca prāg|bhakti|rāgeṇa prabhuṃ jātv arcati svayam
kadā cit preṣayaty asmān, ity emaḥ svāmi|śāsanāt.›
ūce mayā, ‹bhagavatyo, na moghaṃ deva|darśanam,
tad brūt', ârir yo 'śva|rūpo mām iti āpadam ānayat?›

Then I thought, 'Even being carried away by the horse has fulfilled my desire, since it has caused me to meet with the sight of divine women of such appearance.'

Then, after bathing in the lake and gathering lotuses, they went together to the temple, and I rose in respect. They repaid me with a wave of the hand, and when they saw that the lord had been worshipped they said to each other, 'He has worshipped, so he shares our religion.'

On hearing that, I thought, 'They will succor me.' Then 14.485
they removed my offering and worshipped the lord of the universe. They hymned and sang to the Lord of the Ford, and then I approached them. I bowed and then asked them, 'Who are you and why have you come here?'

They said, 'We are maiden demigoddesses who have come here to worship the Jina.' I asked once more, 'Who built this abode for the Jina?'

On their saying, 'The king of the masters of magic,' I asked, 'Why did he make it come to rest in this great forest?'

They said, 'Knowledge was given to the forest tribesmen in the forest in the presence of the lord, and the king of the masters of magic took it and then placed it here.'

I said, 'Why have you come here?' They said, 'My friend, 14.490
Varéndra has become king of the demigods, and is on his way right now. And he ever worships the lord with the passion of his former devotion. And whenever he summons us we come, on the King's instructions.'

I said, 'Blessed ladies, seeing gods is never fruitless, so tell me: who was that enemy in the form of a horse who brought me to disaster?'

‹āstām eṣa te vair" îti, deva, eṣa suhṛt tava.
na c' âiṣ" āpat, kin tu sampan. mā bhaiṣīḥ, puṇyavān asi!›

ity uktvā tās tiro 'bhūvan kṣaṇād ev' êndra|jālavat,
ahaṃ tu vismitas tasmāc caityāt prāsthiṣi satvaram.
14.495 divya|rūpaṃ bhilla|veṣam adhijyīkṛta|kārmukam
sāramey'|ânvitam atha naram adrākṣam agrataḥ.
ten' âpi sahas" âsmy ūce, ‹rāja|kula, namo 'stu te.›
nirbhayena may" âpy ūce, ‹kas tvaṃ, bhoḥ? kuta āgamaḥ?›

‹grāma|svāmi|suto grāmād āsannād,› iti so 'vadat.
‹māṃ nay' âtra,› may" ôktaḥ, ‹samāgacch',› êti so 'bravīt.

tena sārdhaṃ yāmi yāvat, tāvat ku|grāma|sannidhau
śabarāḥ puṅkhita|śarā Yamasy' âpi bhayaṅ|karāḥ
‹māraya māray'› êty uccair giraḥ petur mam' ôpari.
may" âikṣi prāṅ|narasy' āsyaṃ kim etad ati|bhīṣaṇam.
14.500 so 'pi vidyud|ghoṣa|ghoram aṭṭa|hāsam amuñcata.
śunaś ca preṣayāmāsa māṃ prati prati|panthivat.

vyāghravad|datta|phālās te pṛṣṭhataḥ pārśvato 'grataḥ
āgaty' ākulayāmāsuḥ pret'|ēśasy' êva kiṅ|karāḥ.
abhyāyāntaṃ śunaṃ yāvat kṛpāṇyā praharāmy aham,
gāṇḍīvaiḥ śabarās tāvad ājaghnur mūrdhni māṃ samam.
vileguḥ sarvataḥ śvānās te ca me 'th' âsmy acintayam:
‹tābhir uktaṃ, «puṇyavāṃs tvaṃ,» h" âjāyata kim anyathā?›

'That enemy of yours, Your Highness, was actually your friend. And this is not disaster but, rather, success. You are blessed!'

After saying that, they vanished in an instant, really, as if by magic. Struck with amazement, I quickly hurried from the temple. In front I saw a man of handsome appearance, 14.495
wearing the dress of a forest tribesman, holding an arrow with a taught bowstring, and accompanied by a dog. He said to me in a powerful voice, 'Greetings to you, your royal highness.' I fearlessly replied, 'Who are you, and where have you come from?'

He said, 'A village headman's son; from a nearby village.' I said to him, 'Take me there,' and he said, 'Come along.'

I went with him until, near to a wretched village, forest tribesmen with feathered arrows, the cause of fear even to Death, shouting loudly, 'Kill, kill!,' advanced upon me. I saw the face of the first man became dreadful and made me think, 'What is this?' And he let out a laugh as frightening 14.500
as the sound of lightning, and his dog ran toward me like a returning traveler.

They leaped like tigers from the rear, sides and front, and came and crowded around, servants of the lord of the departed. As the dog advanced and I attacked it with my dagger, the forest tribesmen together struck me on the head with their bows. Their dogs fastened on me everywhere. Then I thought, 'The demigoddesses said that I was blessed; alas, why has it turned out otherwise!'

atr' ântare loca|cañcad uttam'|âṅga|tapaḥ|kṛśaḥ
īryā|patha|sthir'|âkṣaś ca mal'|āvila|kalevaraḥ
14.505 nigṛhīt'|êndriya|grāmo nikāmaṃ kāma|jitvaraḥ
tatr' āgaman munir ekaḥ praśamo mūrtimān iva.
tena te śabarāḥ proktā, ‹bhoḥ, kim ity eṣa māryate?›
tair uktam, ‹eṣa bhakṣyaṃ no. bhakṣayiṣyāma eva tat.›
muniḥ punar uvāc' âitān, ‹narako jīva|hiṃsayā.›
te ūcus, ‹tat kim ity evaṃ dehino mārayaty asau?›
ṛṣiḥ punar babhāṣ' âitān, ‹n' âiṣa jīvān haniṣyati.›
muniṃ te vyāharanti sma, ‹tat kiṃ pravrajiṣyati?›
maha"|rṣiṇ" âtha jagāde, ‹'sau dhruvaṃ pravrajiṣyati.›
tair uktaṃ, ‹tad gṛhitv" âmuṃ vraj'. asmābhir amocy asau.›
14.510 tato 'smi muninā prokta, ‹āgacch', āgaccha, bhadra bhoḥ!›
tena sārdhaṃ prasthito 'haṃ gatavāṃs tvarita|kramam.
śrāntaṃ vijñāya māṃ sādhur nirviṣṭaḥ śuddha|bhū|tale.
tato may" ōce, ‹bhagavan, kas tvaṃ?› so 'vag, ‹ahaṃ muniḥ.›
punar ūce may", ‹âṭavyām atra sādhuḥ kathaṃ nanu?
ke v" âmī puruṣā raudrā? māṃ gṛhṇanti kim ity amī?›
munir jagād', ‹âmī mlecchā
bhoktuṃ tvāṃ gṛhṇate tv amī.›
may" ōce, ‹yady amī mlecchāḥ
kim iti tvāṃ na gṛhṇate?

At that moment, his head plucked bald, his face emaciated through his asceticism, his eyes fixed on his path as he trod with care, his body polluted with filth, his group 14.505
of senses restrained, his desire absolutely conquered, a Jain monk arrived at the place, like tranquility personified.

He asked the forest tribesmen, 'Good sirs, why are you killing him?' They said, 'He is food for us. We are actually going to eat it.'

The monk replied, 'A being goes to hell because of violence to beings.' They said, 'Why, then, is he killing embodied beings like this?'

The monk said to them once more, 'This man will not kill beings.' They replied to the monk, 'Is he going to take initiation, then?'

Then the great monk said, 'He is certainly going to take initiation.' They said, 'Then take him and go. We have set him free.'

Then the monk said to me, 'Come, come, good sir!,' and 14.510
I set off with him, leaving at a fast pace.

Seeing that I was tired, the monk halted on clean ground. Then I said, 'Reverend sir, who are you?' He said, 'I am a monk.'

I asked once more, 'Now, how does a monk come to be in this forest, and who are these violent men? Why did they seize me?'

The monk said, 'They are barbarians and they seized you in order to eat you.' I said, 'If they are barbarians, why didn't they seize you? So speak the truth, my lord. I have entire confidence in you. Why was I carried away? Who are you?
Who are these forest tribesmen? Don't deceive me like this 14.515

tat satyam ākhyāhi, vibho, sarvath" âhaṃ tvad|āśrayaḥ.
kim|artham apajahre 'haṃ? kas tvaṃ? ke śabarā amī?
14.515 kṛtrimair vacanair evaṃ mā pratāraya māṃ, prabho!›
tato munir muni|rūpaṃ saṃhṛty' âbhūt sur'|ôttamaḥ.

ūce ca, ‹puri Kauśāmbyāṃ Sudharma|svāmi|sannidhau
vayaṃ daśa parivrajya Saudharme 'bhūma nirjarāḥ.
śrī|Nemi|vacanāc Chūra|nirjaraḥ pretya bodhaye
sarvair amānyata, sakhe, c' âhaṃ Śūra|nirjaraḥ.
prācya|janmani Kauśāmbyāṃ
yo 'bhūc chreṣṭhī Purandaraḥ,
svargāt sa tvam ayaṃ jātas!
tvad|bhodāy' âham āgamam.

para|strī|kāmukas tvaṃ ca na vāṅ|mātreṇa budhyase.
ity aśva|rūpeṇa mayā vyomn" ānīto mah"|âṭavīm.
14.520 mayā mleccha|śvāna|rūpair bahudh" âsi kadarthitaḥ.
āśvāsitaś ca may" âiva kṛtvā rūpaṃ mahā|muneḥ.›
tataḥ, kumāra, jagāde sa mayā vibudh'|ēśvaraḥ:
‹evam evaṃ vyatikare, mah"|ātman, pratyayo 'stu kaḥ?›

deven' ôktaṃ, ‹smarā|bhogaṃ vidhāya sudhiyāṃ, nidhe,›
īh"|ādi sṛjato jāti|smṛtiḥ kānt" âtha me 'milat.
tad|ukti|pratyayāj jāto dev'|ôktau pratyayo dṛḍhaḥ.
tato may" ôktam, ‹atr' âiva dīkṣe, n' âiva vilambyate.›

suro 'vag, ‹dīkṣitasy' êyaṃ dus|tarā te mah"|âṭavī
svayaṃ dīkṣ" âpy a|yuktā tat tvāṃ naye pitṛ|sannidhau.
14.525 tatra prāg|bhava|mitrasya śrī|Jayaśāsan'|ātmanaḥ
sūreḥ Samarasenasya dīkṣethāḥ, saumya, sannidhau.›

with fictitious stories, my lord.' Then the monk removed his appearance as a monk and became a most eminent god.

And he said, 'In the city of Kaushámbi we ten were initiated in the presence of the reverend Lord Sudhárman and became ageless gods in the Good Works heaven. On the command of Lord Nemi, the god Shura came to enlighten and was esteemed by all, my friend. And I am that god Shura. He who was the merchant Puran·dara in his former life in Kaushámbi, after heaven, he was born as you! I have come to enlighten you.

Since, filled with lust for another's wife, you were not able to be enlightened by mere words, in the form of a horse I brought you through the sky to the great forest.
I tormented you in the multiple forms of barbarians and 14.520
dogs, and I reassured you, having taken on the form of a great ascetic.' Then, Prince, I said to the lord of the learned, 'What confidence can there be in reciprocal incident, like so and so?'

The god said, 'Deposit the fortune of memory in your intelligence, you treasury!' As I employed consideration of what was for and against, memory of my former lives, my beloved, came to meet me. Through conviction in what he had said, my conviction in the god's statement became firm. Then I said, 'This being the case, there should be no delay at all in my initiation.'

The god said, 'Once you are initiated, this great forest will be difficult for you to traverse, and self-initiation is inapplicable, so I will take you to the presence of your parents.
There, in the presence of the reverend doctor Sámara·sena, 14.525

ity uktvā māṃ sa utpāṭya Nabhovāhana|bhū|bhujaḥ
srāk|path'|ânveṣiṇo 'raṇye 'śv'|ārūḍhaṃ purato 'mucat.

śrī|Samarasena|sūrer nivedya mama vāsanām
Śūra|devo divam upaid guruḥ Siṃhapuraṃ punaḥ.

a|puṣpa|phalavat prāpte mayi pramudito nṛpaḥ
puram āyan pura|narair gur'|ûdantena vardhitaḥ.

tato vijñāpayāñcakre mayā vasumatī|patiḥ:
‹deva, deva|tarūn etān gurūn vandāmahe puraḥ.›

14.530 atha pṛthv"|īśvaro 'haṃ ca tath" âiva sa|paricchadau
prāṇemiva prabhuṃ gatvā sabhāyāṃ ca niṣediva.

tataḥ kumāra saṃsār'|âraṇya|nistīrṇa|dīpikām
deśanāṃ sūtrayāmāsa gurur moha|giri|svaruḥ.

tathā me prāg|bhav'|ôdanta|vasantena prabhur vyadhāt
jāti|smṛti|latāṃ śraddh"|ôtpuṣpāṃ dīkṣā|phal'|ônmukhīm.

tataḥ saṃbodhya pitarau priyāṃ ca Priyadarśanām
priyayā priya|mitraiś ca sah' âdīkṣe, nṛp'|âṅgaja.»

the soul of your friend in your former life, His Highness Jaya·shásana, you will receive initiation, good sir.'

After saying that, he took me up in the air and set me down in a wood, mounted on a horse, in front of King Nabho·váhana, who advanced quickly along the path.

Having informed the reverend doctor Sámara·sena of my wish, the god Shura went to heaven, but Sámara·sena went to Simha·pura.

Having gained me, like a fruit without a flower, the King was filled with joy, and on entering the city he was congratulated by the citizens with the news of the teacher. Then I informed the ruler of the earth of my intention. 'Your Majesty, we will go pay our respects before the teacher, the divine tree.'

Then the King, and I likewise, both accompanied by 14.530
our entourage, went and paid our respects and sat in the assembly.

Then, Prince, the teacher, a thunderbolt for the mountain of delusion, expounded the teaching that is a light pervading the wilderness of existence. Thus, by means of the spring season of the relation of my former lives, the lord bestowed on me the creeper of memory of my former lives, flowering with faith and expectant with the fruit of initiation.

Then, my parents and my wife Priya·dárshana having been awakened, I was initiated together with my wife and dear friends."

iti śrutvā prabhuṃ natvā śrīmān Kusumaśekharaḥ
gṛhe gatv" āha pitarau, «śrutaṃ bhagavato vacaḥ.
14.535 catur|gatika|saṃsārād duḥkh'|āgārān nirantaram
nirviṇṇo 'haṃ, tāta, mātar, anujānīta māṃ tataḥ.
yen' âsmi guru|sārth'|ēśa|prokta|dīkṣ"|âdhvan" âdhunā
prasthāya nirvṛti|padaṃ yāmi nitya|sukh'|āspadam.»
pit" ākhyat, «te 'dhunā rājyaṃ, vatsa, dīkṣ" ôcit" āvayoḥ.
krama|vyatikramaḥ ko 'yaṃ bhavatā śikṣito 'nagha?
bhavān dhor mama niryāto datta hast'|âvalambanam
mā sma kṣipata tatr' âiv'.» êty uktvā putro 'patat padoḥ.
māt" âbravīc, «chṛṇu, vatsa, tvad|viyog'|ânil'|ōrmibhiḥ
mama prāṇā amī vegād uḍḍāyyante palālavat.»
14.540 putro 'vocad, «amba, tarhi dīkṣyate samam eva hi
yena n' âtra viyogaḥ syān na c' âmutra śiv'|āspade.»
tato 'vādīt Puṣpaketur, «nirbandhaś cet tav' ēdṛśaḥ,
tadā Kusumacūlo 'yaṃ, vatsa, rājye 'bhiṣicyate.
tvayā tu sarve 'pi, vatsa, dīkṣāmahe vayam.»
putro 'brūta, «sādhu, tāta, kṣaṇaṃ n' âtra vilambyate.»
tataḥ sāmanta|saciva|pary|āloca|puraḥsaram
rājā śrī|Kusumacūlaḥ svayaṃ rājye 'bhyaṣicyata.

Having listened to this, His Highness Kúsuma·shékhara, after bowing to the lord, went home and told his parents, "I have heard the preaching of the reverend doctor. I am 14.535
disgusted with existence with its four birth destinations, the perpetual abode of sorrow, so grant me permission, father and mother, so that, having now set out for the place of emancipation along the road of initiation proclaimed by the caravan-leader that is the teacher, I may reach the abode of eternal bliss."

His father said, "Ruling is now right for you, my son; initiation is fitting for us two. What is this you have learned, that transgresses orderly procedure, sinless one? You issued from my arms. Give a supporting hand and don't jump into this business." As his father said that, his son fell at his feet.

His mother said, "Listen, my child. By the gusts of the wind of separation from you, these vital spirits of mine will be forced to fly up in a rush, like straw."

The son said, "Mummy, then initiation will take place 14.540
together at the same time, so that there will be separation neither in this world nor in the abode of bliss."

Then Kúsuma·ketu said, "If such is your insistence, then, my son, Kúsuma·chula here will be consecrated to the kingship. But we all, my son, will take initiation also." The son said, "Excellent, father. There won't be a moment's delay in this matter."

Then, consultation having first been made by the barons and ministers, His Majesty King Kúsuma·chula was himself consecrated to the kingship.

atha śrī|Kusumaketuḥ sarva|tīrtha|kṛt'|ôtsavaḥ
sārdhaṃ Kanakalatayā śrī|sāmanta|śatena ca
14.545 Surasundarī|Ramaṇamatībhyāṃ parivāritaḥ
pañca|śatyā ca mitrāṇāṃ tathā Kusumaśekharaḥ
su|guru|Samarasen'|ācārya|rāṭ|pāda|mūle
sakala|kuśala|lakṣmī|vallarī|sthūla|mūle
Jina|pati|mata|vidhy|ādhāna|pūrvaṃ vitene
caraṇa|hariṇa|netr'|ôdvāha|līlā|vilāsam.

iti śrī|nirvāṇa|Līlāvatī|mahā|kath"|êti|vṛtt'|ôddhāre Līlāvatī|sāre Jin'|âṅke Purandara|śreṣṭhi|jīva|śrī|Surandhara|kumārasya Sulakṣaṇa|rāja|putra|jīva|Kusumaśekhara|kumārasya ca dīkṣā|mah"|ôtsava|vyāvarṇano nāma caturdaśa utsāhaḥ.

Then His Majesty Kúsuma·ketu, having made a festival at every holy place, together with Kánaka·lata and a hundred noble barons, and likewise Kúsuma·shékhara, attended by 14.545
Sura·súndari, Rámana·mati and five hundred companions, at the sole of the feet of the true teacher Sámara·sena, the king of teachers, the thick root of the creeper of fortune for all prosperity, after first performing the ceremony of honoring the Lord Jina, made a delightful appearance at their marriage ceremony to the doe-eyed lady of asceticism.

Here ends the fourteenth canto, entitled "The Initiation Festival of His Highness Prince Suran·dhara, the Soul of the Merchant Puran·dara, and of Prince Kúsuma·shékhara, the Soul of Prince Sulákshana," of the Jain epic *The Epitome of Queen Lilávati*, an abridgment of the events of *The Epic Story of the Auspicious Final Emancipation of Lilávati.*

CANTO 15
THE INITIATION OF HIS HIGHNESS PRINCE KULA·MRIGÁNKA, THE SOUL OF HIS HIGHNESS KÁNAKA·RATHA

15.1 ITAŚ CA BHĀRATE 'tr' âiva vilasad|dharma|nandane
sarva|jña|karmiṇe *bhīma|saha|deva|dhanañjaye,*
Gūrjuratr" êti deśo 'sti sudhā|svādu|phal'|ākaraḥ
rājadhānī vivekasya tri|divasy' êva khaṇḍalam.
yo nānā|vāhinī|ramyo mahā|bhū|bhṛt|kul'|āśritaḥ
deś'|ântarair a|jeyaś ca deśa|rāja iv' âśubhat.
tatra rājā rarāj' ôccair udīṛna|bala|vāhanaḥ
Naravāhana aiśvaryān nāmnā śrī|Balavāhanaḥ
15.5 babhau yadīya|doḥ|stambhe 'vaṣṭambhe rājya|sadmanaḥ
jaya|śrīḥ pañc'|âlik" êva nārācair dṛḍhitā dṛḍham.
śīla|candana|saurabhya|saurabhyita|dhar'|âmbarā chinna
prema|pātram abhūt tasya devī Malayasundarī.
su|kṛt'|âmbhodhi|sambhūṣṇu|mukha|pīyūṣa|pāyinoḥ
ghasrāḥ sahasraśo 'tīyus tayor devatayor iva.
anyedyuḥ Kanakaratha|devaḥ Saudharma|kalpataḥ
kukṣau Malayasundaryā nandanatvam avindata.
rākā|mṛg'|âṅkavat kāntyā samaye 'jāyat' âṅgajaḥ.
Kulamṛgāṅka ity asya nāma cakre mah"|ôtsavaiḥ.
15.10 kramāt kalābhiḥ sarvābhir yaḥ śliṣṭaḥ samadarśanaḥ
līlay" êva Smara|jayī vijigye 'n|īdṛśaṃ Haram.

NOW, IN THIS very continent of Bhárata, rejoicing in the manifestation of righteousness, fit for an omniscient one, *where victory over terrible things is won with the help of the gods: where Bhima, Saha·deva and Árjuna won their victories,** is a country named Gurjuratra, an abundant source of the fruit with the sweetness of nectar, a metropolis of good judgment, like a portion of heaven, which, delighting in its armies in the form of its various rivers, resorted to by families of kings in the form of its ranges of mountains, and not able to be overcome by other countries, prospered, like the king of countries. 15.1

There ruled a king, the vehicle of his power raised extremely high, a god of wealth in his sovereignty, named Bala·váhana. The goddess of victory seemed like a marionette, 15.5
whose arms were pillars supporting the King's palace, firmly fixed by iron arrows.

Clad in a garment that was scented with the fragrance of the sandalwood perfume that was her morality, a vessel of affection, his queen was Málaya·súndari. As they, like a couple of gods, drank the nectar produced from the ocean of their good deeds, their days passed thousandfold.

One day the god Kánaka·ratha, fallen from the Good Works heaven, attained the state of being a son in the womb of Málaya·súndari. When her time was full, a son was born with the splendor of the full moon; he was named Kula·mrigánka (Full Moon for His Family) with great festivity.
In due course, he was embraced by the digits of all the arts. 15.10
Being of the same appearance, he surpassed Love, as if with ease; he surpassed the Destroyer,* who was of a different appearance to him.

kalā|pātrīr bhūpa|putrīr aṣṭ' âṣṭ'|āśā|ramā iva
mahīyas" âtha mahasā pitā ten' ôdavāhayat.
tāsāṃ samāsāṃ su|bhagaṃ|karaṇyā yuva|rāṭ|śriyā
tam udvāhya kṛta|kṛtyaṃ|manyo, manye, 'bhavan nṛpaḥ.

aty|unnate viśāle ca sudhā|nirmala|nirmalaiḥ
a|bhinne 'pi nṛpād bhinne saudhe 'dīvyat sa tat|sakhaḥ.

jñātvā Kulamṛgāṅkasya cāritr'|āvaraṇ'|âtyayam
bodhaye su|guruḥ s' âiṣo 'nyadā taṃ devam ādiśat.

15.15 maṅkha|rūpaṃ vidhāy' āgān nagaraṃ so 'tha nirjaraḥ
jagac|citra|karaṃ citra|paṭam ādarśayaj jane.

tathā hi:

«a|kṛte randhane śvaśrvā snuṣ" âiṣā, paśya, piṭṭyate
nanāndrā khinsyate c' âsau bhrātṛ|jāyā yadā tadā!
eṣā snuṣā kalaha|kṛt bhintte svasy' âmbaraṃ svayam
śvaśrūr eṣ" âdhunā vadhvā piṭṭyate hā niraṅkuśam!»

tathā:

«‹kṣāraṃ rāddham idaṃ kim adya, dayite?›
‹rādhnoṣi kiṃ na svayaṃ?›
‹dhik tvāṃ krodha|mukhīm!› ‹alīka|mukharas
tvatto 'pi kaḥ kopanaḥ?›
‹āḥ pāpe, pratijalpasi prati|padaṃ›

Then his father married him at a very great festival to eight princesses, vessels of the arts, like delighters of the eight quarters of the heavens. Having married him to the fortune of the rank of crown prince, the cause of felicity to his other wives, the King, I suppose, became one who considered his duty fulfilled.

Accompanied by them, he enjoyed himself in a very lofty and extensive palace, which, although unbroken in its purifying applications of spotless whitewash, was broken away from the King.

Knowing that there was danger to Kula·mrigánka in confining him to that way of life, one day that same true teacher ordered that god to awaken him.

Assuming the form of an itinerant displayer of pictures, 15.15
the god went to the city and showed the people a painted scroll with a picture of the universe.

Just like so:

"Look! Whenever the cooking isn't done, this daughter-in-law is beaten by her mother-in-law and this wife is being struck by her sister-in-law! Here is a daughter-in-law crying and rending her own garment. Here is a mother-in-law now being beaten by her daughter-in-law, alas, without restraint!"

Like so:

"'What is this bitter food you've cooked today, my wife?' 'Why don't you cook yourself?' 'Shame on you and your angry face!' 'You are unpleasant and foulmouthed. What's the cause of this anger of yours?' 'Ah, you bad woman, you answer back at every word.' 'It's your father who's bad.' See,

‹pāpas tvadīyaḥ pitā.›
dam|patyor iti nitya|danta|kalahaṃ
bho bho janāḥ, paśyata.»
tathā:
«‹śvaśrūḥ krūratayā kaṭākṣayati māṃ,
duṣṭā nanānd” âpi me,
bhartur bhagny ati|vallabh” âsti na cirān
me garbha|rūpaṃ hale
āste krodha|mukhī ca devara vadhūr
dagdh” âsmy ahaṃ karmabhiḥ
prāyo bhojyam an|iṣṭam.› ity ayam, aho,
brūte vadhūṭī|janaḥ.»
15.20 ity|ādi hāsya|kṛc|citraṃ darśayan prākṛte jane
bhūri|bhūri labhaty eṣa, maṅkho gṛhṇāti no punaḥ.
nirlobhanatayā tena rañjitaṃ nikhalaṃ puram
priya|mitraiḥ kumārasya tat tac|citram akathyata.
kutūhalāt kumāraś ca maṅkham etam ajūhavat
so ’py ānaman dūrato ’pi kumāreṇa nyagadyata:
«re, paṭe tava ken’ êdaṃ likhitaṃ? kiñ ca v” asty adaḥ?»
«kumār’, êdam ātman” âiva likhitaṃ vṛttam ātmanaḥ.»
paṭaṃ vīkṣya kumāro ’tha jagāda, «bata, varṇakāḥ!
aho rekhā|prāñjalatvam! aho rūpaka|kauśalam!
15.25 yathā|sva|rūpam etan me pratipādaya, maṅkha, re.»
«kumāra, śṛṇu, vīkṣasva darśyamānaṃ may” âdhunā.»
lambāṃ kanthāṃ kare kṛtvā sa maṅkho darśayaty atha,
kautuk’|ākṣipta|cetās tu niśāmayati rāja|sūḥ.

good people, sirs, the constant bickering of a man and his wife."

Like so:

"Ah, here are young wives saying, 'My mother-in-law is glaring at me fiercely and my sister-in-law is malevolent. My sister-in-law should not be too dear to my husband after she mentioned my pregnancy in a quarrel. She always has an angry face, and, husband, I am a wife tormented by chores. What should be enjoyed is generally spoiled.' "

Saying this and more besides as he showed his amusing 15.20
picture, the displayer of pictures made an ever greater impression among the simple people, but he did not charge. His dear friends told the Prince that the whole city was delighted by this man who made no profit and then told him about his pictures. And the Prince through curiosity summoned this displayer of pictures. He bowed from a distance and was addressed by the Prince:

"Hey, who painted this on your scroll and what is it?" "I myself painted it, Prince; it's the story of a soul."

Then the Prince examined the scroll and exclaimed, "Oh, the colors! Oh, the accuracy in drawing! Oh, the skill in representation!

Come, displayer of pictures; lead me to understand it 15.25
according to its images." "Listen, Prince. Watch as I display it now."

Holding up the scroll in his hand, the displayer of pictures then began to display it, and the Prince, his mind seized with curiosity, watched with attention.

«Arhat|siddha|śruta|caitya|saṅgh'|ādi|prātikūlyataḥ
nṛtvaṃ vihāya niṣpuṇyaḥ sūkṣma|druṣv eṣa h" âgamat.
bādareṣu tatas teṣu hā jagāma tapasvy asau
utsarpiṇy|avasarpiṇyoḥ santāsteṣv asya ca sthitiḥ.
tebhyo, dev', âiṣa udvṛtto jāto hi, paśya! vāyuṣu
tato 'py agniṣu tatr' āsthād a|saṅkhyātam anehasam.
15.30 jāto 'psu, paśy'!, âtha bhūṣv a|saṃkhyātā avasarpiṇīḥ
tataḥ kathañ cid udvṛtya, paśy'!, âsau dv'|îndriyeṣu, bhoḥ.
jātaḥ kṛmi|prabhṛtiṣu saṃkhyātaṃ samayaṃ stithaḥ.
paśy'!, âth' āgāt tr'|îndriyeṣu kīṭikā|matkuṇ'|ādiṣu.
ath' âiṣa catur|akṣeṣu makṣikā|vṛścik'|ādiṣu,
kumāra, vīkṣasva! tasthau saṃkhyātān hāyayān khalu.
sammūrcchima|nṛ|tiryakṣu pañc'|âkṣeṣu yayāv ayam,
tataḥ, kumāra, paśy'!, âsau prathame narake 'gamat.
tatra ca cchidyate s' âiṣa, pacyate, bhidyate muhuḥ.
sāgar'|ôpamam ekaṃ tu tasthau tatra, nṛp'|âṅgaja.
15.35 sarīsṛpeṣv ath' ôtpady' âsau godhā|nakul'|ādiṣu.
nānā|jīvāṃs tatra hatvā dvitīye narake 'patat.

"Through his opposition to the holy congregation, holy places and the teachings perfected by the Worthy, deprived of human birth, devoid of merit, here he has gone, alas!, among vegetation matter with minute, multiple bodies. After that, alas, he has gone, being mortified, among gross bodies, and that is his state for upward and downward revolutions of the cycle of time.

Having arisen from them, Your Highness, look!, he has been born now among wind-beings and after that among fire-beings, and there he has remained for an unreckonable aeon.

Look! Now he has been born among water-beings for 15.30
unreckonable downward descents of the cycle of time and having arisen from there somehow, look!, he is one of the two-sensed beings, sir.

He remains being born among worms and such for a reckonable age. Look! Now he has arrived among three-sensed beings, insects and bugs, et cetera.

Look, Prince! There he is among four-sensed beings, bees, scorpions and such, remaining for reckonable years, for sure.

There he has gone among beings with five senses, self-generating beings, men and animals. After that, look, Prince!, he has gone into the first hell.

And there he is, being continually cut, roasted and pierced. And, Prince, he remained there for a full aeon.

He is born among reptiles, alligators, crocodiles and such. 15.35
Having there destroyed many beings, he has fallen into the second hell.

cheda|bhed'|ādi tatr' âpi soḍhv" âyaṃ sāgara|trayam
tataḥ pakṣiṣu hiṃsreṣu jajñe, paśya, nṛp'|ātmaja.

atha pṛthvyāṃ tṛtīyasyāṃ sapta|sāgara|jīvitaḥ
nārako 'bhūt tatra ghora|ghoraṃ duḥkhaṃ sa soḍhavān.

tataḥ, paśy'!, âiṣa siṃho 'bhūd Yamasy' êva sahodaraḥ.
samhṛtya jīvān nān" âsau turīye narake 'gamat.

daś'|âbdhīṃs tatra ca sthitv" ânubhūy' â|sukham utkaṭam
kumār', âth' âiṣa sarpo 'bhūt, paśya!, hanti tanūmataḥ.

15.40 tataḥ pañcama|narake sapta|daś'|âbdhi|jīvitaḥ
tatra soḍhvā mahā|duḥkhaṃ jāto matsyo, nar'|ôttama.

pañc'|êndriya|vadh'|ādeś ca ṣaṣṭha|pṛthvyām ayaṃ yayau
dvā|viṃśatiṃ sāgarāṇi sahate, paśya!, vedanāḥ.

mahā|matsyas tato jātaḥ, paśy'! ayaṃ matsya|lakṣa|bhuk.
tato 'bhūt saptama|pṛthvyāṃ trayas|triṃśy abdhi|jīvitaḥ.

tatra nāraka|hiṃs'|āder matsī|garbhe samāgataḥ
antar|muhūrtaṃ sthitv" âtra saptamyāṃ punar apy agāt.

a|pratiṣṭhāna|narake ṣaṭ|ṣaṣṭim iti toyadhīn
antar|muhūrt'|ântaritān varākaḥ, paśya, tasthivān.

Having suffered there, too, cutting and piercing and such for three aeons, after that, look, Prince!, he has been born among birds of prey.

Then he became a hell-being in the third hell-ground, living for seven aeons, and there he has endured dreadful, dreadful pain.

After that, look!, he has become a lion, like the twin of Death. Having slaughtered many beings, he has gone into the fourth hell.

And having remained there for ten aeons, experiencing excessive unpleasantness, then, Prince, look!, he has become a snake, and so he is killing people.

Then, after living in the fifth hell for seventeen aeons and 15.40
there suffering great pain, he is born a fish, eminent sir.

And because of his slaughter of five-sensed beings and such, he has entered the sixth hell-ground for twenty-two aeons. Look, he is suffering agonies!

After that, he is born a big fish. Look! There he is, eating a hundred thousand fish. Then he lives in the seventh hell-ground for thirty-three aeons.

After the violence and such of the hell-beings there, he has been conceived in the womb of female fish. Having remained there for less than a moment, he has returned to the seventh hell-ground.

Having thus remained in the hell without a solid ground for sixty-six aeons, look!, he remains in a wretched state for less than a few moments.

15.45 tato bhrāmyaṃś ca tiryakṣu siṃh'|êbh'|âsva|gav'|ādiṣu
kṣut|tṛṣṇ"|ādi|mahā|duḥkhaṃ hī varākaḥ sahaty ayam.
śar'|âṅkuśa|kaś'|ār'|ādi|ghātair guru|bharais tathā
asāv a|sātaṃ siṃh'|ādi|bhave santatam anvabhūt.
śrī|kumār', âiṣa mahiṣo jāta|mātraḥ kṣudh" âmṛta.
punaś ca mahiṣo jātaś, Cāmuṇḍāyā baliḥ kṛtaḥ.
s' âiṣo 'bhavat kharo, bhāraṃ
vāhyate, paśya!, hanyate.
kharīṃ vīkṣya bharaṃ kṣiptvā
bhuṅ|kurvan dhāvate 'dhamaḥ.
tato gartā|śūkaro 'bhūd viṣṭh"|ādy|a|śuci|bhakṣakaḥ.
an|āryo jananīṃ bhuktvā mṛtas, tad|garbham āgamat.
15.50 ath' âyaṃ śv" âbhavad, deva, kṣudh"|ārtto vraṇa|candrakī
samprayukto hahā śunyā varāko hanyate 'dhamaiḥ.
jātaś chāgo yāyajūkair yāge 'hanyata pāpmabhiḥ.
māṃs'|āśibhiḥ, paśya, jaghne hahā mṛga|bhave 'py asau.
sa eṣa vana|kolo 'bhūd aśva|thaṭṭena veṣṭitaḥ.
bhittv" âśva|thaṭṭaṃ praṇaśyan hataḥ śalyena kena cit.

After that, forced to wander among the lives of animals, lions, elephants, horses, cattle, et cetera, in a wretched condition he suffers that great pain indeed of hunger and thirst. There he is. 15.45

In the lives of lions, et cetera, he has continually experienced pain, through the blows of arrows, hooks and thonged whips, and likewise through heavy burdens.

Your Highness the Prince, there he is, a buffalo. Just born, he has died through hunger, and, born a buffalo again, he has been killed as a sacrifice to the goddess Chámunda.

There he is; he's become a donkey. He's being made to carry a burden. Look, he's being beaten! Having seen a female donkey, he's cast down his burden. He's making a braying noise as he runs, the poor wretch.

After that, he has been born a diseased hog, an eater of filth: shit and suchlike. Devoid of honor, he's died after sexually enjoying his mother and been born in her womb.

Now he has become a dog, Your Highness. Oppressed 15.50
by hunger, covered in boils and spots, joined in intercourse with a bitch, alas, in a pitiable condition, he's being beaten by inferiors.

Born a goat, he's been slaughtered at a sacrificial ceremony by wicked practitioners of sacrifices. Look, in the life of a deer, too, he's being slaughtered, alas, by seekers of meat.

There he is. He's become a forest boar beset by a troop of horsemen. He has broken through the troop of horsemen, but as he flees he's been struck by some spear.

kalaviṅk'|ādi|bālo 'yaṃ jātaḥ śyenā|dvik'|ādibhiḥ,
jala|cārī ca kaivartair varāko 'hanyat' âsakau.

ath' ôtpede varāko 'yaṃ manuṣyeṣu kathañ cana
raṇḍā|proṣita|paty|āder garbhe, 'gāli kad|auṣadhaiḥ.

15.55 raṇḍ"|ādi|garbhe punar apy āyāto na mṛtas tathā;
hī kumāra, varāko 'yam ujjhāñcakre śmaśānake.

strī|garbhe dvādaśa|samāḥ sthitvā mṛtvā sva|varṣmaṇi
jātaḥ sthito dvādaś'|âbdīṃ trir|âṣt"|âbdy eva jātavān.

nārī|garbhe sthitaś c' âiṣa tiryak sthitvā na nirgataḥ
kumāra|vara, jajñe 'sau mātuḥ svasya ca mṛtyave.

ayaṃ garbhe sthita eva vikṛtya pṛtanāṃ ghanām
yudhvā mṛtvā ca hā garbha|narakān narakaṃ gataḥ.

kumāra, jāta ev' âyaṃ revatī|doṣato 'mṛta,
punar utpanna ev' âyaṃ vinaṣṭo danta|pīḍayā.

15.60 ayaṃ ca jāto viṇ|mūtr'|â|pavitro rodano '|sakṛt
makṣikābhiś ca śūkavān mātuḥ kleśāya kevalam.

daridra|gehe jāto 'yaṃ śuṣk'|âṅgo garbhago 'pi hi
jāta|mātre ca jananī hā, kumāra!, vyapadyata.

Born the young of sparrows and suchlike, in a pitiable state, he has been slaughtered by hawks, crows and suchlike, and, born a fish, by fishermen and suchlike. There he is.

Now the wretch has somehow taken birth among human beings, in the womb of a slut whose husband is away or suchlike. He has been made to abort by noxious potions.

And, born once again in the womb of a slut or suchlike, 15.55
he has not been killed like that; no, Prince, he has been aborted in a cremation-ground.

Having remained in the womb of a woman for twelve years, he has died and been born in his own body. Having remained there for twelve years, he has been born twenty-four years old, for sure.

And, situated in the womb of a woman, he has remained lying sideways and not issued out. Excellent Prince, he has become the death of his mother and himself.

By remaining in a womb he has become deformed. After fighting an unending battle he has died, alas, and gone from the hell of the womb to hell.

Prince, born again, he has died through the disease of smallpox, and here he is, born once more and killed by toothache.

And here he is, befouled with shit and piss, continually 15.60
weeping and bristling with flies, born only for his mother's pain.

He has been born in the home of a poor man, his body shriveled, although indeed issued from the womb, and as soon as he has been born, his mother, alas, Prince!, has died.

pitr" âyaṃ c' âj'|ādi|dugdhair avardhyata pit" âstam ait.
eṣa karpara|hastas tu bhikṣate prati|mandiram.

ku|bhojanād eṣa kuṣṭha|galan|nāś'|âuṣṭha|karṇakaḥ
makṣikā|piṇḍako nirbhartsyate bhikṣ"|ârtham āgataḥ.

s' âiṣa mṛtvā punar jāto naro dāridrya|mandiram.
parā|bhava|mahā|pātraṃ jīvann api na jīvati.

15.65 kṣaireyīṃ vīkṣya bhuñjānān yācate sm' âiṣa mātaram
rudatī s" âpi duḥkh'|ārtā bāṣpair ev' ôttaraṃ dadau.

tata eṣa kṣudhā mṛtvā kathañ cit karma|lāghavāt
jātavān ibhya|tanayo vyuvāhe 'nya|sutām asau.

tad|vyaye hṛta|sarva|sva iv' âsau, paśya, roditi
‹kva gat" âsi? prativada, kānte kānta|vilocane!›

n' âiṣa bhuṅkte na pibati tato vātena pūritaḥ
mṛty|avasthām iva prāptaḥ parityaktaś ca vaidyakaiḥ.

tato 'sya pārśve jananī pitā bhrātā ca roditi
ayaṃ t' ûtpatya patati tapt'|ōrvyām iva matsyakaḥ.

15.70 kathañ cid eṣa praguṇībhūtaḥ pitr|ādayo 'hṛṣan
eṣo 'nyadā gato dyūte '|saṃkhyaṃ dhanam ahārayat.
tataś c" ākruśyate mātrā, pitā kiñ cid dadāti na,
gṛhe praveśaṃ n' âiv' âsya bhrātaro 'pi dadāty atha.

He has been raised by his father on goat's milk and suchlike. His father has died. Now he begs from house to house with a bowl in his hand.

His nose, lips and ears crumbling away with leprosy because of his bad diet, a ball of flies, he is being abused, having come to beg.

There he is. He's died and been born a man. Although alive, in a poor man's house, a great vessel of his former life, he does not survive.

Seeing people eating porridge, he demands some from his 15.65
mother, but she, crying and oppressed with pain, in tears even, gives him a refusal.

After that, having died through hunger, he has been somehow born, through the lightness of his karma, the son of a rich man, and has been married to the daughter of another.

At her passing away, as if at the loss of all his wealth, look!, he is crying, 'Where have you gone? Answer, my dear pretty-eyes!'

And he isn't eating or drinking. Then, filled with wind, he looks as if he's reached the state of dying and he's given up by his doctors.

After that, his mother, father and brother are weeping at his side, but he jumps up and falls down, like a fish on heated ground.

Somehow he has been restored to health, delighting his 15.70
father and the others. One day, he has gone and lost a countless amount of money at gambling. Then he is scolded by his mother and not given anything by his father. He is not even granted access to his brother's house. And the gamblers

dyūta|kāraiś ca gartāyāṃ nikṣipy' ādāyi mūrdhani
etasya dhūlī|piṭakaṃ. pitā mocayate na hi.

mahā|janena melanyā mocito 'sau na yāvatā.
eṣa jajñe, paśya, cauraḥ, khātraṃ khanati pātakī.

ārakṣakair eṣa dṛṣṭaḥ kharam āropitas tataḥ
sarvatra bhramitaḥ puryām udbadhya pitṛ|mandire.

15.75 patitaḥ pāśataḥ s' âiṣa śūlāyām adhiropitaḥ!
kathañ cic chubha|mṛtyoś ca jajñe rājño 'yam aṅgajaḥ.

saṃprāpta|yauvanaḥ kām'|āturo mantri|pitṛ|priyāḥ
sāmanta|loka|kāntāś ca pāpo 'bhuṅkta balād asau.

pitrā nirvāsito deśān niḥsahāyo 'tha nirdhanaḥ
kāma|vajr'|ânal'|ôttaptas tiryaścīr api sevate.

naṣṭāṃ raṇḍām ṛddhimatīṃ dharaty eṣa smar'|āturaḥ
jātair apatyaiḥ kliśyeta kramato niṣṭhite dhane.

vārddhake muṇḍita|śirā varāko jīrṇa|mañcake
suptaḥ pūt|kurute bhāry"|ādayaḥ śṛṇvanti no punaḥ.

15.80 nṛ|duḥkha|varṇanāy' ôktā bhavā ete nirantarāḥ
sapt'|âṣṭa|nṛ|bhavebhyas tu jñeyam antar|bhav'|ântaram.

have cast him into a hole and placed a basket of ashes on his head. His father is not at all able to procure his release.

A deputation of such great men has not been able to procure his release. Look, he has become a thief, digging under a wall, the criminal.

He has been seen by the police, and then mounted on a donkey, paraded everywhere in the city and tied up at his father's house.

He has been pulled down by a noose. There he is, im- 15.75
paled on a stake! And because of his death being somewhat auspicious, he has become the son of a king.

Having attained youth, sick with lust, the criminal has forcibly enjoyed the wives of his father's ministers, and the wives of the barons and the people.

Banished from the country by his father, now devoid of assistance and money, heated by the fire of the thunderbolt of love, he even resorts to female animals.

Sick with lust, he maintains a corrupt and wealthy slut. He is tormented by the offspring that are born, his money in due course having been given over.

In his old age, the poor wretch is sleeping on an old bed. He is making a noise, but his wife and the others pay no heed.

These continual existences have been related to explain 15.80
the sorrow of human existence, but, after fifty-six human existences, further intermediate existences must be understood.

tato 'yaṃ vyantaro jajñe strī|puṃs'|ādi|graha|spṛhaḥ
nān"|ân|artha|karatvāc ca māntrikeṇa nyagṛhyata.
kilbiṣik'|âbhiyogy eṣa, kumār', âjani pāpmataḥ
so 'yaṃ jāto vyantar'|ādi|vāhanaṃ, hā nirūpaya.
gandharv'|ādiś ca gandharv'|ânīke tu na rajaty ayam,
para'|rddhi|darśanād eṣa deva|bhāve 'pi khidyate.
prāpte 'p' Îndr'|âham|indratve cyavanād eṣa duḥkhitaḥ.
ete deva|bhavā bodhyā nara|tiryag|bhav'|ântarāḥ.
15.85 itaś ca Bhṛgukacche 'sau jas'|Âditya'|âṅgajo 'bhavat.
vaṇig Jasaraviḥ s' âiṣa kadaryo lobha|sāgaraḥ.
gṛhe śaṭita|dhāny'|ādi jarac|cīraṃ ca yacchati.
potena Ratnadvīpe 'sau yayau pitṛ|ādy|a|sammateḥ.
paśya, tatr' âiṣa ratnāni prabhūtaśa upārjayat,
cakre vaṇijaṃ mitraṃ Ratnadvīpa|nivāsinam.
pāpman" ânena so 'bhāṇi, ‹Bhṛgukacche mayā saha
āgaccha ratnāny ādāya mahā|lobho bhaviṣyati.›
sa ca mugdhaḥ sah' ânena potena prasthito 'mbudhau
antaḥ|samudraṃ tāmbūle viṣeṇ' âmāry anena saḥ.

After that, he has become an interstitial god, desirous of seizing men, women and children. And he has been overpowered by a soothsayer with various evil means.

Because of his wickedness, Prince, he has become employed on unpleasant tasks. There he is, alas! He's become one made to perform fetching and carrying for the interstitial gods and others.

As a heavenly musician god and suchlike, he is not delighted by the splendor of the heavenly musicians, but through the sight of the wealth of others, there he is, depressed even in the existence of a god.

Even having attained the power of saying, 'I'm Indra, king of the gods!', he is pained by his fall from heaven. These existences as gods are to be regarded as the other existences as men and animals.

Now he has become the son of excellent Adítya in Bhrigu·kaccha. There he is, the merchant Yasho·ravi, miserly, an ocean of greed.* 15.85

He is keeping moldy grain and old clothes in his house. He has sailed in a ship to Jewel Island, although his parents did not agree.

Look, there he is. He's obtained jewels in great amounts, and he has befriended a merchant who lives on Jewel Island.

And that criminal has said to the merchant, 'Bring jewels and come with me to Bhrigu·kaccha; the profit will be great.'

And he has been fooled and set out to sea with him on board a ship. Out at sea, he has been murdered by Yasho·ravi by means of poisoned betel leaves.

15.90 rodity eṣa Jasaraviḥ. sa vaṇig vyantaro 'jani.
jñātv" âvadheḥ sa sva|vṛttam etaṃ cikṣepa vāridhau.
tīrtv" ârṇavam ayaṃ daivān milito dhātu|vādinoḥ.
tābhyām hantum ayaṃ ninye. kumār', âiṣa palāyata.
nidhaye taru|pādaṃ ca khanan n' âiṣa nivāritaḥ
adhiṣṭhātṛ|vyantareṇa kopād dūre nicikṣipe.
yakṣiṇīṃ sādhayaty eṣa, pāpaḥ prārthayate ca tām.
tayā grahilitaḥ prāpto gṛhe pitrā paṭūkṛtaḥ.
svayaṃ svaṃ pitaraṃ hatvā viṣeṇ' âiṣa Yaśoraviḥ
mukta|kaṇṭhaṃ śaṭho rodity. avadhāraya, dhī|nidhe.
15.95 punaḥ karpāsam ādāya yayau Garjanakaṃ prati.
davena dagdho 'sau pāpaḥ prāpan naraka|dur|gatim.
Vasumitra|vaṇik|putro Vasunando 'bhavat tataḥ.
kurvann asau dhātu|vādaṃ pitr" âvāri na tiṣṭhati.
bhāgaṃ datvā pṛthak|cakre.
nirdhano 'tha nidhiṃ khanan
yogin" âsau hataḥ kiñ cit
paścāt tāpād vyayaṃ gataḥ.
rājñaḥ Padmarathasy' âṅgabhūḥ Kanakaratho 'bhavat.
asau pitrā samaṃ mantraṃ, bhoḥ kumār', ânyad" âkṛta.

And here is Yasho·ravi weeping. The merchant has become an interstitial god. Having found out what happened to him by means of his supernatural knowledge, he has hurled Yasho·ravi into the ocean. 15.90

And, carried across the ocean, two alchemists have chanced to meet him. They are carrying him away to be slaughtered. There he is, Prince; he's escaped.

And he is not able to be prevented from digging the root of a tree for treasure. The protective interstitial god in anger has hurled him far.

And he is worshipping a demigoddess, and here the criminal is soliciting her. Driven mad by her, he has arrived at his home and been cured by his father.

Having himself killed his father by poison, here is Yasho·ravi, that irritant removed, falsely weeping. Think on, you ocean of intelligence.

Once more taking cotton, he has gone to Gárjanaka. 15.95
Burned by a fire, that criminal has attained the bad rebirth destination of a hell-being.

After that he has become Vasu·nanda, the son of the merchant Vasu·mitra. Forbidden by his father, he does desist from practicing alchemy.

Having given away his money, he has gone off alone. Lacking money, he is now digging for treasures. He has been struck a blow by a magician and after has passed away through pain.

He has become Kánaka·ratha, the son of King Padma·ratha. Prince, good sir, here he is, one day holding a conversation with his father:

‹deva, sāmanta|mantry|ādyāḥ paurā jāna|padās tathā
ek'|âikaśaḥ svaṃ gṛhyante, yasya kośaḥ sa hi prabhuḥ.›

15.100 cetyā bhinnaṃ rahasyaṃ tat. sāmant'|ādyaiḥ sapady api
rājā dāru|gṛhe kṣipto, 'yaṃ ca Kanakaratho 'naśat.

prāptaś ca puri Kauśāmbyāṃ śrī|Sudharm'|āsya|paṅkajāt
svaṃ caritraṃ niśamy' âsau jātiṃ smṛtvā nirakramīt.

Kauśāmbyāṃ prāvrajann ete daśa te ca divaṃ gatāḥ.
śrī|Nemi|pārśve 'mī pṛcchanty āgāmi|bhava|sādhanam.

prabhur ūce, ‹Śūra|devāt prabodho vo bhaviṣyati,
pradīpād iva dīpānāṃ. prapadyadhvaṃ mudaṃ tataḥ.›

ayaṃ ca Kanakarathaś cyutv" âbhūn Nagare pure
Balavāhana|Malayasundaryor eṣa nandanaḥ.

15.105 sa ca tvam eva, kumāra, n' âtra saṃśayaḥ
Śūra|devo 'haṃ maṅkha|rūpeṇ' âtra samāgamam.
paṭo 'yaṃ tava bodhāya may" âracyata citra|kṛt.
tat, kumāra|var', êdānīṃ budhyasva, kuru saṃyamam!
ete 'nanta|bhavāś c' âtra proktāḥ sambhava|mātrataḥ
vastutas tu Jasaravi|mukhyā bhava|catuṣṭayī.»

'Your Majesty, he who has the treasure, the wealth possessed by the barons, ministers and such, the townspeople, and likewise the countrypeople individually, he's the one who is actually king.'

The secret has been revealed by a maidservant. The barons 15.100
and the others have immediately cast the King into a wooden cage, and here is Kánaka·ratha; he's escaped.

And he has arrived at the city of Kaushámbi. Having heard his story from the lotus of the mouth of reverend Sudhárman, he has remembered his former lives and taken initiation.

In Kaushámbi these ten are taking initiation, and they have gone to heaven. In the presence of Lord Nemi they are asking about the fulfillment of their future existences.

The lord has said, 'Your enlightenment will happen by means of the god Shura, like that of lamps by means of a lighter. So enter a state of joy!'

And here is Kánaka·ratha, having fallen from heaven. He's become the son of Bala·váhana and Málaya·súndari in the city of Nágara.

And he is you, certainly. There is no doubt whatsoever 15.105
about it. I am the god Shura. I have come here in the form of a displayer of pictures. This scroll of paintings was designed by me to enlighten you. So, excellent Prince, be enlightened now! Perform asceticism! And these endless existences portrayed on it are by way of possibility only. But the fourfold existence starting from Yasho·ravi is by way of actuality."

ity etat tad|vacaḥ śrutv" âsy'
ēh"|âpohaṃ vitanvataḥ
mūrcch" âmūrcchat kumārasya
lokair maṅkho 'jighāṃsyata.
jāti|smaraṇa|mitre ca
milite rāja|nandanaḥ
tān niṣidhy' âvadan maṅkhaṃ,
«svaṃ rūpaṃ darśaya, prabho.»

15.110 sa ca devo divya|rūpaṃ darśayitvā tiro 'bhavat.
tāṃ vārtāṃ pitarau śrutv" ōcatur, «mā, vatsa, niṣkramīḥ.»
putro 'vadat, «tāta, mātar, idaṃ vām api yujyate,
niṣedhayanta yan mām apy etan moha|vijṛmbhitam.»
dvitīye 'hni śrī|Samarasena|sūriḥ sahasra|ruk
prātaḥ sahasr'|āmra|vaṇe parāpad udaya|śriyam.
tataḥ sadyo 'pi sa|bala|vāhano Balavāhanaḥ
śrīmān Kulamṛgāṅkaś ca prabhuṃ nantuṃ prajagmatuh.
bhagavantaṃ namaskṛtya yath"|ôciti niṣedatuḥ.
dharmaṃ śrutvā nṛpo jajñe dīkṣ"|êcchuḥ śrī|kumāravat.
15.115 laghu|putraṃ śrī|Amaramitraṃ nyasy' ātmanaḥ pade
akārayat tīrtha|mah"|ādikaṃ Vijayasenavat.
tataś ca:
sma vahati Balavāhano mah"|îndraḥ
sa|Kulamṛgāṅka|kumāra|rāḍ|jayantaḥ
caraṇa|bharam aho tato mun'|îndrā hy
ahuta Jin'|ēśvara|līlayā guruś ca.

Having heard this account of his, as the Prince extended due consideration on what was for and against, a swoon took hold of him. The people wanted to kill the displayer of pictures.

Having met the friend that was his memory of his former lives, the Prince restrained them and said to the displayer of pictures, "Show your actual form, Lord."

And the god, having revealed his divine form, vanished 15.110
from sight. When his parents heard his story, they said, "Don't take initiation, our child."

Their son said, "Father, Mother, it is fitting for you, too, since they are warding off from me the consequences of this delusion."

On the following day, in the morning the thousand-rayed sun that was the reverend doctor Sámara·sena caused the brilliance of his rising to settle in the grove of the thousand mango trees. Then straightaway Bala·váhana, with a powerful escort and His Highness Kula·mrigánka, went forth to pay their respects to the lord.

Having bowed to the lord, they sat in appropriate places. Having heard the religious teaching, the King became desirous of initiation, like His Highness the Prince. Having 15.115
placed his younger son, His Highness Ámara·mitra, in his own rank, the King ordered a surpassingly great festival to be prepared, as Víjaya·sena had done.

And then:

Lord of the earth Bala·váhana, together with the moon for the King that was Prince Kula·mrigánka, bore the burden of asceticism. Ah! Then the lords of monks, yes, and the teacher emulated the appearance of the Lord Jina.

iti śrī|nirvāṇa|Līlāvatī|mahā|kath"|êti|vṛtt'|ôddhāre Līlāvatī|sāre Jin'|âṅke Kanakaratha|kumāra|jīva|śrī|Kulamṛgāṅka|kumāra|dīkṣā|vyāvarṇano nāma pañcadaśa utsāhaḥ.

Here ends the fifteenth canto, entitled "The Initiation of His Highness Prince Kula·mrigánka, the Soul of His Highness Kánaka·ratha," of the Jain epic *The Epitome of Queen Lilávati*, an abridgment of the events of *The Epic Story of the Auspicious Final Emancipation of Lilávati.*

CANTO 16
THE INITIATION OF HIS HIGHNESS PRINCE SUSHÉNA, THE SOUL OF HIS HIGHNESS VAIRI·SIMHA

16.1 ATH' ÂTRA BHARATA|kṣetre Kuru|maṇḍala|maṇḍanam
trai|lokye 'py a|prati|rūp" Âpratirūpā purī babhau.

rājā Duryodhanas tatra vireje Dhṛtarāṣṭra|sūḥ.
sa|karṇaś ca paraṃ dharm'|ātmaja|pakṣa|priyaṅ|karaḥ.

yudhi|ṣṭhiro dviṣāṃ bhīmaḥ kīrti|pūraiḥ sad" ârjunaḥ,
saha|devo, nakulaś ca sa śrī|Duryodhanaḥ param.

padm'|ôtpala|mṛg'|âkṣīṇi n' ôpamānāni yad|dṛśoḥ
manye vilāsa|vandhyatvāt, s" âsya devī Sulocanā.

16.5 su|keśī su|smitā sv|āsyā yā su|hastā su|vāk su|pāt
sv|īryā sv|aṅgī ca kiṃ tad|āhūti|mātraṃ Sulocanā?

tau c' ânyonyaṃ vapuṣ|pātre sukha|pīyūṣa|pāyiṇau
ast'|ôdayau na hi vidāncakrāte amarāv iva.

sa Vairisiṃha|jīvo dyor devyāḥ kukṣāv avātarat
su|svapna|dohadaś c' âiṣa samaye samajāyata.

praty|ahaṃ nava|navo 'sya daś'|âhaṃ janan'|ôtsavaḥ
ekādaśe 'hni Suṣeṇa iti nām'|ôtsavo 'bhavat.

saubhāgya|sundara|vapus tataḥ param ayaṃ svayam
divā|niśam, aho!, jajñe sarveṣāṃ nayan'|ôtsavaḥ.

Now, in this continent of Bhárata, adorning the Kuru country, its beauty incomparable in the triple universe, lies resplendent the city of Apratirúpa (Incomparable in Its Beauty). 16.1

And there King Duryódhana ruled, the son of Dhrita·rashtra. He was attentive, and a companion of Karna, but the cause of delight to the offspring of righteousness.

Now, His Majesty Duryódhana was firm in battle, formidable against enemies, ever bright with the upward billowings of his glory, accompanied by the gods, and of unbroken lineage.*

Her eyes surpassing those of a roe or an opening lotus because of their absence of playfulness, I suppose, his Queen
was Sulóchana (Pretty Eyes). Since she had pretty hair, a 16.5
pretty smile, a pretty face, pretty hands, pretty feet, pretty posture and a pretty body, why only address her as Sulóchana?

And as the two drank the nectar of bliss from the vessels of each other's bodies, like a couple of gods, they did not know if the sun was setting or rising.

And the soul of Vairi·simha* descended from heaven into the womb of the Queen, and at that moment this auspicious dream and pregnancy-longing was produced. It was repeated every day. On the tenth day, the dream of the festival for the birth of a son, and on the twelfth day the festival of naming him Sushéna.

But then he himself, his body handsome and charming, was born, day and night, oh yes!, a festival for the eyes of everyone.

16.10 ā|janma sakalo 'py eṣa kalpa ity eṣa bhūbhujā
kal"|ācāryāya sakala|kal"|ârthaṃ dhruvam ārpyata.

udūḍha|niḥśeṣa|kalaṃ niṣkalaṅka|kul'|âṅganāḥ
taṃ pāṇau kārayāñcakre rāṭ sva|kīrti|kṛte dhruvam.

tatra śrī|yauva|rājya|śrīḥ svayam eva samakramīt,
tāṃ rāṭ saṃkramayan snehāt paunar|uktyam viveda na.

ahar|niśam asau rāja|citta|saudhe vasann api
sva|vadhū|kāraṇān, manye, 'dhyāsta saudh'|ântaraṃ punaḥ.

anyedyur Jayapur'|ēśa|Jaya|putrīṃ Nṛsundarīm
svayaṃ|varām upayeme kumār'|êndur niśām iva.

16.15 śvetayitv" âbhitaḥ kīrtyā śaṅkh'|âbhraka|valakṣayā,
citrayitvā pratāpena kuruvinda|sanābhinā,
ājñā|lākṣ"|âvatāreṇa projjvālya bhuvan'|ôdaram,
nyāya|dauvārikeṇ' ôccai rakṣyamāṇe 'tra sarvataḥ,
ratna|rocir|viphalita|pradīpa|dyuti|maṇḍale
pradhāne 'bhyantar'|āsthāne nidhāne sarva|sampadām,
puṇya|lakṣmī|sakhī|rājya|kamalā|kamal'|ākare, chinna svarṇa|ratn'|ôtkar'|ôdāre śrī|sāraṅg'|âdhip'|āsane;

Thinking he was entirely capable, from his birth he was entrusted by the King to a master of arts so that he would firmly acquire all the arts. 16.10

The King, in order to make firm his own renown, married him, now married to all the arts, to ladies from stainless families.

At that point, the fortune of the rank of crown prince stepped forth to meet the Prince actually of her own accord, as the King was leading her forward; in his affection the King did not notice the repeated statement. And day and night he stayed in a palace designed by the King; but it was for the sake of his wives, I suppose, that he remained inside the palace.

One day, at her ceremony of choosing her own husband, the moon of a prince married Nri·súndari, the daughter of Jaya, the King of Jaya·pura, like the moon marrying night.

In that country where everywhere had been made white with the white shell-powder that was glory and had been colored with majesty that was akin to a ruby; where the vault of the universe had been made bright by the descent of the red dye of authority; in that place which was everywhere highly protected by the heavenly rampart of justice; in that country the light of whose splendor made otiose the rays of jewels; in its capital, situated in the interior, a treasury for those who had achieved every success; which contained a mass of lotuses of the fortune of the kingdom, the companion of the fortune of merit; which was lofty with heaps of gold and jewels, which was the seat of the splendid royal parasol; 16.15

adhyāsām āsuṣas tasya śrī|Duryodhana|bhū|pateḥ
śrī|Sulocanayā devy” âlaṅkṛt’|ârdh’|āsana|śriyā,
16.20 kumāre śrī|Suṣeṇe c’ âny’|āsann’|āsana|maṇḍane
yath”|āuciti|niviṣṭaiś ca varya|sāmanta|mantriṣu,
prakrāntāyāṃ ca sāmrājya|kiṃ|vadatyāṃ samantataḥ,
antar|antaḥ parīhās’|ôdante ca pravisarpati,
ratna|karburita|svarṇa|daṇḍ’|âlaṃkṛta|pāṇikaḥ
Priyaṅkaro ’nyadā dvāḥ|sthaḥ pādau natvā vyajijñapat:
«deva Garjanak’|âdhīś’|Âpratiśatru|mahī|pateḥ
siṃha|dvāre ’sti dūto ’yaṃ, prabho, yat kṛtyam ādiśa.»
«drutaṃ praveśay’,» êty ukte rājñā dūtaḥ sabhām upait
natv” āsīno «vijñāpay’,» êty ādiṣṭo bhūbhuj” âbhyadhāt:
16.25 «vijanaṃ kāryatāṃ, deva,» rāj” ōce, «vijanaṃ hy adaḥ.
yaste rahasyaṃ kim api tan niśaṅkam udīraya.»
dūto ’brūta, «bhuv’ îdānīṃ yat|prātapa iraṃ|madaḥ
vairi|nār”|īkṣaṇ’|êrābhir mādyan saty’|ânvayo ’bhavat.
so ’pratiśatru|bhūm’|îndro garjan Garjanak’|âdhipaḥ
ājñāpayati te samyak sāvadhānaṃ niśāmaya:
yāṃ Narasundarī|kanyām upayeme tvad|aṅgajaḥ,
āsīn me sā vṛtā, tat tāṃ preṣaya drutam eva, bhoḥ.
yad vā giriṃ vā darīṃ vā jalaṃ vā sthalam eva vā
śaraṇaṃ pratipadyasva, n’ ânyathā jīvitaṃ hi te.»

one day, Priyan·kara, the doorkeeper, his hand adorned 16.20
by his gold staff studded with jewels, bowed to the feet of His Majesty King Duryódhana, who was seated in assembly, with half of the royal throne ornamented by Her Highness Queen Sulóchana; as His Highness Prince Sushéna was decorating another throne nearby, and as the eminent barons and ministers were seated in their appropriate places; as the news of the King's majesty was proceeding in all directions, and as the report of amusement was being diffused within, he announced:

"Your Majesty, there is a messenger from King Apratishátru, the lord of Gárjanaka, at the lion-gate, so command what is to be done, sire."

On the King's saying, "Show him in immediately," the messenger entered the assembly, bowed and sat, and, commanded to speak by the King, said:

"Let it be done in private, Your Majesty." The King said, 16.25
"This is certainly private. Isn't the secret in a safe place? So speak without fear."

The messenger said, "He whose majesty is now lightning for the world, who rejoiced with the tears of his enemies' wives, a follower of truth, he, King Apratishátru, the thundering lord of Gárjanaka, commands you to pay proper attention:

The maiden Nri·súndari, whom your son married, was chosen by me, so send her right now, good sir. Or else obtain refuge by mountain, cave, water or by land, otherwise you certainly won't live."

16.30 smitvā dūtam ath' âbrūta śrī|Duryodhana|bhū|patiḥ:
«re, prabhus te sa me pattiḥ kuta evaṃ|taro 'sya tat?
puṇya|kṣayād vā tasy' êti matir adya vyajṛmbhata?
kandarāsu sthitaṃ siṃhaṃ re|kārayati kaḥ su|dhīḥ?»
tataḥ prakupito dūto bhūt'|āviṣṭa iv' âvadat:
«sadā tvam eva me svāmi|tīrtha|pād'|ambuj'|ârcakaḥ.
tan na kiñ cid idaṃ, rājan, bhavad|uktaṃ. tato drutam
Nṛsundarīm imāṃ dehi, śaraṇaṃ vā samāśraya.»
śrī|Suṣeṇa|kumāro 'tha vyājahre 'muṃ su|dur|mukham:
«pador gṛhītvā kṣipata purī|nirdhamanena, bhoḥ.»
16.35 tataḥ kṣiti|patiḥ prāha, «vats', âitan na khal' ûcitam.
dūte daṇḍo na hi ślāghyaḥ kin tu tatr' âiva ku|prabhau.»
tatas tātam anujñāpya catur|aṅga|camū|vṛtaḥ
taṃ prati śrī|Suṣeṇaḥ srāk pratasthe stheya|mandaraḥ.
dūtaṃ c' ākhyad, «drutaṃ gaccha
sva|prabhoḥ pratipādayeḥ,
‹idānīṃ puruṣo bhūyāḥ,
pātāle 'pi na mokṣyase.›»
nirvilambaiḥ prayāṇaiś ca kumāraḥ prāpa sīmani,
sva|dūtena tam ūce ca, «prāpto 'haṃ. kṣatriyo bhaveḥ.»
tatas taṃ sarva|pracchanna|tādṛg|vigraha|kāriṇam
para|strī|lipsum a|sama|vairaṃ mantry|ādayo 'mucat.

His Majesty King Duryódhana smiled and said to the messenger, "Hey, your master is my foot soldier; whence comes this strength of his? Or is his mind wandering like this because of the decay of his merit? What intelligent person challenges a lion standing in its lair?" 16.30

Then the messenger, enraged as if a spook had got into him, said, "You're the one who is ever worshipping at the holy place that is the lotus of the foot of my master. So what you have said is nothing at all, King. Therefore hand over Nri·súndari here immediately or seek refuge."

Then His Highness Prince Sushéna, with a very angry face, said to the King, "Grab him by the feet and throw him out by the city sewer, sir."

Then the King said, "My son, this is not at all proper. 16.35
Although by no means to be praised, the messenger should not be punished but, rather, his wicked master."

So His Highness the Prince obeyed his father, and, an abode of firmness, surrounded by his army of four divisions, immediately set out against him.

And he said to the messenger, "Go quickly and give this reply to your master. 'Now be a man. You won't be released even in the underworld.'"

And with unbroken marches the Prince reached the border, and by means of his messenger informed him, "I have come. Be a warrior."

Then his ministers and the others abandoned that King, entirely revealed to be the cause of such a war, and whose manliness was not equal to his lust for others' wives.

16.40 sāmantā mantriṇaḥ sarve śrī|Suṣeṇasya te 'milan
tataḥ pradhāna|tyaktaḥ sa praṇanāśa śṛgālavat.

śrī|Suṣeṇo Garjanake pravartya pitṛ|śāsanam
mahā|balāṃs tatra deśe 'sthāpayad daṇḍa|nāyakān.

vardhāpakaṃ prāhiṇoc ca śrī|Duryodhana|bhūbujaḥ,
rāja|dhānyāṃ svayaṃ sthitvā sausthyaṃ sarvatra c' âtanot.

tataḥ sva|rājy'|âbhimukhaṃ vavale sa bal'|ēśvaraḥ
śrī|Suṣeṇo nija|bhuvi Vasantapuram āpa ca.

tatra śrī|nandan'|ôdyāne skandh'|āvāraṃ nyaveśayat
krīḍan śrī|Narasundaryā tasthau ca kati cid dinān.

16.45 itaḥ, śrī|Siṃha|rāj', Suṣeṇam avabudhya tam
prabodha|yogyaṃ Samarasena|sūrir ih' āgamat.

tatr' âiva nandana|vane tasthau ca sa|paricchadaḥ
prabhuṃ vandāravaḥ paurāḥ śuśruvur dharma|deśanām.

tathā paur'|ādibhir vandyamānān nidhyāya tān gurūn
śrī|Suṣeṇa|kumāraṃ taṃ papraccha Narasundarī.

«ārya|putra, puraḥ ke 'mī, kim ācārāṃ caranti vā?»
kumāro 'vag, «ime Śvet'|âmbarā dharmaṃ ca kurvate.»

His barons and ministers all came to terms with His 16.40
Highness Sushéna, thereupon, abandoned by his chief men, he ran away like a jackal.

His Highness Sushéna, having extended his father's rule over Gárjanaka, established in that country judges with big forces.

And he sent congratulation to His Majesty King Duryódhana, and, having established himself in the King's palace, spread well-being everywhere.

Then that chief of generals His Highness Sushéna set off to return to his own kingdom and reached Vasánta·pura in his own country.

There, in the lovely garden of delights, he placed his royal headquarters and remained there for several days sporting with Her Highness Nri·súndari.

And then, Your Majesty King Simha, having perceived 16.45
that Sushéna was capable of being enlightened, the reverend doctor Sámara·sena arrived there.

And he remained in that very same grove of delights together with his entourage. The citizens paid their respect to the lord, eager to hear his teaching of religion.

Nri·súndari, perceiving that the citizens and such were thus paying their respects to the teacher, asked His Highness Prince Sushéna:

"Noble husband, who are they in front, and what way of life are they practicing?" The Prince said, "They are White-clad Jain monks and they are practicing religion."

priy” â|śāstra|kṣuṇṇa|gatiḥ kumāraṃ punar abravīt:
«ārya|putra, dharma iti kaḥ śabd’|ârtha udīryate?»

16.50 śāstr’|âbhyāsī kumāro ’pi pratyuvāca Nṛsundarīm:
«priye, dur|gati|pāty|âṅgi|dhāraṇād dharma ucyate.»

priy” āha, «dur|gatiḥ k” êyaṃ?» priyo ’vaṅ, «narak’|ādikā.»
«kathaṃ nāth’, âtīndriyaṃ hi narak’|ādy avasīyate?»

«anumānād,» iti prokte kumāreṇa priy” âvadat,
«pratyakṣ’|â|viṣaye, nāth’, ânumānaṃ na pravartate.

anumān’|ântarād eva tat|pravṛttau, vid’|âmbara.
itar’|êtar’|āśrayaṇ’|ânavasth”|ādi prasajyate.»

priyaḥ prāha, «priye, n’ âtra pūrva|doṣaḥ sthitir, yataḥ
pūrv’|ânumānaṃ n’ ânty’|āśrin, kin tu pūrvatar’|āśrayam.

16.55 anavasth” âpi n’ âiv’ âtr’ âvatārituṃ pragalbhate.
dvi|tra|jñān’|ôdaye ’vaśyaṃ jijñās” â|vinivṛttitaḥ.

kiñ ca:

dṛṣṭa|sādharmyato vṛtty” âdhyakṣam apy anumānakam
pravartakaṃ tatas tan na bhaved ḍūṣy’|ânumānavat.

His wife, who trampled on ignorance of scriptural learning as she walked, replied to the Prince, "What is said to be the meaning of the word religion?"

And the Prince, who was practiced in scriptural learning, 16.50
replied to Nri·súndari, "My dear, religion is said to arise through the need to protect the embodied being from falling into a bad destination."

His wife said, "What is this bad destination?" Her husband said, "Hell and so on." "How, husband, is the knowledge of what is certainly beyond the range of the senses, hell and so on, ascertained?"

On the Prince's replying, "By inference," his wife said, "Husband, inference can't take place in what is beyond the sphere of the senses.

By means other than inference, then, it must be investigated in its manifestation, you sky of knowledge. Otherwise it results in an endless series of mutually dependent propositions."

Her husband said, "My dear, there is no situation of previous fault in this, since the previously inferred is not applied at the end but is applied very early on.

And the problem of infinite regress can by no means 16.55
come into it. An inquiry does not surely end when we have knowledge of subsequent stages.

And besides:

Through the occurrence of something of similar properties which has been seen, the result can be inferred by the senses, therefore there would be no fault in the inference.

svapna|pratyaya|dṛṣṭ'|ântāt pratyakṣaṃ na pram" êti cet,
tad" âkhila|vyavahār'|ôccheda|doṣas tav' āpatet!
api c' Āpta|gir" âpy eṣā dur|gatir budhyate budhaiḥ.»
s" ākhyad, «Āptaḥ ka?» ūce 'sau, «vīta|rāga|tri|loka|vit.
na mṛṣā bhāṣaṇe 'muṣya kāraṇaṃ kim ap' īkṣyate.
rāg'|ādi|dūṣito hy ajaḥ puruṣo bhāṣate mṛṣā.»
16.60 preyasy ūce, «tarhi, nātha, śṛṇumaḥ, kiṃ vadanty amī.»
tatas tau dam|patī prāptau sūri|rājasya sannidhau.
a|paśyatāṃ praviśantau prathamaṃ tau mahā|munīm
kāy'|ôtsarga|vīra|vraja|paryaṅk'|ādy|āsana|sthitān,
nānā|labdhi|taṭiny|abdhīṃs tapaḥ|kraśita|vigrahān
rāja|sāmanta|mantr'|îbhya|śreṣṭhi|sārthapa|nandanān.
prekṣāṃbabhūvatur atha vadatas tau mun'|īśvaram
saumyaṃ sudhā|karam iva prabhā|karam iv' ôjjvalam,
payo|dhim iva gambhīraṃ, dhīraṃ kāñcana|śailavat,
kalpa|dru|cintā|maṇy|āder māhātmya'|rddhi|vijitvaram.
16.65 tato bhaktyā namaskṛtya taṃ sūriṃ sa|paricchadam
āsāṃbabhūvatur imau prāñjalī sad|guroḥ puraḥ.

If you argue that direct perception acquired in a dream, for example, is not accurate perception, then you would be faced with the problem of completely denying common sense!

And this bad destination is understood by the wise by means of the teaching of the Worthy." She said, "Who is the Worthy?" He replied, "The omniscient one of the triple universe whose passions are subdued.

And no reason at all can be seen for that man's speaking falsely. But a goat of a man who is corrupted by passions and such is the one who speaks falsely."

His wife said, "Then, husband, let's listen to what he is 16.60
saying." So then the couple, man and wife, arrived near the presence of the king of reverend doctors.

As they approached at first they did not see the great monk, who was assuming the postures of standing bolt upright, sitting with his hand placed between his body and his crossed feet, taking a seated position without a chair, et cetera, who was an ocean of the rivers of various attainments, whose body was emaciated by asceticism, and who was the delight of kings, barons, ministers, wealthy men, merchants and caravan-leaders.

Then they saw him speaking, the lord of monks, placid like the moon, radiant like the sun, as profound as the ocean, as firm as a mountain of gold, surpassing in the wealth of his magnanimity wishing-trees, wishing-jewels and such.

Then the two paid devoted respects to the reverend doc- 16.65
tor and his entourage and sat, their hands folded in salutation, in front of the teacher of truth.

atr' ântare 'vadhi|carāt taṃ vijñāya nṛp'|âṅgajam
śrīmat|Samarasenasya mun'|îndrasy' ôpajānukam,
pañca|varṇa|vimānānāṃ dhoraṇībhiḥ samantataḥ
dyāṃ bhuvaṃ c' ântarā ramyāṃ sṛjann iva navāṃ divam;
kalaśaiś ca vimānānāṃ tāma|rasa|mayīm iva
div" âpi ca patākābhir jyotsnā|śreṇi|mayīm iva;
nāndī|tūrya|ninādaiś ca śabdāyita|mayīm iva
gāyadbhir gāyana|stomair gāndharvaika|mayīm iva;
16.70 nṛtyadbhir nartikā|vṛndair vidyun|mālā|mayīm iva
maṅgala|pāṭhināṃ pāṭhaiḥ san|maṅgala|mayīm iva;
kaṇṭhīra|dvīpa|dvīpi|śārdūla|sarabh'|ādibhiḥ
yānair haṃsa|hay'|ādyaiś ca' rbhā|vismaya|mayīm iva;
amarair amarībhiś ca gaṇanām ati|gāmukaiḥ
rūp'|ântarair iva nijaiḥ paritaḥ parivāritaḥ;
mano|van'|êbha|śravaṇa|dṛk|kuraṅg'|âika|kārmaṇam chinna
pade pade sthiraṃ paśyan puraḥ saṅgīta|kautukam;
bhāsvantam apy a|bhāsvantaṃ tanvaṃs tanu|vibhā|bharaiḥ
śrī|Śūra|devas tatr' āgāt saudharm'|êndra iv' âparaḥ.

16.75 tāvad deva|parīvāraḥ sa prādakṣiṇayat prabhum,
guru|bhakti|bhar'|ākrānta iva nīcair nanāma ca.

At that moment, having perceived by means of his supernatural perception that the Prince was at the knees of reverend Sámara·sena, the lord of the monks, as if, with unbroken series of five-colored celestial vehicles on all sides, he was producing a lovely new heaven between heaven and earth; as if made of gold by the pinnacles of the celestial vehicles, as if made of a multitude of lights by brilliance and banners; as if made of sound by the playing of rhythmic lutes, as if made of vocal performance by the singing of people singing hymns; as if made of wreaths of light- 16.70
ning by the dancing of troops of dancing girls, as if made of true felicity by the recitations of reciters of blessings; as if made of the wonderful craftsmanship of the vehicles drawn by camels, bull-elephants, cow-elephants, panthers, monkeys and such, preceded by swans and horses; as he was surrounded on all sides by gods and goddesses beyond counting, like other forms of himself; as he watched the musical performance that continued at each of his steps, a show for the antelopes of sight and for the elephants of hearing in the forest of the mind; spreading light into darkness with the masses of light from his body, the god Shura arrived there, like the supreme king of the gods of the Good Works heaven.

Meanwhile the god's retinue circumambulated the lord, 16.75
and bowed lowly as if bent down by the weight of its devotion to the teacher.

bhagavantam anujñāpya siṃh'|āsane niviśya ca
ek'|âika|bāhoḥ srī|puṃsa|pātrair dvātriṃśatā kṣaṇāt,
ṣoḍaśa ṣoḍaśa nāṭyāny ādhaya purataḥ prabhoḥ
upadarśy' ôpasaṃhṛtya natvā stutvā punaḥ prabhum,
vinayāt praśnayitvā ca śrutvā nirvacanāni ca
yath"|āgataṃ jagām' āśu sa śrī|nirjara|śekharaḥ.
kumāras tad idaṃ vīkṣya vismaya|smera|mānasaḥ
dadhyāv, «aho bhagavato bhagavattā mah"|âdbhutā!»

16.80 papraccha ca, «prabho, ko 'yaṃ
mahā|māhātmya|mandiram
a|mānaṃ mahimānaṇ yaś
cakār' êti prabhoḥ puraḥ?»
prabhur jagāda, «Kauśāmbyāṃ
Sudharma|svāmino 'ntike
vayaṃ daś' âpi niṣkrāntā
ity|ādi prāg|gata|kramam.
śrī|Vairisiṃha|jīvas tvaṃ Śūr'|ātmā tv eṣa nirjaraḥ.
Jayaśāsana|jīvo 'haṃ tvad|bodhy|artham ih' āgamam.»
ath' ēh"|âpoh'|ādi kṛtas tasya śrī|rāja|janmanaḥ
prāg|bhava|vyañjik'|ôdbuddhā srāg jāti|smṛti|dīpikā.
a|māna|jñāna|śraddhāna|saṃveg'|āvegatas tataḥ
bhaktyā vijñāpayāmāsa guruṃ Kuru|nṛp'|ātmajaḥ:

16.85 «sambodhya mātā|pitarau rucir'|āucitya|yuktibhiḥ,
prabho, yuṣmat|pad'|âmbhoje śrayiṣye rāja|haṃsatām.»

Having sat in a lion-throne after asking leave of the holy one, and having performed thirty-two dramas before the lord with thirty-two male and female actors at each of his arms, then having put on a show, having withdrawn, having bowed and having praised the lord, and having respectfully questioned him and listened to his reply, that splendid crest of the gods quickly returned whence he had come.

And when the Prince saw this his mind was blown and he thought, "Oh, the great wonder of the glorious one's glory!"

And he asked, "Lord, who is this abode of great mag- 16.80
nanimity who has performed immeasurable majesty before your lordship?"

The reverend lord said, "In Kaushámbi, in the presence of Lord Sudhárman we ten took initiation and so on in the course of our former existences.

And you are the soul of His Highness Vajra·simha and this god is the soul of Shura. I am the soul of Jaya·shásana. I have come here to enlighten you."

Then His Highness the Prince made due consideration of what was for and against, and gained the instant illumination of memory of his former lives, produced from the manifestation of his former existence.

Then, with an intense desire for final emancipation because of his faith produced by supernatural knowledge, the son of the king of the Kurus addressed the teacher with devotion:

"Having informed my parents by appropriate and agree- 16.85
able means, I shall resort to the state of being a royal swan at the lotus of your feet, Lord."

tatr' âmātyair ath' āhūya pitarāv anvajijñapat,
ati|saṃvega|vairāgy'|âti|nirbandha|prabandhataḥ.
atha varivasita|śrī|sarva|dev'|âdhidevaḥ
pravíracita|yath"|êcch"|â|māna|dān'|âvadānaḥ
Jina|mahima|juṣo 'sya śrī|guroḥ pāda|padme
caraṇa|madhu sa|kānto 'pāt Suṣeṇa|dvi|rephaḥ.

iti śrī|nirvāṇa|Līlāvatī|mahā|kath"|êti|vṛtt'|ôddhāre Līlāvatī|sāre Jin'|âṅke Vairisiṃha|rāja|putra|jīva|śrī|Suṣeṇa|kumāra|dīkṣā|vyāvarṇano nāma ṣoḍaśa utsāhaḥ.

Then, having summoned his parents to that place by means of his minister, he informed them, with uninterrupted insistence on his disgust for existence and desire for emancipation.

Then, having worshipped His Majesty the Jina, the supreme god of all the gods, and having performed a glorious act of making immeasurable donations in accordance with his desire, at the lotus of the feet of the reverend teacher, who was devoted to the greatness of the Jina, the bee that was Sushéna, together with his beloved, drank the honey of initiation into asceticism.

Here ends the sixteenth canto, entitled "The Initiation of His Highness Prince Sushéna, the Soul of His Highness Vairi·simha," of the Jain epic *The Epitome of Queen Lilávati*, an abridgment of the events of *The Epic Story of the Auspicious Final Emancipation of Lilávati.*

CANTO 17
THE INITIATION OF HIS MAJESTY KING SIMHA AND HIS APPOINTMENT TO THE RANK OF REVEREND DOCTOR

17.1 Itaś ca Magadh'|âbhidhe
janapade sudām'|āspade 's-
ti Rājagṛha|pattanam
vasumatī|śiro|maṇḍanam
ih' āsta Jayadharma|rāṭ
krama|parākrama|svargi|rāṭ
satī subhagatāvatī
priyatam" âsya Padmāvatī.
tadīy'|ôdar'|ântare hariṇa|rāja|su|svapnato
'vatāram akarot suro Vijayasena|rāja'|rṣi|sūḥ.
praśasya|samaye 'sakau samajaniṣṭa diṣṭ"|âmbudhiḥ
sa Siṃha|nṛpa|śekharo vijayate bhavān' êva hi.
ya eṣa kathitaḥ pur" âtra Vasudeva|devaḥ sako
'rimardana|sut" âbhavan nibha|lavena Līlāvatī,
sa sādhu Dhanadevako 'jani sur'|ālayāt pracyuto
'sakau Kamalakesaras tava su|nandanaḥ samprati.
prabodha|samayo 'dhunā, nṛpa, tav' êty asau preṣitaḥ
prage paṭhitavān suras tava ca dharma|rāgo 'bhavat.
vayaṃ ca tad ih' āgatās tata idaṃ mayā mūlato
virāgam ati|kāraṇaṃ nijam udīritaṃ vistarāt.»
17.5 iti śrutavatāṃ kṣaṇān nṛpati|Siṃha|devī tanū|
ruhāṃ hṛd|udaye januḥ|smṛti|tamo|nudaḥ prodagāt.
tato 'khila|vilokanāj jagur amī «bhav'|âbdhes tvayā
vayaṃ, munipa, tāritās tad adhunā vidheyaṃ diśa.»
tadā ca sahas" āgato
gurum uvāca Śūr'|âmaraḥ
«prabodhayitum eṣa māṃ
nṛpa|sutaḥ pratiśrāvyatām,
suto 'sya bhavit" âsmy ahaṃ
yad.» atha rāja|sūr abravīd

NOW, IN THE country named Mágadha, an abode of bounty, is a capital city, Raja·griha, the crest-ornament of the kingdom. And there ruled King Jaya·dharman, a king of heaven in the courage of his proceedings. His very dear and beautiful wife was Padmávati. 17.1

Into her womb, as she had an auspicious dream of a lion, the god who was the soul of the royal monk Víjaya·sena made his descent. At an auspicious moment he was born, an ocean of good fortune. He, the crest of kings Simha, conquered like a lion as at his conception.

And he whose story was previously related, the god Vasu·deva, became in an instant Lilávati, the daughter of Ari·márdana. And the god who was the monk Dhana·deva fell from heaven and has now become your son, Padma·késara.

And, Your Majesty, that reciter in the morning was a god sent for the purpose of enlightenment now. And a passion for religion was born in you. And we arrived here, and I related this, the complete reason for my renunciation, in detail right from the start."*

When King Simha and his queen heard this, their bodily hair thrilled, and memory of their former lives, dispelling darkness, was produced in their leaping hearts. Then, after perceiving all, they said, "You have caused us to cross the ocean of existence, lord of monks, so now teach what is to be done." 17.5

And then suddenly the god Shura arrived and said to the teacher, "Make the Prince promise to enlighten me, since I shall become his son." Then the Prince said, "I, too, want to take the vow of asceticism right now, so how can this happen?"

«vrat'|êcchur adhun" âpy ahaṃ,
tata idaṃ kutaḥ sambhavi?»
jagāv atha sa nirjaraḥ, «sphurati te caritr'|āvṛttis
tad āśraya nṛpa|śriyaṃ tvad|apare tu dīkṣā|śriyam.
tataḥ sva|samaye bhavān api hi dīkṣitā Siṃhatas.»
tad etad amar'|ôditaṃ sapadi te same menire.

nṛpaḥ sapadi Padmakesaram atha sva|rājye nyadhāt
suro 'sya vidadhe 'dbhutaṃ nṛpatit"|âbhiṣek'|ôtsavam.
pit" âsya nṛpater adāt samanuśāsti|dambhān nijān
taraṅgam api vaibhavaṃ. bata, mah"|āśayāḥ sarva|dāḥ!

tataḥ paṭaha|pūrvakaṃ matam adāpayat sarvato
nṛpo vyaracayat|tarāṃ Jina|gṛheṣv ath' âṣṭ'|âhikāḥ,
nitāntam aparādhinām api hi bandi|mokṣaṃ vyadhād
a|mārim udaghoṣayat tri|bhuvan'|â|bhay'|ārambhavat.

17.10 su|candana|vilepanaiḥ kila yaśobhir āpāṇḍuro
dukūla|vasanaiś ca phenila|payo|'bdhi|līlāṃ dadhiḥ
sa|mauktika|pariṣkṛti|cchala|samakṣa|bhāsvad|guṇaḥ
prasūna|vikaca|srajā srajita eva dīkṣā|śriyā;
sureṇa saha Padmakesara|nṛpeṇa kḷpt'|ôtsavaḥ
sura|druma iva pravartita|mata|pradān'|ôddhavaḥ
dig|antara|caraj|jan'|āgamana|kāri|nāndī|ravaḥ
puro Magadha|maṇḍal'|ôcchalita|kāvya|kolāhalaḥ;

Then the god said, "Your aversion to asceticism is evident, so resort to the rank of king, those other than you will resort to the rank of asceticism. Then, at the right time for you, you too will certainly take initiation, like Simha." So then they all agreed to this statement of the god.

The King forthwith established Padma·késara in his own kingship. The god created a wonderful festival for his consecration to the kingship, and his father, in the guise of his thorough instruction, gave him billowing glory. Oh, the magnanimous are all-giving!

Then the King first announced his intention at the beat of a drum, arranged for eight-day acts of worship to be performed continually in the Jain temples, arranged an extraordinary release from prison even of criminals, and proclaimed a ban on killing animals, as making an effort to free the triple universe from fear.

Pallid with the anointments of excellent sandal unguent, 17.10
very fine indeed; giving the appearance of an ocean of foaming milk with his garments of *dukúla* fibers; garlanded with a garland of blooming flowers, and, yes, with the splendor of initiation;

with a festival prepared by King Padma·késara together with the god; like a wish-giving tree of the gods, with a holiday of giving to celebrate the undertaking of his intention; with an acclamation of joy effecting its reaching the people who proceed in the sky, preceded by a hubbub of poetic recitation springing up from the country of Mágadha;

sahasra|nara|vāhikāṃ su|śibikāṃ samadhyāsitaḥ
kṣit'|īśvara|kara|sphurac|camara|puṇḍarīk'|âdbhutaḥ;
pura|pravara|sundarī|kṣapita|lāja|puṣp'|ârcitaḥ
su|kaṇṭha|sa|dhav'|âṅganā|sa|tata|gīta|tan|maṅgalaḥ;
vrat'|ôdyad|Arimardana|
pramukha|mukhya|sāmanta|yuk
Subuddhy|Amalabuddhika|
prabhṛti|mantri|varg'|ânvitaḥ
su|sādhvy|anupama|vrat'|ā-
caraṇa|citta|Līlāvatī|
priyā|prabhṛtin" âvaro-
dhana|janena saṃsevitaḥ;
vayasya|varivasyitaḥ sa|Jinadatta|su|śrāvakaḥ
parivrajitum utsukaḥ sapadi Siṃha|bhūm'|īśvaraḥ,
purāt svar|upamān tataḥ pracalito 'tha Nandīśvare
mah"|ôtsava|cikīrṣayā sura|patir yathā vidyute.

17.15 ath' ôpavana|tīrtham ait su|guru|daivat"|âlaṅkṛtaṃ
vihāya śibikām asau sapadi pāda|cārī yayau.
pradakṣiṇayatā guruṃ saha paricchadena tridh" â-
munā vasumat"|īśinā tri|gatikā kil' âkuṇḍali.
praṇamya pada|paṅkajaṃ Samarasena|sūrer guror
vratāya samupasthitaḥ saha paricchaden' âmunā
sa Siṃha|nṛpatir yadā khalu tad" âiva moha|dviṣo
mahā|pura|vare 'bhavat satatam eva bhaṅgānakam.

seated on a fine palanquin drawn by a thousand men; distinguished with a parasol and a fly whisk wafted by the hand of the King; having worshipped with flowers and rice grains, with a previous observance of abstinence from women; the singing of his blessing diffused by women and their sweet-voiced husbands;

joined with his chief barons, Ari·márdana at their head, eager to take the vows; accompanied by his ranks of ministers, Subúddhi, Ámala·buddhi at their head; attended by the ladies of the royal women's quarters, LiláVati at their head, their minds on the undertaking of the incomparable vow of becoming Jain nuns;

waited upon by his companions; with the Jain layman Jina·datta; eager to take initiation, Simha, the lord of the universe, forthwith left the city, and in the beauty of his appearance was just like the king of the gods in the brilliant Island of Rejoicing,* intent on performing a celebration.

Then he came to the holy grove ornamented by the god- 17.15
hood of the good teacher. He immediately abandoned his palanquin and proceeded on foot. Together with his retinue, he thrice circumambulated the teacher; that lord of the world actually encircled the threefold universe.

When King Simha bowed to the lotus-feet of the reverend doctor Sámara·sena, the teacher, and with his entourage approached to take the vow, at that very moment complete was the rout of the enemy delusion in the environs of that great city.

vimucya vasan'|ādikaṃ
su|muni|veṣam eṣo 'dadhāt
sam'|âṅga|kavacaṃ kila
prabala|moha|nirjitvaram.
rajo|hṛti|mukh'|âṃśuke
sadasi|kheṭake 'nvagrahīt,
kac'|ôddhṛtim iṣāt kil' ākh-
yad, «iti śātrav'|ônmūlanam!»
namaskṛti|puraḥsaraṃ samayikasya sūtraṃ jagau
su|mantram iva moha|rāṭ|sakala|camv|avasthāpakam.
pradakṣiṇayā punaḥ Samarasena|sūrer guror
jagāda, «karaṇa|trik'|ântarayam eva me 'taḥ param.»
sa Siṃha|nṛpatir muniḥ sapadi sā ca Līlāvatī
take nṛpati|mantriṇaḥ sa|Jinadatta|su|śrāvakaḥ
maha"|rṣi|padavī|vṛtāḥ sa|sura|dānavair mānavaiḥ
pramoda|guru nemire. kim api jigyire 'ntar|dviṣaḥ?
17.20 praṇamya sa|paricchadaṃ Samarasena|sūriṃ guruṃ
jagāma puri Padmakesara|nṛ|śekharas tatra ca
pratāpa|vijit'|â|hitaḥ kim api kīrti|bhāgī|rathī|
pavitrita|jagat|trayo 'nvaśiṣad Indravat svaṃ padam.
vilāsa|sukham anvabhūt saha sad" âiva Padmaśriyā
tadīya udare 'nyadā nigaditaḥ śubhaḥ sv|alāhalaḥ.
itaḥ:sa Śūra|muni|nirjaraḥ sutatay" âvatāraṃ yayāv
asūta samaye ca taṃ kamalin" îva līlā|âmbujaṃ.

Having removed his apparel and such, he put on the garment of a Jain monk, armor for the whole body defeating the power of delusion. He then took the broom and the cloth mouth-covering, the two shields for heaven and earth. He actually pulled out his hair and said, "Thus the enemy is uprooted!"

Having first bowed, he recited the vow of self-restraint, a good spell for making firm all of heaven and earth against the king of delusion. Having once more circumambulated the reverend doctor Sámara·sena, the teacher, he declared, "Now, after this my body will have the threefold restraint."

King Simha the monk and Lilávati, the ministers of the King and the Jain layman Jina·datta, with respectful joy, bowed to the footsteps of the great ascetic, thronged by men and by blessed gods. Had they not conquered their internal enemies?

Having bowed to the reverend doctor Sámara·sena, the 17.20
teacher, King Padma·késara returned to the city, and there, whatever enemy conquered by his majesty and the triple universe purified as he rode in the chariot that was his possession of renown, he indeed governed his country like Indra, the king of the gods.

He enjoyed amorous pleasure ever with Padma·shri. One day an auspicious blessing was recited within her womb.

And then:

That god who was the monk Shura made his descent in the form of a son, and when her time was due she gave birth to him as easily as a lotus plant does a lotus.

cakāra nṛpa|Padmakesara udāra|janm'|ôtsavāt
paraṃ nija|tan'|ûdbhave sapadi Kārtavīry'|abhidhā.
kramāt sa sakalāḥ kalāḥ śubha|kalāś ca rāṭ|putrikā
mud" âṣṭa pariṇītavān yuva|nṛpa|śriyaṃ c' āptavān.
itaś ca sa mahā|munir guru|mukh'|âmbujād dvādaś'|â-
ṅgikāṃ ca catur|arṇavīm iva sukhān mud" âdhītavān.
tataś ca nije pade Samarasena|sūr'|īśvaraiḥ
śiv'|āspada|nibandhane guru|mahair avasthāpyata.
tad anu sa muni|Siṃha|sūriḥ samāntāt
skhalana|virahit'|ôdyat|sat|kram'|ôdāra'|rcayaḥ
sapadi vijaya|dev'|âpāsta|dur|darśan'|êbho
'vṛjinam iha vihāraṃ sāram uccaiś cakāra.

iti śrī|Līlāvatī|sāre Jin'|âṅke śrī|Siṃha|mahā|rāja|dīkṣā|sūripada|vyāvarṇano nāma saptadaśa utsāhaḥ.

King Padma·késara, after the munificent birth-festival for the birth of his son, forthwith named him Karta·virya. In due course he was joined to all the arts and to eight princesses possessed of auspicious signs. And he obtained the rank of crown prince.

And then that great monk with joy easily learned from the lotus of the mouth of the teacher the twelve limbs of scriptural knowledge, like four oceans. And then Sámara·sena, the lord of reverend doctors, the great teacher, established him in his own place, the foundation of the abode of bliss.

After that, the reverend doctor Simha, the monk, hymning everywhere the exalted conduct that is the effort to abandon error, an elephant against the bad view that disregards the god who provides victory, forthwith began the strenuous course of his undeviating wandering in this world.

Here ends the seventeenth canto, entitled "The Initiation of His Majesty King Simha and His Appointment to the Rank of Reverend Doctor," of the Jain epic *The Epitome of Queen Lilávati.*

CANTO 18
THE FINAL LIBERATION OF THE REVEREND DOCTOR SÁMARA·SENA AND THE GREAT MONK VÍMALA·SENA

18.1 Atha śrī|Samaraseno vihit'|âihika|sat|kṛtaḥ
śrī|Vimalasena|Surandharau Kusumaśekharaḥ
Kulamṛgāṅkaḥ Suṣeṇa iti pañca'|ṛṣibhiḥ saha
santata|kṣata|ṣaṣṭakair iti duṣ|karma varṣmavat.

tathā hi:

dvādaśa pratimā mukt"|āvalī ca, kanak'|āvalī
ratn'|âik'|āvalyau ca, guṇa|ratna|saṃvatsaraṃ tathā,
laghīyaś ca mahīyaś ca siṃha|niṣkrīḍitaṃ tathā,
mahīyaś ca laghīyas ca bhadraṃ bhadr'|ôttaraṃ tapaḥ,
18.5 ācāmāmla|vardhamānaṃ, tapaś cāndr'|āyaṇaṃ tathā,
itthaṃ tapobhiḥ su|kṛśāḥ śive mātuṃ nu te 'bhavan.

jñātv" âtha Samarasena|sur'|îndraḥ śeṣam āyuṣaḥ
Sammeta|śaila|śikhare mahā|śuddha|śilā|tale,
saṃstārakaṃ samāruhy' ân|aśanaṃ pratipadya ca,
padm'|āsana|sthaḥ pūrv'|âbhimukho maulī|kṛt'|âñjaliḥ,
garīyastara|saṃvega|taraṅg'|ôttuṅga|mānasaḥ
madhura|dhvanin" ārebhe vaktum ārādhanām iti:
«namo 'rhate bhagavate jñāna|darśana|śāline,
nṛ|sur'|âsura|pūjyāya jyāyase jagatām api,

THEN VENERABLE Sámara·sena, benevolent for the good of the world, with the five sages, venerable Vímala·sena, Suran·dhara, Kúsuma·shékhara, Kula·mrigánka and Sushéna, wearing away bad karma, like their bodies, with sixty continuous ascetic practices. 18.1

Just like these:

The twelve-stage ladder of ascetic practice, the necklace of pearls fast, the necklace of gold fast, and also, the jewel necklace and the single necklace fasts, and the yearlong fast of the jewel of excellence,

also , the lesser and greater lion austerities, and the greater and lesser excellent superior auspicious austerities,

18.5
also the increasing rice-water fast, and the moon's course fast. Thus, well worn away by austerities, they indeed began to measure up to final emancipation.

Then Sámara·sena, knowing how much of his life was left, on the peak of Mount Samméta, on a well-purified stone slab,

took his seat, stopped eating and drinking, and, seated in the lotus position, his hands folded in adoration at his head,

his mind swollen with waves of very profound desire for emancipation, in a very sweet voice began to recite this hymn:

"Reverence to the Worthy, the blessed, possessed of the highest omniscience, to be worshipped by men, gods and demigods, most excellent in the whole universe,

18.10 Yādav'|ânvaya|sūryāya samprāpt'|âkṣaya|sampade
pravādyat|kīrti|tūryāya sarvato 'pi nirāpade,
saṃsār'|ârṇava|nirmagna|jantu|santāna|tāriṇe
karma|vallī|vitān'|âika|nemaye 'riṣṭanemaye.

Arhatāṃ sarva|siddhānāṃ manaḥ|paryava|śālinām
avadhi|jñāninām sarva|śruta|kevalinām api
purataḥ parama|prīty" âti|cāra|malam ātmanaḥ
prakṣālayāmi parito nindā|garh"|ādi|vāribhiḥ.

tathā hi:

a|kāl'|ādiḥ śruta|jñāne darśane śaṅkit'|ādikaḥ
cāritre tv a|samity|ādis tapasy a|karaṇ'|ādikaḥ
18.15 vīrye tu nigūhan'|ādir yo 'ticār'|āmayo mama
saṃjātas, taṃ cikitsāmi nindā|garh"|ādi|bhaiṣajaiḥ.

yac ca sūtr'|ârtha|pauruṣyoḥ pratilekhan'|ādiṣu
kaṣāy'|êndriya|yogeṣu duś|cakre, śodhayāmi tat.

mahā|vratāni pañc' âpy ādade teṣāṃ puraḥ punaḥ,
aṣṭādaś' âgha|sthānāni kṣālayāmi muhur muhuḥ.

sun for the descendants of Yadu, the one who has attained 18.10
the fulfillment of asceticism, whose resounding glory is proclaimed by fanfare, the cause of success even everywhere,

who enables the human race to cross the overwhelming ocean of existence, the unique thunderbolt against the spreading creeper of karma, Aríshta·nemi.

With supreme affection, in the presence of the Worthy, who accomplished all objects, who is possessed of the ability to know the thoughts of others, who is possessed of the ability to perceive what is beyond the normal range of the senses, who is omniscient of all learning also, I shall wash away the stain of transgression from my self, all over, with the waters of blame and reproach.

Just like this:

I shall cure this disease that developed in me, of not 18.15
finding the right time and such for scriptural knowledge, of distrust and such of religion, of incongruity and such with asceticism, of the non-accomplishment and such of austerities, of hiding away and from manly activity, with the drugs of blame and reproach and such.

And that of manliness and the meaning of the aphorisms on reality which has been spoiled in daily cleaning and such, in the application of the passions and the senses, I shall purify.

Although I have taken the five great vows, I shall continually purify the abodes of the eighteen types of sin I committed before them.

kṣamayāmi sarvān jīvān. kṣāmyantu mayi te same,
teṣāṃ kṣāmyāmy aham api. maitrī sarveṣu me 'dhunā.
āhāram upadhiṃ sarvaṃ vapuś ca carama|kṣaṇe
samakṣam Arhad|ādīnāṃ vyutsṛjāmi.» tridhā tridhā.

18.20 parameṣṭhi|namaskāra|pratyāhāra|vidhānataḥ
dhyāyann antar|muhūrtaṃ sa pādap'|ôpagamaṃ vyadhāt.

vidadhad iti ca pañc'|ācārik'|ārādhanāṃ sa
prati|samayam udīt'|ôttuṇga|saṃvega|vegaḥ
kṣapaka|muni|padavyā prasthito ghāti|ghātān
nirupamitim avāpat kevala|jñāna|lakṣmīm.

tad anu tad anuyātaḥ pātayitvā kṣaṇ'|ântar
dur|abhibhava|lav'|ôpagrāhi|karm'|âri|vāram
samam a|sama|munīnāṃ pañca|śatyā vyalāsīt
su|guru|Samarasenaḥ śrī|mahā|nanda|puryām.

evaṃ Vimalaseno 'pi buddhv" āyuḥ|śeṣam ātmanaḥ
gurūn anujñāpya sārdhaṃ gīt"|ârthaiḥ praticāribhiḥ,
śrī|Sammeta|gireḥ śṛṅge su|puṣkala|śilā|tale
padm'|āsany" âivam ūce 'tha mauli|kuḍmalit'|âñjaliḥ:

I have forgiveness for all beings. May they have forgiveness for me likewise. I, too, ask forgiveness of them. I have friendship for all now.

I abandon food, all sustenance and my body to its final destruction in the presence of the Worthy and the others." He said this nine times over.

Having prayed to the supreme beings and withdrawn his 18.20
mind from sense objects according to precept, he meditated for forty minutes and undertook the fast until death.

Since he had performed the propitiation of the five vows of ascetic conduct, according to stipulation, as the current of his desire for final emancipation swelled loftily, having set out along the path of an abstinent monk, through doing violence to violence, he attained the incomparable fortune of omniscience.

After that, undertaking that practice, he caused to fall away within a moment the obstruction of the enemy karma, who had met with the destruction of his evil power. Together with five hundred unparalleled monks, the good teacher Sámara·sena shone forth in the lovely citadel of the eternal bliss of final emancipation.

Thus Vímala·sena, too, knowing how much of his life was left, took leave from the teacher, and with his followers, whose purpose was to sing hymns,

on the peak of Mount Samméta, on a well-purified stone slab, took his seat in the lotus position with his hands folded in adoration like buds on his head, and then spoke thus:

18.25 «namo bhagavate Nemi|svāmine śiva|gāmine
bhūr|bhuvaḥ|svas|trayī|pūjya|pādāya param'|ātmane.

tathā:

namo 'rhadbhyo 'sta|rāgebhyaḥ
samyag|vāgbhyaś ca kevalāt
Arhat|siddh'|ādi|bhedebhyaḥ
siddhebhyaś ca namo namaḥ.

gaṇa|bhṛt|pramukhebhyaś c' āryebhyas tān namo namaḥ
up'|āryebhyaḥ sarv'|âṅg'|âdhyāpakebhyo namo namaḥ.

mahā|vrat'|âdr'|îndra|bhṛdbhyaḥ
sādhubhyo 'pi namo namaḥ
manasā vapuṣā vācā
vande 'smi parameṣṭhinaḥ.

teṣāṃ ca purataḥ sarvān ati|cārān viśodhaye,
yad ete dharma|prāsāda|sūtra|dhāra|sahodarāḥ.

18.30 yan may" ân|ādau saṃsāre mithyātv'|āvṛta|buddhinā
an|āryam upadiṣṭaṃ, tad garhe nindāmi sarvataḥ.

‹n' âsti jīvo n' âsti dharmaḥ sarva|jño n' âsti kaś cana›
nāstikena may" ōce yad, garhe nindāmi tat tridhā.

yat strī|śastr'|âkṣa|sūtr'|ādi|rāg'|ādy|âṅka|kalaṅkitāḥ
devatvena may" āucyanta, garhe nindāmi tat tridhā.

pāpa|śrutaṃ yac ca may" âdhītam adhyāpitaṃ tathā,
pratikrāmāmi tat sarvaṃ sarvath" âpi hi samprati.

"Reverence to blessed Lord Nemi, who has attained eternal bliss, whose feet are to be revered by the threefold earth, sky and heaven, whose soul is supreme. 18.25

Likewise:

Reverence also to the Worthies, their passions cast aside, who speak truly because of their omniscience, and reverence, reverence, to the perfected ones of different kinds to the perfection and such of the Worthies.

Therefore, reverence, reverence, to the leaders of the troop, foremost in honor. Reverence, reverence, to those following in honor, the teachers of all the limbs of scripture.

Reverence, reverence, too, to the monks, bearers of the Himálaya mountains of the five vows. In mind, body and speech I give reverence to the supreme beings.

And in their presence, since they are akin to the architect of the temple of religion, I purify myself of all transgressions.

What inferior teaching I taught, not knowing the course 18.30
of wrongfulness in the ever-existent cycle of existence, that I blame and I reproach entirely.

What I said as a materialist, 'There is no soul, there is no religion, there is no omniscient one at all,' that I blame and I reproach three times over.

What I said as a god about those who are defiled by such sins as passion for women, weapons, and gambling, that I blame and I reproach three times over.

What evil I heard, and learned and taught in the same way, I take it all back in its absolute entirety, right now.

iṣṭ'|āpūrt'|ādi pāpaṃ yat kv' âpi dharmatayā mayā
upadiṣṭam anujñātaṃ, garhe nindāmi tat tridhā.

18.35 samyaktvaṃ mahā|vratāni gṛhītāny api sad|guroḥ,
punaḥ siddh'|ādi|pratyakṣaṃ gṛhṇāmy eṣa viśuddhaye.

Arhat|siddh'|ācārya|caitya|saṅgha|śruta|sa|dharmasu
y" āśātanā kṛtā kā cit, tāṃ nindāmi muhur muhuḥ.

chadma|stho mūḍha|cetās tu kiyan|mātraṃ smared iha?
yan na smarāmi, tatr' âpi mithyā|duṣ|kṛtam astu me.

kṣamayāmi sarvān jīvāṃs trasa|sthāvara|bhedinaḥ.
pāpa|prakṣālanād evaṃ śuddho 'haṃ sarvath" âdhunā.

muñce caturvidh"|āhāraṃ dharm'|ôpakaranaṃ tathā.
vapuś ca prāntya|samaye parakīyam iv' âdhunā.»

18.40 ity evaṃ parameṣṭhi|pañcaka|namas|
kṛd dhyāna|dhārā|jala|
prakṣāla|pragalan|malaḥ su|vidhinā
garhā|kṛta|śrāvaṇaḥ
lātvā śrī|Jina|pāla|vidhy an|aśanaṃ
divyaṃ su|śuddhiṃ gataḥ
prāpa śrī|Vimalādisena|ṛṣi|rāṭ
sat|kevalām nirvṛtim.

What evil I desired and fulfilled, et cetera, anywhere, and as a judge ordered and authorized, that I blame and I reproach three times over.

Although I received true insight and the great vows from 18.35
the teacher of truth, I here take them again for the purpose of complete purification.

And whatever aspersion was made among the followers of the religion taught by the holy congregation, the teachers, the perfected ones and the Worthies, I reproach it continually.

Now a deluded mind, situated in darkness, is mindful of things of small account in this world. What sins I have committed but don't remember while in that state, too, let them have been committed vainly.

I have forgiveness for all beings, of both mobile and stationary categories. Through purification from sin, I am now pure in every respect.

I abandon the four types of food, and likewise my implements of religion, and now, at the final moment, my body as if it belonged to another."

Thus, having given reverence to the five supreme beings, 18.40
his impurity falling away through the purification of the waters of the streams of his meditation, very much according to precept, hearing nothing but his reproaches, having obtained the divine knowledge of the holy Lord Jina, having reached the state of absolute purity, reverend Vímala·sena, the king of sages, attained the only true liberation.

iti śrī|nirvāṇa|Līlāvatī|sāre Jin'|âṅke śrī|Samarasena|sūri|Vimalasena|maha"|rṣi|nirvāṇa|vyāvarṇano nāma aṣṭādaśa utsāhaḥ.

Here ends the eighteenth canto, entitled "The Final Liberation of the Reverend Doctor Sámara·sena and the Great Monk Vímala·sena," of the Jain epic *The Epitome of Queen Lilávati.*

CANTO 19
THE FINAL LIBERATION OF THE GREAT MONKS KÚSUMA·SHÉKHARA AND VÍMALA·SENA

19.1 Tathā Surandhara|munir jñātvā paryantam āyuṣaḥ
namaskṛtya caitya|sādhūn kṣamayitv" âkhilaṃ gaṇam,
vitīrṇ'|ālocanaḥ kḷpt'|ânaśano gīta|sādhu|yuk
Sammete padm'|āsana|sthaḥ su|viśālā|śilā|tale,
pūrva|puruṣa|dik|prāptyai pūrv'|āś"|âbhimukhaḥ kila
mūrdhany asta|hasta|kośo 'pāṭhīd ārādhanām iti:
«namo mithyātva|timira|vidhvaṃs'|âika|vivasvate
krodh'|ôṣar|budha|meghāya mān'|âmbhoda|nabhasvate,
19.5 māyā|vallī|paraśave lobh'|âmbhodhi|ghaṭ'|ôdbhave
Ariṣṭanemine bhaktyā dvāviṃśāya Jin'|ēśine.
api ca:
sur'|âsura|nara|svāmi|kṛtām arhanti ye 'rhaṇām
bhūr|bhuvaḥ|svas|tray'|īśānās te 'rhanto maṅgalaṃ mama.
trailokya|jayino rāga|dveṣa|moha|mah"|ârayaḥ
yair hatās, te 'ri|hantāro bhavantu mama maṅgalam.
dhyān'|âgninā bhava|bīja|mithyātv'|ādi|pradāhataḥ
ye na rohanti saṃsāre, te rohantaś ca maṅgalam.
kṣīṇ'|âṣṭa|karm'|ârayo ye bhuñjate śiva|sampadam,
kṛta|kṛtyā bhagavantaḥ siddhās te mama maṅgalam.

LIKEWISE THE monk Suran·dhara, knowing how much of his life remained, having paid his respects to the holy monks and asked forgiveness of the entire troop, 19.1

having made due consideration, began to fast, and accompanied by singing monks, on Mount Samméta, seated in the lotus position on a very capacious stone slab,

facing the east, of course, to attain the region of the men who had gone before, the bud of his hands set on his head, began to recite this hymn of praise:

"Reverence to the unique light for shattering the gloom of wrongfulness, the cloud for the fire of anger, the sun for the ocean of pride,

the axe for the creeper of delusion, the jar-born ocean swallower for the ocean of greed; reverence with devotion to Aríshta·nemi, the twenty-second reigning Jina. 19.5

And also:

Those Worthies who deserve the name of lord of gods, demigods and men, who are the lords of the threefold earth, sky and heaven, increase my blessing.

Victorious over the threefold universe, they by whom the powerful enemies of passion, hatred and delusion are destroyed, may they, the destroyers of my enemies, be my blessing.

They who destroy wrongfulness and such, the seed of existence, by the fire of meditation, they do not arise in existence, attaining blessing.

They whose enemies of the eight kinds of karma are destroyed, whose purpose is attained, who enjoy the abode of bliss, the blessed perfected ones, they are my blessing.

19.10 mati|śrut'|âvadhi|manaḥ|paryava|keval'|âbdhayaḥ chinna
pratyeka|buddh'|ādayaś ca sādhavo mama maṅgalam.

kṣānty|ādi|darśa|dhā dharmaḥ śuddhaḥ sarva|jña|bhāṣitaḥ
bhav'|âmbudhau nirapāyaḥ potaś ca mama maṅgalam.

nārak'|âmara|tiryaṅ|nṛ|samudaye 'tra niścitam
Arhanta uttamā ete bhū|dhareṣu Sumeruvat.

vyavahāryās tad|anyebhyaḥ sūkṣmakebhyas tu bādarāḥ
paryāptās tv a|paryāptebhyo nigodebhyaḥ parīttakāḥ;

nārakebhyaś ca tiryañcas tebhyo martyās tataḥ surāḥ
devebhyo dev'|âdhidevā Arhanto dhruvam uttamāḥ.

19.15 yeṣāṃ garbhe janane ca vrate kevala|mokṣayoḥ
trailokyaṃ kṣubhyati yathā pramoda|bhara|meduram,

tathā Hari|Har'|ādīnāṃ kasy' âpy anyatarasya na
Arhanto bhagavanto 'mī tato 'pi jagad|uttamāḥ.

And the oceans of omniscience, knowledge of the thoughts of others, knowledge of what lies beyond the normal range of the senses, scriptural knowledge and devotion, the monks, the self-enlightened ones and the others, are my blessing. 19.10

And the pure religion, which provides the teaching of forbearance, et cetera, which is proclaimed by the omniscient ones, an imperishable boat in the ocean of existence, is my blessing.

Among this aggregate of hell-beings, gods, animals and humans, certainly the Worthies are supreme, like auspicious Mount Meru among the mountains.

Just as due processes are superior to those which are other than them; just as cotton garments are superior to flimsy garments; just as capacious spaces are superior to uncapacious k spaces; just as circumscribed areas are superior to minute organisms;

as animals are superior to hell-beings, and human beings are superior to them, and gods to them; and as the kings of gods are superior to gods, the Worthies are constantly supreme.

And as the threefold universe totters, cloyed with the weight of its joy at the birth of their offspring, the twin vows of omniscience and liberation, 19.15

but not so for the offspring of Vishnu or Shiva or anyone else whatsoever, thus these blessed Worthies are supreme over the universe.

trailokya|mūrdhni koṭīrāḥ śāśvatāḥ śarma|bhājanam
kṛta|kṛtyā bhagavantaḥ siddhās tad bhuvan'|ôttamāḥ.

sur'|âsura|narāḥ sarve Smara|vīrasya kiṅ|karāḥ
taj|jetāraḥ sādhavo 'mī bhavanti jagad|uttamāḥ.

sarva|jña|bhāṣito marty'|âmartya|pūjyaś ca śāśvataḥ
tri|koṭī|doṣa|muktaś ca dharmo lok'|ôttamaḥ sphuṭam.

19.20 dur|vāra|duḥkha|sambhār'|āgārā|saṃsāra|cārataḥ
yair mocyate jagat sarvaṃ, te 'rhantaḥ śaraṇaṃ mama.

yeṣāṃ nām'|ôtkīrtanena bhakti|rāgān namas|kṛteḥ
siddh'|āspadaṃ prāpyate, te siddhāś ca śaraṇaṃ mama.

sahāyā a|sahāyānāṃ ye dharme śiva|vartmani,
ratna|trayī|bhūṣitās te sādhavaḥ śaraṇaṃ mama.

yaj jagad|bāndhavair diṣṭaṃ sarva|jñaiḥ sarva|darśibhiḥ,
nity'|ārogyāya tat kurve śaraṇaṃ dharma|bhaiṣajam.

sarvān jīvān kṣamayāmi, teṣu kṣāmyāmi sarvataḥ.
dade, ‹mithyā duṣ|kṛtaṃ› ca, tyajāmi malavad vapuḥ.»

19.25 catuḥ|śaraṇikām imāṃ dṛḍhatamāṃ catuṣ|potikām
niruddha|nikhil'|āsravāṃ sita|paṭ'|âñcitāṃ saṃśritaḥ
vyatīta|bhava|vāridhiḥ parama|vitti|śṛṅgāritaḥ
Surandhara|muniḥ śiv'|āspada|rasāṃ samāśiśriyat.

Diadems at the head of the universe, perpetually partaking of bliss, having attained their purpose, the blessed ones are perfected; thus they are supreme over the universe.

Gods, demigods and men are all servants of the power of Love. These monks, triumphant over him, are supreme over the universe.

And the Jain religion, proclaimed by the omniscient ones, reverenced by humans and gods, eternal, having freed thirty million from fault, is supreme in the world, manifestly.

The Worthies, by whom the whole universe is freed from 19.20
the course of cycle of existence, the abode of irresistible sorrow, are my refuge.

And the perfected ones, by the praising of whose names with respectful salutation and affectionate devotion the abode of final emancipation is obtained, are my refuge.

The monks who are the companions of those who lack companions on the road to final emancipation, the Jain religion, who are ornamented by the three jewels of the Jain religion, are my refuge.

That religion which is taught by the omniscient, all-seeing kinsmen of the universe for the purpose of eternal health, that medicine of religion I make my refuge.

I have pardon for all beings, and I seek pardon for everything among them. I recite, 'May my sins be in vain,' and I abandon my body as if abandoning filth."

Having resorted to this fourfold refuge, the most stable 19.25
foursquare boat, its influx of karma completely obstructed, distinguished by the white garment, Suran·dhara the monk, having crossed the ocean of existence, adorned by supreme

atha prānty|ārādhanāyā jñātv" âvasaram ātma|vit
prāg|ukta|yuktyā Sammeta|girau śuddha|śilā|tale
prāṅ|mukhaḥ padm'|āsana|stho muniḥ Kusumaśekharaḥ
paryant'|ārādhanām evaṃ madhura|dhvavin" âpaṭhat:

«namo dev'|âdhidevāya bhuvana|traya|bandhave
nistīrṇ'|âvastīrṇatam'|â|pāra|saṃsāra|sindhave.

jagat|tritaya|dīpāya niṣpratīpāya tāyine
Ariṣṭanemaye nityaṃ nitya|nirvṛti|dāyine.

19.30 prāṇ'|âtipātam akhilaṃ mṛṣā|vādam a|dattakam
mithunaṃ parigrahaṃ ca sarvato rātri|bojanam
guroḥ puraḥ pratikhyātaṃ varam apy adhunā punaḥ
pratyākhyāmi prabhor agre prasadya prekṣatāṃ prabhuḥ.

aśanaṃ pānakaṃ svādyaṃ svādimaṃ sarvam eva hi
yāvaj|jīvaṃ vividhen' āpathyadaṃ vyutsṛjāmy aham.

yad ap' îdaṃ vapuḥ pūrvaṃ śīt'|āder yan na rakṣitam
sarvathā tad ap' îdānīṃ vyutsṛjāmy asmi pāṃśuvat.

tath" ânādau bhave nānā|vimāna|bhavan'|ādiṣu
yan mamatvaṃ mayā cakre, tat tyajāmi ku|mitravat.

19.35 yac ca kiñ cin me mamatvaṃ mānavīṣv amarīṣu ca
tiraścīṣu ca, tat sarve vyutsṛjāmi palālavat.

omniscience, attained the dry land that is the abode of final liberation.

Then, knowing by his devotion to his final end that the time was right, the monk Kúsuma·shékhara, who knew the nature of the soul, in accordance with his former utterance, on Mount Samméta, on a purified stone slab, facing the east, seated in the lotus position, began to recite in a sweet voice this hymn of praise extending in all directions:

"Reverence to the god of gods, the kinsman of the triple universe, who has traversed the immense boundless ocean of existence,

The light for the threefold universe, the one without a contrary, the protector, Arísht̤a·nemi, ever granting final liberation.

And the vow of renouncing all harm to life, speaking falsely, taking what is not given, copulation, and any eating at night, which I took in the presence of the teacher, I now take again in the presence of the lord. May the lord graciously observe. 19.30

I renounce food, drink, savories, sweets, absolutely all. For the rest of my life I abandon nourishment of all kinds.

And this body, too, which previously was not protected from cold and such, I now abandon entirely, like dung.

Likewise, that self-pride I experienced in the ever-existent cycle of existence, in my various mansions, palaces, et cetera, I abandon like a bad friend.

And whatever self-pride I had in my women, goddesses and female animals, I abandon it all like straw. 19.35

yan me mamatvaṃ putreṣu pavitreṣu guṇa|śriyā,
tad idānīṃ vyutsṛjāmi sva|jāmi|prabhṛtiṣv api.
yan mamatvaṃ parīvāre priya|mitreṣu bandhuṣu
sarva|kālīnam adhunā dhunāmi pada|dhūlivat.
catur|aṅgeṣu sainyeṣu bhāṇḍ'|āgāre pure jane
mayā mamatvaṃ yac cakre, tac cakre thūt|kṛtaṃ yathā.»
sa ity ārādhanam uktvā niṣaṇṇas tṛṇa|saṃstare
ārukṣat kṣapaka|śreṇīṃ niḥśreṇīṃ śiva|sadmani.

19.40 amuṃ Kusumaśekharaṃ śubha|samādhi|sūra|prabh"|â-
prahastita|moha|ripuṃ sapadi kevala|śrīḥ svayam
svayaṃvara|vara|srajā varayati sma tad|bhājinaṃ
tam āśu śiva|sundarī samam upāyata premataḥ.

iti śrī|nirvāṇa|Līlāvatī|sāre Jin'|âṅke Surandhara|Kusumaśekhara|mahā|muni|nirvāṇa|vyāvarṇano nāma ekonaviṃśatitama utsāhaḥ.

That self-pride I had in my sons, pure, with the radiance of excellence, and in my sisters, et cetera, I now abandon.

That self-pride I had in my retinue, dear friends, and kinsmen, for all time I now free myself from like dust from my feet.

That self-pride I had in my armies of four divisions, my troops, my treasury, city and country, I have likewise spat out."

Having recited this hymn of praise, he sat on his bed of grass and undertook a successive fast, the ladder to the abode of final liberation.

The Fortune of omniscience of her own accord forthwith 19.40
chose as her husband, by throwing a garland around his neck, Kúsuma·shékhara, whose enemy of delusion had been repelled by the light of the sun that was his meditation on auspicious matters. As he was partaking of her, the wife that is final liberation immediately also came forward to meet him, full of affection.

Here ends the nineteenth canto, entitled "The Final Liberation of the Great Monks Kúsuma·shékhara and Vímala·sena," of the Jain epic *The Epitome of Queen Liláváti.*

CANTO 20
THE FINAL LIBERATION OF THE GREAT MONKS REVEREND KULA·MRIGÁNKA AND REVEREND SUSHÉNA

20.1 Atha Śrī|Kulamṛgāṅkaḥ śaśāṅka iva pārvaṇaḥ
jñātv" âsta|kālaṃ Sammet'|âsta|giriṃ samaśiśriyat.
śilā|paṭṭe dṛḍha|padm'|āsana|sthāyī puro|mukhaḥ
mauli|stha|kara|mukulo vaktum evaṃ pracakrame:
«Ariṣṭaneme, bhagavan, bhuvan'|âika|vibhūṣaṇa,
ādi|kartar, loka|nāth', ālok'|ôttama, tamo|'paha,
tubhyam abhyantar'|ôllāsi|bhaktito 'stu namo namaḥ
śṛṇu prasadya, bhagavan, bruve kiñ cin mano|gataṃ.
20.5 tav' âiva purato, nāth', âdhunā nindāmi duṣ|kṛtam
āsravān sakalān eva pidadhāmi ca sarvataḥ.
prāṇa|prahāṇaṃ, re jīva, tvayā prāṣṭaṃ muhur muhuḥ
tat paricitasya prāptau kṣobhitavyaṃ tvayā na hi.
narake mārgitam api na tvay" êdaṃ parāpyata.
sampraty a|mārgite tatra labdhe harṣo vidhīyatām.
garbha|stho 'tha jāyamāno bālo 'tha taruṇo jaran
muhur bhṛto 'si tat sampraty artiṃ m" âiva vṛthā kṛthāḥ.
cakr'|ēśvara|śrī|dhar'|ādyā ye c' âtr' âpara|pauruṣāḥ
śāśvatās te 'pi n' âbhūvaṃs tat kiṃ tvam iha khidyase?
20.10 ye vajra|kāyā dev'|êndra|prātihārya|sa|paryitāḥ
ye 'py Arhantaḥ sthirā n' âtra tat k" ârtis te vyay'|āgame?

THEN REVEREND Kula·mrigánka, like the full moon, knowing that his time was waning, resorted to Mount Samméta. 20.1

Sitting fixed in the lotus position on a stone slab, facing the east, the buds of his hands placed on his head, he began to recite this hymn of praise:

"Aríshta·nemi, reverend lord, unique ornament for the universe, prime mover, lord of the world, supreme in the world, remover of darkness,

may reverence with devotion flashing up from the interior be yours; reverence. Please listen, reverend lord, while I state my intention.

In your actual presence, Lord, I reproach all my wrong- 20.5
doings, and I prevent all influx of karma entirely.

Hey, soul, you have arrived at the end of your life, time and again, so don't falter now at the hope of gaining one similar.

You will not gain your desire in hell again. Let joy be spread at this present attainment of non-desire.

Situated in the womb, the being born, a child, then a youth and an old man, you are continually borne away, so don't make this present suffering in vain.

The emperors, possessors of fortune, and other such men in this world do not live forever, so why are you depressed about this?

Even the Worthies, their bodies of adamant, and attended 20.10
on by the king of the gods, cannot perdure here, so why should you become depressed when decay ensues?

Indr'|âham, indrāḥ sarve 'pi cyavante sv'|āyuṣaḥ kṣaye.
tad, ātmann, ātman" ātmānaṃ dhairya|varmitam ātanu.

tathā rādhnuhi paryantaḥ samayaṃ samyag ātmanaḥ
paṇḍita|mṛtyunā mṛtyuñ|jayaḥ syā a|bhavo 'pi yat.»

itthaṃ Kulamṛgāṅkasy' ārādhanāṃ paṭhato 'pi hi
ārūḍhasya samādhi|droḥ kṣapaka|śreṇi|vīrudham,
kevala|jñāna|stabaka|saurabhaṃ jighrataḥ kṣaṇāt
mah"|ôdaya|phalaṃ hasta|kuśeśayam upāgamat.

20.15 «prabho, jagad idaṃ gilaty alam a|nityatā|rākṣasī
tad etad|an|upadrute naya pade kva cin mām» iti
su|vijñapanato 'munā su|muninā dhruvaṃ Neminā
prahitya paramāṃ vidaṃ dhruva|pade 'yam āvāsyata.

evaṃ kiyatsv apy ahassu Suṣeṇo 'pi mahā|muniḥ
paryālocy' āyuḥ|paryantaṃ Sammet'|âdrau śilā|tale,
tṛṇa|saṃstāram āstīry' ôttam'|âṅga|kara|kuḍmalaḥ
paryant'|ārādhanām uccārayāmāsa mṛdu|dhvaniḥ:

«śrī|Yādava|kul'|âmbhodhi|śarat|parva|sudh"|âṃśave
ā|janma|sīma|mathita|dur|vāra|viṣam'|êṣave;
karpūra|pūra|surabhi|kīrti|vyāpt'|âbdhi|nemaye
namasyāya tri|jagatām, oṃ namo 'riṣṭanemaye.

All the kings of the gods who can state 'I am Indra!' also fall from heaven at the decay of their lives, so, soul, gird yourself in the armor of self-fortitude.

So at all points apply proper restraint to yourself. The conquerers of death arise by means of a wise death. In this way you, too, may become liberated from existence."

Thus Kula·mrigánka, while actually reciting this hymn of praise, a tree of meditation, put forth the shoot of uninterrupted abstinence, and instantly gained the fragrance from the blossom of omniscience, and the lotus for the hand that is the fruit of great success approached him.

"Lord, the demoness of impermanence is like one swal- 20.15
lowing this universe, so lead me to some place that is unassailed by her." Through the constant fitting requests of that good monk, Nemi, having sent supreme knowledge, established him in the constant place of final liberation.

And thus within some days Sushéna also, the great monk, knowing how much of his life was left, on a stone slab on Mount Samméta,

having strewn a bed of grass, the buds of his hands placed on his head, in a sweet voice began to utter an extensive hymn of praise:

"To the nectar-rayed autumn moon for the ocean of the honorable family of Yádavas; to the one whose five senses, dangerous and difficult to subdue, have been ground down by his morality from birth;

to the one surrounded by an ocean filled with the fragrance of rivers of camphor that is his fame; to the one reverenced by the triple universe, om, reverence to Aríshta·nemi.

20.20 tat|puraḥ prāṇ'|âtipātaṃ mṛṣā|vādam a|dattakam
a|brahma|parigrahaṃ ca sampāraya|catuṣṭayam,
bandhane kalah'|âbhyākhyānake māyā mṛṣā tathā,
paiśuny'|ânya|parivāda|mithyātv'|âriti|raty atha,
ity aṣṭādaśa|pāpānāṃ sthānakāny akhilāny api
moha|rāṭ|sthānakān' îva nāśayāmi samantataḥ.

catur|vidhaṃ tath" āhāraṃ pratyākhyāmi tridhā tridhā,
sarv'|âbhīṣṭam api vapus tyajāmi tṛṇa|khaṇḍavat.

kiñ ca:

eka|dvi|tri|catuṣ|pañc'|êndriyā jīvā bhav'|âṭavau
a|trāṇā a|śaraṇāś ca nihanyante parasparam.

tathā:

20.25 pitā mātā sutā bhrātā bandhu|mitra|nṛp'|ādayaḥ
śaraṇaṃ na bhavanty atra svayaṃ hy a|śaraṇā amī.

tad a|sāre 'tra saṃsāre sarva|jñ'|ôpajña āgamaḥ
kṣānty|ādir daśadhā dharmaḥ śaraṇaṃ n' âparaḥ punaḥ.

tac ca, jīv', âdhunā labdhaṃ su|dur|labdham api tvayā.
tataḥ paryavasāne 'pi kā cintā tava sāmpratam?»

ity evaṃ bhāvayann eva śrī|Suṣeṇa|mahā|muniḥ
śukla|dhyāna|Ratna|sānum āruroh' âti|raṃhasā.

In his presence, harm to life, false speech, taking what is not given, unchastity, possessiveness and fourfold passion, also illusion about injuring, strife and calumny, and backbiting and complaining about other, falsehood, intemperance and lust—all divisions on the eighteen sins I now destroy on all sides, like the divisions of the king of delusion. 20.20

So I renounce the four kinds of food, nine times over, and I abandon my body and all its desires like a piece of grass.

And besides:

Beings with one, two, three, four and fives senses, lacking protection and refuge in the wilderness of existence, are destroyed by each other.

So:

Father, mother, sons, brother, relatives and friends, the king, et cetera, are no refuge in this existence, since they themselves lack refuge. 20.25

Therefore, in this worthless cycle of existence, the teachings, the tenfold conduct of forbearance and the others, and the religion, taught by the omniscient one are the refuge; there is no other besides.

So, soul, since you have now gained what is extremely difficult to gain, why do you have concern about also coming to an end right now?"

While actually thinking thus, the great monk reverend Sushéna with great eagerness began to ascend the Mount Meru of meditation on brilliant matters.

ardh'|âdhirūḍhe tatr' âiṣa parāpat kevala|śriyam
sarv'|âdhirūḍhe tv a|dvaita|mudaṃ kaivalya|sampadam.

20.30 «saṃsāra|cāraka|gṛhe '|śaraṇas tamo|'ndho
duḥkh'|āturo 'smi tad adh'|īśvara mām av'» êti
etad|gir" êva vimal'|â|vṛjina|prabodha|
dhamnā sva|pārśvam anayat prabhur Nemir etam.

iti śrī|nirvāṇa|Līlāvatī|sāre Jin'|âṅke śrī|Kulamṛgāṅka|śrī|Suṣeṇa|mahā|muni|nirvāṇa|vyāvarṇano nāma viṃśa utsāhaḥ.

When he had climbed it halfway, he attained the splendor of omniscience, but when he climbed to the top he attained the unique joy of the accomplishment of final liberation.

"I am in the prison of existence, lacking refuge, blinded by 20.30
darkness, sick with sorrow. So, supreme lord, accept me with favor." As if by means of this invocation, fraught with the power of pure and true enlightenment, Lord Nemi brought Sushéna to his own side.

Here ends the twentieth canto, entitled "The Final Liberation of the Great Monks Reverend Kula·mrigánka and Reverend Sushéna," of the Jain epic *The Epitome of Queen Lilávati.*

CANTO 21
THE OMNISCIENCE AND FINAL LIBERATION OF THE TRUE TEACHERS, THE VENERABLE REVEREND DOCTOR SIMHA, THE VENERABLE ROYAL MONK PADMA·KÉSARA, LILÁVATI, SURA·SÚNDARI, RÁMANAMATI AND THE VENERABLE KARTA·VIRYA

21.1 ŚRĪ|SIṂHA|SŪRI|NṚPATIḤ paratīrthak'|ājñām
utthāpayan prati|padaṃ draḍhayan Jin'|ājñām
grām'|ākar'|ādiṣu vihṛtya|tarāṃ paredyuḥ
śrī|Rāji|rāja|gṛha|kānanam ājagāma.

sadyaḥ Priyaṃvada iti prathit'|âbhidhāna
udyāna|pālaka|varaś ca tad|āgamena
śrī|Padmakesara|nṛpaṃ saha|putra|pautra|
gotraṃ sma vardhayati tasya paricchadaṃ ca.

rājā pramoda|bhara|nirbhara|hṛn niśāntaḥ
svarṇ'|âṃśuk'|ādi|nikara|pratipādanena
udyāna|pālakam amuṃ saha|putra|pautra|
gotraṃ sma vardhayati tasya paricchadaṃ ca.

sāmanta|mantri|vara|paura|jan'|ânuyātaḥ
s'|ântaḥpuraś ca catur|aṅga|camū|vṛtaś ca
śrī|Siṃha|sūri|guru|rāja|namasyanāya
śrī|Padmakesara|dhar"|âdhipatiś cacāla.

21.5 he, śeṣa|kūrma|pati|dig|dvi|radā idānīṃ
sarv'|âujasā kṣiti|talaṃ sakalaṃ pradhatta.
śrī|Padmakesara|nṛ|śekhara eṣa sarva|
ṛddhyā prayāti guru|rāja|sabhā|janāya!

gatv" ôdyānam asau vihāya nṛpateś
cihnāni sūr'|īkṣaṇe
mūrdhany asta|suhasta|kuḍmala|miṣāt
saṃgīrṇa|tac|chāsanaḥ
tat tāvat parivāra|yuk kṣiti|pati|

VENERABLE Simha, the king of reverend doctors, continued to promote the authority of the Jain order in every place, establishing the teachings of the Jina, wandering incessantly among villages, multitudes, et cetera. One day he arrived at the palace garden of His Majesty Padma·késara. 21.1

Forthwith, the head gardener, well known by the name of Priyam·vada, congratulated King Padma·késara, together with his sons, grandsons and family and his attendants on his arrival.

The tranquil king, his heart full of masses of joy, congratulated the gardener, together with his sons, grandsons and family and his attendants, with the bestowal of a gratuity of gold and fine garments, et cetera.

Attended by the barons, chief ministers and townspeople, together with the royal ladies, surrounded by his army of four divisions, His Majesty King Padma·késara set out to pay his respect to the reverend doctor Simha, the king of teachers.

Hey, primeval serpent, tortoise and elephant, lord of the four quarters, attend to holding up the entire surface of the earth with all your might—His Majesty King Padma·késara is advancing with all his resources to join the assembly of the king of teachers! 21.5

On arriving at the garden he relinquished his symbols of kingship in the sight of the reverend doctor. By the appearance of the buds of his hands properly placed on his head, he signified his acceptance of the teacher's instruction. Then, as that sun for the kings of the earth, accompanied

jyotiṣ|patiḥ śrī|guruṃ
Meru|kṣoṇi|dharaṃ pradakṣiṇayati
sm' ānanda|rom'|âñcitaḥ.
pañc'|âṅga|saṃspṛṣṭa|mahī|talaś ca
tat|pāda|padmaṃ sa namaścakāra
tatra sthira|sthāyuka|puṇya|lakṣmyā
bhāla|sthale saṃkramaṇāya manye.
yathā|sthān'|āsīne nṛpati|tilake tatra bhagavān
sudhā|dhār'|ādhār'|ādhara iva su|gambhīra|ninadaḥ
kṣaṇād bāhy'|â|bāhya|prabalatara|santāpa|śamanīṃ
su|dharma|vyākhyān'|âmṛta|rasa|mahā|vṛṣṭim atanot.
tathā hi:
«kule janma kṣīr'|ârṇava|nava|nav'|ôllola|vimale
su|lakṣmīr a|kṣīṇā sva|para|janat"|ānanda|vasati
su|pātre śrī|dānaṃ praśama|paripākaḥ pariṇatau
parīpākāḥ puṇya|śriya udayate śrī|Bharatavat.
yathā:
21.10 Mahāvidehe kila Puṇḍarīkiṇī|
puryām abhūt Tīrtha|patiḥ śriyo nidhiḥ
śrī|Vajrasenas tri|jagat|pati|sphurat|
koṭīra|koṭī|maṇi|cumbita|kramaḥ.
putrās tadīyā dhuri Vajranābho,
bāhuḥ Subāhuś, ca tataś ca Pīṭhaḥ,
tato Mahāpīṭha, iti krameṇa
krameṇa jajñuś ca dhuran|dharās te.

by his entourage, circumambulated the Mount Meru that was reverend teacher, he thrilled with joy.

Touching the ground with his head, hands and feet, he bowed to the lotus-feet of the teacher, in order, I suppose, to transfer to the flat of his brow the fortune of the teacher's firmly abiding merit.

When that forehead ornament of kings had sat in an appropriate place, the reverend doctor, his voice very deep, like a rain cloud for a reservoir of streams of nectar, immediately began to spread forth a heavy rain shower of the essence of nectar that was his exposition of the true religion, that provided soothing for the heat of very dangerous pains, both external and internal.

Like so:

"Birth in a family purified by the ever-renewed waves of the ocean of milk, the imperishable good fortune for one abiding with joy among one's subjects, the giving of wealth to worthy recipients, the ripening of tranquility in maturity, the ripening of the wealth of merit at the end, like Bharata.

Thus:

Now, in the city of Pundaríkini in Maha·vidéha, the foot- 21.10
steps of the Lord of the Ford, His Majesty Vajra·sena, an ocean of splendor, were kissed by the diadem jewels of the gods of the triple universe.

His sons, in order, were, at the head, Vajra·nabha; at the arms, Subáhu; then Pitha; and then Maha·pitha. In due course they became fit for the burden of leadership.

śrī|Vajranābhaṃ viniveśya rājye
pradāya sāṃvatsarikaṃ ca dānam
prabhur didīkṣā|kṣata|moha|śatrur
jaya|śriyaṃ tv āpa ca kevala'|rddhim.
abhyāyayāv āyudha|śālikāyāṃ
śri|Vajranābhasya ca cakra|ratnam
ṣaṭ|khaṇḍam asmād vijayaṃ prasādhya
svīkṛtya cakri|śriyam atyabhuṅkta.
ath' ânyadā tatra pure vyahārṣīt
śrī|dharma|cakrī prabhu|Vajrasenaḥ.
śrī|Vajranābha|pramukhāś ca sarve
pituḥ samīpāj jagṛhur vrata'|rddhim.
21.15 śrī|dvādaś'|âṅgīṃ prathamo 'dhyagīṣṭ' âr-
jīṃ dviśati|sthānakato 'rhad|ṛddhim
ekādaś'|âṅgīm apare tu peṭhuḥ
sarve tapasyāṃ vividhāṃ vitenuḥ.
vaiyāvṛttya|dhanena Bāhu|su|muniś
cakr'|îndirām ārjayat
sad|viśrāmaṇayā Subāhu|yatir apy
ūrjasvalaṃ Dorbalam
sarv'|ârthe sukha|śevadhau yayur amī
tatra trayas|triṃśataṃ
sthitv" âbdhīn Bharate yug'|ādi|Jina|rāṭ
śrī|Vajranābho 'bhavat,
Bāhuḥ śrī|Bharat'|ēśvaro 'jani Subā-
hū Bāhubaly ākhyayā
Pīṭho Brāhmy ajaniṣṭa so 'pi ca Mahā-
pīṭho 'bhavat Sundarī
sve rājye Vṛṣabh'|ēśvareṇa Bharataḥ
saṃsthāpitaḥ svāmy upait

Having appointed His Highness Vajra·nabha to the kingship and made donations for a year, the lord, the enemy of delusion shattered by his desire for initiation, attained the fortune of victory and the prosperity of omniscience.

The discus jewel appeared in His Majesty Vajra·nabha's armory. Having attained by its means victory over the six regions, and made it his own, he enjoyed the rank of universal emperor.

Now one day Lord Vajra·sena, the universal emperor of the fortune of religion, came to that city in the course of his wanderings. And all his sons, His Majesty Vajra·nabha at their head, attained the prosperity of initiation in the presence of their father.

The eldest studied the twelve-limbed holy scripture, 21.15
which, by means of its two hundred sections, brings the fortune of a Worthy, but the others recited the eleven limbs of scripture. They all practiced the various kinds of asceticism.

Through the wealth of his performance of asceticism, the good monk Bahu attained the fortune of rebirth as a universal emperor. Through the righteous striving of his asceticism, the monk Subáhu also attained the fortune of rebirth as the powerful Bahu·bali. They all went to the Treasury of Happiness heaven, and, after remaining there for nine hundred aeons, reverend Vajra·nabha was born in Bhárata as King Ríshabha, the first Jina of the current era.

Bahu was born as His Majesty Bharata, and Subáhu born as Bahu·bali. Pitha was born as Brahmi, and Maha·pitha became Súndari. King Ríshabha established Bhárata in his kingship. The lord took initiation and attained omniscience. Bharata became universal emperor.

dīkṣāṃ kevalam āsadac ca Bharataś
cakr'|ēśvaro 'jāyata.
śrī|Nābheya|Jin'|ēśvare śiva|gate
śrī|Bhārat'|âdh'|īśvaro
rājyaṃ prājyam abhukta tīrtham atanot
tat|tādṛg Aṣṭāpade
vātsaly'|âmṛta|kulyay" âpi ca paro|
lakṣāṃś ca sādharmikān
samprīṇan gṛha|medhitām api vahat-
tais tīrtha|bhūyaṃ bhuvi.
sa c' ânyedyuḥ snātaḥ
pratipada|dhṛt'|âlaṅkṛti|bharaḥ
kil' ādarś'|āgāre
sva|vapur abhipaśyann ita itaḥ
viśoṣaṃ nirvarṇy|ā-
bharaṇa|rahitām aṅgulim asau
samantād apy āgan-
tuka|suṣamam ev' âṅgam abudhat.
21.20 tatas tad|dṛṣṭ'|ântād
akhilam api saṃsāram abhito 'py
a|sāraṃ manvānaḥ
śubhatama|pariṇāma|vaśataḥ
dalitvā ghātīni
prabalatama|karmāṇi sahasā
gṛha|stho 'py āśliṣyad,
bata!, batatamāṃ kevala|ramām.»

When His Majesty the King of JinasRíshabha attained final liberation, His Majesty King Bharata enjoyed the kingdom very much. Gratifying with masses of the nectar of affection more than one hundred thousand of his fellow Jains, he built the same number of temples on Mount Ashta·pada. And the tears of the domestic sacrificers formed a river crossing for the world.

And one day after bathing, while putting on his clothes and jewelry, since he was in his hall of mirrors, he looked at his body here and there and saw that his finger, deprived of its ornaments and coloring, was withered. He realized that even a handsome body is subject to accident at every point.

Then, considering, as a result of that example, that the 21.20
entire cycle of existence was completely worthless, he all at once subdued the murderers, the extremely powerful karmas, and, even though a householder, behold!, embraced the most wonderful fortune of omniscience."

śṛṇvann eva hi Padmakesara|nṛpas
tat|sarvam ity adbhutaṃ
vairāgy'|âdbhuta|bhaṅgim aṅgy|akṛta tām
ātm'|âika|vedyāṃ tataḥ
uccair vīrya|vilāsataḥ pavanataḥ
karm'|âmbud'|ālī kṣatā
sadyaḥ kaivalikaḥ prakāśa udagāt
tasy' âvanī|bhāsvataḥ.

atr' âiv' âvasare pramoda|vikasan
netr'|âravindo hariḥ
sarva'|rddhyā sa|paricchado 'tha sahas" ā-
yāsīd, «an|āyāsy aho!»
kṣveḍā|nāda|jay'|āravaiḥ kila tadā
devā jagarjur ghanā
gandh'|âmbho vavṛṣuḥ sumāni ca tataḥ
sadyaḥ pupuṣpye ca bhūḥ.

āgū ratna|vimāna|mālita|mahī|
pīṭhāś caturdh" âmarāḥ
Śakreṇ' āucyata Padmakesara|nṛpo,
«dhatsva' ṛṣi|veṣaṃ, prabho.»
kṛtvā locam adhatta veṣam ṛṣi|rāṭ
Śakr'|ādibhir vanditaś
cakre kaivalik'|ôtsavaś ca jagatī|
kautūhal'|âik'|ākaraḥ.

Even as he was listening to this entire wonder, King Padma·késara gained the wonderful appearance of disgust for the world, and then unique self knowledge. The mass of the clouds of his karma was broken up by the purification of the manifestation of his strenuous vigor. Suddenly, the brilliance of omniscience arose upon him, like the sun upon the earth.

At that very moment, Indra, the king of the gods, suddenly arrived, accompanied by his entourage and all his resources. Then the massed gods boomed out a cry of victory just like the roaring of lions, "Oh, his unweariedness!" A shower of perfumed water and flowers fell, and then the earth suddenly flowered.

The gods signified their assent by garlanding the supports of the earth four times with their jeweled celestial vehicles. Indra said to King Padma·késara, "Put on the garment of a monk, Lord." The king of monks plucked out his hair and put on the garment. Indra and the other gods bowed to him and celebrated a festival for his omniscience, the single origin of rejoicing for the universe.

Indro vyajñapayad gurūn, «praṇamat' â-
mum keval'|ôdbhāsvaraṃ»
sūriḥ, «sādhu! phale|grahir mama jahāy'
âsau 'dhun" âbhūd!» iti
ānand'|âika|mayaḥ pradakṣiṇayituṃ
taṃ yāvad ev' ôtthitas
tāvac chukla|samādhin" ân|-
avadhinā tasy' âpy udait kevalam.

21.25 «vandāpya eṣa na hi hanta pitā guruś c'» êty
ālocya kevala|ram"|â|samatāṃ kil' ādhāt
pitr" ârjya|kevala|sudhāṃ yadi vā tapobhiḥ
prāg|bhojitaḥ suta imāṃ svayam anvabhuṅkta.

a|prayukta|vara|vainayikatvāt
sūrir āsta Harir āha, «kim evam?»
Padmakesara uvāca, «sur'|êndraṃ
keval'|îndram amum ity abhidh" âsau.»

tau jāta|kevala|vidau sahasā viditvā
harṣa|prakarṣa|paripūrita|mānasās tāḥ
Līlāvatī ca Surasundarikā|mukhāś ca
bhaktyā pradakṣiṇayituṃ drutam ārabhanta.

śubhatama|hṛdo Līlāvatyāḥ pradakṣiṇane guroḥ
samagatarāṃ nityaṃ jñānaṃ tato niviveśa sā
dhruva|cid udayam anyāsām apy ajānata cakrire
parama|mahimāṃ prītā jñāni|trikasya surās tataḥ.

Indra said to the teacher Simha, "Pay your respects to that son of omniscience." Just as the reverend doctor, thinking, "Excellent! Success is mine now that he has renounced the world!," a unique form of joy, his meditation on brilliant matters unlimited, stood up to circumambulate him, omniscience arose upon him, too.

However, reflecting that this father and teacher should by no means be made to bow, the son, it is said, held his immeasurable omniscience, or perhaps he followed in partaking of that nectar of omniscience which was to be gained by the father through his previous partaking of asceticism. 21.25

Not employing his excellence because of his modesty, the reverend doctor continued. Indra asked, "What's happening?" Padma·késara said, "This lord of reverend doctors is to be addressed as lord of the omniscient ones."

And having suddenly realized that the two had become omniscient ones, Lilávati and Sura·súndari, and the others, their minds overflowing with intense joy, immediately began to circumambulate them with devotion.

As Lilávati circumambulated the teacher, her mind on highly auspicious matters, everlasting omniscience tightly embraced her and then, her soul immovable, she achieved the good fortune aimed at by other women. The gods perceived this and thereupon performed a celebratory festival of supreme majesty for the three omniscient ones.

tathā hi:

vādyante divi deva|dundubhi|gaṇā
nṛtyanti divy'|âṅganā
gīyante tri|daś'|âṅgajābhir abhitas
tāra|svaraṃ maṅgalāḥ
ūrdhvyante divi ketavaḥ phala|maṇi|
svarṇ'|ādikaṃ vṛṣyate
yad vā Rājagṛhaṃ tadā dhruvam abhūt
śrī|deva|rājaḥ puram.

21.30 prāsāde 'gur apare sur'|âsurā
Vāsavas tu Bharat'|ātmajaṃ yathā
Kārtavīryam uru|vīrya|sampadaṃ
Padmakesara|pade 'bhyaṣiñcata.

Indro jagāma sura|dhāma|lalāma te tu
śrī|Siṃha|kevali|mukhā vara|keval'|îndrāḥ
mahyāṃ vijahrur akhila|pratibodha|hetor
jajñe ca kevala|vidaḥ paritaḥ su|kālaḥ.

śrī|Padmakesara|nar'|ēśvara|sārathitvaṃ
samprāpuṣo Dṛḍharathasya sutaś ca kīraḥ
saṃjātavān abhidhayā nanu Nāgaśarmā
śrī|Kārtavīrya|nṛ|varasya babhūva sūtaḥ.

ath' âgra|mala|kevalā muni|dhunī|sahasr'|ânvitā
sad" âiva jagat|īśvar'|ôddhura|śiro 'vataṃs'|ôpamā
jagat|tritaya|pāvanī sura|sabhājitā Jāhnavī|
vad|udyata|vihāriṇī bhuvi rarāja Līlāvatī.

Like so:

Troops of the gods' drummers beat their drums in the sky; divine women danced; all around the daughters of the gods sang hymns with finely modulated voices; banners were erected in the sky; a shower of fruit, jewels, gold, et cetera, rained down; thus at that time Raja·griha certainly became the city of His Majesty the king of the gods.

The gods and demigods entered the palace, and Indra, as 21.30
he had done the son of Bharata, anointed Karta·virya, that consummation of great heroism, to the place of Padma·ké-sara.

Indra, the forehead ornament of the abode of the gods, left, but the lords who were the excellent omniscient ones, Simha, the venerable omniscient one, at their head, wandered through the earth, for the sake of enlightening all, and everywhere there became an excellent opportunity for omniscience.

And the parrot, who had been reborn as the son of Dridha·ratha, who had attained the rank of charioteer to His Majesty King Padma·késara, became the charioteer of His Majesty King Karta·virya; Naga·sharman by name, of course.

Then, purified from subsequent defilement, accompanied by a thousand rivers of monks, ever indeed like a garland from the yoke-free head of the lord of the universe, purifying the triple universe, surpassing the assembly of the gods, like the Ganges, increasing as she traveled, Lilávati was illustrious throughout the earth.

bhav'|ârṇava|mahā|tarī bhagavatī vihṛty' âbhito
yad" ânaśana|su|sthitā sthitavat" îha Līlāvatī
tad" âiva Surasundarī|Ramaṇamaty upait kevalaṃ
suraiḥ kṛta|ṃahā|mahā yuga|pad eva tisro 'sidhan.

21.35 kiṃ prāg|janur|guru|Sudharma|vibhor bhav'|ântaraṃ
mūrty|antaraṃ Samarasena|mun'|īśvarasya vā
śrī|kevala|śriya uta pracalan|niketanaṃ
śrī|Siṃha|sūrir iha siṃha iv' âjayac ciram.

s' âiṣa śrī|Siṃha|sūris
taraṇir iva bhuvo bhāskaras tārakaś ca
s' âiṣa śrī|Siṃha|sūrir
vidhur iva jagatas trāyakaḥ prīṇakaś ca
s' âiṣa śrī|Siṃha|sūris
tri|daśa|śikharivat pronnato 'bhīṣṭa|daś ca
s' âiṣa śrī|Siṃha|sūris
tri|jagati yadi vā niḥsamāno, bat'!, âbhūta.

ciraṃ vihṛtyā jagatīṃ bibodhya
śrī|Siṃha|sūr'|īśvara āyur|alpam
vedy ādi|karm'|âdhikam ākalayya
sadyaḥ samudghātam iti vyadhatta.

tad yathā:

cakre pūrva|kṣaṇe 'sau
nija|tanu|pṛthulaṃ daṇḍam ātma|pradeśair
ūrdhv'|âdho|lokamānaṃ
tad itara|samaye tv īdṛśaṃ srāk kapāṭam
sphāraṃ pūrv'|āpareṇ' êty
atha para|samaye dakṣiṇen' ôttareṇa
kṣubdhaṃ tādṛkṣam ev' ân-
tara|bharaṇam ath' ânukramāt saṃjahāra.

When, after the venerable lady Lilávati had wandered all about, a great helper for crossing the ocean of existence, firmly established in fasting, had halted in this world, at that very time omniscience arose in Sura·súndari and Rámana·mati. The gods celebrated three festivals simultaneously.

On the other hand, the venerable reverend doctor Sim- 21.35
ha, like a lion, a wandering abode of the fortune of blessed omniscience, another existence of the teacher Lord Sudhárman, his former birth, or another image of Sámara·sena, the lord of monks, lived in this world for a long time.

That very reverend doctor Simha was like the sun, an enlightener and a savior for the world; that very venerable reverend doctor Simha was like the moon, a protector and a delighter of the universe; that very venerable reverend doctor Simha was like the peaked mountain of the gods, lofty and granting what was desired; or, rather, that very reverend doctor Simha was without equal, indeed!, in the triple universe.

Having wandered for a long time, wishing to enlighten the universe, the venerable reverend doctor, Lord Simha, knowing that his life was short, reckoned the amount of his original karma and determined on its immediate destruction.

Then, like so:

At the first moment he formed the limbs of his body like a stick, seen from top to bottom. Then, at the next moment he likewise made it quickly into a plank, expanding it forwards and backwards. Then, after that, he pushed it towards the left and right for a moment. Then he withdrew it.*

kṣamayitvā parito 'pi saṅgham anagham
prāpto 'tha śail'|êśikāṃ
kṣapayitvā nikhilāni tāni ca bhav'|ô-
pagrāhi|karmāṇy api
rucite 'nantaka|pañcakena satataṃ
lok'|âgra|cūḍā|maṇau
śiva|saudhe samayena rājyam alabhat
śrī|Siṃha|sūr'|īśvaraḥ.

21.40 Padmakesara|mun'|îndra|kevalī
maṇḍaleṣu su|ciraṃ vihṛtya saḥ
Kārtavīrya|nṛpater anugrahaṃ
vīkṣya Rājagṛham anyadā yayau.
taṃ namasyitum ath' âbhyagān mudā
Kārtavīrya|nṛpatir maha"|rddhibhiḥ
Padmakesara|guruś ca deśanāṃ
kleśa|kanda|khananīṃ vinirmamau.
abudhyata mahī|patir jhaṭ|iti Kārtavīryo yato
mahat|su|guror vaco bhavati sākṣi|mātraṃ param
vidhāya vasudhā|dhavaṃ sapadi Padmacandraṃ sutaṃ
svayaṃ tu sa nirakramīt sa ca śuk'|ātmakaḥ sārathiḥ.
abhūc ca sakal'|āgam'|ôpaniṣadāṃ padaṃ so '|cirāt
tataś ca guruṇā vyadhīyata|tarāṃ sa gacch'|âdhipaḥ
svayaṃ tu gurur anyadā vidadhad eva sad|deśanām
upākramata satvaraṃ kim api sarva|yoga|cchide.
tathā hi:
ādau vāṅ|manase sa c' ādare tanu|yoge na sa tādṛś" âdhīt
eken' âiva nihanti patriṇā kṛta|hasto hy a|bhaye śaravyake.

And, having everywhere asked forgiveness from the faultless congregation, he then resorted to a stone slab strewn with grass and abstained from even the actions that support existence. In due course venerable Simha, the king of reverend doctors, attained a kingdom in the palace of final liberation, the eternal crest-ornament for the summit of the universe, made brilliant by the five eternal ones.

Padma·késara, the king of monks, the omniscient one, 21.40
wandered through countries for a very long time. One day, having regard for the benefit of King Karta·virya, he arrived at Raja·griha.

Then King Karta·virya, with copious resources, joyfully went to pay respect to him, and the teacher Padma·késara began to mete out the religious teaching that is a spade for the tuber of distress.

Whoosh! In an instant Karta·virya was enlightened, since the statement of a great teacher of truth is the supreme eyewitness. He forthwith appointed his son Padma·chandra king, but he himself, together with his charioteer, the reborn soul of the parrot, renounced the world.

And he soon became an abode of the doctrines of all the scriptural teachings. So then the teacher firmly placed him in charge of the congregation. But the teacher himself, one day, as soon as he had expounded the teaching of truth, resorted to mortificatory postures of all kinds.

Like so:

First of all he suppressed speech and mind and carefully applied ascetic postures, unlike any. He stretched out his hand to strike as if with a single sword at the target that is fearlessness.

21.45 kāya|yogena sūkṣmeṇa taṃ bādaraṃ
so 'jayad dantinaṃ tad|raden' êva, bhoḥ!
sūkṣma|vāk|citta|yogāv asāv ekadā
kāya|yogena sūkṣmeṇa nirjigyivān.

klpta|kāryaṃ tato 'sau muniḥ sūkṣmakaṃ
kāya|yogaṃ kṣaṇād geha|ratnaṃ yathā
svena vidhyāpayāmāsa yog'|īśvaraḥ
so 'tha śail'|êśī (- - - - - - -)

niruddha|nikhil'|āśrayaḥ sapadi pādap'|āupamyakaṃ
vidhāya vidhinā kṣaṇāt kim api varya|paryaṅkam
nihatya (- - - - -) nibiḍa|karma|vidviṅ|ghaṭām
asidhyad anurūpatāṃ, bata, yayau ca Vīra|prabhoḥ.

śrī|Kārtavīryo gaṇa|dhāri|ratnaṃ
prabodhya tāntaṃ viṣayeṣu bhavyān
paryāyam uccaiḥ pratipālya c' ânte
saṃlekhanām ārabhat' âivam evam.

catvāri varṣāṇi tapo 'ṣṭam'|ântaṃ
tat|pāraṇe sarvam ih' âiṣaṇīyam
punaś ca catvāri tapo 'ṣṭam'|ântaṃ
vinā vikṛtyā tv iha pāraṇam syāt.

21.50 saṃvatsarau dvau ca tapaś caturtham
ācāmam ev' âtra ca pāraṇe syāt
ṣaṇ|māsam anyac ca tapo 'ṣṭam'|ântam
ācāmam atr' âpi hi pāraṇe, bhoḥ.

With acute ascetic postures he conquered that cotton elephant as by its tusk, oh! With his one acute bodily mortification he subdued acute speech and thought. 21.45

The monk performed what was necessary to be done, in a moment acute bodily mortification, like a jewel in a house. The lord of bodily mortification resorted to a stone slab strewn with grass.

All influx of karma obstructed, he forthwith disposed himself to wait for death according to precept, and, fixed in the excellent squatting position, he accomplished the destruction of his inimical dense karma. Oh, he attained the likeness of Lord Maha·vira!

Venerable Karta·virya, the jewel of leaders of the troop, continued to wander incessantly, teaching beings who were capable of enlightenment to have weariness among the senses. In the end he undertook a wasting-away fast as follows:

He performed a fast for four years, eating a meal only every eighth day, and at the end of it he took what was allowable in that case. Then he fasted for another four years without eating on the eighth day, and with a restriction on what was allowable at the end of it.

And then he fasted for two years, eating on the fourth day, and at the end of the fast taking rice-water. And then he fasted for six months, eating every eighth day, and then only rice-water and at the end of the fast, too, sirs. 21.50

ṣaṇ|māsam anyad daśam'|ādikaṃ tapa
ācāmam atr' âpi hi pāraṇ'|ādine
syād dvādaśe 'bde khalu koṭi|saṃhitam
ācāmam atr' âpi tapo vikṛṣṭakam.
saṃlekhanām iti vidhāya kṛt'|âṣṭamo 'sau
svādhīnatām agamayat kila kevala'|rddhim
evaṃ tapobhir abhipaśyati yat sakhīyaṃ
sā k" âpy, aho, vijayate, bata, mukti|kāntā!
āruhya niṣpratima|vīrya|rathaṃ sa|sūtaḥ
śrī|Kārtavīrya|munir āyata|mukti|saudham
sā sadya eva kila kevala|lakṣmik'|ākhyā
sāṃmukhyam, aṅga, gamitā ramitā ca tena.
ataḥ peyaṃ geyaṃ
na nava|vasanaṃ sparśa|sukhanaṃ
na visphārā hārā
na ca parimalaḥ ko 'py apamalaḥ
ras'|ôdārā sārā
na ca rasavatī n' âpi su|datī
samunmīlal|līlā
smara|nivasatir yatra yuvatiḥ,
21.55 ku (-) śaṃso (-) sminn
ati|hata|gatir bhrāmatutarāṃ
paraṃ tyaktv" âśeṣaṃ
viṣaya|paṭalaṃ nistuṣa|dhiyaḥ
niṣaṇṇā adhyātmaṃ
śama|śama|niśaṃ śānta|manaso
labhante tad yasy' ā-
varaṇam api n' ōcur viṣaya|jam.
a|varṇair a|sparśair
a|rasajani|saṃsthāna|tanukair

Then he fasted for another six months, taking rice-water on the tenth day and at the end, too. Then he fasted for a further six months, taking rice-water at the end also. As a cusp to be applied to the twelfth year, he performed an extended fast of rice-water only.

Having thus undertaken a wearing-away fast, taking sustenance on the eighth day only, he was united with self-mastery, yes indeed, the fortune of omniscience. Behold, the desired beloved of final liberation, who had seen that he had been made a companion by austerities, she too was won!

Having mounted, together with his charioteer, the chariot of inimitable heroism, the venerable monk Karta·virya proceeded to the palace of final liberation. At that very moment, she, with the appearance of the fortune of omniscience, face to face, yes!, was united with and enjoyed by him.

So, not drinking and singing, not new garments, pleasant to the touch, not pendulous necklaces, and by no means perfumed baths, not nectar with a noble taste, not tasty meals, and not a woman with a pleasant smile, with a blossoming appearance, the abode of love, in which is youth,

... in which the transient course of embodiment is very 21.55
wretched. But having abandoned the entire mass of pleasure, those whose minds are purified, wearied of the world, their selves perpetual nights of tranquility, their minds at peace, also do not obtain the mental blindness which they say is produced by sensuality.

Therefore, unrivaled bliss is found in the final liberation obtained by the kings of monks whose bodies lack color, are

a|gandhair niḥsaṅgair
hata|sakala|vedair api tataḥ
mun'|îndrais tair muktau
sukham anupamaṃ syād yata idaṃ
vaś'|īśā karṣanti
praśama|sukha|bhaṅgy" âtra yad|aṇum.

na śoko 'pi stoko
na ca khalu mṛṣā n' âpy aśiśiṣā
na c' âdhir na vyādhir
jani|mṛti|jarā na prasṛmarāḥ
sad"|â|mand'|ānand'|â-
mṛta|rasa|ghan'|āsvāda|vidhinā
samastā apy astā
iva samabhavaṃs teṣv api lavam.

a|mānaṃ vijñānaṃ
vigamita|malaṃ darśana|malaṃ
nirīryaṃ sad|vīryaṃ
pramada|muditaṃ dṛg|vilasitam
(- - - -) pañca|
vrata (- - - - - -) palavat
sad" âśnanto ye 'ntar-
vidadhati takaṃ siddhir|a|mitam.

always unwashed, who are unperfumed, who are free from attachment, and have abandoned all possessions. Hence the possessors of self-mastery, through their partaking of the bliss of tranquility, obtain a minute part of it in this world.

Not the slightest sorrow, certainly not falsehood, not desire for enjoyment, not anxiety, not sickness, not the cycle of birth, death and aging—as if they had gathered together and vanished through the effect of the taste of the mass of nectar of their intense and eternal bliss—none has appeared in them even for a moment.

Those who thus keep the five vows, attaining lack of pride, understanding, the possession of abstention, the possession of insight, lack of arousal, true heroism, delight in indifference, and the manifestation of insight, develop within themselves that infinite bliss of final liberation.

tad idam anupamānaṃ
mukti|śarm'|âti|mānaṃ
satatam anubhavantaḥ
sarvataḥ kṣemavantaḥ
su|guru|Samarasen'|ād-
yā mun'|îndrāś caturviṃ-
śatitama|Jina|ratna|
śrī|su|saṅghaṃ pṛṇantu.

So, eternally experiencing this incomparable, highly honored abode of final liberation, possessed of entire happiness, may the true teachers, Sámara·sena and the others, gods of monks, bless the good and holy congregation, the jewel of the twenty-four Jinas.

AUTHOR'S COLOPHON

22.1 TĪRTHE śrī|Vardhamānasya Sudharma|svāmino 'nvaye
śrī|Vardhamānaḥ su|guruḥ su|dharma|svāmy udaiyata.
tac|chiṣya|mauli|maṇir aidhata Gurjaratrā|
sutrāma|Durlabha|nar'|ēśvara|mūrdha|sevyaḥ
śrīmān Jineśvara|gurur guru|dhāma|pūraiḥ
sūraṃ vijitya, bata, sat|patham aikṣayad yaḥ.
san|nīti|ratn'|ākara|mukhya|tarkān
śrī|Aṣṭak'|āder vivṛtīś ca mṛṣṭvā
campūm i (- -) vṛta|vāg|vilāsāṃ
Līlāvatīṃ yaḥ su|kathām asūta,
tat|pāda|padma|madhupo Jinacandra|sūrir
ādyo dyutan|nikhila|vāṇ|maya|sindhu|sindhuḥ
«Saṃvega|sāra|sarite» (- - - - - -)
yat tan nibandha|miṣataḥ parito nirīyuḥ.
22.5 śrī|stambhan'|âbhidha|su|tīrtha|maṇi|pradīpo
'bhū (- - - - -) varo 'bhayadeva|sūriḥ
ā śaiśavād api hi yo vimukho nav|âṅgyā
vṛtiṃ (- - -) m iti kāñ cid, aho, nav'|âṅgyāḥ.
tat|paṭṭa|net" â|tula|sauvihitya|
jñān'|âmbudhiḥ śrī|Jinavallabho 'bhūt
yad datta|sad|grantha|sudhā|prapās tāḥ
(- -) samastair api mukti|pānthaiḥ.

IN SUCCESSION to reverend Lord Sudhárman, in the ford of venerable Vardhamána, the good teacher reverend Vardhamána, the master of the good religion, arose. 22.1

The crest-jewel of his pupils, reverend Jinéshvara swelled with good fortune. He was the head servant of King Dúrlabha, the protector of Gurja·rátra, and he overcame, indeed!, a powerful man with the effusions of his venerable appearance, and made him see the true path.

After composing works on philosophy, eminent among jewel mines of true behavior, and commentaries on Hari·bhadra's eight-part treatise and other works, he composed the fine epic poem in mixed styles and meters, the Lilávati, charming with the poetic language with which it was filled.

The chief bee at the lotus of his feet was the reverend doctor Jina·chandra, a brilliant ocean consisting of entire eloquence. He composed "The River of the Essence of Disgust for the World" ... since, in emulation of this composition, they departed in all directions.

The excellent reverend doctor Ábhaya·deva was a jewel- 22.5
lamp for the ascetic lineage known as the support of excellence. Intent, even from pupilage, on the nine limbs of scripture, he composed commmentaries, gosh!, on every part of the nine limbs.

His disciple was reverend Jina·vállabha, an ocean of knowledge and unrivaled asceticism. The roadside wells filled with the nectar of the books on religion written by him are enjoyed even by all travelers along the road to final liberation.

tadīya|gacch'|âmbuja|khaṇḍa|caṇḍa|
bhānur babhau śrī|Jinadatta|sūriḥ
yat|pāda|sevā, bata, rājabhis taiḥ
sa (- -) sampūrṇatamair vitene.

tad anu ca Jinacandra|sūri|siṃhaḥ
samajani śaiśa|śālin" âpi yena
prabala|mada|bhara|pravādi|dant'|
āvala|dalanā khalu līlay" âiva cakre.

tat|paṭṭa|pūrv'|âcala|heli|keliḥ
pradyotana|śrī|Jinapaty adhīśaḥ.
yasy' ôdaye saṃprasasāra dhāma
n' ânyasya kasy' âpi hi sarva|dikṣu.

22.10 ath' âbhyudayam āsadat
prabhu|Jineśvaraś candram ā-
ramā|mada|bhidaṃ gaṇ'|âm-
budhi|vilāsa|jāgrat|karaḥ
Jin'|êndra|bhavan'|âcalāḥ
prati|padaṃ yadīy'|ôdaye
babhuḥ prathama|candrikā|
kanaka|kumbha|caṇḍ'|âdbhutāḥ;

yas tātkālika|navya|kāvya|kusumair
ārcīt trisandhyaṃ Jinān,
nānā|labdhi|nadī|nadī|parivṛdho
yo 'nuvyadhād Gautamam,
śrī|kṣm" âbhūṣyata yat|pratiṣṭhitatamaiḥ
śiṣyair vihārair dvidhā,
yad vā yo vidhi|dharma|sīmni su|kṛt'|â|
dvaitaṃ, bat', âdhāt Kalau.

The reverend doctor Jina·datta became the sun for the mass of lotuses that were Jina·vállabha's ascetic followers. His foot-service, remarkable!, was performed by kings in large number.

And after him Jina·chandra became the lion of reverend doctors, who, even while in the state of pupilage, with consummate ease actually caused to shatter the rows of teeth of his opponents in the battle of debate, who were exulting in their strength.

Having achieved the likeness of a sun for the eastern mountain that was Jina·chandra's turban, the brilliantly radiant Jina·pati became chief. At his arising, not of anyone else at all, glory indeed spread in every direction.

Then Lord Jinéshvara began his ascent, a moon for de- 22.10
stroying the madness of passion, awakening the charm of the ocean of his ascetic followers. At whose arising, everywhere, mountains that were the temples of the Lord Jina shone with the wonderful brilliance of the pots of gold that was the light of the new moon;

who thus, morning, noon and night, worshipped the Jina with the flowers of a fresh poem, appropriate for the season; who, an ocean of various attainments, conformed to Gáutama, the first pupil of Lord Maha·vira; by whose pupils, flourishing in great numbers, wandering in two companies, the lovely earth was ornamented; or who, rather, produced benefit, unique indeed!, for the present degenerate age, parted from precept and religion.

su|guru|sura|tarus tato 'bhyuditaḥ
pṛṇati jaganti Jinaprabodha|sūriḥ
sama|yama|su|mati|prabhāvanābhir
bata suṣamā|suṣamām naya!
sa vyākhyāt satataṃ manīṣita|latā|
vistāra|dhārā|dharāt
śrī|sūr'|îndra|Jineśvarasya su|guroḥ
śiṣy'|âvataṃs'|âgraṇīḥ
eṣa śrī|Jinaratna|sūrir asṛjan
«Nirvāṇa|Līlāvatī|
sāraṃ» sāram udāra|bhakti|madhuraḥ
prāk|sūri|pād'|âmbuje.
stumaḥ prabhu|Jineśvara (- - - - - -) guruṃ
kavitva|pada|vid|guruṃ yati|pa|Sarvadeva|prabhum
pramāna|padavī|guruṃ Vijayadeva|sūriṃ mah"|â-
bhiṣeka (- - - -) āgama|guruṃ namaskurmahe.

22.15 Līlāvatī dvi|navate śaradāṃ sahasre
śrī|Vaikrame 'raci Jineśvara|sūri|pādaiḥ.
tasyāś ca saṃcitir iyaṃ punar eka|catvā-
riṃśat|trayodaśa|śateṣu mayā vitene.
sah' âiva Lakṣmītilak'|âgra|jena
«Pratyeka|buddha|caritaṃ» vyadhāma
«Līlāvatī|sāram» amuṃ tu Jaine-
śvara|prabandhena sah' âgra|jena.
prācīna|sad|guru|Jineśvara|śūri|baddhaṃ
Līlāvatī|samabhidhāna|kath" êti vṛttam
pīyuṣa (- - - - -) vidadhe may" êti
haste pragṛhya tad idaṃ su|dhiyo dhayantu.

Then the reverend doctor Jina·prabódha, a sacred tree of good teachers, arose and blessed the three worlds. Bring forth the age of extreme happiness by your promulgations of restraint and benevolence!

He, through his continuous preaching, a rain cloud for the growth of the desired creeper, became the foremost crest of the pupils of the good teacher, the lord of reverend doctors, venerable Jinéshvara. I, the venerable reverend doctor Jina·ratna, composed the "Epitome of the Final Liberation of Queen Lilávati," a bee devoted to its exalted essence, at the lotus of the feet of the former reverend doctor.

I praise Lord Jinéshvara, my teacher and my teacher Lord Sarva·deva, lord of ascetics, highly conversant with literature. I honor my teacher Víjaya·deva, highly skilled in logic, and with great unction my teacher of canonical scripture.

The Lilávati was composed in the year one thousand and 22.15
ninety-two of the Víkrama era* by the venerable reverend doctor Jinéshvara, and this epitome of it was prepared by me in the year thirteen hundred and forty-one of the same era.

Together with my senior, Lakshmi·tílaka, I composed "The Deeds of the Self-Enlightened Ones," and together with the senior composition of Jinéshvara I composed this "Epitome of Queen Lilávati."

Thus I composed this essential cream, the abridgment of the events of the epic poem called "The Final Emancipation of Queen Lilávati" of the teacher of truth of yore, the venerable doctor Jinéshvara. May the wise take it in their hand and reflect on it.

Mārgādi (- - - - - -) śi Puṣya|yoge
Jābāli|pattana|vare ca samarthito 'yam
praty|akṣaraṃ gaṇanayā (- -) sāyut'|ârdhaṃ s'|ârdhaṃ
triśaty|adhikam uktam anuṣṭubhāṃ bhoḥ.
aṅkato 'pi 5350.

vyākaraṇ'|ādi|śruta|patha|pathikena Jinaprabodha|yati|patinā
samaśodhi Rājagaṇin" âsau Saumyamūrtigaṇinā ca.

22.20 chando|vyākaraṇa|pramāṇa (- -) a-
laṅkāra|pārīṇa|dhīḥ
kāvya|jñāna|vidhāna|śodhana|kalā|
cāturya (- - - -)
ādarṣe prathame mama kramyat" â-
muṃ Saumyamūrtir gaṇiḥ
sāhāyyaṃ (- - - -) Sāgaragaṇi|
praṣṭhāḥ sa me vyādadhuḥ.

yāvad dvīpa|sarasvatāṃ kṣiti|bhṛtām
melaṃ mitho vidyate
yāva - nara|janma|ratna|kanaka|
prāg|bhāra|sāra|śriyam
yāvat prāñcati ratna|sānu|śikharī
nirvāṇa|Līlāvatī|
sāras tāvad ayaṃ nitānta|mudiyād
vyākhyāyamāno budhaiḥ.

iti grantha|kāra|praśastiḥ sampūrṇā.

śubham astu caturvidha|śrī|śramaṇa|śaṅghasya.

And it was completed in November, as the moon was in the flourishing mansion in the excellent city of Jabáli. Putting the reckoning in writing, it consists of five thousand three hundred and fifty verses, good sirs, and in numerals, 5,350.

And it was corrected by Jina·prabódha, the lord of ascetics, my guide along the path of the knowledge of grammar, et cetera, and by Raja·ganin and Saumya·murti·ganin.

Saumya·murti·ganin, completely versed in metrics, 22.20
grammar, logic and rhetoric, skilled in the art of correcting according to literary rules, and Ságara·ganin, eminent men, according to my arrangement, prepared it for first publication.

As long as there is mutual meeting between the mountains and the rivers of the island, as long as there is the wealth of the essence of the mountains of gold and jewels of human birth, as long as the peak of Mount Meru endures, for so long may this Epitome of Queen Lilávati continue to give extraordinary delight as it is related by the wise.

Here ends the author's colophon.

Blessings on the fourfold congregation of holy strivers.

NOTES

Bold *references are to the English Text;* ***bold italic*** *references are to the Sansrkit text. An astersik (*) in the body of the text marks the word or passage being annotated.*

9.22 **Víjaya·puri** was famous for its temple dedicated to the demigod Ashóka.

11.26 The chief power of the masters of magic is their ability to discern what lies beyond the normal range of the senses.

11.188 Sense perception, inference, and scripture form here a hierarchy in which each depends on the former, so that if there is no sense perception of an omniscient person, none of the other means of knowledge can operate.

11.189 Another argument against the possibility that scripture can prove that an omniscient being exists.

11.192 The point of course is that you can never have seen your mother's birth.

12.161 Nemi was betrothed to Princess **Raja·mati** but he renounced the world instead on seeing the caged animals that were to be sacrificed to celebrate his nuptials.

15.1 Leading characters of the Maha·bhárata; see note on 2.17.

15.10 The god Shiva, who bears a single digit of the moon on his forehead.

15.85 The story of **Yasho·ravi**, Vasu·nanda and Kánaka·ratha was related in detail in Canto 6.

16.3 Some puns on the names of the chief characters of the Sanskrit epic, the Maha·bhárata. **Duryódhana** was the leader of the Káuravas. With his ally Karna he fought against the five Pándavas—Yudhisthira, known as the son of righteousness, Bhima, Árjuna, Saha·deva and Nákula, who were the sons of Dharma. See notes on 15.1 and 2.17.

16.7 He was initiated by Sudhárman at the end of Canto Five.

17.4 Sámara·sena here concludes the narrative as he began at the end of the first canto.

17.14 See note on 7.171.

21.38 It is not clear what is going on in this verse. For further discussion see our website.

22.15 The **Víkrama era** began in a year equivalent to 58/7 BCE.

INDEX

Sanskrit words are given in the English alphabetical order, according to the accented CSL pronunciation aid. They are followed by the conventional diacritics in brackets.

THE CLAY SANSKRIT LIBRARY

The volumes in the series are listed here in order of publication.
Titles marked with an asterisk* are also available in the
Digital Clay Sanskrit Library (eCSL).
For further information visit www.claysanskritlibrary.org

1. The Emperor of the Sorcerers (*Bṛhatkathāślokasaṃgraha*) (vol. 1 of 2) by *Budhasvāmin*. SIR JAMES MALLINSON
2. Heavenly Exploits (*Divyāvadāna*). JOEL TATELMAN
3. Maha·bhárata III: The Forest (*Vanaparvan*) (vol. 4 of 4)* WILLIAM J. JOHNSON
4. Much Ado about Religion (*Āgamaḍambara*) by *Bhaṭṭa Jayanta*. CSABA DEZSŐ
5. The Birth of Kumára (*Kumārasaṃbhava*) by *Kālidāsa*. DAVID SMITH
6. Ramáyana I: Boyhood (*Bālakāṇḍa*) by *Vālmīki*. ROBERT P. GOLDMAN
7. The Epitome of Queen Lilávati (*Līlāvatīsāra*) (vol. 1 of 2) by *Jinaratna*. R.C.C. FYNES
8. Ramáyana II: Ayódhya (*Ayodhyākāṇḍa*) by *Vālmīki*. SHELDON I. POLLOCK
9. Love Lyrics (*Amaruśataka, Śatakatraya & Caurapañcāśikā*) by *Amaru, Bhartṛhari & Bilhaṇa*. GREG BAILEY & RICHARD GOMBRICH
10. What Ten Young Men Did (*Daśakumāracarita*) by *Daṇḍin*. ISABELLE ONIANS
11. Three Satires (*Kaliviḍambana, Kalāvilāsa & Bhallaṭaśataka*) by *Nīlakaṇṭha, Kṣemendra & Bhallaṭa*. SOMADEVA VASUDEVA
12. Ramáyana IV: Kishkíndha (*Kiṣkindhākāṇḍa*) by *Vālmīki*. ROSALIND LEFEBER
13. The Emperor of the Sorcerers (*Bṛhatkathāślokasaṃgraha*) (vol. 2 of 2) by *Budhasvāmin*. SIR JAMES MALLINSON
14. Maha·bhárata IX: Shalya (*Śalyaparvan*) (vol. 1 of 2)* JUSTIN MEILAND

15. Rákshasa's Ring (*Mudrārākṣasa*)*
by *Viśākhadatta*. Michael Coulson
16. Messenger Poems (*Meghadūta, Pavanadūta & Haṃsadūta*)
by *Kālidāsa, Dhoyī & Rūpa Gosvāmin*. Sir James Mallinson
17. Ramáyana III: The Forest (*Araṇyakāṇḍa*)
by *Vālmīki*. Sheldon I. Pollock
18. The Epitome of Queen Lilávati (*Līlāvatīsāra*) (vol. 2 of 2)
by *Jinaratna*. R.C.C. Fynes
19. Five Discourses on Worldly Wisdom (*Pañcatantra*)*
by *Viṣṇuśarman*. Patrick Olivelle
20. Ramáyana V: Súndara (*Sundarakāṇḍa*) by *Vālmīki*.
Robert P. Goldman & Sally J. Sutherland Goldman
21. Maha·bhárata II: The Great Hall (*Sabhāparvan*)
Paul Wilmot
22. The Recognition of Shakúntala (*Abhijñānaśākuntala*) (Kashmir Recension) by *Kālidāsa*. Somadeva Vasudeva
23. Maha·bhárata VII: Drona (*Droṇaparvan*) (vol. 1 of 4)*
Vaughan Pilikian
24. Rama Beyond Price (*Anargharāghava*)
by *Murāri*. Judit Törzsök
25. Maha·bhárata IV: Viráta (*Virāṭaparvan*)
Kathleen Garbutt
26. Maha·bhárata VIII: Karna (*Karṇaparvan*) (vol. 1 of 2)
Adam Bowles
27. "The Lady of the Jewel Necklace" & "The Lady who Shows her Love" (*Ratnāvalī & Priyadarśikā*) by *Harṣa*.*
Wendy Doniger
28. The Ocean of the Rivers of Story (*Kathāsaritsāgara*) (vol. 1 of 7)
by *Somadeva*. Sir James Mallinson
29. Handsome Nanda (*Saundarananda*)*
by *Aśvaghoṣa*. Linda Covill
30. Maha·bhárata IX: Shalya (*Śalyaparvan*) (vol. 2 of 2)*
Justin Meiland
31. Rama's Last Act (*Uttararāmacarita*) by *Bhavabhūti*.
Sheldon Pollock. Foreword by Girish Karnad

32. "Friendly Advice" (*Hitopadeśa*) by *Nārāyaṇa* &
"King Víkrama's Adventures" (*Vikramacarita*). Judit Törzsök

33. Life of the Buddha (*Buddhacarita*)
by *Aśvaghoṣa*. Patrick Olivelle

34. Maha·bhárata V: Preparations for War (*Udyogaparvan*) (vol. 1 of 2)
Kathleen Garbutt. Foreword by Gurcharan Das

35. Maha·bhárata VIII: Karna (*Karṇaparvan*) (vol. 2 of 2)
Adam Bowles

36. Maha·bhárata V: Preparations for War (*Udyogaparvan*) (vol. 2 of 2)
Kathleen Garbutt

37. Maha·bhárata VI: Bhishma (*Bhīṣmaparvan*) (vol. 1 of 2)*
Including the "Bhagavad Gita" in Context
Alex Cherniak. Foreword by Ranajit Guha

38. The Ocean of the Rivers of Story (*Kathāsaritsāgara*) (vol. 2 of 7)
by *Somadeva*. Sir James Mallinson

39. "How the Nagas were Pleased" (*Nāgānanda*) by *Harṣa* &
"The Shattered Thighs" (*Ūrubhaṅga*) by *Bhāsa*.*
Andrew Skilton

40. Gita·govínda: Love Songs of Radha and Krishna (*Gītagovinda*)*
by *Jayadeva*. Lee Siegel. Foreword by Sudipta Kaviraj

41. "Bouquet of Rasa" & "River of Rasa" (*Rasamañjarī & Rasataraṅgiṇī*) by *Bhānudatta*. Sheldon Pollock

42. Garland of the Buddha's Past Lives (*Jātakamālā*) (vol. 1 of 2)*
by *Āryaśūra*. Justin Meiland

43. Maha·bhárata XII: Peace (*Śāntiparvan*) (vol. 3 of 5)*
"The Book of Liberation" (*Mokṣadharma*). Alexander Wynne

44. The Little Clay Cart (*Mṛcchakaṭikā*) by *Śūdraka*.
Diwakar Acharya. Foreword by Partha Chatterjee

45. Bhatti's Poem: The Death of Rávana (*Bhaṭṭikāvya*)*
by *Bhaṭṭi*. Oliver Fallon

46. "Self-Surrender," "Peace," "Compassion," and "The Mission of the Goose": Poems and Prayers from South India (*Ātmārpaṇastuti, Śāntivilāsa, Dayāśataka & Haṃsasaṃdeśa*) by *Appayya Dīkṣita, Nīlakaṇṭha Dīkṣita & Vedānta Deśika.* Yigal Bronner & David Shulman
Foreword by Gieve Patel
47. Maha·bhárata VI: Bhishma (*Bhīṣmaparvan*) (vol. 2 of 2)* Alex Cherniak
48. How Úrvashi Was Won (*Vikramorvaśīya*) by *Kālidāsa* Velcheru Narayana Rao & David Shulman
49. The Quartet of Causeries (*Caturbhāṇī*) by *Śūdraka, Śyāmilaka, Vararuci & Īśvaradatta.* Csaba Dezső & Somadeva Vasudeva
50. Garland of the Buddha's Past Lives (*Jātakamālā*) (vol. 2 of 2)* by *Āryaśūra.* Justin Meiland
51. Princess Kadámbari (*Kādambarī*) (vol. 1 of 3) by *Bāṇa.* David Smith
52. The Rise of Wisdom Moon (*Prabodhacandrodaya*)* by *Kṛṣṇamiśra.* Matthew T. Kapstein
Foreword by J.N. Mohanty
53. Maha·bhárata VII: Drona (*Droṇaparvan*) (vol. 2 of 4)* Vaughan Pilikian
54. Maha·bhárata X & XI: Dead of Night & The Women (*Sauptikaparvan & Strīparvan*).* Kate Crosby
55. Seven Hundred Elegant Verses (*Āryāsaptaśatī*)* by *Govardhana.* Friedhelm Hardy
56. Málavika and Agni·mitra (*Mālavikāgnimitram*) by *Kālidāsa.* Dániel Balogh & Eszter Somogyi

k	ṭ	t	p	ṅ	n	m	(*Except* āḥ/aḥ) ḥ/r	āḥ	aḥ	*Permitted finals:* / *Initial letters:*
k	ṭ	t	p	ṅ	n	ṃ	ḥ	āḥ	aḥ	k/kh
g	ḍ	d	b	ṅ	n	ṃ	r	ā	o	g/gh
k	ṭ	c	p	ṅ	ṃś	ṃ	ś	āś	aś	c/ch
g	ḍ	j	b	ṅ	ñ	ṃ	r	ā	o	j/jh
k	ṭ	ṭ	p	ṅ	ṃṣ	ṃ	ṣ	āṣ	aṣ	ṭ/ṭh
g	ḍ	ḍ	b	ṅ	ṇ	ṃ	r	ā	o	ḍ/ḍh
k	ṭ	t	p	ṅ	ṃs	ṃ	s	ās	as	t/th
g	ḍ	d	b	ṅ	n	ṃ	r	ā	o	d/dh
k	ṭ	t	p	ṅ	n	ṃ	ḥ	āḥ	aḥ	p/ph
g	ḍ	d	b	ṅ	n	ṃ	r	ā	o	b/bh
ṅ	ṇ	n	m	ṅ	n	ṃ	r	ā	o	*nasals* (n/m)
g	ḍ	d	b	ṅ	n	ṃ	r	ā	o	y/v
g	ḍ	d	b	ṅ	n	ṃ	*zero*[1]	ā	o	r
g	ḍ	l	b	ṅ	l̃[2]	ṃ	r	ā	o	l
k	ṭ	c ch	p	ṅ	ñ ś/ch	ṃ	ḥ	āḥ	aḥ	ś
k	ṭ	t	p	ṅ	n	ṃ	ḥ	āḥ	aḥ	ṣ/s
gg h	ḍḍ h	dd h	bb h	ṅ	n	ṃ	r	ā	o	h
g	ḍ	d	b	ṅ/ṅṅ[3]	n/nn[3]	m	r	ā	a[4]	*vowels*
k	ṭ	t	p	ṅ	n	m	ḥ	āḥ	aḥ	*zero*

[1]ḥ or r disappears, and if a/i/u precedes, this lengthens to ā/ī/ū. [2]e.g. tān+lokān=tāl̃ lokān.
[3]The doubling occurs if the preceding vowel is short. [4]Except: aḥ+a=o '.